Reflexive Historical Sociology

This book opens up new theoretical ground at the point of intersection of social theory and historical sociology. A follow up to Szakolczai's earlier work, *Max Weber and Michel Foucault: Parallel Life Works* (Routledge, 1998), it brings together the writings of a series of major contemporary thinkers whose works so far have remained disconnected. It is argued that, taken together, the work of such thinkers as Elias, Voegelin, Borkenau and Mumford, in conjunction with the work of Weber and Foucault, lays the ground for a coherent field called 'reflexive historical sociology'. This field carries a unique potential for understanding the modern condition.

The book consists of two main parts. The first reconstructs the themes and dynamics of the life works of Elias, Voegelin, Borkenau and Mumford using a new method developed by Szakolczai for the understanding of authors. The second part explores the 'visions' of modernity contained in their best-known works, and those of Weber and Foucault. It is argued that these visions and interpretations of modernity can be brought together in the concept of 'permanent liminality', which the author offers as a new diagnosis of the modern condition.

Reflexive Historical Sociology is a discipline-defining text. It will be of essential interest to scholars and students in social and political thought, and historians and philosophers seeking new theoretical perspectives.

Arpad Szakolczai studied in Budapest, Hungary and Austin, Texas. After teaching social theory for eight years at the European University Institute in Florence, Italy, he has taken up the chair of sociology at University College, Cork, Republic of Ireland.

Routledge Studies in Social and Political Thought

Reflexive Historical Sociology

Arpad Szakolczai

London and New York

First published 2000
by Routledge
11 New Fetter Lane, London EC4B 4EE

Simultaneously published in the USA and Canada
by Routledge
29 West 35th Street, New York, NY 10001

Routledge is an imprint of the Taylor & Francis Group

© 2000 Arpad Szakolczai

Typeset in Baskerville
by Curran Publishing Services Ltd
Printed and bound in Great Britain
by MPG Books Ltd, Bodmin

British Library Cataloguing in Publication Data
A catalogue record for this book is available
from the British Library

Library of Congress Cataloging in Publication Data
Szakolczai, Arpad.
Reflexive historical sociology / Arpad Szakolczai.
304 pp. 23.4 x 15.6 cm
Includes bibliographical references and index.
1. Historical sociology. 2. Civilization, Western. 3.
Civilization – Philosophy. 4. Europe – Civilization. I. Title.
HM487.S93 1999   99–18441
301'.01—dc21   CIP

ISBN 0–415–19051–7

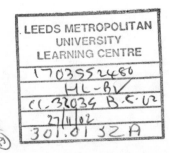

To Knut

Contents

Acknowledgements

Most of the research on which this book is based was completed while I was teaching at the European University Institute (EUI) in Florence, Italy. The Institute and the hills and valleys around Fiesole were a most congenial environment for the work. For their personal support, I am grateful to Patrick Masterson, principal of the EUI, Karl Ulrich Mayer from the Research Council, and Stefano Bartolini who was Head of Department during my last two years.

Much of the actual writing was done once I became Professor of Sociology in 1998 at the University College, Cork, Ireland. The book could not have been finished without the support I received there, matched by the West Cork scenery.

I am most grateful to the Foucault Archives which at the time of my research were still housed at the Bibliothéque de Saulchoir, a Dominican library in Paris, and the Voegelin Archives, The Hoover Institution, Stanford, California, for permitting me to use their material. I am especially grateful to Daniel Defert, Stephen Mennell, Geoffrey Price and Brendan Purcell for sharing material in their possession with me.

A number of people gave invaluable help with this work, either through conversation or by commenting on draft chapters. I am grateful to Zygmunt Bauman, Shmuel Eisenstadt, Bernd Giesen, Harvey Goldman, Elemér Hankiss, Alessandro Pizzorno, Gianfranco Poggi, Dennis Smith, Peggy Somers, Godfried van Benthem van den Berg and Dennis Wrong for their insights, and to Colin Gordon, Kieran Keohane, Richard Kilminster, Paddy O'Carroll, Stefan Rossbach, Valeria Russo and Roberta Sassatelli for taking the trouble to read parts of the manuscript and for giving precious advice. I am especially grateful to Paul Caringella for his detailed and relentlessly critical response to an earlier draft of Chapter 3, which saved me from a series of blunders, and to Agnes who was as merciless a critic as anybody else, as always.

It was my special privilege and fortune to share a series of seminar meetings with particularly bright and receptive audiences in both Florence and Cork: especially, though not restricted to, the two courses devoted to reflexive historical sociology in 1997–8 in Florence and 1998–9 in Cork.

This book owes more to Knut Mittendorfer than to anyone else, for his comments, his presence, the inspiration drawn from his work. He is also the only one who did not see it completed. The book is therefore dedicated to his memory.

Arpad Szakolczai
Kilbrittain, 9 May 1999

Abbreviations

The following abbreviations are used for major or frequently mentioned books. They are used only in the reference sections, while in the main text a shortened version of the title is given. For book series and collected writings, an attempt has been made to harmonize the demands of simplicity, coherence, and compatibility with usage in the existing literature on individual thinkers.

For Franz Borkenau

EB   *End and Beginning: On the Generations of Cultures and the Origins of the West*, ed. R. Lowenthal, New York: Columbia University Press (1981).

UFB   *Der Übergang vom feudalen zum bürgerlichen Weltbild: Studien zur Geschichte der Philosophie der Manufakturperiode*, (referred to as *Transition*), Darmstadt: Wissenschaftliche Buchgesellschaft (1976 [1934]).

For Norbert Elias

CS   *The Court Society*, Oxford: Blackwell (1983 [1969]).

CP   *The Civilising Process*, Oxford: Blackwell (1994 [1939]).

EO   *The Established and the Outsiders*, Cambridge: Polity (1994 [1965]). (With J. L. Scotson.)

ER   *The Norbert Elias Reader: A Biographical Selection*, ed. J. Goudsblom and S. Mennell, Oxford: Blackwell (1998).

GE   *The Germans: Power Struggles and the Development of Habitus in the Nineteenth and Twentieth Centuries*, ed. M. Schröter, Cambridge: Polity (1996 [1989]).

ID   *Involvement and Detachment*, Oxford: Blackwell (1987 [1983]).

RL   *Reflections on a Life*, Cambridge: Polity (1994 [1987]).

ST   *The Symbol Theory*, ed. R. Kilminster, Cambridge: Polity (1991).

WIS   *What Is Sociology?*, London: Hutchinson (1978 [1970]).

For Michel Foucault

BC   *The Birth of the Clinic: An Archaeology of Medical Perception*, New York: Vintage (1975 [1963]).

CF75 *Les anormaux: Cours au Collège de France (1974–1975)*, Paris: Gallimard/ Seuil (1999).

CF76 *'Il faut défendre la société': Cours au Collège de France (1975–1976)*, Paris: Gallimard/ Seuil (1997).

DE   *Dits et écrits*, 4 vols, ed. D. Defert and F. Ewald, Paris: Gallimard (1994). (Texts from this collection are cited either by volume and page number, or by the chronological number given to them.)

DP   *Discipline and Punish*, New York: Vintage (1979 [1975]).

EST   *Ethics: Subjectivity and Truth*, vol. 1 of *The Essential Works of Michel Foucault*, ed. P. Rabinow, New York: New Press (1997).

FR   *The Foucault Reader*, ed. P. Rabinow, New York: Pantheon (1984).

HF   *Histoire de la folie à l'âge classique*, Paris: Gallimard (1972 [1961]). (Partial English translation: *Madness and Civilisation*, New York: Mentor (1965)).

HSI   *The History of Sexuality, vol. 1: An Introduction*, New York: Vintage (1980 [1976]) (referred to as *The Will to Know*).

HSII *The History of Sexuality, vol. 2: The Use of Pleasure*, New York: Vintage(1986 [1984]).

HSIII *The History of Sexuality, vol. 3: The Care of the Self*, New York: Vintage (1987 [1984]).

OT   *The Order of Things*, New York: Vintage (1973 [1966]).

PK   *Power/Knowledge: Selected Interviews and Other Writings by Michel Foucault, 1972–1977*, ed. C. Gordon, Sussex: Harvester (1980).

PPC   *Politics, Philosophy, Culture: Interviews and Other Writings*, ed. L. D. Kritzman, London: Routledge (1988).

TS   *Technologies of the Self*, ed. L. H. Martin, H. Gutman and P. H. Hutton, London: Tavistock (1988).

For Lewis Mumford

CLH   *The City in History*, London: Secker and Warburg (1961).

GD   *The Golden Day: A Study in American Literature and Culture*, New York: Dover (1970 [1926]).

MB   Miller, D. L., *Lewis Mumford: A Life*, Pittsburgh: University of Pittsburgh Press (1989).

MMI   *Technics and Human Development*, vol. 1 of *The Myth of the Machine*, New York: Harcourt (1967).

MMII *The Pentagon of Power*, vol. 2 of *The Myth of the Machine*, New York: Harcourt (1970).

MR   *The Lewis Mumford Reader*, ed. D. L. Miller, New York: Pantheon (1986).

SL *Sketches from Life: The Autobiography of Lewis Mumford: The Early Years,* New York: Dial (1982).
SU *The Story of Utopias,* New York: Viking (1962 [1922]).
TC *Technics and Civilisation,* New York: Harcourt (1963 [1934]).
TM *The Transformations of Man,* New York: Collier (1956).

For Eric Voegelin

AN *Anamnesis,* Notre Dame, Ill.: University of Notre Dame Press (1978 [1966]).
AR *Autobiographical Reflections,* ed. E. Sandoz, Baton Rouge: Louisiana State University Press (1989).
ER *From Enlightenment to Revolution,* ed. J. H. Hallowell, Durham, N.C.: Duke University Press (1975).
FPP *Faith and Political Philosophy: The Correspondence Between Leo Strauss and Eric Voegelin, 1934–64,* ed. P. Emberley and B. Cooper, University Park, Pa.: Pennsylvania State University Press (1993).
HPI *Hellenism, Rome and Early Christianity,* vol. 1 of *History of Political Ideas,* ed. A. Moulakis, Columbia: University of Missouri Press (1997). (Volumes 1–8 of the *History of Political Ideas* are published as volumes 19–26 of *The Collected Works of Eric Voegelin.*)
HPII *The Middle Ages to Aquinas,* vol. 2 of *History of Political Ideas,* ed. P. von Sivers, Columbia: University of Missouri Press (1997).
HPIII *The Later Middle Ages,* vol. 3 of *History of Political Ideas,* ed. D. Walsh, Columbia: University of Missouri Press (1998).
HPIV *Renaissance and Reformation,* vol. 4 of *History of Political Ideas,* ed. D. L. Morse and W. M. Thompson, Columbia: University of Missouri Press (1998).
HPV *Religion and the Rise of Modernity,* vol. 5 of *History of Political Ideas,* ed. J. L. Wiser, Columbia: University of Missouri Press (1998).
HPVI *Revolution and the New Science,* vol. 6 of *History of Political Ideas,* ed. B. Cooper, Columbia: University of Missouri Press (1998).
HPVII *The New Order and Last Orientation,* vol. 7 of *History of Political Ideas,* ed. J. Gebhardt and T. A. Hollweck, Columbia: University of Missouri Press (1999).
NSP *The New Science of Politics,* Chicago: Chicago University Press (1952).
OHI *Israel and Revelation,* vol. 1 of *Order and History,* Baton Rouge: Louisiana State University Press (1956).
OHII *The World of the Polis,* vol. 2 of *Order and History,* Baton Rouge: Louisiana State University Press (1957).
OHIII *Plato and Aristotle,* vol. 3 of *Order and History,* Baton Rouge: Louisiana State University Press (1957).
OHIV *The Ecumenic Age,* vol. 4 of *Order and History,* Baton Rouge: Louisiana State University Press (1974).

OHV   *In Search of Order*, vol. 5 of *Order and History*, Baton Rouge: Louisiana State University Press (1987).

SPG   *Science, Politics and Gnosticism*, Chicago: Henry Regnery (1968 [1959]).

For Max Weber

ES   *Economy and Society*, Berkeley: University of California Press (1978 [1921–2]).

FMW   *From Max Weber*, ed. H. Gerth and C. W. Mills, London: Routledge (1948). (Contains the *Einleitung*, translated as *The Social Psychology of the World Religions*, and the *Zwischenbetrachtung*, translated as *Religious Rejections of the World and their Directions*.)

GARS   *Gesammelte Aufsätze zur Religionssoziologie*, 3 vols, Tübingen: J. C. B. Mohr (1920–1). (Contains the *Vorbemerkung*, the PE, the essay on Protestant Sects, and the 'Economic Ethic of World Religions' (*Die Wirtschaftethik der Weltreligionen – WEWR*) essays.) (Referred to as *Sociology of Religions*.)

MSS   *On the Methodology of the Social Sciences*, ed. E. A. Shils and H. A. Finch, Glencoe: Free Press (1949). (Contains the 'Objectivity' and the 'Value Freedom' essays.)

PE   *The Protestant Ethic and the Spirit of Capitalism*, Los Angeles: Roxbury (1995 [1904–5]). (Also contains the *Vorbemerkung*, translated as 'Author's Introduction'.)

PE2   *Die protestantische Ethik*, vol. 2, Gütersloh: Mohn (1978). (Contains the 'anticritical essays'.)

MWG   *Max Weber Gesamtausgabe*, ed. H. Baier, M. R. Lepsius, W. J. Mommsen, W. Schluchter and J. Winckelmann, Tübingen: J. C. B. Mohr (1981–). (Roman number II is given to the letters. Texts from this collection are cited by volume and page number.)

WB   Weber, Marianne, *Max Weber: A Biography*, Oxford: Transaction Books (1988 [1926]).

Introduction

As its title indicates, this book is positioned at the point of intersection of social theory and historical sociology. It aims to bring together and discuss jointly a series of major social thinkers whose work was historically oriented. According to the perspective of contemporary common sense wisdom, the pairing of social theory and historical sociology is not at all self-evident. Sociology is often considered as the modern social science *par excellence*, dealing with the problems faced by contemporary society. From this perspective, historical sociology may provide some information from the past about the background of contemporary processes, but is not central to the task of theorizing. And yet, some of the most important and influential social theorists, both classical and contemporary, like Marx and Weber, Foucault and Elias, were definitely historical sociologists of one kind or another. The taken for granted status of these figures helps to hide the puzzling character of the close links revealed between social theory and historical sociology.

The puzzle is increased by extending the argument to anthropology. It seems that if there were another social science as distinct from sociology as history, it would be anthropology. In so far as sociology deals with the problems of contemporary society, the links to economics or political science are evident, as social, economic and political problems can never be separated completely. According to this logic, anthropology – which deals mostly with non-modern or non-Western societies – should be much more distant from sociology. Yet again, the works of a series of major classical and contemporary social theorists like Durkheim, Mauss, Bourdieu, Goffman and Girard are all anthropologically based.

The two considerations and the two lists support and reinforce each other. Taken together, the two social science disciplines that should be furthest away from sociology are evidently closest (Calhoun 1992: 140). And taken together, the two lists contain many of the classic figures and the most exciting, innovative contemporary representatives of social theory.

At this point, it is possible to reverse the line of questioning followed so far and turn against the common sense wisdom that was taken for granted. This involves theoretical, even metatheoretical issues (Ritzer 1992), and problems related to the history and constitution of the discipline of sociology.

On the theoretical level, the puzzle concerning the close links between social theory and history on the one hand, and anthropology on the other, can be solved by reassessing the balance of closeness and distance. Events and processes belonging to the distance past, or to distant cultures, can become relevant in the sense of holding up a mirror to the present: the mirror of the 'other', or the mirror of our own past selves. In this way they help to shed – often suddenly and unexpectedly – new light on aspects of present practices that are taken for granted and unseen not because they are so distant, but exactly because they are so close. This brings home the point that the task of social theory is not simply to explain facts and processes, but to act as an exercise in self-understanding. It is therefore not surprising that the 'historic turn' (McDonald 1996) in social thought is so close to the 'interpretive turn' (Rabinow and Sullivan 1987) or what could be called as the 'reflexive turn' (Bauman 1997, Gouldner 1971).

The recognition of the presence of a self-reflexive component in all social theory implies some affinities with philosophy. This is especially true of the concern with philosophy as a way of life and with philosophical exercises, which were characteristic of the work of Pierre Hadot. These had a major impact on the last period of Foucault (Szakolczai 1998b), and have close parallels with Wittgenstein or Voegelin. However, it is just as important to emphasize that all this does not imply a simple return to philosophy, the breach of the dividing line between sociology and philosophy which was so important for both Durkheim and Weber. This is because the task of sociological self-understanding has as its primary task the understanding of modernity: this solid block of reality rendering impossible the simple pursuit of the classical task of philosophy, understanding the human condition. Modernity intervenes between the single human being searching for understanding and the central and universal experiences and emotions of human existence. Its understanding requires reliance on a series of empirical and collective studies, as it cannot take as its starting point the reflexions and meditations of the individual self. Any such attempt is doomed, as it is rooted in the misconstruction of the specifically modern experience of the self as being a universal, an anthropological given.

However, the novelty of this historical (and anthropological) turn still requires some explanation. Though the list of social theorists includes both classical and contemporary figures, there is a wide gap between them in terms of the effect of their works. The classical period in sociology closed around the end of the First World War, with the deaths of Durkheim, Simmel and Weber. The work of most historically and anthropologically minded social theorists, however, did not become effective in sociology until the 1980s. In between, there were the decades of the Great Depression and the Second World War, of totalitarianism and the Cold War, a contemporary 'dark age' in both political and intellectual history, and a period in which 'The best lack all conviction, while the worst/Are full of passionate intensity' (Yeats 1990: 100). In sociology, this was the era of structural-functionalism, based on the classical synthesis of Parsons, and the Freudo-Marxism of critical theory, with the balance between the two shifting from the 1940–50s to the 1960–70s. In this semantic field the crucial historical and anthropological insights of Weber and Durkheim, and the related work of Simmel, were largely overlooked, and those thinkers who pursued these directions like Elias or Goffman were marginalized within the field for a very long time.

This book is therefore both programmatic and analytical. It is programmatic, as its main aim is to reconstruct the history of sociological thought and reorient contemporary social theory. In this sense, the undertaking of which this book is a part is both conservative, even traditionalist, and radically innovative. It is traditionalist because it is rooted in the works of Weber and Durkheim and recognizes the epochal significance of Parsons in bringing the two seminal thinkers together. It is opposed to those revisionist attempts that question the role of Durkheim or Weber, the relevance of classical social theory for the present, or the central formal insight of Parsons (Arjomand 1999, Connell 1997). However, it is also radically different from the substance of Parsonian sociology and the entire kind of social theory built upon it. It takes as its starting point the late substantive works of Weber and Durkheim, their sociologies of religions, in opposition to the Parsonian synthesis of the spirit of early Durkheim and the form of late Weber, and tries to bring together those thinkers who, in considerable isolation, took up these works in an innovative manner.

The central argument is that these works define two branches of sociology, reflexive historical sociology and reflexive anthropological sociology. Reflexive historical sociology takes its departure from Weber's historical sociology and attempts to bring together the work of those thinkers who, beyond the paradigmatic dividing lines of structural functionalism and critical theory, took inspiration from his work, or went ahead in parallel lines, irrespective of intellectual fashions, and thus created life-works which today can be used as valuable, indeed priceless reference points. The thinkers discussed in this book, Elias, Borkenau, Voegelin, Mumford and Foucault, are representative figures of the field. Further names such as Reinhart Koselleck, Albert Hirschman, Philippe Ariès or Norman Cohn could be added to the list.

Reflexive anthropological sociology similarly takes off from Durkheim's last period. It includes among its main figures such anthropologically oriented social theorists or sociologically interested anthropologists as Mauss, Bateson, Goffman, Girard, Turner, Bourdieu and Geertz. Apart from relying on Durkheim, some of the most important thinkers in this group also took up the work of his main opponents, Tarde and van Gennep.

The two expressions, like any similar label, are imperfect, and may create all sorts of objections. They can be defended on the following grounds. The work of all thinkers listed, whether they were primarily anthropologists, political scientists, philosophers or historians, had a socio-logical angle in the sense that they had an interest in the question of under-standing the character of modernity; and a reflexive angle in the sense of using historical or anthropological evidence as a mirror to get a better grasp of this problem.

The parallel expressions are useful as they help to identify the works of Weber and Durkheim as the main sources of the two branches. This is important in order to underline the tradition-respecting component of the argument. Sociology today is increasingly threatened by a characteristic of its own conditions of emergence, the attempt to shake off all preceding forms of thought and look for a new start, another *tabula rasa*. Such mani-festos dismissing the interest in classics as meaningless exegesis are always popular, but dangerous and misleading. All social scientific disciplines are rooted in a fundamental problematics which they have not yet overcome, and never will. Philosophy never went beyond the questions of Plato and Aristotle; political science can never relegate Machiavelli or Hobbes to the dustbin; and similarly in so far as there is modernity – whether it is provided or not with the prefixes 'late' or 'post' – there will be sociology and an interest in Weber and Durkheim. Far from declaring a break with the clas-sics, reflexive historical sociology and reflexive anthropological sociology only proclaim a shift of attention to the most important mature part of their substantive work.

However, it is also argued that for long decades, partly for personal reasons, partly because of a series of political experiences like the Great Depression and its political consequences, the Second World War and the Cold War, and partly because of academic politics, the most fashionable versions of social theory did not follow the footsteps of Weber and Durkheim as thoroughly as they might have done. It is therefore necessary to bring together the work of a series of thinkers who have to date often been considered either as marginal, or as unrelated to each other.

Such a reorientation may encounter objections both from the perspec-tives of established mainstream social theory and the different alternative theoretical groups. In fact, in a book promoting a reflexive approach in sociology, it seems appropriate to turn this tool to the discipline itself; and in a book attempting to revitalize Weber's thought, it is only proper to do it with the help of a Weberian concept, the conceptual pairing of Church and sects. Mainstream social theory perfectly fits the concept of a secular Church, with Durkheim and Parsons quite consciously working on the establishment of canonical texts and playing the role of high priests, with all the merits and problems such an undertaking entails. In opposition to their theses there were the Marxian and Freudian sects of the past, and various contemporary sect-like groups, loose or quite well organized, formed around a single, charismatic social theorist. An attempt to build bridges between these sects, and to reconnect them to the canonical sources, is therefore bound to generate objections. This reconnecting and bridge-building, though, is exactly what this book aims to accomplish.

Because of the kind of programme the book pursues, it is strictly analytical. Its aim is to reconstruct, and not to construct a new theory or comment upon existing theories. It also refrains from drawing out implications and pursuing the argument further, beyond reconstructing the actual links between the works of different reflexive historical sociologists. The only exception is the Conclusion to Part II, which provides an interpretative framework for some of the main findings and draws out implications for the condition of modernity, by introducing the concept 'permanent liminality'.

This book is both an independent monograph and part of a series. It is a follow-up volume to an earlier book on the life-works of Weber and Foucault (Szakolczai 1998a), but both its parts comprise a new whole.

Part I is not simply about four additional thinkers, but reconstructs the life-works of four representative figures of a generation. Elias, Borkenau, Voegelin and Mumford belong together as a close-knit generation. They were born within a very short time of each other, between late 1895 and the first days of 1901, but they also form a generation in the sociological sense (Mannheim 1953). Their birth dates define with mathematical precision the generation who went through the most important initiation rite in modern societies (at least for the educated strata), the passage from youth to adulthood, the leaving of high school with the *Abitur* or *maturità*, and the entry to university at the age of eighteen, during the First World War.

Part II similarly has its own coherence and independence. It focuses on the most influential works of reflexive historical sociology, such as Weber's *Protestant Ethic*, Foucault's *Discipline and Punish*, Elias's *The Court Society* and *The Civilizing Process*, or Mumford's *The City in History*. The individual chapters focus on reconstructing the central ideas of these epochal thinkers about the modern condition, or – using a term that will be elaborated in the Introduction to Part II – their visions of modernity. The chapters build on each other. They demonstrate in detail how much these works, and these visions, are connected. To a large extent this is due to a common source of inspiration in Weber and in Nietzsche, and also in some or other of the main background figures of reflexive historical sociology such as Marx, Kierkegaard and Freud.

Finally, the book contains both formal and substantive analysis. Part I continues the formal analysis of the previous volume, focusing on the reconstruction of the entire life-trajectories of selected thinkers. This analysis is formal in the sense that it concentrates on the characteristics of the trajectory itself, its sources and moving forces, the animating experiences and the moments of reflection and redirection which punctuate it, partly altering its shape but to a large extent only providing further precision and clarity. The approach followed in pursuing this analysis is elaborated in the Introduction to Part I.

In these formal analyses, matters of content are discussed only in so far as they are linked to the shape of the entire trajectory. However, the formal analysis is not a goal in itself, but is a prelude to a detailed joint reconstruction of the content of these works. It is necessary, both to recognize the proper emphases and accents for the individual works, and to lay down the foundations for connecting them, through direct influence, common sources, or the type of reflexive relationship connecting the thinkers to their works. In Part II, the book moves to matters of content, reconstructing the visions of modernity contained in the most influential works of reflexive historical sociologists, which in almost all cases belonged to their early or middle periods.

In spite of its attempt to study in some depth, and to contrast, the life-works and some of the main ideas of six major social thinkers, and its programmatic aim, the book has obvious and major limitations. The chapters of Part I restrict attention to the formal characteristics of the dynamics of the life-works, and do not go into matters of substance. Part II, on the other hand, only reconstructs internally the main argument of each thinker. It alludes to parallels, but does not integrate these ideas in detail, nor does it present a critical commentary. These restrictions are partly owing to methodological considerations, and partly a result of the attempt to keep the book to a reasonable size.

The author is well aware that many details of the life and thought of the thinkers discussed will have escaped his attention. Nevertheless, the material as collected together has its own weight and momentum, both in its individual parts and especially as a whole. It would only gain and not lose by further research. He is therefore quite happy to take on board any clarification or improvement in precision.

Part I

Reflexive historical sociologists

Introduction to Part I

Reflexive historical sociologists are social thinkers who were engaged in detailed empirical and long-term historical studies in their self-reflexive quest for understanding modernity. It would seem that such an undertaking, involving not only much of the social sciences but also history and philosophy, would lie beyond the realm of possibilities for single individuals living and working under modern academic conditions. Yet, apart from Weber and Foucault, there are a series of other thinkers who meet most or all of the criteria.

Starting with the social sciences, there is Albert Hirschman who was born in 1915 in Berlin and who began his academic career as an economist of development before moving into political science and producing milestone theoretical works (Hirschman 1959). He also wrote a series of widely-read and influential historical books that gave an original interpretation about the emergence of modern economic society (Hirschman 1977, 1991).

One could continue with Reinhart Koselleck who was born in 1923. He was a German political scientist who became famous through the method he worked out for the history of thought called *Geschichtliche Grundbegriffe* (Koselleck 1985, 1989; Tribe 1989) and who also wrote an influential interpretation of the emergence of modernity focusing on the role of intellectual clubs as his doctoral thesis (Koselleck 1998 [1959]).

There is also the sociologist Shmuel Eisenstadt, who was born in Poland in 1923 and received a somewhat unusual introduction to the work of Weber through Martin Buber. As a result, his work became oriented to the comparative study of civilizations and their dynamics. The first major results of his research are contained in the classic book *The Political Systems of Empires* (Eisenstadt 1963) while, in the last decades, his research focused on the question of the axial age civilizations (Eisenstadt 1986, 1995, 1998).

As far as historians are concerned, one may start with two Germans who fit into the best Weberian traditions. The first is Otto Hintze (1861–1940) who was the great comparative institutional historian of Prussia. Hintze and Weber were contemporaries and shared a common interest in the joint emergence of absolutism and Protestantism. Hintze's work became a major resource for much work in historical sociology. Gerhard Oestreich (1910–1978) further pursued some of the themes pioneered by Hintze and Weber, focusing on reason of state, police and social disciplining as key moments in the emergence of modernity.

The line can be continued with two French historians who were quite well-known and influential, yet their names create some perplexity, as they did not belong to the *Annales* school which became almost synonymous with French historiography in the twentieth century and which was strongly influenced by structuralist Durkheimian sociology. They are Philippe Ariès (1914–1984) and Alphonse Dupront (1905–1990). Ariès was a 'Sunday historian', ignored by the establishment, working at a centre studying the population problems of the third world who was not given a proper academic position in France until his last years. Yet, animated by an original and profound vision of the destiny of modernity, he undertook long-term reconstructive historical studies of Western attitudes and mentalities regarding to the most important experiences of human life like childhood, family, education, sexuality and death in a series of highly-influential works (Ariès 1974, 1975, 1977, 1993). In contrast to Ariès, Dupront was very much part of the academic establishment. Between 1971 and 1976, he was first president of the new University of Sorbonne (Paris-IV). However, even though his colleagues recognized his extraordinary achievements, his name is much less known than those of the *Annales* historians, partly because he had a tendency to hide his most important works in relatively obscure publications or even keep them in manuscripts and partly because his interests and methods were different from the dominant, structuralist and secular concerns of his contemporaries. His main interest was in religious experiences, which he studied not in the manner of positivism but as the outbreak of obscure unconscious forces. His historical studies were strongly influenced by concepts and concerns taken over from anthropology and Jungian analytical psychology.

The subset can be closed by two historians of the Low Countries, the Dutchman Johan Huizinga (1872–1945) and the Belgian Henri Pirenne (1862–1935). Huizinga gained his degree in philology studying Sanskrit texts, before he became a historian. He wrote works much influenced by, and much read in, the social sciences (especially Huizinga 1955), and also a widely-read work belong to the 'crisis literature' of the 1930s (Huizinga 1936). His most important work, however, was the *Autumn of the Middle Ages* which rooted the Renaissance, as a movement of spiritual revival, in a period of dissolution of order, the collapse of the Middle Ages. Pirenne was a historian of the Middle Ages, writing an influential work of the emergence of medieval cities. His most important book was *Mohammed and Charlemagne*, which was based on the highly controversial thesis that the joint appearance of two movements of spiritual revival, the Carolingian Renaissance and Islam, had its roots in a period of dissolution of order, the long decline following the collapse of the Roman Empire.

Finally, there is a historian of ideas with similar concerns, Norman Cohn who was born in 1915. Cohn was one of those thinkers who were trying, shortly after the Second World War, to dig out the joint intellectual origins of the totalitarian mass movements and ideologies and the idea of progress from their own personal experience. However, he not only produced one of the most important and original works of this literature, *The Pursuit of the Millenium* that studied the movements from their medieval origins, but stayed with the theme, and after revisiting his earlier work, leaped further back in history and traced the apocalyptic form of thought to its Zoroastrian origins (Cohn 1993).

Though all these thinkers produced works that are not only extremely valuable sources for reflexive historical sociology but also reflect place in this discipline, in this first part of the book the life-works of four other thinkers will be reconstructed in detail. This is partly due to evident limitations of space and the subsequent need to rank and select. It was furthermore decided that only those thinkers will be covered whose work has already been closed. In the end, four thinkers were singled out for attention as it seemed that their work individually had special importance and that the small group, taken together, was quite homogenous. They were Eric Voegelin (1901–1985), Norbert Elias (1897–1990), Lewis Mumford (1895–1990) and Franz Borkenau (1900–1957).

It seemed that the character, depth and breadth of the work of these four thinkers was closest to the kind of tradition for which the inspiration or the spark was derived from Nietzsche (1844–1900), the classic formulation of the problem and body of work was provided by Weber (1864–1920) and the most important and influential contemporary contribution was given by Foucault (1926–1984). The four thinkers produced, just like Weber or Foucault, an outstanding contribution in every single dimension of reflexive historical sociology. As opposed to most of the other historians or philosophers belonging to the field, they have accomplished important empirical studies and even complementary work in journalism. As opposed to most of the other protagonists of the field, their historical work did not stop at the sixteenth and seventeenth centuries but went back in time to the collapse of the Roman Empire, the axial age or even beyond. Finally, the vision they presented about the emergence of modernity was particularly convincing and influential and specifically centred on the two main themes of reflexive historical sociology; the historicity of the forms of subjectivity and the historicity of forms of thought.

Part I therefore reconstructs the dynamics of the life-works of Mumford, Elias, Borkenau and Voegelin. It follows the methodological considerations as laid out in Chapter Two of my previous book, *Max Weber and Michel Foucault: Parallel Life-Works*.

The major principles of this reconstructive analysis are very simple. They amount to the treatment of an intellectual trajectory as a performance where the actual script is the *curriculum vitae*, using the concept of liminality as developed by Victor Turner. The central idea is that most breakpoints of an individual life are not that difficult to identify. In most cases they correspond to the major 'rites of passage' in one's life and are available in any reasonably accurate and detailed *curriculum vitae*. In our contemporary world, due to the excessive formalization and emptying of all rites of passage, it is forgotten that such rituals do not simply perform a formal-legalistic function but are emotional and experiential breakpoints, liminal experiences. Dates of initiation, maturation, appointment, promotion and publication are not just trophies to be collected in a *curriculum vitae* but provide the emotional and existential context of the work. They have a fundamental impact on the form in which it is eventually put, on the character of the projects pursued, the style in which the books and papers are written, or the polemics in which they are embedded in their reception. Such formal occasions, like inaugural speeches, also present an opportunity and pose a challenge to reflect on one's own work. Experiences that directly have a professional character must be complemented with other experiences like illness, death or war whose relevance may be less apparent but nevertheless could be just as central, for much the same reasons (see also Greco 1998, Rinken forthcoming, Rossbach forthcoming).

The four chapters of Part I will have unequal lengths. The Borkenau chapter is the shortest, because of the paucity of available information. Next comes the Mumford chapter, partly for the opposite reason as Mumford is the only one of the four for whom we have a published biography, an autobiography, and a series of other autobiographical works. The two longer chapters are on Elias and Voegelin. This is partly due to the amount of material available on them, reflecting their relative importance. But their work is also closest to the line of research as represented by Weber and Foucault.

Part I ends with a long concluding section which makes a detailed comparison between the intellectual trajectories of all six thinkers.

1 Norbert Elias

Norbert Elias was born on 22 June 1897 in Breslau (now Wroclaw), in Silesia. Though the town now belongs to Poland and he was born into a middle-class Jewish family, he was brought up as a German.

His early years were marked by profound, almost timeless stability and security. Being the only child in the period of the 'child king' (Ariès 1975), and in a Jewish bourgeois environment which was famous for the huge amount of loving attention paid to children, he had a childhood which was particularly rich and rewarding emotionally.[1] The sense of stability also extended to the surrounding world, where he felt completely safe, and where '[o]ne could not imagine that the world would ever be different' (RL: 13). In the autobiographical interview, he immediately connected this sense of stability to his later ability of persisting with his work for decades, despite the almost complete lack of recognition (RL: 14).

The only threatening events in his childhood were the illnesses which he caught with great regularity and which only reinforced maternal care around him. His fragility had a significant consequence as his parents considered that he was unfit for formal schooling and hired a private teacher. Because of this, he started independent work, in the sense of reading and browsing through a huge number of books on his own, at a very early age (RL: 3, 84–5). No doubt it was through these readings that he soon felt the world of his town and family to be suffocating, below his intellectual level, and he wanted to escape as soon as possible (RL: 6–7).

The opportunity came eventually and with a vengeance. The outbreak of the First World War represented the wholesale collapse of his entire world, a 'change from the complete security of my family to the complete insecurity of the army' (RL: 14). The shock was so great that, in his biographical interview, Elias kept returning to the event saying that he still could not understand how he had been able to cope with it at that time; that most of his memories seem to be forgotten, blocked; and that his preoccupation with historical change must be rooted in these experiences (RL: 14–15, 26–8). This is the first, but not the last, occasion when Elias would have particular difficulties in reliving his own past.

Like all his classmates, Elias enlisted as a volunteer as soon as he finished secondary education and remained in the army until the end of the war (Korte 1997: 74). He was released from military service on 4 February 1919 and immediately started his higher education at the University of Breslau. In fact, he had already been enrolled on his eighteenth birthday, 22 June 1915, just before going to the front.

Though the main facts about the studies for his first degree are well known, the most important impulses and reading experiences of the period remain surprisingly clouded in silence even in the autobiographical interview. Elias enrolled jointly in medicine and philosophy, following gentle parental encouragement to read the former, but after his first medical exams in April 1919, he decided to concentrate on the latter (Korte 1997: 75).

His professor of philosophy in Breslau was the well-known neo-Kantian Richard Hönigswald, whom Elias much respected but whose approach he could not accept. His formation was broadened and amplified by the two summer semesters he spent in Heidelberg (1919) and Freiburg (1920). The first of these took place at a particularly liminal moment of his life. It was the first year after the First World War, right after his first regular university semester in Breslau, in a new environment where he was only a visiting student and just after he made a commitment to focus on philosophy (Korte 1997: 75–7).

The most important experience of the Heidelberg semester was his encounter with Jaspers for whose seminar he prepared a presentation on the current debate about 'civilization', studying the writings of Thomas Mann. Given that Jaspers had a degree in psychiatry and belonged to the faculty of medicine, though already more interested in philosophy (he became a professor of philosophy in 1921), he was an evident choice to be associated with. During a long walk, Jaspers also 'initiated' Elias to Max Weber, of whom he had not heard before (RL: 35, 83; Korte 1997: 77–8). In Freiburg, Elias listened to Husserl (Korte 1997: 77), and gained an understanding which, though critical, was very different from the extremely negative view pronounced by Hönigswald (RL: 92). However, it remains the case that, apart from these few bits and pieces, very little is known of the main formative experiences of Elias.

One can only conjecture that a main reason for this silence was not simply his war experience but also his participation in the Zionist movement. Though he participated in the activities of the Youth Movement before the war (Hackeschmidt 1997), his deep commitment came only after and particularly when he was named as leader of the Breslau group in November 1918 (Korte 1997: 83). Elias certainly omitted this chapter of personal history in the biographical interview, just as he was very sparing in details about his formative experiences. Based on the available information, and focusing on the breaks in Elias's career during these and later years and on the character of his trajectory, I will attempt a short, hypothetic reconstruction of these influences.

The question of intellectual formation, especially in terms of reading experiences, is central to this book. This is the way in which the launching could become possible of a certain type of highly innovative research project, which involves a long-term commitment but therefore also implies loneliness and neglect, and is subsumed in the expression 'untimeliness'. Elias himself was always much concerned about the conditions of possibility of sequences of events. Indeed, this was his definition of a process and a question central to the last piece of work he ever wrote, the unfinished *Introduction* to *The Symbol Theory*. It is only fair to ask therefore: what made the work of Elias possible? But while for most other protagonists of the field, the detailed reconstruction of these experiences is possible through the available pieces of evidence, for Elias most of this information is missing. All what we know is the clearly-identified influence of Freud which, somewhat mysteriously, is never dated, and the candid remark made in a letter (see in Goudsblom 1977: 78) about the lack of his in-depth familiarity with much of sociology while writing *The Civilizing Process*. The remark about sociology can be easily misunderstood, as by that time Elias was evidently profoundly familiar with both the accepted authorities of German sociology of the times, and a few less well-known names.

This section will suggest a dating of his first reading of Freud, and two further major encounters for Elias. Both will be based on analogies with the careers of other reflexive historical sociologists. One will concern the early, formative years, and will hypothesize an in-depth encounter with Nietzsche, possibly a 'reading experience', in the 1910s. The other will be less speculative and will argue for the joint development of his project with his long-time friend, Franz Borkenau, during the 1930s. As these aspects are closely related, they can be characterized by the term 'formative figuration'.

The safe path to start this exercise is by referring to two points which can be taken for granted, namely that Freud was the single most important source of inspiration for Elias, and that in his formative years he was strongly involved in the Zionist youth movement. The next step comes by relating the two facts. Freud became much discussed in both the German and Jewish youth movements exactly at the time when Elias's involvement started. In the following, as a historical background, a small sketch will be given of the emergence of youth movements in the first decades of the century.

The term 'youth movement' today often conjures images of 1968 and the counterculture, and of the Boy Scouts. However, a full-fledged youth movement and a counterculture had already emerged in the first years of this century in Central Europe. The first independent youth movement, the *Wandervogel*, was founded on 4 November 1901 in Berlin (Laqueur 1978: 3). The movement was originally concerned mostly, as its full title reveals, with the organization of schoolboy excursions. However, it possessed a romantic, confrontational ideology from the start. It was a challenge to the adult world, based on a spirit of recklessness, and a rejection of the 'bourgeois' values of parental upbringing and school discipline.

In spite of its original apolitical and asexual character, both politics and sexuality soon caught up with it. As far as the former is concerned, the movement developed a nationalist, *völkisch*, anti-Semitic rhetoric, while other factions were influenced by Marx, came close to the socialists and after the First World War even the Communists. After the First World War, the rift between the left and the right became the main issue dividing the movement (Laqueur 1978), and following the transitory period of 1918–23, the *Wandervogel* movement became closely allied with the Nazis. The issue of sexuality first caused concern due to a strong latent tendency to homoeroticism and the high esteem of male physical beauty (Stachura 1975: 3). Open discussion of the issue started in 1912–13 (Laqueur 1978). The main forum was Gustave Wyneken's journal *Der Anfang*, published in Vienna. One of the editors, Siegfried Bernfeld, who was one of the main ideologues of the youth movement, was strongly influenced by the ideas of Freud. Papers openly condemned the philistinism of the ruling morality, discussed taboo issues like masturbation, and presented a view according to which man was by nature bisexual with the transition to heterosexuality being only a recent development. At that time Wyneken, who was the main, strongly charismatic ideologist of the movement, still preached a 'heroic asceticism' of restraint, but by 1915 he was also converted to the dominant Freudian mood (Laqueur 1978).

The year 1912 was also when, at the same time as Freud, the presence of Nietzsche became more marked in the German youth movement. In a way Nietzsche was already present in the *Wandervogel*, but attitudes towards him were ambivalent, as his ideas were incompatible with the nationalist rhetoric, and were especially opposed by the anti-Semites in the movement who wanted to 'exorcise' his influence (Aschheim 1992: 115). Arguably he became a dominant force only with the foundation of the more progressive *Freideutsche Jugend* movement, which emerged as a response to the nationalistic rhetoric of the *Wandervogel* in 1913.

Given the later history of the twentieth century and the subsequent development of the different youth movements, it seems to lie beyond the bounds of comprehension that the origins of the German and the Zionist youth movements were closely interrelated. This was due partly to direct influence and partly to a common outlook. Much as the Christian youth movements, both in the Anglo-Saxon world and in Germany, were created in order to fight the image of Christianity as weak and effeminate (Springhall 1977: 22), the Zionist movement also fought against the similar stereotyped image of the Jews and promoted physical education, especially athletics, boxing, swimming and skiing (Laqueur 1972: 485). The two movements also had common heroes, and again paradoxically, one of the most important was Nietzsche. In spite of his outbursts against the priestly type and *ressentiment*, the second generation of the Zionist movement, in contrast with the strong hostility of the first generation, was among the most enthusiastic readers of Nietzsche (Aschheim 1992: 103–4; Kaufmann 1974: 419). The paradigmatic figure here is Martin Buber who, by the first years of the century had become the intellectual leader of Zionism with an especially strong impact on the youth movements (Laqueur, 1972: 166–8), and whose main reading experience, as he tells in his autobiography, was Nietzsche (Buber 1967: 12).

Zionism was a movement that always had a particular appeal to the young generation. However, two independent youth movements, the *Hashomer Hatzair* and the *Blau Weiss*, played a special role in the history both of Zionism and of two main reflexive historical sociologists, Elias and Borkenau. The parallels between the two movements are quite striking. Both were founded in 1912–13, the former in Galicia although it moved and was 're-founded' in Vienna in 1916 (Aschheim 1992: 105), the latter in Breslau, Silesia, and both also had origins in Berlin (Laqueur 1972: 485). Though Galicia and Silesia are now in Poland, at the turn of the century they both belonged to Germanic states and cultural settings, the former being the North-Eastern province of Austria and the latter the South-Eastern part of Prussia. Even though both movements were attached to Zionism, neither was politically and religiously fully committed, airing 'dangerous', dissident voices. Both were very strongly influenced not only by the 'scoutist' character of the German youth movements but by German culture in general. Instead of a simple return to Jewish traditions, their aim was rather a type of cultural and spiritual development which was closely modelled on the German *Bildung*. This was because most of their members belonged to the educated middle classes. Their beliefs were strongly romantic and influenced by Marx, Freud, Nietzsche, Buber and the two main intellectual leaders of the German youth movements, Wyneken and Bernfeld (Laqueur 1972: 297–8).

The last relevant chapters in the history of these movements also ran parallel. Ending the period of hesitation, both decided to make a full political commitment after the First World War (respectively in 1919–20 and in 1922), and their members emigrated to Palestine.

Elias became a member of *Blau Weiss* even before the First World War, and was elected as its Breslau leader in 1918. This helps to shed light on some of the unclear episodes of his youth, starting with the dating of his reading of Freud. As far as the genesis of *The Civilizing Process* is concerned, it is usually pointed out that Freud's *Civilization and its Discontents*, which evidently had a huge impact on *The Civilizing Process*, appeared in 1930. But Elias must have read Freud earlier in his life. His involvement in the Zionist youth movement would date this encounter to his late teens. Similarly, though by now it has been publicly stated that Elias had strong homoerotic tendencies (Schröter 1997: 225, fn 48), he was also attracted to women, and therefore had a bisexual erotic life, which can again be located in the same context. (It should be seen in this perspective, not as directly comparable to present-day bisexuality.) One could add mastur-bation, which he had to leave out of the published 1939 volume with much regret (Mennell 1996), and which was another much-discussed theme in the youth movement. Another aspect left out completely from the biographical statements is Elias's interest in physical education. He was a formidable swimmer (Albrow 1990: 372), skied, even damaged his eyesight during a skiing incident, and boxed at a professional level for two years (Tabboni 1993: 11). Apart from athletics, which was the generic sport at that time, these were exactly the three activities singled out for attention by the Zionist movement. Finally, one should mention Buber, whose 1922 book *I and Thou* may well have been a major source for Elias's interests in personal pronouns, just as it could have inspired Mannheim (1982).

From Buber, Nietzsche is only at a short step. Elias never gave any sign of Nietzsche having had an impact on him during these formative years, but occasional references in his works, especially *The Civilizing Process*, betray a familiarity with Nietzsche's ideas. Given the circumstances, it is more than probable that Elias knew about the writings of Buber and Nietzsche. Furthermore, an impact by Nietzsche seems present in Elias's works, at least in two respects. One concerns the historicization of Freud. We do not know the inspiration behind such an idea, but it may well have been *The Genealogy of Morals* which was one of Nietzsche's most widely-read books in Zionist circles around the First World War. Hebrew was indeed among the first foreign languages into which the book was translated. The other concerns the evident untimeliness of Elias's ideas as shown by their difficult reception. The reading of Freud, together with Nietzsche and the sociology of Weber, could have provided the experiential basis for the untimeliness of Elias's work, while the *Untimely Meditations* could have given him a model and further support in persisting in his path.

One could still argue that all this is hypothetical, and that there is no proof for Elias ever seriously reading Nietzsche. This may well be true. However, in that case, the similarities between *The Genealogy of Morals* (and Foucault's work which was strongly based on his Nietzsche reading experi-ence) and *The Civilizing Process* must be seen as purely fortuitous, and it is necessary to look to other possible sources which made possible the untimely work on which Elias was engaged.[2] In this case, however, we have to explain how Elias could have escaped reading Nietzsche, given the strong presence and therefore availability of Nietzsche in the circles where Elias moved, and the close affinities which Elias was bound to recognize.[3] It seems much easier to explain why Elias never talked about his reading of Nietzsche. Apart from his general silence concerning anything related to his involvement in the youth movement, there are the professional dif-ficulties associated with Nietzsche, as shown by the example of Max Weber. Both in Breslau and in Heidelberg, Elias would have realized early on that the mention of Nietzsche would create further obstacles to his difficult aca-demic career. The use made of Nietzsche by the Nazis, and the further tragic experiences that Elias had to go through at that period, could also easily have drawn a curtain over this formative experience.

1922

Whatever the exact figuration of Elias's formative experiences, their first main output was his dissertation. Though retrospectively one can read much of the themes and interests of the later Elias into this work, it does not seem to contain his later project. Its main values seem rather negative. First of all, he distanced himself from the ruling neo-Kantian orthodoxy, which at that time meant a definite closing of his academic horizons in philosophy. His professor much resented his straying from the trodden road. Elias had to delete certain passages from his thesis and even then, though he fulfilled all requirements on 26 June 1922, he only graduated as a Doctor of Philosophy on 30 January 1924 (Korte 1997: 79, RL: 32).

Interestingly enough, at exactly the same time another chapter of his life closed. In 1922, at its Prünn meeting, the *Blau Weiss* decided to opt for emigration to Palestine (Laqueur 1972: 486). Elias did not support the move and his political involvement ended at that point. At the same time, his parents experienced financial difficulties owing to the after-effects of the First World War, so he had to work for a living. For two years, he worked in a metal goods factory (RL: 31–3). All this added up to a peculiar two-year transitional or liminal period in his life. All his past commitments were suspended, there was nothing stable in his life, and there was no possibility of engaging in something new.

If the dissertation was more the ending of a chapter than a new opening, the main question becomes the identification of the moments in which Elias's project started to take shape. For other protagonists in the field, this usually happened through a reading experience which eventually led them to the problem of finding a field of study into which their work could be fitted. This was something which, given the experientially-based character of their work, was never easy. In this respect, Elias was an exception. For him, the choice of discipline came before the project and was never again questioned. Once his family overcame the financial difficulties caused by the First World War and Elias could resume his studies, he went to Heidelberg and made a definite commitment to sociology. The firmness of this decision and the way in which he never looked back to his past must have been very much conditioned by the peculiar, two-year long liminal period separating his earlier and later involvement.

1924

The exact conditions and consequences of this decision require a few explanatory comments. First, the contrast between his first and second stays in Heidelberg is quite illuminating. His 1919 stay was liminal in all respects, in that it was a short-term visit just after the War, linked to a Zionist conference, after which he would return to Breslau, his university, a degree in philosophy and work in the local Zionist youth movement. The 1924 trip, however, represented a point of no return. It was a definite farewell to Breslau, his family, the university, his career in philosophy and the political–religious involvement of his youth. The break was so complete that, in both a symbolic and a very real sense, Elias never turned back to it. It was as if a curtain was drawn at this point in his life. He lost all interest in what he had done in the past and was often positively hostile to anything connected to it. For over sixty years, he did not even know about the existence of a copy of his thesis (Korte 1997: 81). Philosophy, especially its neo-Kantian version, became an anathema for the rest of his life. He could not imagine a more negative judgement on a piece of work than to claim that it was philosophical. Though overcoming the dichotomist thinking which dominated much of contemporary academic life was a major asset to his work, his refusal to be engaged in even discussing the philosophical aspects of his work became rather a liability (see also Mennell 1992: 284–5).

His attitude to religion and politics would similarly become prohibitive. He refused to take part in even the smallest political activity, and was unable to recall whether he had ever voted in his life (RL: 45–6). Though this does not have a direct influence on his life-work, it is at least highly peculiar in view of both his later life experiences and the very strong political involvement shown by most reflexive historical sociologists. His attitudes with respect to religion were much more prejudicial to his work. In his entire body of writings on the civilizing process, Elias would never acknowledge any positive impact of religious factors. His statements range from outright denial to more cautious later remarks in which he would simply claim that this should be a matter for empirical sociological research, though while writing *The Civilizing Process*, he did not encounter significant religious factors (Elias 1985: 19). As well as the strong and unnecessary conflict this entailed with the main 'founding fathers' of sociology, it represented an undue limitation on the scope of his work. It is simply not possible to write a comprehensive history of the civilizing process if all prophetic and salvation religions, the churches and sects and especially the monasteries are left out.

Taking some cues from Elias himself, Stephen Mennell argued at length about Elias and the fact that he often acted as his own worst enemy, his 'counter-ego' (Mennell 1996). I believe that this disposition, this peculiar combination of forgetfulness and active repression of the past can and should be located here, with the contrast between the two moves to Heidelberg and the curtain falling on the past. It is not just connected with the War, as the experiential part of the autobiographical interview suggested (RL: 28). The explanation is partly theoretical–structural, and partly personal–emotional. As far as the former is concerned, there had been a complete switch of roles between the orderly normal and the transitory liminal between 1919 and 1924. Whatever was normal in 1919, his Breslau family home, professional and political background, became liminal, distant or completely abandoned; and whatever was liminal in 1919, Heidelberg and sociology, now became his normal 'home'. Liminality is known to have an impact on identity. Such a full-scale reversal is therefore bound to leave strong marks on identity and memory.

But there is something more involved here. At this point, another unavoidable hypothetical point must be made. Elias not only left his university career and political friends, but also his family, especially his parents. Today it seems only natural but then and there, especially in the concrete family situation of Elias, it was by no means common. The painfulness of this separation only revealed its true dimensions and its irreversibility between 1938 and 1940. Elias was then even further away and exiled. Within a few years both his parents died, his mother in Auschwitz. This, arguably, made the curtain steel-hard.

The move to Heidelberg in late 1924 (Korte 1997: 92, fn 51) was therefore a decisive moment, an existential choice which constituted a move away from his past and an opting for a new profession, sociology. In a very real sense, Elias was 'born again' as a converted sociologist.[4] He was also hoping to support himself as a writer. At the same time this was also a return, as it was in Heidelberg that he had first heard about sociology and Max Weber. Paradoxically, however, his change of allegiances prevented him from returning to the Heidelberg he had left. In 1919, as a student of philosophy and medicine, it was natural that he attended the seminars of Jaspers. However, for someone who wanted to study Max Weber and his sociology, the road lay through Alfred Weber.

Elias soon had to contend with a series of brute facts. Before coming to Heidelberg, he had hardly any knowledge of sociology (RL: 83). He also became aware of the differences between Max Weber's sociology and the approach of his younger brother though, strangely enough, he could not recall a tension here. Alfred Weber had a number of students already signed up for the *Habilitation* and Elias also had to get himself accepted in the salon of Marianne Weber (RL: 97–8). Together with the standard difficulties that Jews had to face in an academic career, the figuration was not particularly promising, and it looked as if he would have to wait at least ten years before he could even have a hope of getting the position he was looking for.

However, though his career as a writer failed to materialize, he did not have financial problems because of his parental background, and could afford to spend years mostly reading on his own, familiarizing himself with sociological literature. Simmel, Weber and Marx were certainly among his main readings at that time (Goudsblom 1977: 78), and he read Durkheim during his stay in Paris, if not earlier. He was evidently slow in finding a suitable theme for his thesis but he was not under pressure. The first topics he selected are quite revealing because of their affinities with other reflexive historical sociologists who were developing their interests at the same time, though they were not at all timely. As a theme for his initiatory speech in Marianne Weber's salon, he chose Gothic architecture, as it could be related 'to the development of the towns' in Germany which is closely akin to the interests of Mumford (RL: 41, 97–8). He finally settled on writing his thesis on the transition from pre-scientific to scientific modes of thinking, focusing on Florence, an interest close to Mumford, but also to Borkenau, and evidently taking a hint from Max Weber (RL: 41, 98).[5]

1930

The next breakpoint in Elias's career came in 1930, with the appointment of Karl Mannheim to the chair of sociology at the University of Frankfurt (Kilminster 1993). In Heidelberg, Elias had found more sympathy and common interest with Mannheim, a refugee from Hungary interested in the sociology of knowledge, than with Alfred Weber. After the famous 1928 row between Alfred Weber and Mannheim his position in Heidelberg was even more precarious. As he was offered an assistantship and the prospect of a *Habilitation* in three years, he was ready to follow Mannheim. With the move, he not only changed the theme of his thesis, but his work soon gained a novel focus. Mannheim suggested that he focus on the eighteenth century but he soon stumbled upon the courts of the sixteenth and seventeenth centuries and recognized a so-far unnoticed link with the present. In doing so, he received a significant impulse from the publication of Freud's *Civilization and its Discontents*. However, the decisive impact for the new project and its manner of development was due to the intellectual encounter with Franz Borkenau.[6]

1933

Elias managed to finish his thesis on court society within the planned three years. However, all this was in vain. Owing to the Nazi take over, the public defence could not take place and in any case he had no hope of ever gaining a chair under the new political conditions. Thus started a long period of odyssey and exile. First there was an unsuccessful search in Switzerland, followed by a two-year stay in Paris and finally, from the end of 1935, in England. For our purposes, the main question concerns the extent of break this represented in the work of Elias, and here one immediately enters a mystery (Mennell 1992: 17–18).

In his own account, Elias places emphasis on the break. According to this, he would only have started to work on *The Civilizing Process* once he arrived in England, where for a long while he did not know what to do or even how to make a living. Once he received a scholarship from an emigré

Jewish foundation, he first started to read casually in the British Library without any clear purpose. Finally, after picking up a few books on etiquette, he suddenly launched himself into this new project on which he worked for three years (RL: 53–6).

This account has two problems. First, there are clear continuities between *The Court Society* and *The Civilizing Process* (Mennell 1992). This contradiction could be solved by arguing that though Elias believed the change to be a break, he was only picking up the project he had abandoned when forced to leave Germany. The other problem, however, is more cumbersome. The Preface of the book is dated September 1936. It is not just a trivial formal piece, but was recently judged as still the best available introduction to the entire work (ER: 40). Furthermore, a pre-print of the first volume was circulated in 1937; and it does not seem humanly possible to complete a *magnum opus* like *The Civilizing Process* within the little more than six-month time-span implied by Elias's account. This only underlines the fact that very little is still known about the formative experiences of Elias and the conditions under which his life-project emerged.

That this is not merely a trivial philological exercise is demonstrated by the reception of the work. Elias managed to write a book which was, exactly in the sense of Nietzsche, profoundly untimely.[7] The question of what rendered such a work possible is therefore of particular substantive and methodological interest, and calls for further research.

However, if the central and still unanswered question of Elias's life and work up to writing *The Civilizing Process* is the conditions of possibility of this work, the main issue of the remaining half-century of his life became the effect of this work, or rather its lack of effect, and the question of its reception. Elias singled this out, without any hesitation, as the first question to be asked of him in an important interview in March 1985 (Elias 1985: 1). But it is also betrayed by his publication list. Apart from two articles published in the *British Journal of Sociology*, which were no doubt vital for securing a teaching position in Leicester in 1954, he did not publish a word on his own until the second edition of *The Civilizing Process* came out in 1969. The lack of recognition granted to his book, which he rightly believed then to be, and which is recognized now as, a masterpiece of social analysis in the twentieth century, made him to a significant extent into a *homo clausus*, unable to 'get rid of' his ideas in a proper form.

The remaining part of this section will try to reconstruct, in so far as it is possible now, the dynamics of the remainder of Elias's work, centring on the question of recognition and reception.[8]

It would be completely mistaken to argue that Elias was only searching for instant recognition and fame. First, he never stopped working. The problem rather was that he was not able to finalize his ideas in writing. He was constantly preoccupied with this fact and even went through psychoanalysis to improve his condition. This, however, was and could have been of no help, as no doctor could secure him an understanding audience.

Though writing can be a technique of self for therapeutic reasons, in terms of the message it is a means of communication and if it does not find an 'intended reader' (Iser 1980), the activity becomes pointless and impossible. All untimely work carries within itself the possibility of silence in one way or another.[9] This can be through madness (Nietzsche), breakdown and illness (Weber) or a partial abandonment of the project (Foucault).[10]

Elias's life-work was a quest, a *zetesis*, the persistent relentless pursuit of a coherent set of problems which were rooted in events through which he lived. He went 'where the spirit move[d him]' (Schröter 1997: 237). But his work ethos was incompatible with a *literati* posture of a project: 'I never planned my life. I went along like the rider on Lake Constance, without fear that I might fall through the ice. That is my basic feeling of life' (RL: 67). He pursued the problem he simply *had* until he found a solution (ibid.: 76), based on his self-recognition that 'I see connections that many other people do not see, and therefore have a duty to say so' (ibid.: 76).[11] This required courage which Elias never lost, as he 'never threw in the sponge' (ibid.: 67) and '[did] not let [himself] be corrupted'(ibid.: 75). It was a long-term task which involved ignoring fashionable views: 'It was always clear to me that the prevalent opinions were a fraud' (ibid.: 76). It also assumed almost boundless self-confidence: 'I have never doubted what I was doing' (ibid.: 76). This empowered him to diagnose the present as he saw it in 1984:

> It shocks me again and again to find so many people losing heart, as if nothing was worth the trouble. There is so much to be done, and so many people are wasting their time with nonsense or being intellectually corrupted. . . . I find it terrible – this lack of courage, this nihilism, this whining.
>
> (RL: 75–6)

The fact that Elias kept working during the long period of complete neglect and lack of recognition made it possible for him to publish major works in relatively quick succession at an age when other scholars have long stopped working. However, the prolonged lack of response left a profound mark on his published work. Based on certain formative experiences and the argued dialogue with Borkenau, Elias developed an original approach to and vision of sociology. It was not a system, but it had its own circular, figurational systematicity. The steps by which he arrived there, however, remained unpublished, undiscussed and inaccessible. Therefore, when presenting his argument in later life, he was often caught up in giving endless versions of his own cycle without being able to present his work in an accessible, concise form.

There were two further reasons preventing him from doing so. One has to do with age and aging. Owing to a sporting accident suffered in his youth, Elias had damaged vision in one eye, and by his old age he was hardly able to read. He therefore could not go through his own notes and had to dictate his work. This rendered a certain repetitiveness inevitable. But even before this loss of sight, the lack of previous publications prevented him from engaging in a major 'technique of self', the writing of late prefaces to earlier published works. This was all the more unfortunate as Elias was very much aware of the value of such an exercise in enhancing creativity (Schröter 1997: 239–41). The few occasions which did present themselves, together with the stimulus of autobiographical recollections, were the major sources structuring the last two decades of Elias's active life.

1968

This era starts with the first such exercise, the new *Introduction* to *The Civilizing Process*. The edition was a facsimile reprint of the 1939 edition with the only change being the new *Introduction*, completed in July 1968 in Leicester. It responded to a new public interest in Elias's writing, an interest which was further manifested in the almost simultaneous demands for a final printed edition of his 1933 thesis, *The Court Society*, and for him to write an introductory book on sociology. The effects of writing the *Introduction* are shown in the fact that Elias complied with these requests, and the manner in which he did so.

First of all, both books were published very quickly. *The Court Society* came out in 1969, while *What Is Sociology?* which had been in the making since 1965 (Korte 1997: 31), appeared in 1970. Second, they contained major conceptual developments. By the time Elias completed the new *Introduction*, *The Court Society* was already in production, but he practically rewrote the entire book at proof stage (Mennell 1996, Schröter 1997).[12] *What is Sociology?*, fortunately for Elias and especially his publishers, was not yet at such an advanced stage, so he was able to work in his new concepts more calmly. The effect of the technique of self is best visible in the introduction of two new concepts which became major Eliasian trademarks, figuration and *homo clausus*, both of which are contained in the *Introduction* written in July 1968.

But the effects can also be seen through the stream of other publications coming out at that time. In 1966 he published with Eric Dunning a short article on sport, based on a 1966 seminar given in Cologne, and between 1969 and 1971 a series of articles on sport appeared. Most of them were published jointly with Eric Dunning, with one significant exception: a major theoretical statement on the genesis of sport which took Elias back in his interests and published work to ancient Greece, apparently for the first time. Roughly during the same period, another series of articles appeared on a concern that had been close to Elias since his Heidelberg years, the sociology of science and of scientific knowledge. But the most important new project of his was a book manuscript he finished around 1971 on 'The balance of power between the sexes' (Mennell 1992: 25).

The relevance of the manuscript for Elias, and the potential impact the book could have had, is shown by what is known of its content. While his 1969 and 1970 books were based on earlier manuscripts and existing notes, this was a brand new research work. Having as its theme the problem of gender, an issue on which classical sociology had precious little to say and which was just becoming a major issue, the book could easily have brought major fame to Elias, the kind of recognition he only enjoyed in his last years, and which grew after his death. Finally, this manuscript again took Elias back to antiquity, this time to Rome, as was shown when the only part of this work that was ever published came out in a reconstructed version in 1987. Thus, writing a late Preface as a 'technique of self' led to exactly the same result for Elias as it did for Nietzsche, Weber, Foucault, Mumford and Voegelin: a sudden shift of the time horizon of research back to antiquity.

One could speculate about the possibility of Elias undertaking a major new research project at this point, similar to the multi-volume works of the other protagonists. However the manuscript was lost, and this evidently closed any such opening.

The problem was rendered more acute by the reception of the second German edition of *The Civilizing Process*, which was far from overwhelming (Korte 1997: 27, Goudsblom 1977: 57–60). Elias's real breakthrough would only come in 1976–7. The combination of the loss of the new manuscript, and the lack of an enthusiastic reception for the old work, led to another major stumble in Elias's career. This is visible first of all again through the publication track. The tide of publications which had just begun to flow ebbed. Between 1972 and 1977 few new pieces were published, and most of those were in edited collections which had probably been committed years before.

A major opportunity lost, in terms of both reception and self-reflexion, was the publication of a French edition of the two main works. Between 1973 and 1975, Callman-Lévy published both volumes of *The Civilizing Process* and also *The Court Society*. The French interest is not surprising given the themes of the books and Elias's general attachment to things French. The books were quite well received by major French intellectual figures (Goudsblom 1977: 68–72; Eribon 1994: 343, fn 3). Elias had the opportunity to produce a new preface, but in fact the first volume was published without either the *Introduction* or the *Preface*. Given the importance of both pieces, the shortness of the *Preface* and the definite need for an introduction for the French audience, it is unlikely that the omission was a choice of the publishing house. It is much more probable that Elias promised a new version but because of his current state of mind was unable to deliver it.

During the same period, little progress was made with the English translations of Elias's works. Given both his academic situation and the international market, these were even more important for his career. A manuscript translation of *The Civilizing Process*, made by Eric Dunning, had been circulated in the 1960s, and by the 1970s publishers were showing interest in bringing out the main books in English. The experience, however, proved to be a nightmare for translators. Elias was not simply difficult to accommodate; he gave the distinct impression that he was not interested in appearing in print in England (Mennell 1996).

This puzzling fact can partly be explained by referring again to the cases of other reflexive historical sociologists. Weber and Foucault were both reputed to be involved frequently in polemics. However, to contextualize these affairs, they only happened when they encountered major difficulties with their work or its reception. The situation was similar for Elias: his conflict with Mannheim can safely be associated with the first reception of *The Civilizing Process*, while his row with Ilya Neustadt, who was a close friend and with whom he jointly managed the sociology department in Leicester for over a decade, can be linked to its second reception.[13]

This indicates that his reluctance to publish was not a result primarily of perfectionism, or caused by a purely individualistic, Freudian framework (the role of the superego) (see Schröter 1997: 229ff). After the decades-long wait, he could only go into print if he was confident and assured of a proper reception. In England, after his recent row with Neustadt, this was not the case. Furthermore, he evidently laid most store by the German reception of his work. Perhaps because *The Civilizing Process* was first published in German and because of his background in German culture, it seemed that he 'pegged' the English publication of his books, especially in the context of the recent row, to a triumphal German reception.

These ideas receive support from his only major new work and his only new 'late Preface', both published during this period in the Netherlands. The new work was his essay on time, written in English but published in Dutch in 1974–5. The theme reflected on his own experience of the passing of years. The new introduction was to the Dutch translation of the only other book he published before 1969, *The Established and the Outsiders*. This new edition therefore provided an opportunity for another 'technique of self'. The new introduction is widely acknowledged as a major theoretical statement.

It was also at the University of Amsterdam that Elias gave, in November 1976, a lecture on the 'Theory of Social Processes' which was another significant theoretical piece (Elias 1997). Around that time, Elias became a major figure in Dutch sociology, much more influential and recognized than in France, England or Germany. In the Netherlands he could take for granted a sympathetic, waiting audience.

1977

The spectacular breakthrough in the reception of Elias' work happened around 1977. This was again owing to a combination of factors. In 1977, Elias celebrated his eightieth birthday. This gave rise to a *Festschrift* (see

Gleichman *et al.*, 1977) and stirred general interest in his work. In 1976 a cheap pocketbook edition of *The Civilizing Process* appeared in German (Korte 1997: 28). It received laudatory praise in a 7 February 1977 article in *Der Spiegel* (Schröter 1997: 264) and soon became a major best-seller. Within a short time, Elias was named as the recipient of the Adorno Prize of the City of Frankfurt. The success had been delayed for almost forty years but finally it had come.

This recognition gave rise to a burst of creativity and also to existential choices. In Elias's case, creativity and publications did not mean the same thing, as many of the new publications were translations or printed versions of texts written earlier. An abundance of new projects started in 1977; Michael Schröter lists no less than six new projects which were launched between the summers of 1977 and 1978 (Schröter 1997: 278–9). At this period, any external stimulus could launch him immediately into a new project which was often quickly completed. Thus his essay *The Loneliness of Dying* was written in a spurt, provoked by a brainstorm-interview for a journal (Schröter 1997: 236). While Elias often worked decades on a project before it appeared in print, this essay was published shortly after the original idea came and within a few years it was translated into Dutch, French, Danish, Italian, and English.

Apart from this outburst of creativity, quick progress was made in the translations of his works that had been lagging behind for such a long time. The first volume of *The Civilizing Process* and *What Is Sociology?* were brought out in English by different publishers in 1978, ending years of stalemate (Mennell 1996). At the same time the German translation began of Elias's works written in English. A translation of his 1956 essay on 'Involvement and detachment' started in early 1977 (Schröter 1997: 227). It was eventually published as a book in German in 1983 and in English in 1987, while the essay on time appeared in 1979.[14]

Just as happened with Foucault in 1955, 1961, 1966 and 1971, changes in his work and its recognition also led to a move of residence for Elias. In summer 1978 he moved to Bielefeld, becoming a fellow at the *Zentrum für interdisziplinäre Forschung* (Schröter 1997: 284). He stayed there until 1984 when, again in the context of a major reorganization, he moved to Amsterdam.

Perhaps the most significant choice Elias made at that moment, however, was further to delay the publication of Volume Two of *The Civilizing Process*. The reason was that in 1978, Elias tried to do the same thing as he had done with much success in 1968: to write a new *Introduction*. As Elias considered the re-reading of his own work a main technique for enhancing creativity (Schröter 1997: 239–40), there can be no question about the deliberateness of the strategy. Over the years he accumulated piles of notes, but the undertaking did not lead to a proper result. After about three years, Stephen Mennell attempted to cut the material into a reasonable shape, but the result failed to satisfy Elias (Mennell 1996). This failure, however, succeeded in convincing him that the undertaking was impossible and he finally gave the green light to publication without a new *Introduction*.

The main reason for the failure was that in the voluminous draft version Elias produced, he conflated a technique of self with its effects. The manuscript not only contained reflections on the work but also tried to encompass the effect of that work of reflection, elements of the remodelled research project launched by the self-reading experience. The conflation is visible from the fact that the manuscript contained copious sections on the history of the civilizing process, going back to Sumeric cities (Mennell 1996), which clearly had nothing to do with an *Introduction* to the published Volume Two. However, it is just as clear that it would be most unjust to blame Elias for the 'error', as the main cause was beyond his control. By that time, his eyesight had deteriorated to the extent that he could hardly manage to read. He was no longer able to launch a new project concerning the more distant origins of the 'civilizing process'.

The exercise, though unsuccessful, was by no means futile. Most of the works which he managed to complete and publish in the period were, in one way or another, tied to this exercise of self. One of the most important was a return to and revisiting of the question of civilization and the civilizing process. It seems that, until this moment, Elias was not able or willing to present in print further reflections on the question. It does not mean that he did not keep reflecting on the matter. The first version of *The Society of Individuals* was finished even before Volume Two of *The Civilizing Process* was published, and in the 1940s or 1950s he even wrote a second draft version. Furthermore, the Eichmann trial in 1961 induced him, just like Hannah Arendt, to a series of reflections that led to the first version of 'Civilization and Violence'. But none of these saw print. The decisive impetus to commit himself to a long-term research project came in the autumn of 1977 (Schröter 1997: 278). It was soon followed by a stream of related publications and in the last decade of his life remained one of the central preoccupations for Elias, eventually leading to the publication of his book *The Germans*, one of his conclusive statements.

A second stream of works can be traced directly to Elias's reflections on the very experience of writing this new *Introduction*, especially the painful realization of his lack of success. His essay on death belongs in this stream, along with the German translation of his essay on time and an essay on the elderly, published in 1980.

Finally, at this time Elias also started work on a subject not touched by him before, the question of Utopia. He was both giving talks on this topic and writing an utopia on his own (Schröter 1997).

1984

The last major reorientation of Elias's life and work, together with an additional creative upsurge, came around 1984 when he was already eighty-seven. This time, it was not related directly to the reception of his work, which suffered no further bad fortune, though neither was it unrelated to matters of recognition. It was a consequence of fame, with the recurrent concern of others with questions about his life and intellectual predecessors which eventually helped Elias to turn to another 'technique of self', one which was better suited to his condition but which he was very reluctant to use for a long time.

Techniques of self can be oriented to two different targets: to one's own past work or to one's life. Owing to his poor eyesight, the first became impossible for Elias to practice fully. For the second, such limitations were less inhibiting. It is certainly easier to remember what one lived through than what one actually wrote down.[15] However, this type of autobiographical undertaking, even restricted to intellectual history, was an undertaking Elias repeatedly refused to engage upon (Mennell 1996).

The comparative perspective used in this book helps to locate this resistance in a proper setting. With the singular exception of Mumford who rather represented an opposite excess, all main protagonists of the field were very reluctant to discuss themselves as opposed to their works, owing to a combination of privacy, an unwillingness to push their personality into the foreground as opposed to their work, and their upbringing.[16] In an age when biographies and autobiographies became particularly fashionable, Elias, like Voegelin or Foucault, was only willing or able to treat his own life in the form of biographical interviews, and even then with much reluctance (Tabboni 1993: 26, 31).

The demand for knowledge about Elias's intellectual formation and personal background had been increasing since 1977. Still in 1980, he was quite reluctant to meet the demand though even the little information he leaked about himself had the effect of a 'revelation' (Mennell 1996). However, in 1984, the ice was finally broken. He wrote a short statement mostly dealing with issues of intellectual autobiography, and also granted a series of seven long autobiographical interviews to two of his research assistants, which were published together in *Reflections on a Life*. Around the same time he moved from Bielefeld to Amsterdam where he would spend the remaining years of his life.

The effects were immediate and significant, and gave Elias the chance of completing a series of significant new publications, based both on already completed manuscripts and on new ideas. They also help to single out his priorities. Part of the new work represented a successful completion of work started in the early 1980s. This is especially true for the two major books which took up the line of research started with *The Civilizing Process*, *The Society of Individuals* and *The Germans*. Others were directly produced by the anamnetic exercises. One of his most important new writings was indeed a work of recollection and recovery. Elias was now able and willing to reconstruct from memory at least parts of the lost manuscript on the balance of power between the sexes. This was the part dealing with

Rome, serving as a further indication of the close ties between self-reflexivity and an intensified interest in antiquity (Elias 1987a).[17] This was not an isolated incident. In a major interview he gave around the same time, Elias claimed that the breakdown of the Roman Empire greatly interested him at that moment (Elias 1985: 34).

If on the one hand the new reflexive exercise launched Elias towards the distant past, helping him to put into print at least some of his related ideas, it also made him reflect again on the experience itself and helped him towards a new understanding of the importance of life and biographical information. This led to one of the other end-projects of his life, a biography of Mozart which occupied him much in his last years and which appeared in print shortly after his death. This project was started in the creative upsurge of 1977–8. However, the emphasis was more on the context of the court society and the book only gained its strongly biographical inspiration after Elias's anamnetic exercises of 1984.

In the mid 1980s, Elias produced a series of synthetic essays and short books. However, probably the most significant and without any doubt the most daring, almost breathtakingly courageous, new undertaking was the idea of writing a theory of symbols.[18] The stakes were quite high, as a failure could have jeopardized Elias's steadily rising reputation.[19] He certainly placed a great deal of emphasis on this new work and considered any voice of doubt a personal betrayal. This was no doubt because these voices alluded to the most painful part of his life, and the fact that by the time he was being given recognition and was in the position of working properly, physically he became too old.[20]

The stunt came off. In 1989, there appeared in the German original the long book of essays entitled *The Germans*, and in the English original the three essays forming *The Symbol Theory*. The biography on Mozart was also basically ready by that time, and appeared in print in 1991. The last piece of work Elias was engaged in, literally until the time of his death on 1 August 1990, was the *Introduction* to the book version of *The Symbol Theory*. He was in his ninety-fourth year.

2 Franz Borkenau

Of the six main protagonists of this book, without any doubt Franz Borkenau is the least known. Weber and Foucault are representative thinkers of their age, Elias and Voegelin are major figures in their field and have developed a considerable following, while Mumford is also a widely known public, academic and even literary figure. Borkenau, however, is only known as having written some classic works in the obscure and mostly forgotten field of communist studies, and as a peripheral figure of the early Frankfurt School, deserving perhaps a few footnotes.

Thus, it is not surprising that there is neither a biography on Borkenau nor a book-length discussion of his work available. In fact, the situation is even worse. Among circles that knew about him or his work, his name rather often provokes rare animosity.[1] Being half-Jewish but going through a strict Catholic education (which he then renounced), joining the Communist Party early but then becoming a staunch anti-Communist, being a member of the early Frankfurt School but then going in a different direction, writing a dissertation on the philosophy of history but publishing books on contemporary history and journalism, he was disliked by both Catholics and Jews, Communists and anti-Communists, the friends and foes of the Frankfurt School, academic historians and political philosophers. In addition he married and divorced three times and was considered a womanizer.

He had his supporters, though. His work was highly praised by Lucien Febvre and later by Raymond Aron. Bronislaw Malinowski helped him to a teaching appointment in Panama, while in 1946 he obtained a chair in contemporary history at the University of Marburg. Georg Lichtheim considered him as a man of extraordinary erudition.[2] In the late 1970s his work was championed by the odd couple of the conservative American sociologist Daniel Bell and the ultra-radical Italian thinker Toni Negri (1978).[3] However, some of his 'friends' had few friends of their own, while the prestige of the others often only fuelled the envy and hatred that seem to have followed him everywhere.

Still, in spite of all this, I will claim both that his work was highly significant, especially when read together with that of the other protagonists of the field, and that his life had the character of a coherent quest, a *zetesis*, as 'in this driven and restless life, there was one abiding passion: the thirst for truth, for learning, for a never-ending approach to knowledge' (Lowenthal, in EB: 8). In this section, I will try to support this latter point, using the quite sketchy information available.

Franz Borkenau was born on 15 December 1900 in Vienna.[4] His family was Jewish on his father's side, the grandparents coming from Hungary and Rumania, while his mother was a Catholic. His father became a civil servant and one of his uncles achieved notoriety as head of the political police both in the Habsburg Empire and during the First Republic. Borkenau was educated in the elite *Schotten Gymnasium* run by the Jesuits but based on an old Irish monastery.

Though both his grades and conduct were good in his high school years, around the end of the First World War the spirit of the times moved Borkenau and he became involved in the emerging German youth movement. Furthermore, he was one of the youngest members of its most radical wing, run by Siegfried Bernfeld (Lowenthal, in EB: 2) who attempted to create a synthesis between Austro-Marxism and psycho-analysis (Russo 1981: 291). Given the predictable reactions of his parents, this was most probably the context in which he was informed of his Jewish origins, which was a 'great shock to him' (Brenan 1974: 328; see Tashjean 1984: 289). Here one can add a further speculative point: as Bernfeld was highly influential in the Jewish youth movement *Hashomer Hatzair* which had moved to Vienna in 1916, it is quite possible that Borkenau made contact at that moment. At any rate, he certainly encountered not only the works of Freud, but also those of Marx and Nietzsche at that time, and responded to the 'shock' with a series of existential decisions. He left Vienna and his family, moving to Leipzig in order to study history and philosophy at the university. There, in 1921, after being first involved with the socialist students' movement, he joined the German Communist Party.[5]

In the Party, he continued his involvement with the youth movement. He became national leader of the communist students in Germany under an alias (Lowenthal, in EB: 3). In 1924, he joined the staff of the Communist International, working secretly in Berlin in a research section led by the Hungarian economist Eugen Varga. This experience left a profound mark on him, as even in the late 1930s though '[h]e was a courageous man, [he was] so extraordinarily nervous that he could not sit or walk without continually turning his head to see if he was being watched or followed' (Brenan 1974: 328). This concern with secrecy has also contributed much to the paucity of information available on his life and activities.

Borkenau became disillusioned with the Communist Party during its Stalinization around 1928 and was finally expelled at the end of 1929. At that point he intensified his contacts with the Frankfurt *Institut*, most probably through its first director, Carl Grünberg, who also came from Vienna (Bottomore and Goode 1978: 9–10, Jay 1973: 16).[6] However, Grünberg soon became ill and had to be replaced. Borkenau thus remained without a protector which represented particular difficulties for him, as '[h]e was an uncouth, clumsy man with . . . little aptitude for getting on with people. A Nietzschean romantic rather than a Marxist' (Brenan 1974: 328). Furthermore, he soon became engaged in a complex work, straying far away from the safe waters of orthodox Eastern or Western Marxism, going where the dynamics of his project led him.

This attitude was bound to lead to conflicts in an institute organized expressly on the principle of single-person responsibility, giving quasi-dictatorial powers to its director (Jay 1973: 19). In addition, Borkenau committed the sacrilege of not only referring approvingly to the work of Carl Schmitt, who belonged to the opposite camp, but even preferring this work to Horkheimer's. These 'clumsy' acts of unorthodoxy could not and did not remain unpunished.

First, once the manuscript of *Transition from the Feudal to the Bourgeois World Image* was submitted, Borkenau was 'tricked' into a relatively minor though not insignificant alteration of the text. Given that Marx connected the rise of the machine and of the mechanistic view of modern science to the age of manufacture, Borkenau was reminded that he omitted to pay service to this work and it was suggested that he rectify his error. He complied with the request and added a short chapter to appease criticism.[7] This, however, was a mistake as, in the second round, the economic historian Henryk Grossman was charged with reviewing the book. Not surprisingly, he focused much of his criticism on this chapter, the only one on which he could claim competence, and which was indeed below the standard of the others.

The book appeared in 1934 in Paris, where the entire Institut, including Borkenau, had taken temporary refuge. Though at first it received favourable reviews from Lucien Febvre in *Annales* and Christopher Dawson in the *Sociological Review*, Grossman's violent attack reversed the trend. Even today, the book is mostly known 'filtered through' (Russo 1985: 114, fn5) this most 'unfair' (Lichtheim, quoted in Jay 1973: 306, fn45), partial and 'bitterly doctrinaire' (Lowenthal, in EB: 6) review.[8] In the given circumstances, this criticism did not simply dismiss a work which had taken several years, and which raised 'highly original questions' (Lowenthal, in EB: 4) and answered them by an erudite knowledge of Western political thought going back to the Middle Ages, marshalled in over 550 pages, but rendered Borkenau an exile among exiles.[9]

At that difficult moment, instead of collapsing or giving up his independence, Borkenau bounced back immediately, partly by using whatever support his book received before the fatal blow, and partly by returning to his roots. As far as the first is concerned, his only 1935 publication was an article in *Annales*, where the favourable review of Febvre appeared earlier; while his only 1937 article came to light in the *Sociological Review*, no doubt with the help of Christopher Dawson, where he continued to publish book reviews in 1938 and 1939. As far as the second is concerned, through his old Vienna connections, he managed to obtain the support of Malinowski in getting a teaching position in Panama (Russo 1981: 302, 1985: 112).

During this highly liminal year (being an exile of exiles in an exotic country, recovering from the negative reception of a major work and fighting against illness), Borkenau both completed a major work and did even more important work on his self. Returning to his knowledge gained while studying Italian fascism, he put together a book on Pareto (Borkenau 1936).[10] Pareto at that time became highly fashionable in the Anglo-Saxon academic world.[11] Though this book was widely read and reprinted as late as 1979, it certainly did not do full justice to the range of Pareto's ideas (W. D. Jones: 1992: 459).

However, from the perspective of Borkenau's life-work, its flaw proved to be its main asset. While writing this book, Borkenau was less interested in reproducing Pareto's ideas than in elaborating a view he gained under the liminal conditions of his Panama year, based on both his work and life experiences. This view was that in spite of taking up the opposite extremes in the political scene, fascism and communism shared many common features that could be described in the word 'totalitarianism'. Even though details of his historical analysis can be questioned, Borkenau came up with a new vision of the politics of his times. He was 'an unorthodox [and] also a "premature" anti-totalitarian', presenting a comparison between communism and fascism that 'would become commonplace during the early Cold War years, but . . . was hardly an attitude typical of European leftist intellectuals in 1936' (W. D. Jones 1992: 463).

The 'visionary' character of the book on Pareto, which is both its asset and its liability, reveals that Borkenau's liminal conditions in Panama stimulated reflexivity, and that this led to unusual, experientially-based combinations and insights. The strong presence of self-reflexivity, involving both life and work, is also revealed by the publication in 1936 of an essay on the free youth movement in which Borkenau himself played a part. This no doubt is the reason why he selected the pseudonym 'Jungmann' here, though the fact that he used such a device remains to be explained. Given the 1935 incidents with Horkheimer and Grossman, one could understand that his name was not welcome in an *Institut* publication. In fact, in 1935 he told Grossman that he would not publish his reply to the criticism in the *Zeitschrift* (Russo 1985: 112) and this was indeed his last piece associated with the *Institut*. Yet, it is difficult to believe that Horkheimer, who edited the volume, did not know who was the author of this essay.[12]

Because Borkenau developed health problems in Panama, he returned to Europe in 1936 and stayed, just like Elias, in England until the outbreak of the Second World War. As a further commonalty with Elias, he made a living by giving courses in adult education in London and Cambridge. However, even before he could settle in England, he grasped a singular chance and went to Spain in order to give 'an eye-witness account' on the outbreak of the Civil War (Borkenau 1937). The book became a huge success and even today remains the single best known work of Borkenau still in print.

The reception of the book included another indication of the bad luck which pursued Borkenau throughout his career. The book was reviewed by George Orwell, who praised it in the highest possible terms (Orwell 1968, I: 276–7).[13] He characterized the book as an exemplary, calm and lucid sociological analysis and added that it managed to capture the entire atmosphere of the situation. He reviewed Borkenau's subsequent book on the Communist International in similar terms (Orwell 1968, I: 348–51). The two became friends and Orwell started to champion Borkenau as one of the most incisive writers and intellectuals of his generation.

At this moment, fate intervened again. In 1940, Borkenau was deported as enemy alien to Australia. The connection with Orwell was broken and it was not resumed even after 1945. After the war Borkenau returned to Germany, while Orwell fell ill and died in January 1950. Given that the two novels that brought most fame to Orwell, *Animal Farm* and *Nineteen Eighty-Four*, were conceived and written in the early to mid-forties, one may wonder to what extent the comet-like appearance of Borkenau in the life of Orwell may have left a decisive stamp on them.

At this point, it is worthwhile returning to the comparison with Elias. There was a huge difference between the productivity of Borkenau and Elias at the period, when both were suffering from the fate of the reception of their major book. The difference was recognized by Elias with emphasis and evident envy even decades after (Papcke 1991: 136) and one wonders about the extent to which this can be attributed to the different way they dealt with their own similar pasts and their involvement in the youth movement. The contrast between the repression and forgetting of the past done by Elias and his difficulties in writing, and the memory recovering and the ease of writing characteristic of Borkenau, is certainly not spurious. However one may wonder whether the strong, almost obsessive involvement of Borkenau in the problems of communism, towards which his anamnetic exercises launched him, did not slow down and deviate from his long-term historical work.

Such an argument is all the more appropriate as it was exactly at that moment, again liminal on several counts, when Borkenau had a major reading experience which projected him on to his major research path lasting for the last two decades of his life.[14] It was during his first year in England, just after his traumatic experiences in Frankfurt, Paris and Panama, shortly before the outbreak of the Second World War, and just after gaining fame with his book on Spain and starting his career as an interpretive historian of communism. To make the circle full, the book was the major new work of his old friend Norbert Elias, *The Civilizing Process*.

Borkenau read the first volume of *The Civilizing Process* when the second was not yet available, but he knew that it was in the making. It made a substantial impact on him; it was a genuine reading experience. It built up a huge expectation, an intellectual tension in him. At the end of his review, he stated that for a full assessment of the underlying theoretical question, it was necessary to wait for the second volume (Borkenau, 1938: 311). This volume, however, as Goudsblom (1977: 42) recognized, did not fully satisfy Borkenau. But it did not mean that he turned away from the underlying problem. Quite the contrary, it was this combination that made him launch his major life-project. It was *The Civilizing Process* that genuinely 'projected' Borkenau into starting *End and Beginning*, where he traced back the roots of the European 'civilizing process' to the monastic spurt of the sixth to eighth centuries.

Information about the remaining two decades of Borkenau's life is scarce. However, perhaps it is not too risky to claim that for the purposes of this book, little that happened is of much interest. It seems that most if not all of what Borkenau did in this period revolved around the two main projects launched by the pattern of events of 1935–38 that related to recognition, reflexivity and liminality: the shock of the reception of his 1934 book, the suspended year spent in Panama which was conducive to anamnetic exercises, his two travels in Spain shortly after his return to Europe, and his reading of the two volumes of *The Civilizing Process* around the same time.

In a way, these projects complemented each other, one being contemporary and political, the other purely academic, related to the distant past. In fact, according to Lowenthal, 'he lived *on* the first but largely *for* the second' (in EB: 7). However, one wonders whether this was so simple, whether he needed to do so much journalistic work in order to make a living and whether he found eventually a proper balance. It would seem that the answer is no.

In fact, after the Second World War Borkenau got his chance to devote himself to the pursuit of his research interests because in 1946 he obtained a chair in Marburg. But in 1948 he gave it up and returned to live as an independent writer and journalist, which meant to write about communism. It is extremely difficult, and almost by definition unjust, to pronounce a judgement on this point. Due to his life experiences, and especially thanks to the reflexive dynamics of his life-work gained by his relation to these experiences, Borkenau was decades ahead of his contemporaries, both in his work and in his political assessments. Classic figures of the so-called 'Western Marxism' such as Lukacs or Sartre, though older or not much younger than him, would preserve their affiliation with the Communist Party until the 1960s and a rather dogmatic orthodox Marxist stamp was left on all their work.[15] Borkenau certainly knew the Party better and felt it his duty to make his views known and to act on them. Just like Weber, he was caught between science and politics, or perhaps rather science and political journalism, as a vocation but in his case the cards of fate were stacked slightly differently.

The Cold War had just started, and under such conditions Borkenau was not able to gain the peace of mind necessary for academic work (Lowenthal 1957: 59). The fact that his chair was in contemporary history may have contributed. Though in 1947 he published a book on German history which contained a first version of his ideas on the 'I-form of speech', in 1948, with the communist takeover spreading in East Europe, he gave up his chair and immersed himself in political activities. This meant active membership in intellectual movements like the Congress for Freedom led by Arthur Koestler which belonged to the charismatic wing of anti-Communism (Hochgeschwender 1997). But most of all, it meant journalistic activities.

After giving up his chair, Borkenau made his living out of political journalism and produced a vast output. His work contained unusual insights, like his 1952 prediction of the imminent split between Russia and China (Tashjean 1983). But his interest in communism became obsessive and it led to inaccuracies in detail and occasionally excessive speculations (Lowenthal, in EB: 7).

The most important consequence of leaving Marburg was his withdrawal from academic life. This is clearly visible in the structure of his publications. While before, he mostly published books with some articles and reviews in scientific journals, from now on he published only one real book which was received much less well then his classic 1938 work, many journalistic articles and short pamphlets.[16] More problematically, even pieces of his historical work were published in political journals. This prevented a proper circulation of his ideas, as those interested in the daily affairs of the communist countries had no interest in the early Middle Ages, while academic historians or historically-oriented social theorists did not turn to these journals for new ideas. As a consequence Borkenau got no proper feedback, his ideas did not gain circulation, and the work remained an unpublished fragment, all the more so as its two parts were written in different languages. He wrote the part on the origins of German mythology in German, while the other thread of his genealogical design covering Irish and Anglo-Saxon monasticism was written in English.

Franz Borkenau died suddenly of a heart attack in a Zurich hotel on 22 May 1957, in the fifty-seventh year of his life.

3 Eric Voegelin

Eric Voegelin was born on 3 January 1901 in Cologne. His father, a civil engineer, was Lutheran, while his mother was Catholic. As the family was not affluent, problems of money influenced much the character of his studies.

As no Voegelin biography is available, information about his early years and formative experiences are scarce and are mostly confined to autobiographical discussions with Ellis Sandoz (AR) and a few scattered remarks. However, a unique set of documents exists, the anamnetic exercises Voegelin made in autumn 1943 which cover the first nine years of his life.

The anamnetic exercises, published in *Anamnesis* (AN: 38–51), brought to the surface 'childhood experiences of wonder, awe, fear, perplexity, and longing' (Webb 1981: 38), which rendered Voegelin, at a very young age, sensitive to the 'problematicity of existence' (Patocka 1981). They were, first and foremost, related to the experience of time (numbers 1, 2, 4) and space (numbers 8, 14). This covers partly the recurrence and reversal of time, as captured in the story about the calendar (number 2) and the Prussian history book (number 15), or the reversibility of perspective (number 8). Even deeper impressions, however, were left by the experience of endlessness, the infinity of the time and space horizon, the anxiety in face of the beyond (numbers 5, 6, 7 and 13).[1] Still, even at that age, Voegelin found the utopias attempting to cover this tension with illusory solutions singularly unappealing, representing too high a price. This anticipated his later, relentless rejection of all type of utopianism, in the name of 'reality' (Sebba 1982: 9).

Apart from concerns with perspective and infinity, however, several of the recollections were connected to properly liminal experiences. They were about travelling and ships (numbers 9, 10, 11, 17), and about a famous monk who got lost in the forest for a hundred years during a meditation (number 4), while another involved a scene from the *Mardi Gras* carnival (number 3). This last closely recalls the similar childhood experience of Huizinga, which also came back to him during a major breakpoint of his intellectual career.[2]

The list of recollections ends with Voegelin's first 'trauma of emigration', the move of the entire family from Germany to Vienna in 1910 which disrupted the timeless stability of his childhood.

Schooling

Very little is known about Voegelin's high-school years, as the anamnetic exercises end at the age of nine and the *Autobiographical Reflections* start with the university years, giving only a short glimpse backwards later. Contrast and comparison with Borkenau, Elias, Foucault, Mumford and Schutz, however, provide some help for analysis and interpretation.

Voegelin's career deviated from the standard pattern of Central European intellectuals by the age of ten. He was enrolled at a *Real-gymnasium*, thus studying more sciences and less humanities. In this way, he missed out on Greek, which he would have to pick up at the age of thirty, but gained in mathematics and English. Then came the First World War, and many of his teachers came to be casual staff. This experience, however, far from being a disruption, gave him the opportunity to encounter new and unusual ideas which were way beyond the bore of the standard curriculum. These 'listening experiences' were complemented with a pair of 'reading experiences' (Szakolczai 1998a: 28–30) an encounter with the works of Schopenhauer and Nietzsche, 'the only philosophers who were widely read in the German-speaking countries . . . neither of them academically fashionable' (Webb 1981: 24, paraphrasing Voegelin).

The far-from-ordinary high school years, lived in a foreign country during a world war and increasingly surrounded by non-regular teaching staff, were concluded not by a return to order and stability but by a genuine escalation of liminality. In November 1918 'a political order that to the Austrians of the early part of the century had seemed virtually indestructible' collapsed (Webb 1981: 21). This happened during Voegelin's last year at high school so that his *Abitur* and first university year corresponded to the first year of post-war reconstruction, just as occurred to Elias, Borkenau and Foucault. The political events did not fail to leave deep marks on his intellectual development but they did so in a highly peculiar manner, through two major encounters with the *Upanishads* and Marxism.

During winter 1918–19 Paul Deussen, the foremost specialist in Hindu philosophy and translator of the *Upanishads* and also a friend of Nietzsche since the Pforta years, came to Vienna to deliver a series of lectures on the *Upanishads* in an adult education institute. Voegelin came to the lectures and it was there, and not in the Protestant Sunday school, that he become touched by and drawn to the experience of transcendence (Voegelin 1980: 153–4; 1984: 106). At the same time, Max Weber was giving his first university course in Vienna after a break of exactly twenty years, but Voegelin still attended high school and the next year Weber was lecturing in Munich. During the summer of 1919 Voegelin read Marx and for a short time became a convert to Marxism. Though he admitted this fact, in a rather self-desultory manner, in his *Autobiographical Reflections*, the significance of this event is still little realized.

This can be assessed by reconstructing the exact figuration, taking into account its highly liminal character, and also by making comparisons with other protagonists in the field. Voegelin read Marx in August 1919 and considered himself a Marxist until the end of the year (AR: 9–10). In political time, this was still the year after the First World War, the time of the Soviet republics in Bavaria and Hungary, with the Weimar Republic being founded in August 1919. In Austria, the Social Democrats were in government and the new constitution of the country was accepted on 1 October 1919. The situation was no less liminal as far as Voegelin's own 'personal time' was concerned. August 1919 was the time of summer vacation, between finishing high school and starting university, while autumn 1919 was his first university semester. As evidence from the comparable life periods of Weber, Mumford, Elias and Foucault shows, for each of them similar conditions rendered possible a major intellectual encounter which shaped, positively, the dynamics of their future life-work. This was the moment when Weber was initiated into political economy by the lectures of Knies and read Lange, when Mumford read Geddes, when Elias was 'initiated' into Max Weber through Jaspers and when Foucault listened to Hyppolite. Voegelin came under the sway of Marx for a short time, probably 'initiated' by the singularly boring, doctrinaire figures of Max Adler and Carl Grünberg.[3] Though the episode was short, one could argue that it was bound to leave lasting scars especially in matters of style.

The crucial stamp left by this figuration during the liminal period on the substance, as opposed to the style, of Voegelin's later work can be seen by assessing the impact of the sequence of these encounters that rendered Voegelin's formation unique in a generation undergoing a series of common formative experiences. At the height of political mobilization and of abandoning religion, which was considered outmoded and bourgeois, Voegelin was drawn to a mystic kind of non-Western religion.[4] In this way, far from seeing politics and religion, especially mysticism, as opposites, he recognized a basic connection between them. Furthermore, far from seeing Christianity (his background) and Eastern mysticism (his current experience) as opposites, he recognized the commonality between the two kinds of religious experiences, rendering him sensitive to the 'equivalences of experiences' and their 'symbolization'.

Voegelin's formative years, which extended to the entire 1920s, his twenties, can be characterized both by the unusual variety of intellectual encounters and influences, and by their strongly personally-mediated character. Voegelin did not simply read a series of thinkers but intensively discussed them with friends in closely-knit intellectual communities. The broad scope was partly due to the extraordinary intellectual fermentation that encompassed Vienna at that time, as this was the Vienna of Freud and psychoanalysis, of the Vienna Circle and 'Wittgenstein's Vienna' (Janik and Toulmin 1973). Even further, while in most other places like Frankfurt the different intellectual and political groups were distant and hostile to each other, in Vienna they kept talking to each other until the last minute. However, even in this context, the 'ecumenic' interests of Voegelin were exceptional. He had two supervisors, Hans Kelsen and Othmar Spann, who belonged to opposite areas in the intellectual landscape, while his 1922 dissertation *Wechselwirkung und Gezweiung* combined key words from the sociology of Simmel and Spann (AR: 26; see also Petropulos 1997: 6–11). He belonged to the main intellectual circles at the university, a seminar of the economist Ludwig von Mises on '"the understanding of understanding"' (Webb 1981: 52–3, fn 1), the *Geistkreis* founded by Hayek and Herbert Fürth in 1921 but soon led by Voegelin, and he was close to the Stefan George *Kreis*. These groups were not only places of intellectual exchange but also gave rise to lasting friendships. Finally, a major formative experience of Voegelin was his encounter with Karl Kraus (AR: 17–19; see also Janik and Toulmin 1973, Johnston 1972: 203–7). Kraus was some kind of a modern reincarnation of ancient Hebrew prophets, a relentless critic and polemical adversary who was always ready for a fight to serve a just cause. He founded the satirical journal *Die Fäckel* in 1899 which he wrote alone between 1910 and 1936. His was an extraordinary one-man show but it was also part of the same world he detested, as he 'denounced faults that he himself shared', taking 'refuge in a fortress of solipsism' (Johnston 1972: 207). His example, and especially his excessively polemical style that may be acceptable in journalism but is out of place in academic work, proved a very mixed blessing for Voegelin.

Of all personal encounters, the most important was no doubt his friendship with Alfred Schutz (Voegelin 1981, Weiss 1997), while the dominant intellectual impact was exerted by Max Weber. Not surprisingly, the two were closely related. As the details of Schutz's encounter with Weber are better known, they can also be used to indicate the sequence for Voegelin.[5]

Though Schutz was almost two years older than Voegelin they started university together in the first post-war year, owing to his military service. Though Weber was no longer there, his charismatic presence had already become a living legend (Wagner 1983: 14). During their first university years, there was little Schutz and Voegelin could read from Weber, as his works were still scattered in the *Archiv* and not available in a book form. As they were both very busy studying for their degrees in the Faculty of Law and finishing the requirements with unusual speed, they had little time to read articles that were relatively difficult to access.

The decisive moment of reading Weber came in 1922. By that time they had finished their degrees and *Economy and Society*, *Sociology of Religions* and his 'methodological' writings were all available in book forms and 'were of course devoured by us students' (AR: 11). The first major theoretical article of Voegelin, published in 1924, was indeed 'On Max Weber'.

Travelling

Though in the 1920s Vienna could rightly be considered as the centre of Europe, at least in an intellectual sense, the intellectual career of Voegelin in the period was rendered further unique by the amount and the kind of travelling abroad he did. Spending a few semesters outside home was a standard practice of students at German universities. But in the highly receptive period of his twenties, Voegelin was constantly on the move. In the summer 1921 or 1922 he went to Oxford, mostly to perfect his English, but he also used the opportunity to listen to the lectures of the great classical scholar Gilbert Murray. During the 1922–3 academic year, he was in Berlin for a semester and took a course on Greek history with Eduard Meyer (AR: 15).[6] These listening experiences reinforced and deepened his interest in comparative history already acquired through his reading of Weber (AR: 14–15). But the most important study trip, without any doubt, was the two years he spent with a Rockefeller Fellowship in the United States. He was among the first Austrians to ever receive the award (AR: 28).

He studied at Columbia, Harvard and Wisconsin. He met Giddings, Dewey, Whitehead and Commons and had the chance of encountering not only new ideas but also the persons propagating them. This link proved to be crucial for Voegelin's entire later work, and is already visible in the last chapter of his 1928 book on the work and personality of John Commons (AR: 32). The encounter with these persons and their works amounted to a genuine intellectual shock. In Vienna, Voegelin was intellectually socialized through the marginal utility theorists in economics (Hayek, von Mises, Machlup, Haberler), the logical positivists in philosophy, and especially the legal positivism of Kelsen, into the neo-Kantian school, though he had some reservations even then. The encounter with American constitutional and legal life and through it the American forms of thought and their roots in common sense, liberated him from the sterile intellectualism of his native environment: 'The experience broke for good (at least I hope it did) my Central European or generally European provincialism without letting me fall into an American provincialism' (AR: 32–3). Voegelin thus overcame another of the 'opiums' of Central European intellectuals, the fascination with neo-Kantian philosophy and methodology.[7] Upon his return to Vienna after spending 1926–7 in Paris, he wrote his first book *On the Form of the American Mind*.

However, before returning home, the fellowship allowed him to spend an additional year in France where, apart from attending lectures by Brunschvicg the famous Pascal scholar and reading Mallarmé and Valéry the Lucretian poet, he met Russian refugees and even learned the language. Finally, in 1929, he spent a term in Heidelberg.

This episode, strangely, received only scattered references in the *Autobiographical Reflections*. However, it had its own significance, as this study trip that happened at the age of twenty-eight represented another major turning point in Voegelin's career. The importance of this moment in recent years has increasingly been recognized. For Paul Caringella, the first chapter of the unpublished manuscript '*Herrschaftslehre und Rechtslehre*', discussing Augustine, Descartes and Husserl, provides the background to Voegelin's 1943 anamnetic exercises.[8] Sandro Chignola emphasizes the same manuscript but puts the emphasis on Voegelin's reading of Carl Schmitt (Chignola 1997). However, none of them roots this development experientially in the encounter that engendered it, meeting Jaspers in Heidelberg and the subsequent return to Weber. The clue to the solution is contained in a crucial, experiential conversation of 27 April 1978 which Voegelin had with Eugene Webb (Webb 1981: 20–7). These few pages are of crucial, almost free associational importance.[9]

By 1929, Voegelin was already initiated into Weber but Jaspers revived his memories and directed him towards Nietzsche, Kierkegaard, Heidegger and Husserl (Webb 1981: 20).[10] This helps to show us the full weight of the encounter and also the reasons for Voegelin's later reluctance to return to this moment. After the revelatory impact American thought had exerted on him during his stay there, it was the Heidelberg semester that helped him to return to his own roots.

These roots were in continental German philosophy, but it was a special kind of continental philosophy to which he returned through Jaspers. It was a type of thought that, as opposed to the neo-Kantians, was not satisfied with matters of discourse, proposition and method, but considered philosophy as a way of life, a quest for truth, and did not shy away from the problem of transcendence. Webb is quoting from and referring especially to Jaspers in these pages (Webb 1981: 20–7), no doubt truthfully sticking not just to the word but also to the spirit of his 27 April 1978 conversation with Voegelin, but he also lists those other philosophers who came to be mis-labelled as 'existentialists'.

Through Jaspers Voegelin returned to his roots in a strictly personal sense as well. Jaspers directed him to Nietzsche, and this evoked not only his earlier encounter with Nietzsche but also the *Upanishads*, into which he had been 'initiated' by Paul Deussen, Nietzsche's life-long friend. The connection came up from the distance of almost half a century so that it cannot be accidental that the account given about the experiences Voegelin had at the ages of fifteen and eighteen is contained in the same pages where the encounter with Jaspers is mentioned. The most important of all, however, was the return to Weber. Soon an opportunity would arise to present the results of his new reflections on Weber. The year 1930 was the tenth anniversary of Weber's death, and the memorial lecture on this occasion in front of the Viennese Sociological Society was given by Eric Voegelin. The *leitmotiv* of the talk was a detailed comparison and contrast between Weber and Nietzsche.

The impact of this exercise, Voegelin's first 'meditation', is discernible from his publication list.[11] With the talk on Weber, the veritable explosion of publications that happened between 1928 and 1930 is brought to an end. Between 1930 and 1932, only a few reviews appeared in print. Instead, he was immersed in his first major attempt at a theoretical synthesis, the manuscript entitled *Herrschaftslehre und Rechtslehre*. The first chapter of the manuscript was a meditation on Augustine, Descartes and Husserl, while the discussion of legal and political theories relied strongly on the work of Carl Schmitt who was influenced by Weber and whose *Verfassungslehre* was a major reading experience for Voegelin.[12]

The work however remained unfinished and unpublished as Voegelin realized that, due to his inability to read Greek, he was not up to the task of covering the philosophical and historical background material. He started to learn the language and this led him to Aristotle and especially to Plato, who became the most fundamental reading experience of his life.

However, at this moment of internal difficulties, the impact of external political factors gave new direction to his work. He lived through an increasing corruption of public and political life and language, the decivilization and coarsening of the political scene, the emergence of a mad rhetoric of race, the 1934 coup and the rise of the authoritarian state. Up to 1938, Voegelin wrote four books related to these topics. The first two, published in 1933, were about the political uses of race, a relentless criticism of the intellectual inanity and political dangerousness of the fascist race ideal. In 1936, he published a book analysing the current practice of the Austrian government, the authoritarian state. As this form of government claimed for itself medieval scholastic roots, he went on to study medieval theology. For this reason, he returned to Paris for another major study visit where he encountered the works of Gilson, Maritain and especially Bergson's *Two Sources of Morality and Religion*. He also collected material for a book on Bodin. Finally, in 1938, literally weeks before the *Anschluss*, he published a short, more synthetic theoretical book entitled *Political Religions*, his first overall attempt to come to terms with the reasons and dynamics of the ideological corruption of his age.

It would be wrong to claim that, in the 1930s, Voegelin had been caught up in the whirlwind of the age. He preserved his distance and managed to produce remarkable books; books that could and should have been used extensively after the war when both the question of the authoritarian state and the religious character of Marxism became much discussed topics. Yet he had little effect, which to a considerable degree was because his books were among the first to be banned by the Nazis and they were later destroyed in aerial attacks.[13] The immediate effects of the books lay elsewhere. Within weeks after the German takeover, Voegelin was sought by the Gestapo and barely escaped. He did not make plans for leaving Austria as could not imagine that the Western Powers would let Hitler get away with the act. His anger to what he considered as a morally cowardly and diplomatically foolish reaction (or lack of it) was barely controllable (AR: 42).

1938

In 1938, at the age of thirty-seven, Voegelin had his second experience of exodus. He escaped in July through Zurich and then through Paris to the United States. The events represented a fundamental break not only in Voegelin's life but also in his work. His forced emigration and the immediate decision to become integrated into American society instead of staying on the east coast with exile groups eliminated the possibility of direct political relevance through his work, while he had to produce professional academic credits in order to make a living. Such novel starts provide an opportunity, but also pose the question of what would happen when memories and concerns of the past suddenly erupt again into consciousness.[14]

From the moment of his arrival, Voegelin duly took up the challenge and gave talks. At the age of thirty-eight and with five books to his credit, he accepted temporary and assistant positions at Harvard, at Bennington College, Vermont, at Northwestern and then at the University of Alabama, and started to publish extensively. Most importantly, on 9 February 1939 (Hollweck and Sandoz 1997: 3), he secured an offer to write a textbook on the history of political ideas (AR: 62).

In a sense, the contract came at the best possible moment for Voegelin. It was a major asset in his difficult fight to get himself established in a new country. However, it also proved to be fateful. It is with this contract that his life-long project started: it 'ended' almost half a century later. Between 1939 and 1953, Voegelin wrote about 4,500 manuscript pages for his *History of Political Ideas*, and then published five volumes of *Order and History* (one posthumously). Even allowing for overlaps, the sheer size of the work is commanding. Much more than a mere question of quantity, this work certainly represents one of the most important and innovative projects in the social and political thought of the twentieth century.

The methodological perspective in which this book was written places a central emphasis on the conditions out of which a particular project emerged, emphasizing the links between liminality, reflexivity, recognition and identity, connecting life and work (for details, see Szakolczai 1998a: 20–33, 83–6). This approach seems particularly appropriate in the case of a work of such vast proportions and all the more so as these conditions were indeed extremely singular in early 1939. A proper reconstruction of these conditions of emergence is also central to understanding the links between the two related projects, *History of Political Ideas* and *Order and History*.

This question gains special importance today for two reasons. On the one hand, after a gap of almost half a century, the manuscript of the *History of Political Ideas* is being published in eight volumes.[15] On the other, the editorial *Introduction* to the series, arguing for an unbroken continuity between the two projects (Hollweck and Sandoz 1997: 11, 16, 17, 26), failed to solve the problem of the relationship between the two related projects.[16] This is because it has committed three major omissions: it failed to pay serious attention to authorial intentions and self-assessment; it ignored other thinkers whose life-work, both in terms of the direction of the project and the posthumous character of the publication, and posed problems similar to Voegelin's; and finally, it neglected to take into consideration the related methodological issues.

First, and most obviously, it goes against authorial intentions and self-assessments (AN: 3, AR: 64–5). The editors do refer to these claims, but find ways to play down their significance by arguing that Voegelin's own remarks obscure rather than clarify the issues for the readers (Hollweck and Sandoz 1997: 16). Second, the problem posed by the posthumous edition of unpublished writings recurs frequently among the most important thinkers of the century, including many of those who had links in one way or another to Voegelin, like Nietzsche, Husserl, Wittgenstein and Foucault. However, the parallels are the strictest for the thinker to whom Voegelin was closest in all respects, Max Weber. As we shall see in detail, Weber's case provides as close a model as it is possible to get for the way Voegelin's project emerged and progressed. The editors, however, failed even to make a allusion to the similarities with Weber's case.[17]

This leads to the third issue that concerns questions of method. The editors do not pay proper respect either to the vast literature on the questions of authorial intentions which is one of the most important recent developments in the field of the history of ideas, or in general to questions which emerge regarding posthumous publications and the internal dynamics of complex life-works.[18] Method is not meant here in a rigid way, only in the sense of being informed about the state of affairs concerning the manner in which to proceed with respect to a particular problem.

Such an editorial perspective is especially puzzling and paradoxical for two reasons. First, it fails to apply to Voegelin's work the perspective he developed while working on the project, the locating of symbols in their engendering experiences. Second, it assumes an unbroken continuity in the case of a project where a several-thousand-page manuscript was written out of an original contract for a short textbook. Consequently, in the account given below, particular attention will be paid to Voegelin's self-assessment, to the character of the break his three key encounter-experiences of 1943, 1945 and 1950 represented for the work, and to the identification of the three major, all but incompatible exigencies which the project tried to meet at the same time.

The analysis will start by attempting to reconstruct the conditions out of which the project emerged.

These conditions, first of all, were liminal in more ways than one. Emigration is a painful event for anybody. It was especially so in the case of Voegelin, for whom the family move to Vienna at the age of nine, as his anamnetic exercises of 1943 would reveal, proved to be the greatest trauma of his childhood.[19] Furthermore, the contract was signed literally in the first moments of his stay in America. The topic and character of the book to be written were also of particular importance. The contract was for a thin textbook with a short deadline (Hollweck and Sandoz 1997: 3). But it was supposed to be written on the history of political ideas, which was exactly the topic on which his attempt to write a 'Herrschaftslehre' stumbled some five years previously.

The combination was explosive: in liminal periods time is suspended, short-circuiting is bound to happen between the different time periods of one's life; the present becomes past and the past present. Indeed, while the textbook meant a break with the concern of his past years and the research projects he had in the spring of 1938, it was also a return: but only in a way, as the contract was for a textbook, not for a monograph. The question, in terms of his life-work, was whether he was now in the position to tackle the problems. However, in terms of his actual existential situation, it was whether this closeness to his in-depth long-term concerns was helpful for writing quickly a textbook which would secure him a stable academic appointment. The answer to this question seems clearly no. The short-circuiting of two different exigencies, the short-term need for a quick book publication and the long-term task of writing his *magnum opus* on political thought would prove to be fateful for Voegelin's entire life-work.

The difficulties appeared almost immediately. Though he was supposed to deliver by September 1940 and a piece of the manuscript was ready by August 1939 (Opitz 1994: 133), the deadline proved to be impossible to meet. This was because the original textbook framework exploded during the first years of work in 1939–40. He ran into the same problem as he did in 1931–2: he discovered that his 'own knowledge of the materials [was] quite insufficient' (AR: 62).[20] This meant the need for much more extensive preparatory work than was previously envisioned and while in Alabama around 1940 he started to learn Hebrew. This is a most telling sign of the way in which Voegelin was carried forward by the dynamics of his work, as it is quite evident that the knowledge of Hebrew is not a primary requirement for writing a college textbook on the history of political ideas.[21] During these years he carried an enormous workload, reputedly working eighteen hours per day (Havard 1978: 14), and gained extensive knowledge in ancient, medieval and Middle Eastern history. Following the example of Max Weber, he maintained connection with the most recent advances in the specialized sciences, especially with the work of Frankfort and his associates in the Oriental Institute of the University of Chicago (Frankfort *et al.* 1949 [1946], Frankfort 1978 [1948]).

Still, in spite of the enormous work, or rather because of it, the textbook project was not progressing properly. This is evident in exchange of letters that took place between Voegelin and his editor, Fritz Morstein-Marx, during the spring of 1941. It is confirmed by the end of summer when, instead of delivering the entire manuscript, Voegelin indicated a new, eight-chapter structure of which the first three chapters alone ran up to 225 manuscript pages (Hollweck and Sandoz 1997: 4–5; Opitz 1997: 120). The final deadline for the book was then set for the end of September but this clearly served only cosmetic purposes. The dilemma of the incompatibility between the exigencies of a textbook and Voegelin's pursuit of his own project has indeed reached a 'critical stage' (Hollweck and Sandoz 1997: 4). There followed the first great silence with the publishers, and for the following two and half years there was no exchange of letters until the correspondence was resumed in the spring of 1944.

Behind this silence, however, there were the tremors of a volcano. The completion of the textbook was almost a matter of life and death for Voegelin. On his arrival in the United States, he had decided that he would settle down and try to integrate into the broad academic community. The fate of his friend, Alfred Schutz, who had to use his legal degree in order to make a living, compromising his ability to pursue his work, showed how right Voegelin was in his assessment of the situation. This, however, implied that he had to play the publishing game.

Pressure was already high at the end of April 1940 when the publisher enquired about the completion date. It only increased by the end of the year when the deadline was broken and the stream of publications, based on his work done in Europe in the 1930s, had run out. After his article on the 'Mongol Orders', written in 1937, appeared in the winter of 1940, Voegelin would not publish anything but book reviews for three years. Even then, this was not exactly the most promising way of securing an academic appointment. Given his upbringing, he played with the continental rules of the game by putting all the stakes on a book. Work on the manuscript continued at a frenetic pace, while his attempts to get papers published were frustrated. Chapter drafts proved to be too long and difficult to read in themselves and he had no time to write separate articles.[22]

His academic position was extremely precarious. From 1939 onwards, he only held visiting and assistant positions. In February 1942, based on his previous publication record, on the impressive talk he gave there and also the support of Rudolf Heberle (Heilman 1996), he got another short-time appointment as a visiting associate professor of government at Louisiana State University, when it was still an agricultural and mechanical university. He was literally surviving from day to day in the academic community of a new country. By April, he had hopes that the appointment would be renewed and by August it had been granted for another academic year.[23] His position was only stabilized slightly in August 1943 when he was appointed as an associate professor. It was a sudden improvement of his situation as his visiting status had only been extended on 1 June 1943 to cover the summer term. This, however, was still not the security of tenure as the appointment was for three years and dependent on a final renewal.

The question of academic status is the fundamental emotional and existential background of Voegelin's work on *History of Political Ideas* and his correspondence and silence with the publishers in the first half of the 1940s.

1943

The project gained its balance only through the effects of three subsequent 'peak experiences' (V. Turner 1985), in 1943, 1945 and 1950. These experiences were not irrational eruptions. They were rendered possible by the relentless efforts of the previous years.[24] Without the shattering impact of these encounters, the work would not have gained its proper shape. In the following, a reconstruction of these experiences will be given, taking into account the fact that the dynamics of the work unfolded itself in a highly charged socio-political and personal-existential situation.

The first experience was set off by his reading of Husserl's *Crisis*, a negative reading experience, and an ensuing dialogue and exchange of letters with Schutz (Voegelin 1981: 463). This well-known and documented episode happened at a moment that was liminal in more ways than one. It came after four and a half years of extremely tense work, when Voegelin 'had arrived at a dead-end' in his work (AN: 3), just when his appointment was extended for three years for the first time during his stay in the US which gave him some breathing space, and when he had a very intense conversation with Schutz during a summer visit to New York.[25] While discussing Husserl's work with Schutz, Voegelin suddenly recognized, through the choice of particularly inappropriate words like the 'functionary of the spirit', that it contained the same type of thinking characteristic of the ideological mass movements which had created the catastrophes of the century. This led him to write his long letter of 17–20 September to Schutz on Husserl (FPP: 19–34), the first of the three writings of the period which form a meditative unit. As a way out, he recognized that consciousness is not an abstract category but is always the concrete consciousness of a human being, and he engaged upon a series of anamnetic exercises between 25 October and 7 November (AR: 70–4; AN: 9–13, 36–51). Finally, during the same period, he wrote his first theoretical essay on consciousness (AN: 14–35).

This essay criticized the phenomenological approach to experience which placed undue emphasis on one particular kind of experience, sensory perception (ibid.: 16). In opposition to this, following James but even more Nietzsche, Voegelin put the phenomenon of attention and the concentration of the limited quantum of energy one is able to control at the centre (ibid.: 20).[26] He thus conceptualized consciousness not on the basis of the *I* (ibid.: 23), the common underlying assumption linking Descartes, Kant and Husserl, but as a process so that 'the experience of consciousness is the experience of a process – the only process which we know "from within"' (ibid.: 21). The central features of consciousness are illumination and transcendence (ibid.: 20–3): consciousness is 'a process that is illuminated within itself' (ibid.: 30).

It follows from this perspective that consciousness is not a monad, it is 'based on the body and on the external world' (ibid.: 31; see also 200). The experience of the present requires interpretation, based on bodily existence. We cannot directly experience being, we only 'experience consciousness itself' (ibid.: 32). The ground of being 'is nowhere a datum in human existence rather it is always strictly transcendent that we can approach only through meditation' (ibid.: 32).

These considerations yield two general principles. First, 'there is no absolute starting point for a philosophy of consciousness'. All philosophizing happens in the consciousness of a human being, is thus an event in a life history:

> Consciousness is given in the elemental sense that the systematic reflection on consciousness is a late event in the biography of the philosopher. The philosopher always lives in the context of his own history, the history of human existence in the community and in the world.
>
> (AN: 33)

Second, as a consequence, the entire question concerning a 'radical philosophy of consciousness', Husserl's project, becomes displaced. Instead of taking the need for such a project for granted, the question becomes why and when such a need emerges at all. This allows Voegelin to root this project in a general civilizational crisis, comparable to the similar crisis of the fifth century BC, and diagnose the undertaking as an insufficient response to this crisis and only a 'symptom of a spiritual nihilism' (ibid.: 35). This is because it implies an 'abandonment of philosophy as the creation of an order of symbols through which man's position in the world is understood' (ibid.), which is exactly the project to which Voegelin wanted to return.

However, in the concrete world of Voegelin, a major task was to secure a stable academic employment and finish the book project. The meditations were much related to these questions and the three-year appointment made it possible for Voegelin to step back finally from the relentless work and reflect on the purpose of the undertaking. In this respect, they had a mixed result: while helping to give a decisive focus to his theoretical work, they only rendered the task of finishing the book more difficult. In the intense months of September to November 1943, the centre of Voegelin's interest decisively shifted towards a theory and history of consciousness, severing any close ties between the dynamics of his own work and the task of writing not simply a textbook but even a standard work for the 'field'. This was quite problematic, as the situation of Voegelin in 1943 was still far from being secure. Within less than a year after his autumn 1943 experience, a series of events would radically underline the precariousness of his situation.

The immediate impact of the September–November 1943 meditations was that the intense reflections on the project led Voegelin to reconsider his strategies. He needed a reformulation of his project and also actual publications. These tasks were accomplished together in three major publications which were brought together within a few months, as the three-year breathing space allowed him to turn him away for a short time from the overwhelming task of finishing the book. One was an essay on Siger de Brabant, cut out of the *History of Political Ideas* project and published in June 1944. This essay relied on research completed while working on his book on the authoritarian state (AR: 52).

For the November 1943 meeting of the political theory panel of the American Political Science Association (APSA) (Cooper, in HPVI: 2), Voegelin prepared a major theoretical statement on his work, published as 'Political Theory and the Pattern of General History' in August 1944. In this paper, Voegelin attempted to make intelligible the basic ideas underlying his book project by situating his work within existing literature. The specificity of the approach was given by the bringing together of two fields which had until then been separated, general history and the history of ideas (Voegelin 1944b: 751). At this point, without giving a single hint about experiences and their symbolization, he only stated that this effort would require the work of generations and not the efforts of a single scholar, and finished the article by listing some of the problems such an undertaking has to face.

The third, and indeed crucial, essay was an article on Nietzsche, published in May 1944. In 1930, when starting his first attempt at a history of political ideas, his talk on Weber contained a detailed comparison and contrast between Weber and Nietzsche (Voegelin 1930: 7–10). This time, at a crucial juncture in his second attempt, he came up with an article devoted to Nietzsche. It was a passionate defence against current Anglo-Saxon interpretations, arguing that those who charged Nietzsche with 'causing' the war and promoting nihilism were simply attempting to execute the messenger of bad news.

The article is organized in an ascending order, starting with the most outrageous misinterpretations, progressing to Santayana (sections IV–V), who was a protagonist of his 1928 book on the American mind, and then to Stefan George (section VI), who was one of the main formative influences of Voegelin's youth (AN: 5, AR: 17). This last section is summarized by the claim that 'George is the only great figure of the last generation who can be said to have entered into the spirit of Nietzsche, not in contemplative understanding, but as the continuator of his task' (Voegelin 1944a: 200). Given the huge role Voegelin assigned to George in his own formation, it is not too risky to argue that Voegelin considered himself as a member of his own generation who took up the task of Nietzsche, and also of George.[27] However, the problems caused by the reception of Nietzsche required some further comments. Here Voegelin took some cues from another of his most important educators, Karl Jaspers, who had analysed the misuses to which Nietzsche so far had been subjected (ibid.: 200–1). Taking a further step, Voegelin did not want to exonerate Nietzsche, suggesting the need to 'explore the structure of thought which produced them' (ibid.: 201). He identified as the sources of these misuses Nietzsche's 'unrestrained' use of 'inappropriate deprecatory language', and his lack of sensitivity to 'the transcendental experiences which are the foundation of the Christian conception of man' (ibid.: 202).

The parallels between the periods 1929 to 1932 and 1940 to 1943 thus go beyond the attempts at writing a history of political ideas and their apparent failure. They also extend to the set of thinkers who were, in close connection, the central encounter-experiences of Voegelin's formative years: Weber and Nietzsche, George, Jaspers and Kierkegaard. It was this figuration which returned in the 1944 Nietzsche paper, which was transitory in terms of both terminology and content.

1944

The break with the textbook format which was evident already in 1941 was finally completed in the spring and summer of 1944 under extremely stressful conditions. After preparing the three articles for publication, Voegelin returned to the book. Work was particularly difficult, as owing to the illness of a colleague – the first in a series of accidents in 1944 – he had to assume a double teaching load (FPP: 36). Still, by 7 April, he managed to all but complete his manuscript (Opitz 1994b: 135). However, it had a serious formal defect: instead of a 200–250 page textbook, it had grown into a major undertaking of 1,400 pages. In his letter to the publisher, Voegelin suggested a three-volume edition. This, however, proved to be unacceptable for McGraw-Hill, a publisher specializing in undergraduate textbooks, and Voegelin had to spend much of summer 1944 in search of a new publisher just as he was desperately trying to finish the work.

As if all this were not enough, when the Voegelins were in Cambridge, Massachusetts, thanks to a loophole given by wartime regulations their landlords sold the house they rented and practically evicted them (Heilman 1996). The situation thus became suddenly precarious and extremely liminal: being not just an exile but temporarily homeless; going up for naturalization without even a rented home, and going up for tenure without a forthcoming book.

Though for a short time the situation looked most frightening, within a few months the troubles were smoothed out. With the help of the Heilmans, the Voegelins found and bought a house in Baton Rouge using a loan received through fellow refugees (Heilman 1996). On 14 November 1944, again with the assistance of Heilman, they successfully passed the naturalization procedures and became American citizens. Finally, on 27 September 1944, Voegelin was offered a contract for *History of Political Ideas* by Macmillan (Hollweck and Sandoz 1997: 5), with publication set for early 1946 (Opitz 1994b: 136).

Under the conditions, it is astonishing that Voegelin kept working at full speed during the summer, sending a new chapter to Engel-Janosi practically every fortnight.[28] On 28 August 1944 Engel-Janosi acknowledged receipt of the 'irrevocably last chapter' of the manuscript on the Middle Ages.[29] Voegelin then turned to the completion of the volume on modernity.

It was during the summer of 1945, when Voegelin again returned to Cambridge to try to complete the volume on modernity (Webb 1981: 6, AR: 63, Gebhardt 1982), that his second peak experience happened.

1945

The moment was again liminal in more ways than one. It was a time away from home and regular duties; it was an attempt to put the finishing touches on a work whose publication was of vital importance given that his tenure would come up soon; and this was also the moment when the war had already ended in Europe and was in its last stages in the Far East. The apocalyptic situation was very strongly present among Voegelin's concerns.[30]

This was the context in which Voegelin read Schelling's *Philosophy of Mythology and Revelation*. 'In Schelling Voegelin recognize[d] a kindred mind', both facing the same task of searching for '"a point of orientation" in the crisis, without being "engulfed in the crisis themselves"' (Gebhardt 1982: 68).[31] Under the impact of Schelling and also of Vico whom he studied at the same time, he gained two major insights into both the concept of a general history and the organization of the work. He overcame the 'pattern of a unilinear development of political ideas' in which his thinking was still imprisoned; while it also 'dawned on [him] that the conception of a history of ideas was an ideological deformation of reality', as '[t]here were no ideas unless there were symbols of immediate *experiences*' (AR: 63).

On the basis of this new reading experience, Voegelin wrote a major, synthetic manuscript, entitled 'Last Orientation', situating his work with respect to 'a time of civilizational disintegration' and 'crisis' which require a 'point of orientation' as 'the starting point for a civilizational restoration' (quoted in Gebhardt 1982: 67–8). The task is analogous to the one Weber set out for himself in 1917–19 and also recalls Voegelin's analysis of Nietzsche given just the year before. Indeed, in the third footnote of his paper, Gebhardt refers to Voegelin's Nietzsche article. However, in this chapter Voegelin takes Schelling and not Weber or Nietzsche as his reference point.

In fact, this is a central part of the story, and in light of his later writings, the presentation of Schelling given there is most important, and also puzzling. Voegelin calls Schelling a 'realist in an age of disintegration' (HPVII: 193). Because of the times, however, a realist is also isolated. In Schelling, Voegelin recognized the same kind of figure of transition that earlier, and even later, he would identify with Nietzsche or Weber. He is a 'seismograph of a civilizational earthquake', who 'marks the end of a period, and not a beginning', just like Plato, Augustine or Aquinas did before (ibid.: 241; see also 235). By assigning a central role in the intellectual tradition in which he is situating himself to Schelling, Voegelin now redraws this landscape.

In this 'great tradition from St Augustine to Pascal' (ibid.: 235), the key figures are the mystics, Eckhart, Angelus Silesius and Boehme (ibid.: 214, 235) and among his direct predecessors, Herder and Baader (ibid.: 212). This tradition is then continued with Schopenhauer and Kierkegaard, and then Bergson, Jaspers, Heidegger, Ortega and Berdyaev among others (ibid.: 1999), but also Nietzsche, George and the diagnosis of the 'last man' (ibid.: 203). Also prominent is the role of Giordano Bruno, as 'Schelling does not return to a Christian ontology, nor to the pneumatocentric anthropology: he returns to the speculative task of constructing the universe as an intelligible whole with the means that can be found in the nature of man' (ibid.: 205).

The relationship between Schelling and Christianity is indeed a basic concern for Voegelin. Schelling starts from within the Christian tradition (ibid.: 219). This provides a basic contrast to Plato, the other major thinker whose work was an attempt to confront the spiritual disintegration of his age (ibid.: 237). The central symbol of Schelling's work, however, is not Christian. It is Prometheus: 'Prometheus is that principle of humanity which we have called spirit (*nous*); he put understanding and consciousness into the souls of those who formerly were spiritually feeble' (ibid.: 217, quoting Schelling's *Philosophy of Mythology and Revelation*). This Promethean experience is central to Schelling's idea of religiosity (ibid.: 221) and the play of Aeschylus is also linked to the development of an eschatological consciousness in late Hellenic civilization (ibid.: 229). Schelling also extensively uses the symbol Dionysus, talking about the polis as the 'third Dionysus' (ibid.: 227), linking it to the Johannite 'third Christianity' and emphasizing the influence of Joachim of Fiore on Schelling (ibid.: 230).

Within the great tradition, the tone changes from Pascal to Schelling: 'Schelling's "goal" is not the Christian *summum bonum* of the eternal beatific vision; it is rather a desire for depersonalisation into a nirvana' (ibid.: 235). The experience one can find in Schelling, the 'Promethean suffering through nature, is a tone of existence which arises *within* Western history, but transcends the Augustinian, Christian tension of *amor Dei* and *amor sui*' (ibid.: 236). In this way, we return to the starting point: Schelling is 'neither a prophet, not the founder of a sect; he is a realist who expresses in his dialectic the existential fact that he, as an individual, is beyond the churches' (ibid.: 237).

Given the tradition in which Schelling is located and given his characterization especially the central symbol of Prometheus, there can be no question that in his later terminology, the Schelling presented here would be a gnostic *par excellence*. This is exactly the way he would be presented later (see NSP: 113, 124; OHIV: 21). However, here, Voegelin is not diagnosing but is speaking from the inside.

Voegelin's identification with this 'gnostic' Schelling marks an 'in-between' situation in his intellectual trajectory. It is a break away from his background formation, dominated by Schopenhauer, Kierkegaard and Jaspers, but especially Nietzsche and Weber. This is still acknowledged in the early forties, for example in the 1944 Nietzsche article or the Nietzsche–Pascal manuscript that dates from the same period (Voegelin 1996, Opitz 1996: 174). A 1942 letter is particularly explicit in this regard: 'We possess the great critiques of our civilization by Nietzsche and Max Weber, and for me at least they are the indispensable starting-point for every work in the field.'[32] But it is not yet his mature formulation that would centre on Plato, the Gospels, Augustine and Aquinas.[33]

The four and a half years from the Schelling reading experience to the preparation for the Vienna trip form a tight unity, with key events clearly marking both its starting and ending points. Borrowing the expression Tenbruck used for Weber, they were also some kind of 'dark years'. In retrospect, Voegelin himself characterized the 'years between 1945 and 1950 as a period of indecision, if not paralysis' (AR: 64).

On a first look, it is not evident why this should be the case. The events in life, work and world marking the starting point are all for the better. Roughly around the same time, in summer 1945, the Second World War ended; Voegelin got a new impetus in his work through the reading of Schelling and Vico; and by the end of the year all existential worries were closed as on 3 December 1945 he was promoted to full professor status.[34]

As a result, he again had the opportunity to reflect on his situation and reconsider his strategies. During the summer of 1945, he was in another rush to finish part of the manuscript on modernity. As he stated in an October 1945 letter to the publishers, written shortly before the crucial senate vote on tenure, he still had a 'lively interest in "publication at the earliest possible date" for reasons "of my position and career"' (Hollweck and Sandoz 1997: 6). Now this issue became less central both for his interests and for his existential situation. He had the opportunity to take another deep plunge into his main theoretical sources. He spent the second half of 1946 working on Vico, and most of 1947 on Plato (Hollweck and Sandoz 1997: 27). Pressure to finish the book was eased not only because of his promotion, but also by his better realizing the difference between the American and continental publication game. The main expectation was to publish one article per year and Voegelin duly complied with this obligation.[35] Every year between 1946 and 1950 he published one article in a major American social or political science journal (*Journal of Politics, Social Research, Review of Politics*), alternating critical articles on Bakunin, positivism and Marx (1946, 1948, 1950) with meditative articles on Plato (1947, 1949), plus the usual series of book reviews (Price 1994). This practice ended with the joint 1951 publication of two articles: one on Machiavelli and one on More.

Such a strategy was all the more appropriate as the Schelling reading experience exploded beyond repair even the Macmillan idea of the 'standard work' in the field. Using his later terminology, this was the moment when concerns with the 'beyond' made their presence with force in his work. Such a question, while increasingly central to Voegelin's own work, simply had no place in a book that was supposed to set the standard in the 'history of political ideas'. One may want to reinvent a field, but not with a book that should immediately guide the readings of graduate students. Indeed, troubles were reappearing about the publication of the book.

Voegelin could not dispense with the need for publication, and thus had to maintain the fiction of the identity of purpose behind the manuscript which was not only continuously growing in size but also, due to the shocks of 1943 and 1945, was gaining depth and changing character. The first two volumes were sent to the publisher in early 1946 who sent it to a reviewer first in 1946 and then in 1948 (Hollweck and Sandoz 1997: 6–7). These reviews, especially the second, made two things evident. First, in spite of his repeated insistence, his work does not simply represent the latest step in the field but is an extremely original and demanding personal philosophy in its own right which was bound to be engaged in an uphill struggle against the established ways of thinking in Anglo-American philosophy and political science. Second, however, it also became clear that the work would not and could not serve its original purpose, to replace the works of Sabine and Dunning as a standard reference in the history of political ideas. It was much more than that.

The result is the second 'great silence' in the correspondence with the publishers. Apart from an accidental personal encounter between Voegelin and Anderson in March 1949 (Hollweck and Sandoz 1997: 8), there was no exchange of letters until 20 October 1953, when the publisher finally enquired about the state of the manuscript.

This silence, however, did not mean a lack of work. Quite the contrary, it was after the frustration created by the second reader's report that Voegelin returned to the task of finishing the volume on modernity. 1948 was spent on feverish work trying to complete this part, writing among others on Marx, Machiavelli and Luther. During this work, the manuscript again gained in size, and Volume Three was eventually split into two volumes (Opitz 1994b: 137).

The additional years of work, especially the reflections on Plato, set off a marked change in Voegelin's style and key concepts. This has been recognized by one of his close friends, Gregor Sebba, according to whom '[a]round 1948 we find the search for the engendering experiences turning up "sentiments" which "crystallize" into "ideas" that engender their "formulation," where "idea" is not a concept but "a symbol that draws its life from sentiments"' (Sebba 1982: 17). A 12 March 1949 letter written to Leo Strauss also contains similar indications. Voegelin was able to formulate in a concise way the underlying 'problem' of his work: 'To restore the experiences that have led to the creation of certain concepts and symbols; or: Symbols have become opaque; they must be made luminous again by penetrating to the experiences they express'.[36] Still, though completion was always on the horizon, it moved away the closer Voegelin came to it.

It was now that external events caught up with Voegelin. He returned to the contemporary part of his work in the same year as the major intensification of the Cold War, the Communist takeover in East-Central Europe. This coincidence between political and work troubles reinforced the stressful character of each, mounting tension. It was in this context that Voegelin's insight on Gnosticism can be located. This happened in conditions where the personal and the political, life and work again became strictly interlinked, fuelling the tension that led to the eventual discharge that can be characterized at the same time by sharpness of insight and high pitches of polemics.

The analysis must again start with reconstructing the context. By the end of summer 1948, Voegelin has finished the manuscript of *History of Political Ideas*. However, he was evidently unhappy with the result. Signs of a crisis are visible in the correspondence and in personal recollections.[37] Most importantly, he was increasingly looking for ways to go back to Europe, to establish and retrieve personal and professional links. During late summer 1948, he made a first enquiry about a possible scholarship, first with the Rockefeller and then on 20 August at the Guggenheim Foundation. He was also trying to update his readings by asking Gurian about major contemporary German journals.[38]

By April 1949, it seemed that all publication plans were settled. In several letters, Voegelin claimed that the manuscript was ready and a publication date was agreed for 1950.[39] In the last days of April, he gave a radio talk on Goethe, characterizing him as 'a man of daemonic qualities himself'.[40] In the first days of May, he settled publication matters with Gurian, related for example to the selection of the exact sections from the Marx chapter. Then, in the summer, he took another plunge into Aristotle.[41]

In October 1949, Voegelin applied to the Guggenheim Foundation for a fellowship for a study visit to Europe.[42] The plans for work enclosed with the application is a unique document, a presentation of self. Its most important aspect concerns the relationship established there between the *History of Political Ideas* and Voegelin's own 'systematic theory of politics'. First of all, Voegelin very clearly separates the two concerns. He claims that he first attempted to do a systematic study of politics back in the late 1920s, but he had to abandon the project as his knowledge proved to be insufficient. Then, upon his move to the US, he started work on *History of Political Ideas*

that is basically complete and should appear in 1950. The crucial statement comes at the start of section II: 'With the work just outlined as a basis
I think that I now can accomplish the task of writing a theory of politics
that I had to abandon in 1930'.[43]

Though in his Guggenheim application the publication dates are considered as given, the deadline was not kept. This was due to a complex
figuration that emerged in the autumn of 1949. A crucial role was played
by the new reading of Aristotle that, according to Vatikiotis, pushed
Voegelin into a dead end.[44] At that time, he was also reworking the 'People
of God' section of *History of Political Ideas*. The existence of the new manuscript is mentioned in a 20 November 1949 letter to Dempf.[45] As in his
earlier 20 August letter, there is no mention yet of this piece so that it must
have been written in the meantime. It is the new version of this manuscript
that contains Voegelin's first major diagnosis of gnosticism.[46] This is also
the moment when Voegelin relocates this manuscript from the volume on
Middle Ages into the start of the planned volume three on 1500–1700.
This happened in the context of a return to his former work *Political
Religions* and a new reading of the Presocratics especially Heraclitus.[47]

These developments seriously jeopardized not only the immediate publication schedule but also the entire status of the manuscript. They serve as
a background for the breakthrough of 1950. They also help to render intelligible its peculiar modality. At the same time as Voegelin was able to
develop his own language of symbols and experiences and recognized the
relevance of the concept 'gnosticism' for his work, another change of style
in his writing happened; a change that was certainly much more controversial and that led to major problems in the reception of his work and the
dissemination of his ideas. This was the emergence of an aggressive,
polemical tone and emotional charge that was not present in earlier private letters and published work. This tone immediately struck his friends
and acquaintances as new and unfortunate and has recently led to a debate
whether Voegelin's interest in gnosticism can be reduced to a kind of cold
war rhetoric (Poirier 1997, Price 1997, Webb 1997).

The exact link between these two changes in vocabulary, and their connection with Voegelin's reading of gnosticism, is therefore a central
question to be tackled. In reconstructing the links between the two types
of changes, the aim is not to establish direct causalities, rather to show the
manner in which slight perturbations reinforce each other under certain
circumstances and are eventually magnified almost beyond repair and certainly unintentionally.

1950

Of the three peak experiences, the third one, though characterized as the
breakthrough, is the least clearly defined. Voegelin claimed that it
occurred 'on occasion of the Walgreen lectures' of 1951 (AR: 64). But the

term 'occasion' remains vague. In the following, emphasis will be given to the identification of the emergence of the polemical tone.

In published articles, reviews or the publicly-available private correspondence, there is no sign of a polemical tone just as there is no stressed reference to gnosticism throughout the 1940s. A book review of 1949 is a particularly telling example, still closing with an understating, ironic tone (Voegelin 1949: 263). The same Weberian control of the underlying passion is characteristic of the article on Marx that appeared in the July 1950 issue of *The Review of Politics*, and was probably finalized around the end of 1949. The first signs of polemics can therefore be dated with precision. They are contained in private correspondence: in a letter of 18 April 1950, when the mere mentioning of the name of Popper by Strauss evokes a most passionate outburst from Voegelin, so much so that at the end of the letter, he asks Strauss to handle this letter with particular confidentiality (FPP: 69); and in a letter to his friend Alfred Schutz, who was so struck by its tone that he took it personally and did not write to Voegelin for almost a year (Voegelin *et al.* 1993: 55). The change can be comprehended through a proper attention to the context, by reconstructing its emotionally highly-charged liminal character.

In the first months of 1950, just when the publication date set for the first two volumes was broken, Voegelin suddenly and unexpectedly received three major acts of recognition that not only acknowledged the efforts he had made so far but also promised to bring them to a satisfactory end. On 7 February, he obtained a grant from LSU for travel to Europe and, less than two weeks later, he received an official invitation to deliver the prestigious Walgreen lectures at the University of Chicago.[48] The most important of the three, however, combining the previous two, came in the first days of April, when he received news about obtaining the prestigious Guggenheim Fellowship. This not only enabled him to make extensive trips to Europe but also granted him an unexpected, and thus all the more precious, recognition of his work.

The personal letter he wrote to Henry Moe, secretary of the Foundation is a most precious and touching document of what this honour meant to Voegelin at the time: 'After more than twenty years of historical studies I feel at last competent to undertake the task of systematic, theoretical formulation in political science'.[49] Though he had already completed a lot of work in this respect, he felt that without a resumption of personal contacts in Europe, he may not have been able to draw it to a conclusion. He made also clear in the letter that he considered the fellowship as a special recognition both to the kind of non-establishment work he was doing, and due to his being a foreigner by birth.

Though he had been preparing since February for the trip to be started on 31 May, these preparations now intensified.[50] It seems highly likely that this was the period in which he wrote a few pages on T.S. Eliot's *Four Quartets* that are a most striking document of this rite of preparation.[51]

Voegelin reads the poem as an autobiographical document, 'the spiritual autobiography of a Christian poet' (section II), an exploration or a quest. Eliot's ideas also rhyme with the central concerns of his work, like the idea that creation is not a once-for-all act but a 'continuous process' where 'the creativeness of man enables him to participate in his humble way in God's creation' (section I); or the idea, central to his theory of consciousness, that '[m]an is the meeting-place of spirit and body, of the invisible and the visible' (ibid.). The two concerns, matters of autobiography and of work are closely related, as '[t]he spiritual autobiography is the history of a spirit joined to a body, and the body lives in the here and now of a definite locale' (section III). However, the other aspect of the autobiographical relevance which the poem had for Voegelin at that moment concerned exactly the suspension of this place, the home, in the experience of emigration as described in the third section of the poem. For Eliot, emigration, like travel, is 'the symbol for a beyond of history' (section III), and is described both in the poem and by Voegelin in a clear paraphrase of liminality, where one is between the closer and the further shore and thus time becomes suspended. This yields a 'suspense between action and inaction where the immediacy of death becomes visible' (ibid.). In the fourth section of the poem, the quest reaches its end. However, the end at the same time represents a beginning. The explorer will arrive at the same place where he started; and not only that, will experience it the first time.

The few pages ended with this as a direct quote. One cannot avoid the recognition that this was the way in which Voegelin prepared for his return to Vienna: to arrive at his starting point, but also to see it with a fresh eye.

Thus, after a twelve year absence Voegelin returned to Vienna in the summer of 1950. It was bound to be a major experience, as it represented a return to his past, evoking especially strong memories of 1910 and 1938 which were his two major moments of exodus, exactly when both his work and its recognition were at a critical juncture.

This was only magnified by the kind of Vienna he encountered. Part of Austria was in the Soviet Occupation Zone until 1955 and the summer and autumn of 1950 happened to be the most critical moment of the entire occupation period. After its disastrous results in the 1949 elections, the Communist Party prepared for the final attack. The opportunity was offered by the economic difficulties due to the termination of the Marshall Plan aid (Bader 1966: 158). In the difficult stabilization and adjustment situation, negotiations with the unions were broken off at the end of July 1950 and were not resumed until late August. In mid-September, the government was in full crisis. The Communists tried to grasp their last opportunity and organized a series of strikes around 25 September. On 4 October, after its failure, with the support of the Red Army they called for a general strike and attempted a communist *putsch*. Though this again failed, tension remained high and the precarious situation of Austria in between East and West was not solved until the signing of the treaty returning sovereignty on 15 May 1955.[52] Finally, it was on 25 June 1950, shortly after Voegelin's arrival in Vienna, that the Korean war broke out.

Voegelin therefore suddenly had a personal encounter with the Cold War. It was the kind that he could not experience in America and it coincided with his return to his roots. At another level, there was also a return to the controversy and polemics represented by Kraus who was such a crucial formative influence for Voegelin. Finally, to close the circle, in 1950 there appeared in the *Dublin Review* an article by Béla Menczer, a Hungarian Catholic thinker whose views were strikingly close to Voegelin's as expressed in the *Authoritarian State*, entitled 'Karl Kraus and the Struggle against the Modern Gnostics'. Though there are no proofs that Voegelin has read this piece, the fit is almost too perfect to be purely fortuitous.

As a document of his trip, a few handwritten pages are available among his papers in the Archive.[53] They further confirm that, apart from meeting people and obtaining books, Voegelin also went to Europe to observe and reflect. He was not just an observer of reality but a 'participatory self-observer', not simply a traveller but a time-traveller into his past. He was prepared for the reality of totalitarianism and the Soviet occupation at the height of the Cold War and he was also prepared to make detailed notes on the trip. However, he was still struck by what he saw as it was so different from what he expected. The most intolerable part of reality was not political oppression or economic misery, but the depressing outlook of the city, and the mood and the behaviour of the people. The real experience of Cold War Austria proved so depressing that the second section of the travel notes was never written.

In late summer 1950, Voegelin returned to the States and his work after a gap of more than six months. However, instead of simply picking up *History of Political Ideas*, he started work on the Walgreen lectures, entitled 'Truth and Representation', to be delivered in February 1951 at the University of Chicago and which would be published in book form as *The New Science of Politics* in 1952. The preparation for these lectures was of course very closely related to work he had done on *History of Political Ideas*. But it was not a simple continuation but a reflexion on work completed, a philosophical exercise. As he would characterize it later, this was a first step towards the theoretical work.[54]

In fact, the figuration presents the main methodological perspective of this book with particular clarity regarding the reconstruction of the dynamics of life-works. There is the long relentless work over a period of more than ten years on a project, punctuated by two major experiences that nevertheless failed to yield a breakthrough. There is the authentic liminal experience, the travel to Vienna that both broke the rhythm of the work and gave further impetus, preceded by a genuine 'rite of separation' (V. Turner 1969, van Gennep 1960[1909]), the anguishing difficulties of the project and the preparations for the trip, and followed by a 'rite of reaggregation', the return to work through the preparation for the Walgreen lectures. These lectures presented exactly the opportunity and the need to reflect on the work accomplished during the past decade and to reassess its priorities and stakes.

The intense work done on his previous work (FPP: 70, Chignola 1991: 148), after the highly charged liminal trip to Europe, produced major effects. It proved to be the third major peak experience for Voegelin, the 'breakthrough' that on his own recognition came 'on occasion' of the Walgreen lectures (AR: 64), and that finally directed his work away from the *History of Political Ideas* project and towards the completion of the first three volumes of *Order and History*. This coincided with a genuine insight that gave focus to the lectures: the sudden recognition of a kind of structural equivalence between ancient gnosis and modern ideologies. This vision came in the same way and had the same character as the similar visions of Weber, Elias, Foucault and Mumford. In a highly charged liminal moment, after years spent with intense work whose end had remained elusive, he recognized the commonality between two types of practices that were widely separated in time and space and that so far were considered unrelated.

The proper symbolization and differentiation of this insight, of course, required time and repeated efforts. Voegelin himself often came back to the question of the gnostic character of modernity and refined his argument by mentioning other, similar trends of thought that also had an impact on modern ideological thinking, like hermetism, neo-Platonism or apocalyptic thought. However, any attempt to question the relevance of this insight, according to which not just Marxism was a gnostic socialism but modern politics and thought was to a considerable extent gnostic, would amount to a denial of the value of the vision that launched Voegelin's entire later work. Thus, the idea of 'salvaging' the work of Voegelin from his 'questionable' opinions concerning the gnostic character of modernity is not possible. The work would not survive the surgical destruction of its core insight (Price 1999).

However, something was indeed problematic in the way Voegelin formulated his thesis in 1952 and this concerned the excessively polemical tone of its presentation. An emotionally-charged, liminal figuration is a double-edged sword: it can help the gaining of insights but it may also contribute to the transference of the emotionally-charged conditions into the style and tone of the work. This combination marks the *New Science of Politics* and would only escalate afterwards.

One of the best illustrations of the modality and effects of this polemics and also of the malleability of liminal condition, is the treatment Voegelin gives to Max Weber. Weber was the most important reading experience of his formative years and returns to Weber would be a source for meditative reflections. The only exception is the *New Science of Politics* where Voegelin gives a mostly negative and quite biased representation of Weber's ideas. This may have been partly due to a temporary conflation of these ideas with the kind of 'positivist Weber' then painted by structural-functionalist sociology.[55] It also recalled the Weber painted by Hans Kelsen, the famous neo-Kantian legal scholar who was Voegelin's professor in Vienna.[56] But all this may not have been sufficient had Voegelin not received a copy of Strauss's 1951 article on Weber during the final stages of his work (FPP: 79–80).

This case be taken as a representative example both for the impact produced by a confluence of coincidences and liminality, and the fallacy of the conventional method of the history of ideas which puts the emphasis on printed words without taking into account their experiential context. For almost half a century, the few pages written on Weber in *New Science of Politics* are considered as Voegelin's authorial and authoritative 'position', a sign of his 'withdrawal from Weber' (Hennis 1988: 198–9). However, though some of the ideas exposed here appeared earlier and later in his assessments of Weber, the version presented in *New Science of Politics* was quite different and may have taken its direction and tone from the Weber presented in Strauss's 1949 Walgreen lectures.[57]

The substantiation of this point requires analysis of both the context and the two texts. First, the outcome was produced by a specific event that happened in a specific figuration. Since September, Voegelin had been feverishly working on *New Science of Politics*, first on preparing the lectures and then writing them up for publication. He received Strauss's text on Weber just when he was completing the text by finishing the Introduction. It was thus at the best, or rather the worst, possible moment.

Furthermore, Voegelin then had a very special relationship with the author of the text. Strauss was senior to Voegelin both by age and by academic standing and the correspondence occasionally reveals a deferential tone on his part. This was bound to be the case now, as the text was an article version of Chapter Two of Strauss's own Walgreen lectures which had been delivered in October 1949. In addition, Strauss was instrumental in helping Voegelin receive the invitation so that, in more ways than one, Voegelin followed in Strauss's footsteps.

In order to show that these aspects of context produced an intellectual effect, one has to compare and contrast the two texts. Strauss's presentation of Weber is a most cunning piece; a reverse of the strategy of Antonius in Shakespeare's *Julius Caesar*. Strauss starts by praising Weber as 'the greatest social scientist of our century' (Strauss 1953: 36) but only to bury him.

Strauss starts by restating the questionable commonplaces of the secondary literature on Weber: that his aim was to establish objective standards which is a misconception of Weber's 'Objectivity' essay (ibid.: 37) or that at the centre of his work was the distinction between facts and values, or 'the Is and the Ought', which is a misconception of Weber's

'Value Freedom' essay (ibid.: 40–1). He also charges Weber with attributing reality only to the individual, thus with methodological individualism which is a misconception of the entire conceptual framework of *Economy and Society* (ibid.: 37).

The fact that Strauss does not really address Weber, only takes for granted the picture painted in the secondary literature, is hidden by his use of references. Though the book was intended for broad audiences, Strauss only refers to the original German editions of Weber's works in seemingly extremely authoritative footnotes where he often listed a dozen pages. This looks very intimidating indeed, except that when looking up the references one finds that the point becomes impossible to trace. This is helped by the fact that Strauss practically never gives a single quotation from Weber's works that goes beyond a word or two. In the smokescreen, it becomes lost that Strauss gives an interpretation of Weber in his long chapter which is not supported properly by textual evidence. The procedure becomes visible in the instance where he refers to Aristotle. There, with genuine scholarship, he both quotes the passages and in the footnote gives the exact line (ibid.: 41, fn 9).

Under normal conditions, Voegelin would have seen beyond appearances. However, the conditions were not ordinary and in more ways than one. His sight was thus obscured and he simply incorporated some of the ideas of Strauss into his book. This happened, furthermore, in the worst possible manner, in introducing and concluding his section on Weber.

Following Strauss, Voegelin fits his Weber section into a discussion of positivism, in particular the distinction between values and facts which is something that he would not do earlier or later. Furthermore, he introduces Weber as the person in whose work this methodological movement 'ran to the end of its immanent logic' (NSP: 13). He repeats the same characterization after this section, in the starting sentence of section four: 'In the work of Max Weber positivism had come to its end' (ibid.: 22). The nine pages devoted to a short discussion of Weber are located between these highly emphatic and untenable claims.

Most of the contents of these pages, as opposed to the sentences coming before and after them, are often close to the Weber Voegelin would present before and after. There are also frequent qualifications referring to the shortness of the treatment (ibid.: 13, 17, 21). In fact they are so frequent in such a short piece that they make one a bit suspicious. However, the entire discussion starts from the wrong note and this weighs heavily on it. Though his characterization of Weber is much sharper than the vague commentaries of Strauss, it contains several untenable claims. Voegelin claimed that a 'value-free science meant to Weber the exploration of causes and effects' (ibid.: 14), and in general attributed an excessive importance to Weber's concern with causality (ibid.: 14), neglecting his interest in 'elective affinities'. He argued that Weber omitted pre-Reformation Christianity from his plans (ibid.: 20), while exactly where Weber made reference to Islam he also listed a planned volume on early Christianity (Schluchter 1989: 425). He claimed that Weber 'religiously observed the positivistic taboo on metaphysics' (NSP: 21), while later he would recognize that Weber was a 'man conscious of transcendence' (Voegelin 1995: 102). Finally, and most untenably, he claimed that Weber's general conception of history was 'obviously derived from Comte's philosophy of history' (NSP: 22). He not only should have known better; he *knew* better.

1951

After finishing the *New Science of Politics*, in summer 1951 Voegelin resumed the work on his manuscript which had suspended for more than a year (Opitz 1994a: 131). When Voegelin set out to complete his research, he realized that his thought outgrew the limits of his previous work. This was because *New Science of Politics* was not simply a preliminary version of the results of his research or a first order work but a reflection on this work and therefore a 'second-order' phenomenon, in the same way as Weber's *Einleitung* (Tenbruck 1980: 348, fn 29). He had to go through another fundamental reorganization. The realization of this necessity is indicated in a 10 July 1951 letter written to his friend, Eduard Baumgarten.[58]

The conditions were again liminal in a multiple sense. Voegelin had just finished a major work, his first book in his fourteen year stay in the US, but was in the period before its publication. This is a state of suspense for any academic, but especially so for somebody who had had to wait so long for the fruits of a particularly arduous and lonely undertaking and who was so much convinced of the validity and relevance of his work and indeed his 'insight'. The difficulties encountered when returning to the book project were therefore all the more stressful. Finally, as another peculiar coincidence, his letter to Baumgarten which was the document of his state of mind of the period was written on the very day that the armistice talks started in Korea.

Of all possible candidates, July 1951 seems to be the moment when the work on the *History of Political Ideas* definitely turned into *Order and History*. This statement is meant in a strong and not in a weak sense and is explicitly challenging the methodological perspective of the editors of the *History of Political Ideas*. It also follows the spirit of Voegelin's work. Voegelin emphasized that the history of thought must be based on the reconstruction of engendering experiences. Experiences are *events*. Events are breakpoints and they erupt into the world. They divide the flow of processes into a before and an after. They are eye-openers which create the impression of a radical gap between the past and the present, a brand new departure. Because of their radical novelty, experiences are open to a gnostic (mis)interpretation, as if they represented a *tabula rasa*, breaking all links with the past. Such an interpretation of experiences and breaks is unacceptable. In this particular case, the work on *Order and History* was clearly based upon and grew out of the *History of Political Ideas* but it is also clear that the two projects are not identical. There is a difference between a fundamental continuity at the level of the work and a radical disconti-nuity in the conceptualization of the underlying project. In the case of Voegelin's work, it is clear from the available evidence that the breakpoint happened after work on *New Science of Politics* was finished.

From 1939 to 1950, he was working with an almost fanatical determina-tion on the *History of Political Ideas*, having little time to step back and reflect upon its direction. When the opportunity presented itself with the major 1943 and 1945 peak -experiences, he was forced to return to the old project within a short time. This time, however, he had a break from the project for more than a year, and this year was extremely full of both new experiences and reflexive exercises. *History of Political Ideas* and *Order and History* are clearly not identical projects. Between the two, a major reorga-nization in Voegelin's work has occurred. And there is no better candidate for this than the moment when he returned to his work after a gap of more than a year and realized that he simply could not go on as before.

The project became unmanageable and impossible to complete as it combined three quite different aims: the writing of an authoritative account of the history of political ideas; the presentation of his own polit-ical philosophy centring not on the personnel and ideas of political thought but on his own vision of the 'beginning' and the 'beyond'; and a diagnosis of modernity that eventually led to an original vision, linking ancient gnosticism and modernity. The change from *History of Political Ideas* to *Order and History* meant a fundamental shift of focus from the first to the second aim. However, even though the shift in his own priorities was accomplished at that time, the question of the publication of his manu-script and its actual status still loomed large in the background. It was adding fuel to the increasingly polemical tones in Voegelin's work.

The situation can again be illuminated by a comparison with Weber. Both started the work that eventually turned out to be their major projects, *Economy and Society* and *Order and History*, as simply charged to produce a textbook in their field. Weber was editor of the third edition of Schönberg's *Handbook of Political Economy*, while Voegelin should have written a simple introductory textbook on the history of political ideas. Both authors failed in their original purpose and this is exactly why their works are still relevant for us today. Even the relationship between Parts Two and One of *Economy and Society* and between *History of Political Ideas* and *Order and History* are analogous down to the minute details. Weber was first editor of a standard textbook, of which he was only supposed to write a few sections then his contributions expanded out of all proportion which resulted in the deadline of the work being continuously postponed (Schluchter 1989: 441). He was only 'saved' by the outbreak of the First World War. Then, after the end of the war, he set down and produced Part One on the basis of the earlier manuscript.[59]

Summer 1951 marks the starting point of another four-and-a-half-year-long period in Voegelin's life-work that would end with the completion of the first three volumes of *Order and History*. This was the moment when the second of Voegelin's mature concerns, the 'beginning' entered forcefully into the work. The unity of the period, however, only becomes visible retrospectively and the road towards completion would be quite bumpy.

Each such period can be identified by the kind of life-work and world links that are unique to it. Between 1939 and 1943, Voegelin was ostensibly working on a textbook on *History of Political Ideas* that soon turned into a standard reference book. This was during a world war and under conditions of utter existential insecurity. Between 1945 and 1950, during the increasingly bitter Cold War years, he was ostensibly working on a standard reference book that soon turned into a deeply personal project, in existential security but still in isolation and with hardly any recognition.[60] Between 1951 and 1955, when the heat of the Cold War was receding, Voegelin's work hardly bore any resemblance to the original *History of Political Ideas* project as it turned decisively into *Order and History* and its completion became entangled in matters of illness, recognition and polemics.[61]

Questions of illness are not often considered as having relevance to the work of a thinker. However, given the examples of Weber and Nietzsche among many other contemporary thinkers, it would be a bit hasty to dismiss such phenomena as lying outside the scope of interpretive understanding. This is all the more so as intestinal difficulties are considered one of the prime examples of psychosomatic illness. It would be also too easy to refer only to matters of overwork, as Marianne Weber argued in Weber's case. Voegelin was always working intensively, both before and after his illness. Furthermore, the outbreak of illness can be closely connected to very specific moments: in Voegelin's case it was the concern with the reception of *New Science of Politics* that started once he delivered the manuscript to the publisher and ended with the actual response upon publication.[62]

There are no major complaints about illness in the correspondence during the busy and extremely stressful time of the 1940s. An indication of a major health problem is contained, however, in an October 1951 letter to Hans Paeschke, the editor of *Merkur*.[63] Voegelin apologises for a delay in responding to Paeschke's letter of 31 July that was due to his being really ill for three months. This puts the start of the troubles back to the time when Voegelin finished work on *New Science of Politics* and returned to *History of Political Ideas* or exactly the moment when he wrote his major letter to Eduard Baumgarten.

The illness looked only transitory, but it returned in the winter of 1951 in the form of a chronic bladder infection.[64] By that time, he was already working on ancient Egypt.[65] Though he was hoping to avoid an operation, between December 1952 and December 1953 he underwent four operations for intestinal problems. The decisive outbreak of the illness, together with a decisive outbreak of high pitches of polemics coincided around the publication date of *New Science of Politics*.

This was in October 1952. However, publication had been foreseen for spring 1952, thus it had been imminent since the summer and this fuelled the polemical tone. It is present in an August 1952 talk, delivered at the APSA meeting, entitled 'Political Science and the Intellectuals'. Voegelin identified the intellectuals as sophists and sleepwalkers and defined the science of politics as far back as Plato as a 'militant enterprise, a defence of truth both political and practical' against their revolt (Voegelin 1999).[66] It is also visible in the two main review essays he finished around that time, 'The Oxford Political Philosophers' written in summer 1952 and on Arendt's *Origins of Totalitarianism*. The polemical tone comes out quite strongly in the texts themselves, but breaks through more directly in the correspondence. In a letter sent to Gurian, he dismisses Arendt outright, claiming that he committed an error by taking her seriously and was just wasting his time.[67] This letter is significant for a series of further reasons. It is here that Voegelin definitely rejects the possibility of the publication of the Bodin essay; suggests instead 'The World of Homer' that would be considered as excessively polemical by de Waal; and indicates that due to the persistence of intestinal problems, he would have to undergo two operations, starting from December.[68]

An exchange of letters with Schutz is also instructive. A letter of 15 September 1952, written a month before publication, is characterized by a particularly aggressive tone (Weiss 1997: 15). In his reply, not fully understanding the reasons, Schutz wonders about what is going on: 'You know how much I admire your work. I esteem it so highly that it does not need any justification. But why, why, why do you take on such a monopolistic-imperialistic attitude?' (Voegelin *et al.* 1993: 74–5). The exchange of letters with Schutz continued with the publication of *New Science of Politics* and in similar tones.[69] If Alfred Schutz, Voegelin's friend of four decades, was suddenly so much troubled with matters of tone and style, then the existence of the problem cannot be dismissed.

However, it certainly does not require the dismantling of the entire idea of modern Gnosticism. In fact, the point of the entire exercise is exactly the opposite. As Chapter 8 will argue in more detail, Voegelin's vision concerning the gnostic character of modernity, together with its later extensions and qualifications, is one of the most important insights of contemporary social thought. The problem, just as in the related cases of Mumford and Foucault, was in the manner of the presentation, its excessive polemics. The aim is to explain this aspect by various issues of context so that the power of the vision could shine through better. The aim is therefore not to use matters of context to explain the substance of the idea and diminish its validity; on the contrary, contextualization serves only the purpose of clearer understanding.

Illnesses are major life experiences offering, especially in the stage of convalescence, possibilities for reflecting upon and changing one's life course. Voegelin evidently made use of this opportunity. This is visible in what he wrote and what he did. The letters written in 1953 contain a series of attempts at self-description, a continuous concern about the links between his mystic-gnostic and Christian-Platonic self-identities. In January, he talked about the need to take Christianity more seriously than even Bergson did and claimed that Plato was a philosopher and not a gnostic, as 'philosophy is not "wisdom" but "love of wisdom" which implies the essential unattainability of the wisdom of the gnostic'.[70] In April, he provided a three-fold classification of contemporary theorizing with Bergson at the top and the huge digests of empirical material like Urs von Balthasar and Toynbee belonging to the second tier.[71] Also in April, he claimed that while in the past he was too obsessed with 'Weberian *Zweckrationalität*' and the Aristotlean concern with the science of ultimate aims, he found a way out with Bergson, recognizing that human societies may have a moral culture without the benefit of theories.[72] At the same time, his polemics arguably also has reached its peak in an unsent letter of 15 April 1953 to Strauss. There Voegelin got so carried away in his invective against Locke that he had to re-write the entire letter five days later.[73]

Paradoxically, both polemics and illness reached their peak at the moment when *New Science of Politics* met unexpected success. The book generated huge interest and, though reception was controversial, it was mostly positive. It arguably reached its highest moment on 9 March 1953 when *Time* magazine ran a feature on the book.

The spring of 1953 marked the end of the hectic period that had started in the summer of 1951. The reception gave secure recognition to his work and this helped Voegelin take heed of the warning given by the operations. Though some polemics continued from the past, from now onwards Voegelin evidently tried to avoid a repetition of those activities that had led to such polemics in the past. Thus, he ended his correspondence with Strauss and even the exchange of letters with Schutz became much less frequent (Weiss 1997: 2). After three more reviews in 1954 and 1955 of books published in 1953, he never published another review. And finally, no more excerpts from *Order and History* appeared until full publication. In fact, he did not publish anything until the three volumes came out in 1956, which was something that he could afford to do after the success of *New Science of Politics*.

However, it meant that at the same time as he was saving his energies from unnecessary polemics and was engaged in finalizing the first volumes of *Order and History*, he was thrust into even greater intellectual isolation after the considerable success of *New Science of Politics* than before. The paradox of Voegelin's case lies in the fact that while the partial derailment of the projects of Elias, Borkenau and Foucault was caused by a perceived negative reception, the basically positive reception of Voegelin's work became overshadowed by the polemics he was engaged upon before actual publication.

Literally the moment the two-year period lived under the shadow of the reception of *New Science of Politics* ended, the problem of the publication of the manuscript that by now reached enormous proportions returned. On 20 October 1953, after a silence of about four and a half years, the publishers inquired about the status of the manuscript (Hollweck and Sandoz 1997: 8–9).

Voegelin's reply to Macmillan on 25 October 1953 makes two things clear. First, the manuscript again bore no similarity to the one contracted; as would soon become as evident for Macmillan as it had to McGraw-Hill in the spring of 1944. The first time, the 250-page textbook expanded into a 1400 page work that was to set the standard on the field for decades to come. Now even this work had mushroomed into an enormous manuscript of 4500 pages. Second, by that time the organization had become identical to the one suggested as the framework for *Order and History* in the 1956 publication of the first volume. That the original idea behind *History of Political Ideas* had long been abandoned is clear from Voegelin's letter which states in plain terms that the work no longer follows the conventions of the field: 'The sequence of subject-matter [. . .] is no longer a simple string of authors and ideas in time.' Accordingly he suggests a new title, 'Order and Symbols', and argues combatively for the outright obsolescence of the very concept of a 'history of political ideas', 'because the liberal ideology on which it was based is by now exploded in critical science by the development of the experiences of order and their adequate symbolization' (Hollweck and Sandoz 1997: 9). If the language used here conflates Voegelin's new work and the entire field, this was to a large extent imposed on Voegelin because of the force of circumstances out of which his project took shape. One could argue that, paradoxically, it was exactly these circumstances that prevented the work from really becoming a pacesetter.

The proposed new Table of Contents, apart from making it clear that Voegelin was by then thinking in terms of *Order and History* and no longer *History of Political Ideas*, also gave paradigmatic clarity to the triple moving forces behind the work that had exploded all time horizons and publication frameworks during the past fifteen years. The 'first volume', running to 1450 manuscript pages and dealing with myth, history and philosophy corresponds to the first three volumes of *Order and History* as it would appear soon. This contains Voegelin's own philosophy of the order of consciousness in history, the continuously re-worked historical material that exploded first in the direction of the 'beyond' and then of the 'beginning'. It basically remained the same from this 1953 formulation through the 1955 letters to various publishers (Hollweck and Sandoz 1997: 12–13) until the eventual publication in 1956. Of course, this work was not written solely after 1950. However, from 1951 onwards, it was *the* exclusive concern for Voegelin.[74]

The suggested 'second volume' on the Middle Ages is 1200 pages long and corresponds to the bulk of the work on the *History of Political Ideas* that Voegelin completed during the early 1940s and never altered significantly. This work, published roughly in the first three volumes of *History of Political Ideas*, has indeed the structure and character of a survey of political ideas. But in this entire body of work, there is not a single reference in the original script to works published after 1940.[75] The 'third volume' follows a quite different kind of structuring. Corresponding to the last five volumes of *History of Political Ideas*, it is focusing on the third and 'critical' stream of Voegelin's work, his diagnosis of modernity.

The identification of the three streams with the three suggested volumes should not be taken mechanically. This is especially valid for the 'third volume', as it also contains elements of the other two streams. Thus, it contains some of Voegelin's most important meditative essays with its analysis of three of the thinkers whose importance he kept emphasizing, Bodin, Vico and Schelling. To some extent it also follows a chronological sequence. However, the difference to the other two volumes in both substance and style is also clear and fundamental.

On the themes discussed, the 'third volume' got increasingly distanced from the standard set of authors discussed in any history of political ideas, culminating in the last parts that bear no resemblance to the standard personnel of the political thought of the eighteenth and nineteenth centuries. It omitted Rousseau, Burke, Hegel, J. S. Mill and de Tocqueville and focused instead on authors whose work was central to proving a diagnosis of the present from a sociological perspective.[76] Even in terms of content, the volume looks much closer to a history of sociological thought with its focus on its main 'precursors', the Enlightenment (Hawthorne 1987), Comte and Marx. However his treatment is just as different from a textbook on sociological thought as it is from a standard history on political ideas.

The question of the fate of this manuscript of gigantic proportions was now in the balance. The attitude of Macmillan was clear enough once they had received Voegelin's first letter after four and a half years: the manuscript was not meeting the contract and they could not publish it (Hollweck and Sandoz 1997: 10–14). Voegelin was trying to save the results of all his hard work. He argued yet again that the original idea of *History of Political Ideas* had been preserved and again proposed that the first 'volume' be published separately (Hollweck and Sandoz 1997: 10). This is what would indeed eventually happen.

Though Macmillan declined publication, the long odyssey of at least the first part of the manuscript would soon end. Voegelin found that there was interest at his local university press and the three volumes appeared duly at the end of 1956 and in 1957. The decisive moment of completion was due to another Guggenheim Fellowship that enabled Voegelin to return to Europe in the summer of 1955. The punctuation is almost too perfect: the third stage of the odyssey would end on the same note, a trip to Europe with a grant from the Guggenheim Foundation, as the second trip.[77]

The books attracted considerable attention. According to Geoffrey Price's bibliography, the first volume alone generated about fifty reviews, of which seventeen had appeared by the end of 1957. The work became a classic in its field within years and the few instances of polemical remarks still contained in the volumes were lost among the wealth of insight and information. However, there was one slight but still perplexing formal peculiarity about the Acknowledgement page. The piece is cryptic as it included reference to an institution which provided 'aid at a critical juncture of the work' but 'wishe[d] to remain unnamed' (OHI: xv). It also thanked only one individual, Robert Heilman, for his help but not for any substantive advice concerning content only for improving its English, in terms of praise that were recognized as excessive (Heilman 1996). This combination of no acknowledgement of substantive help but an extremely generous acknowledgement for assistance in language creates a strange impression which borders on arrogance. This is all the less intelligible as Voegelin received major stimulation and substantial help from quite a few of his close colleagues and friends like Schutz, Engel-Janosi, Sebba and Löwith, to whom he regularly sent draft versions of his ongoing work. The impression thus created concerning the making of the work and even of Voegelin as a person is certainly misleading, though this was not unintentional.

In this light, we can return to the question whether Voegelin had kept to his original purpose throughout all these years and the work had only gained in 'breadth and depth', as the editors argue, or whether the original book project has been 'abandoned' as Voegelin himself claimed repeatedly.[78] This way of posing the question, however, assumes an identity between the book project and the internal dynamics of Voegelin's work that is fictional. The project was both driven and torn apart by the tensions between the three different threads it was trying to keep together. With every deepening of the project, which itself was not simply a continuous process but happened through a series of basic experiences, the fiction of this identity became impossible to maintain. Voegelin's problems have indeed remained identical in his life-work but they have nothing to do with a college textbook on *History of Political Ideas* or even with a standard work of the field. The central concern of Voegelin's work, which first appeared in the 1930–32 *Herrschaftslehre*, and then reappearing through the experiences of 1943, 1945 and 1950, was the same throughout, and it was the concern with the 'beginning' and the 'beyond' as he would eventually call it. Throughout these years, however, he was desperately trying to finish a book whose genre did not suit his purposes, and the 'critical' part of his work, the diagnosis of modernity, was not simply an intellectual concern for him but a pressing matter of the world in which he was living. The abruptness of the transition from *History of Political Ideas* to *Order and History* that Voegelin placed around the writing of *New Science of Politics* and which the previous analysis confirmed as correct, simply meant the decisive abandonment of a format into which he was pressed to put his work due to the force of circumstances.

Behind the insistence of the editors about the identity of the 'core' of the project (Hollweck and Sandoz 1997: 10), there is a serious conceptual problem. This comes to the surface in the assertion that Voegelin's work had an 'ultimately humanistic concern' (ibid.: 28). 'Humanism', however, in the sense of an unbroken, continuous 'education' into the received wisdom of a canonized *Kultur* is the ideal of neo-Kantianism and the *Bildungsbürgertum*, not of Voegelin. This perspective ignores the question of spirituality in the sense of the transformation of the self through experiences and the readiness to respond to the 'drawing' of the 'beyond'. This implies not simply the cumulative acquisition of knowledge, added to an unchanging 'core', but the ability to suddenly look at the world and at oneself in a fundamentally new light. Had the editors paid proper attention to the long passage that they quote from Voegelin in order to support their point, they would have noticed that in his definition of self-education Voegelin talks about discovering 'all of a sudden' that one's understanding increases (Hollweck and Sandoz 1997: 29). This is the old philosophical ideal of the wondering at the world, the *thaumazein*, and not the continuous evolutionary process of gaining 'breadth' and 'scope' which was the ideal of Renaissance humanists and Prussian schoolteachers and was based on the fixed identity of the subject.[79]

1958

The completion of three books was a major achievement. Voegelin was no longer tied to Baton Rouge and he clearly wanted to move to break out of his intellectual isolation. He was in touch with several major American universities but in the end decided to return to Europe to take up the Munich chair of Max Weber left vacant since his death, and also to assume the directorship of the newly-founded Institute for Political Science.

Voegelin suggested three reasons for his choice, namely higher salary, the wish to be with old friends and the challenge to build up an Institute (AR: 91). The latter two allude to the classical concept of *phylia* that combined friendship at the personal level with active and creative participation in the life of a community which was something that American academic life was certainly not equipped to offer. One should also not forget the appeal exerted by Weber's own chair, which parallels the way Weber assumed the chair of Knies in Heidelberg and Foucault that of Hyppolite at the *Collège de France*.

The parallels go even further as far as concerning the polemics which Voegelin got almost instantaneously involved in. The theme of modern gnosticism returned with a vengeance and were the centre stage in his inaugural lecture (SPG), with tones that were among the harshest he had ever used about Nietzsche, Heidegger, Marx and Comte. One must remember the context.

The moment was again liminal as it was not just a new position in a new country but a permanent return to Europe after two decades and to Germany after almost five decades. It was also a special occasion, being an inaugural lecture and also a manifesto for the new Institute he was in charge of creating. Finally, at that time, his work on volume four of *Order and History* centred on ancient Gnosticism.[80]

Shortly after the move, Voegelin came up with a discovery that led to a major reorganization of the project. The substance of the change, which was the recognition of parallel lines of meaning in history and the development of the concept of historiogenesis and was published in a first version in 1960, is well-known. The event can be dated with some precision. 1959 was the year when *Science, Politics and Gnosticism* was published, organizational efforts were particularly heavy and Voegelin spent a lot of time giving talks. He had returned to intensive work by summer 1960, and a letter written to the publisher on 21 July 1960 contains an account of the discovery and also details its effects on the publication schedule (Hollweck and Caringella 1990: xiii).

Much of the rest of the decade which Voegelin spent in Munich was devoted to the working out of the effects of this discovery. The first years of this work, covering the period 1960–3, were devoted to the implications with respect to the question of history. As Voegelin soon realized, the discovery of parallel lines of meaning did not lead to a quick solution of all the theoretical problems which the work posed. The empirical material again became overwhelming (Voegelin 1990b: 234–8). This work culminated in a major unfinished paper entitled 'What Is History?' (in Voegelin 1990b).

1964

The abandonment of work on the manuscript of 'What Is History?, and indeed the suspension of work on volume four, can be connected to a specific event. 1964 was the centenary of Weber's birth and the occasion for a huge conference. Voegelin took part in the commemoration in Munich, just as he did in Vienna in 1930, and on 23 June 1964 he delivered his paper entitled 'The Greatness of Weber' (Voegelin 1995). The tone of this lecture was quite different from that of the 1952 sections in *New Science of Politics*. Voegelin started by listing those four figures of German thought in the second part of the nineteenth century who reached world rank: Marx, Nietzsche, Freud and Weber.[81] According to Voegelin, the most important one was Weber, a crucial threshold figure who closed an epoch and opened a new one.

The notes Voegelin made while preparing for the lectures are illuminating on his new and old interpretations of Weber.[82] Apart from sketches of his argument, they include pages of notes about Nietzsche including allusion to his Nietzsche-Pascal article, and quotes from Eduard Baumgarten's recently-published book. The quote with which Voegelin's Weber talk ends, referring to Weber's self-definition as a mystic, however, is not the end of the notes but it is rather a door to another quite different set. This includes a number of passages from the *Bible*, both the Old and New Testaments, the *Talmud*, the *Babylonian Talmud* and a page of Chinese terms related to the *Tao*.

These notes make it clear that it is quite inappropriate to set Voegelin the mystic prone to mediations against Voegelin the Weberian scholar.[83] The two are one and the same person. Just as his 1930 Weber talk launched his first meditative exercises, his 1964 talk again represented a major break and a reorientation in his work.

Since the publication of the first three volumes of *Order and History*, Voegelin had been working on the fourth volume which was only interrupted temporarily by the move to Germany and his inaugural lecture. Around the time of his Weber talk, however, he took another step back, reorganized the economy of his work and engaged in a series of philosophical-anamnetic exercises which were the second set of meditations identified by Caringella (in Lawrence 1997: 40). The effects are visible in the work as far as both general direction and terminology are concerned. The new encounter with Weber as an 'in-between' or threshold figure coincides with the time when Voegelin discovered one of the central concepts of his entire work, Plato's *metaxy*. This word did not yet appear in 'What is History?', but it took up the central place in a major 1964 article entitled 'Eternal Being in Time' which was based on a 24 October 1962 speech (Hollweck and Caringella 1990: xvi–xvii, fn 4). Soon after came another major meditative piece, 'Immortality: Experience and Symbol', that was delivered as the Harvard Divinity School Ingersoll lecture on 14 January 1965.

As a result, instead of finishing the fourth volume, in 1966 Voegelin published a book outside the series. *Anamnesis* was meditative and not historical in character even though it included translations of some of his related historical essays. These pieces would be duly omitted from the later English version. Its character was described in a letter to Heilman whose importance has been widely recognized.[84]

In this letter, Voegelin singles out Heraclitus as the main inspiration for this book, as the first thinker to recognize the depth of the psyche (see also OHII: 220–39).[85] However, given the 'debris of opaque symbols' characteristic of the present condition, it is not enough to simply take up the path of earlier thinkers like Heraclitus, Aristotle and Augustine, but one 'must start from the current obstacles of human self-understanding.' This requires the development of a new 'literary form in philosophy', which is 'neither pre-Socratic, nor classic, nor Christian, though it has certain affinities to the mysticism of Plotinus and Dionysius Areopagita, not to forget the Cloud of Unknowing.' With the meditative volume, Voegelin again shifted his concerns from Plato the philosopher to Heraclitus the sage and from the Christianity of Aquinas to gnostic and neo-Platonic mysticism.[86]

The most important piece of the book is the long third part entitled 'What is Political Reality' (subordinated in the original German edition to the section title 'The Order of Consciousness'). It was written in the second half of 1965 and both in its title and its content combined interests derived from Plato and Weber. But it also contained in its first part the 1943 letters to Schutz, together with a belated memorial that rendered public their close intellectual friendship and ended the self-created myth of Voegelin as the solitary thinker. Given that Voegelin and Schutz developed their projects, following some kind of 'division of labour', on the basis of their joint reading of Weber, it gives further support for the thesis that the meditation on Weber had a crucial role in launching this book project.[87]

Shortly after, he developed a new and ambitious historical and philosophical project which was based on his Candler lectures delivered between 17 and 20 April 1967 at Emory University Atlanta and entitled 'The Drama of Humanity'. This project, which he emphatically did not associate with *Order and History* (Hollweck and Caringella 1990: xxiii), would include trips to the Neolithic monuments of Malta, Crete, Mycenae, Newgrange, West Ireland and Ankara and occupied Voegelin for several years (Purcell 1996).

1969

At that time, there was another coincidence of personal and political liminality. By the mid 1960s, he got increasingly frustrated with certain aspects of German academic life (Heilman 1996). It was also the time of increased student activism and, given Voegelin's strong feelings about Marx and Hegel, it is not surprising that he became a target of heckling. In 1968, he reached the age of sixty-seven and qualified for a pension. He decided to leave Germany and return to the US where he became Henry Salvatori Distinguished Fellow at the Hoover Institution in Stanford on 15 February 1969. He remained there until his retirement in 1974 and then became Senior Research Fellow until his death (Price 1994: 6).

The liminal years 1968 and 1969, his last year in Europe and the first year back in the States, were times in which a series of major papers were finished at least in a draft version, based upon the meditative exercises published in *Anamnesis*. They include the unpublished manuscripts 'Anxiety and Reason' (1968), 'The Eclipse of Reality' (1969) and 'The Moving Soul' (1969); 'Equivalences of Experience and Symbolization in

History', published in 1970 but delivered as a conference paper in Rome in 1968; 'Gospel and Culture', published in 1971, but delivered as a lecture to the Pittsburgh Theological Seminary in April 1970 and already existing in a manuscript version by December 1969 (Voegelin 1990b: 241); 'On Hegel: A Study in Sorcery', also published only in 1971 but delivered as a conference paper in early September 1969 (Voegelin 1990a: 213); and the meditation on Henry James's *Turn of the Screw*, based on a 1947 letter to Heilman and finalized in December 1969 (Voegelin 1990b: 239).

Upon his return to the States, he also returned to the *Order and History* project or perhaps it was the project that returned to him. It only took shape slowly. At first, he was trying to combine historical work with the American edition of *Anamnesis* into a single volume under the new title 'In Search of Order', while still considering completion of 'The Drama of Humanity' (Hollweck and Caringella 1990: xxvi). However, the separation of the two projects proved difficult to maintain with some essays listed as contributions to both volumes and he was still missing the essay on mysticism. Eventually 'The Beginning and the Beyond' would fill the gap (ibid.: xxiii).

In the organization of the project, the central question was the same as during the 1940s and 1950s, namely the division between the historical material and their reflexive elaboration. The main difference was that the theoretical component had been increased considerably. The historical parts themselves became extremely dense and theoretically sophisticated while theoretical reflection on this material took the form of meditation, close to mysticism. As a result, the delivery of volume four that was supposed to combine both aspects and be completed by July 1970 kept being postponed.[88]

The fourth volume was eventually published in 1974, under the title *The Ecumenic Age* that had 'insinuated itself' by 1973 (Hollweck and Caringella 1990: xxiii). The final push towards publication was arguably given by another anamnetic exercise, the autobiographical interview sessions which Voegelin had between 26 June and 7 July 1973 with Ellis Sandoz, who was then working on his monograph (Sandoz 1981). Like Elias and Foucault, Voegelin was very reluctant to disclose facts about his life. He did so only by answering questions, not by writing an autobiography and still did not allow publication in his lifetime. However, like Elias and Foucault, the exercise did not fail to have a major impact.

The impact was at the most sensitive part of the project, the long *Introduction* that, according to Voegelin, 'has introduced itself as the form which a philosophy of history has to assume in the present historical situation' (OHIV: 57). Most of the other chapters had been finished between 1970 and 1972 and, in his report of 15 February 1973, Voegelin stated that the first volume was finished and would be published by autumn 1973. However, this did not happen and the title foreseen for the publication was still 'In Search of Order'. At the time of the next report, however, the volume gained its final title and it was published as announced.

The effects of these anamnetic exercises go well beyond the publication of the *Ecumenic Age*. They are visible in a major new meditative essay, considered by Caringella as the starting point of the third and last meditative period (in Lawrence 1997: 41). It is the posthumous *chef-d'oeuvre* 'The Beginning and the Beyond: A Meditation on Truth' (in Voegelin 1990b) which was presented at the March 1975 Aquinas lectures at Marquette. This came again at the right moment when, having just completed the *Ecumenic Age*, Voegelin was trying to finalize *In Search of Order*. Work on the final version of this talk preoccupied much of Voegelin's time between 1975 and 1977.

Finally, the appearance of the *Ecumenic Age*, after a gap of seventeen years, also coincided with two other important book publications. In December 1969, Voegelin opted against the American publication of *Anamnesis* as he wanted to incorporate it into *Order and History*. Now, this restriction became meaningless and was lifted. At the same time, as it was now evident that much of the empirical material worked out as part of *History of Political Ideas* would never be published in the new *Order and History* project, Voegelin agreed to the publication of a selection of the chapters on modernity entitled *From Enlightenment to Revolution*.[89]

The English version of *Anamnesis* also gave rise to a new introductory piece which was completed in March 1977. It became another self-reflexive exercise that, apart from containing a comprehensive overview of Voegelin's own path and some of the sharpest formulation on experience, symbolization and language (AN: 11–12), also had an effect on the work. It is around that time (Hollweck and Caringella 1990: xxx) that Voegelin turned from 'The Beginning and the Beyond' to a new meditative exercise, 'Wisdom and the Magic of the Extreme: A Meditation' which was first presented in the July 1977 Eranos conference. According to Caringella, the final volume of *Order and History* grew directly out of this meditation (in Lawrence 1997: 41).

The completion of this volume took up the remaining part of his life and, fighting against failing health, he had completed another substantial manuscript. Work was only suspended in the very last days that were spent on his last meditation, '*Quod Deus Dicitur*', which he kept refining until his death on 19 January 1985 at the age of eighty-four.

4   Lewis Mumford

Lewis Mumford was born on 19 October 1895 in Queens, New York. On his mother's side he was descended from German immigrants who were still ingrained in their home culture, while his father belonged to a well-to-do Jewish family. However, not only were his parents never married, but they only met for a few passing weeks. Mumford was born and raised as an only child out of wedlock.

Such a family situation, especially at that time, could easily have led to either a lack of emotional stability and security, or suffocating, close links between mother and son. However, Mumford grew up in conditions which were both warm and stable but also provided necessary independence. He had close ties to several members of his extended family and one of his earliest recollections is of his grandmother who died soon after (SL: 4). He had especially close ties with one of his grandfathers (in fact, only a step-grandfather) who often took him on long walks and 'introduced' (SL: 13) him to the city, to 'his' New York which was one of the long-lasting loves of his life but for which he also used the expression 'my long incarceration' (SL: 3). Most important of all was his 'second mother', Nellie Ahearn, his Irish nurse from Youghal, who stayed with the family well after there was any direct need for her assistance.

Besides intimacy and warmth, external conditions of stability were not missing. Strange as it seems today for a child growing up in New York: '(t)here was a kind of moral stability and security in the city of my youth that has now vanished' (SL: 5). And in spite of having two 'mothers', Mumford did not miss one of the most precious gifts of any childhood, that of being left alone, learning self-containment and self-sufficiency. As he stated at the age of twenty, if he were ever to write an autobiography, 'I shall not hesitate to attribute what small ability I possess to my mother's fond carelessness . . . By doing nothing for me she accordingly did a great deal' (MB: 19).[1]

Still, his childhood did not fail to contain a series of experiences which shook up his stability and certainty, and provided a proper 'Eliasian' mixture of involvement and detachment. As far as external conditions were concerned, the distancing was provided by the constant moves which at that time were an almost general feature of life for New Yorkers (SL: 9). As far as life experiences were concerned, Mumford went through a very serious illness, a prolonged case of measles with various complications (SL: 20), and the key word he used to characterize the career trajectory of his family was 'dissipation' (SL: 59). These experiences reinforced his self-containment and started a pattern of withdrawal and renewal which would be central not only for his life trajectory but also for his vision of history.

Formal schooling for Mumford, from his earliest age, was marked by two extremes. On the one hand, he hated school and its military discipline (SL: 20), a type of educational experience of which he could only make sense by interpreting it as a punishment (SL: 74–8). Together with his 'long incarceration' in the city and the months he spent training in the Navy in 1918, these were the experiences that rendered him sensitive, according to his own recognition, to the importance of small, compact organizations handed down from the 'pyramid age' (SL: 209). Still, he got hardly anything but A grades, and preserved an extreme work discipline and almost compulsive orderliness in his entire life, a major aspect of which was the practice of reviewing his past year every New Year's Day (MB: 21). His education was also marked by diversity. Though always drawn to the humanities, he was enrolled in the industrial and scientific Stuyvesant High School. He was also made sensitive to the arts by vaudeville theatre (SL: 120–2) and by museums (SL: 122–3) and to literature by his first adolescent love (SL: 109). Finally, owing to an interest he developed in journalism, he started his university years in the City College doing evening classes. The collegial atmosphere and the presence of mature and highly-motivated fellow students left indelible marks on Mumford's intellectual interests and career.

The main breakpoint in his educational career came with his transfer from evening to day classes in the autumn of 1914. Disappointed by the routine, mechanical curriculum and the lack of interest shown by both professors and students, he was unable to find motivation to study and started to develop clearly psychosomatic symptoms.[2] Helped by doctoral advice (SL: 140–1), he realized that proper convalescence required the finding of a proper way of life and not simply physical recovery. Without becoming a '"dropout" in the later 1960s sense' (SL: 141), he gave up the pursuit of a degree and selected instead a combination of training by experiences, exploring further and systematically the city and making the Central Library his 'home' (MB: 64). In developing this strategy, he relied a great deal on the main reading experience of his life, his encounter with the work of Patrick Geddes.

Of all thinkers discussed in this Part, Mumford is the only one who did not properly complete formal education, who was not fundamentally touched by a reading of Nietzsche and/or Weber, and whose main reading experience was a thinker who is not among the most highly-regarded thinkers of the modern age. Furthermore, these characteristics are all related, as Mumford encountered the work of Geddes just in the liminal period when he developed health problems owing to the frustrations of formal schooling, which he gave up with Geddes' help. However, the differences are less radical than they seem.

First, in spite of all antagonism and as opposed to Nietzsche, Mumford did not sever all ties with academia. He continued to do genuine research for his books, although he was notorious for the omission of footnotes. Although he never really took up a full-time teaching position, he was a much sought-after and highly popular visiting professor at major universities.[3] Furthermore, Mumford read and appreciated Nietzsche and even more so Emerson, on whom Nietzsche has written that 'Never have I felt so much at home in a book, and in *my* home, as – I may not praise it, it is too close to me' (quoted in Kaufmann 1974: 12). But most importantly, Mumford read Geddes exactly in the way Weber and Foucault read Nietzsche, focusing less on the content of single ideas than on the entire intellectual trajectory and especially the life-work link. Perhaps the strongest evidence for the claim can be taken from Mumford himself. The chapter of his autobiography summing up his debts to Geddes closes with the following sentence: 'What Nietzsche wrote about his master, Schopenhauer, applies to my intercourse with Geddes: "What he *taught* is put aside: what he *lived*, that will abide"' (SL: 158).

Reading Geddes launched Mumford on a 'four-year pilgrimage', again comparable to Weber's (WB: 146). The fact that Mumford thought of these four years as a unity is of some importance, as from an external perspective the period included such a significant break as his training in the Navy in the spring of 1918. During these years, Mumford 'withdrew' into himself and 'ruminated' on the reading experience.[4] As a result, he was gradually developing his own perspective, tearing himself away from the taken for granted. An idea of Geddes which made a particularly strong impact on Mumford was that civilization is produced not by the individual but by the city (MB: 72). This created sparks between the reading experience and his childhood experiences. The price of this type of formation, however, also had to be paid in both private and public life. In the former, it resulted in a period of loneliness, and prolonged emotional and sexual deprivation. In the latter, the period of maturation was marked by a steady stream of refusals. Mumford wandered off the safe grounds, but was not yet able to break through on his own terms, and was thus not able to get things published. The personal and public difficulties can be subsumed into a lack of recognition and this leaves scars.

Finally, this formative period also included two major visions. The first happened in a moment liminal both in its temporal and spatial dimensions, in 'a twilight hour in early Spring', in 'the middle of the Brooklyn Bridge'. It was a 'sudden revelation of power and beauty', 'raising all my energies by its own vivid promise to a higher pitch' (SL: 129–30). The other experience was even more overpowering, as '[p]erhaps this is what religious people have meant when they speak of communing with God'. It also happened in an unmistakenly liminal 'figuration' during his military training in spring 1918 on an island, walking home just after sunset after a day spent in a library, during weekend leave. The experience of 'love, joy and sorrow', an 'exaltation of pure being' said 'that the world had meaning'; it gave 'an indescribable but exalted sense of my whole future life spreading out before me'. It also provided tighter focus in one sense: 'In that breathless moment past and future, my past and the world's past, my future and the world's future came together. Yes: a glimpse of eternity' (SL: 198–9). The ability of establishing broad and stunning connections between the remote past and the present, pointing towards the imminent future, remained a gift of Mumford for his entire life.

This period of 'pilgrimage' ended in 1920–1 when in both his private life and his written work, Mumford at the end found some stability. He finally managed to get a few of his writings published. In 1920 he became associate editor at *The Dial* (MB: 107) for a short time.[5] He was also offered the post of editor at the *Sociological Review* (MB: 116), which he did not take up.[6] In 1921, he got married to Sophia Wittenberg whom he had met at *The Dial*. However, it should be emphasized that though the 'four-year pil- grimage' had ended, the formative years lasted until 1925 (MB: 231). This was because the closing of this period was largely due to the generational experience of the end of the First World War.

Just as for most Americans, the war in Europe at first meant little to Mumford. It was brought closer by the American involvement from 1917 and he only avoided participation in combat in an almost miraculous way, as he was diagnosed with a serious illness on the morning he was due to be sent to the front (MB: 104–5). Still, the most important impact of the war, just as for most other reflexive historical sociologists, happened in the lim- inal immediate post-war period. This meant that his first works, published in the 1920s, were based not just on the development and maturation of his own internal problematics but also reflected much of the generational post-war experience.

This is visible in both what Mumford did and did not do, in his hesita- tions and the manner in which he defined the scope of his work. These concerned the central theme of his work, its broad relevance, and the status of both this work and himself as its author. In his choice of theme he was guided by his vision of the unity of past and future, and he devoted his first work to an analysis of the manner in which this unity was broken up in the different utopian visions so influential in the European tradition. However, the key underlying idea of this first book was strictly generational because, as critics immediately realized, 'it was a book about the shattering impact of the First World War on the mind and moral outlook of an entire generation, the generation of its author' (MB: 163). As for role, reading Geddes pushed him away from any specialized science. Still, he kept being preoccupied with the question and he flirted among others with the label 'sociologist' but he did not find an intellectual resting point until as late as 1924 (MB: 230). As to the public relevance of the work, he developed a strong interest in regionalism under the impact of Geddes and came to the realization that his 'vocation' was less to become a planner than to enlarge the vision of planners (MB: 88). His first book was also about the impact of ideas on minds, although he was not yet able to be precise about the exact modalities.

A decisive breakthrough in all three areas happened in 1925. Mumford was always precise and clear about the relevance of this year in his intellectual formation (MB: 231). The breakthrough was due to another liminal figuration. In spring 1924 the Mumfords decided to have children, and on 5 July 1925 their only son Geddes was born. The decision also led to an immediate improvement in marital sexual life (MB: 235). In early 1925, Mumford was invited by Alfred Zimmern to give a series of lectures in Geneva, his first experience in teaching. He also visited Geddes in Edinburgh, his first visit to one of his favourite cities and the last time they ever met (MB: 224). In spring 1925, Mumford also wrote a play which he considered as his most important artistic achievement so far. Though it remained unpublished, the writing 'opened him up, releasing creative energies' (MB: 235). Also in 1925 the Mumfords moved house.

This series of experiences were chanelled into the writing of *The Golden Day* and helped him to gain focus in all the three dimensions discussed above. On the central theme of his work, he had a genuinely original vision, perceiving a direct connection between the collapse of the Middle Ages in Europe and the specificity of American culture. On status, he was now able to pin down himself with sufficient conviction as a generalist.[7] Finally, on the public relevance of his work, in a letter written to Geddes a few months earlier, he wrote of seeing his role in the imminent regional transformation (MB: 211).

The sharpening of focus was immediately visible in output. In fact, this sudden gain so much overshadowed his second book that had come out in 1924 that, even in the first draft of his autobiography, Mumford simply forgot about his work on the criticism of architecture. In 1926, he published his most significant work of the decade, *The Golden Day*, one of the first appreciative books written about American culture in a period when it was much more fashionable to claim that such a thing did not exist. The book reconstructed the 'golden generation' of American culture and focused on Emerson, Thoreau, Whitman, Hawthorne and Melville, a generation brought together by the frontier experience of the West and closed by another war experience, the Civil War. In 1929, he published a follow-up book on Melville. In 1931 he closed this series of works by *The Brown Decades*, where he went beyond the Civil War and analysed American culture, especially architecture, in the last decades of the nineteenth century.

Given that in *The Golden Day*, Melville was the last of the five main authors discussed, belonging to the 'night' of 'the golden day' (GD 71–7), it was not evident that Mumford would choose to write a monograph on him rather than Emerson or Whitman whom he liked just as much, if not more. On the publication of the book he experienced enormous exhaustion (MB: 281), just as Melville did upon completing *Moby Dick* though by no means due to simple imitation.

This collapse made 1929 the most desolate year of the pre-1944 period of Mumford's life. The collapse was owing partly to problems experienced exactly in those areas of his life where the year 1925 had brought a change of fortune, and partly to the fact that the issues not yet solved in that year rose forcefully to the surface. In 1929 Sophia had a miscarriage, while their son Geddes became seriously ill, was misdiagnosed and was eventually operated on just a few hours before the illness would have reached a terminal stage (MB: 282). Mumford also went again to Geneva but this trip turned out to be a disaster and in the end he did not even go to Edinburgh as planned to meet Patrick Geddes. Although 1925 represented a significant improvement both in Mumford's private and public activities, it failed to be completely satisfactory. In his work, though guided by a significant vision connecting the Middle Ages and the present, he was still too much under the impact of the post-war generational experience focused on America. On the personal side, his sexual life was still only partially satisfying and his marriage was going through another difficult period (MB: 306). Thus, the deprivations of the 'years of pilgrimage' were still not fully overcome. Upon his return from Europe, Mumford started a major period of self-reflection, guided by his reading of Vossler's book on Dante, and realized that the sources of his depression were his sexual and emotional problems (MB: 285).[8]

The self-reflections of Mumford in 1929 targeted his life, not his work. This was probably inevitable, as meaningful reflexive exercises on one's own work require a distance and a body of work covering fifteen to twenty years. The main effect was that in the 1930s, Mumford had two passionate, emotional and erotic love affairs, first with Catherine Bauer and then with Alice Decker. Still, indirectly, these personal self-reflections also had a major impact on his work, as the start and end dates of both affairs corresponded with the times when Mumford started and ended his two main books of the 1930s, *Technics and Civilization* and *The Culture of Cities*, which formed the first two volumes of the *The Renewal of Life* series.[9]

Apart from the centrality of these two erotic adventures which repeated and deepened the contribution to his creative upsurge in 1925, he also enjoyed other favourable conditions for his work. Thus, in spring 1932, yielding to the pressures of Catherine (MB: 303), he went on a long study trip to Europe, where he spent time in Germany with Catherine and in England with Sophia. The long sea journey back, an archetypal liminal situation, became 'a decisive moment in [his] life', when he saw the whole *Renewal of Life* series 'take form before' him (MB: 321). On 28 April 1935 his daughter Alison was born, and Sophia's pregnancy corresponded with the start of his affair with Alice, something he simply was not able to resist in spite of recognizing its deeply problematic character (MB: 343). This was also the moment of conception for his book on cities.

In these books, Mumford extended his investigation to the entire Western civilization. Going beyond the problematics defined by the post-First World War generation in America, he returned to the centre of his problematics and interest with books on the development of the city and on technology. Even further beyond the heart of his formation and personal experience, Mumford turned to the inner experience of man and the history of the self itself in these books (SL: 443).

These books certainly did not amount to a withdrawal into himself. On the one hand, a return to personal experience for reflexive historical socioligists never represents a purely private interest. On the other, in these years Mumford also increasingly took on a public role both by advising planners and directly by preparing reports on city planning. However, world events would soon bring about another major reorientation in his work as a writer and as a public intellectual.

On his major study trip of 1932, Mumford encountered the unsettling phenomenon of Nazism and was not fully reassured by his German friends, including Karl Vossler, according to whom Hitler was not to be taken seriously (MB: 390; see also RL: 38). On two occasions in 1935, he publicly voiced his concerns. Finally, in early 1938, he expressed his opinion in writing that the menace of Nazism could only be confronted by military means. The article created a huge uproar among his liberal, pacifist and leftist friends. From that moment, questions of war, violence and power entered the centre stage of his public life, as both a writer and an intellectual.

The exact conditions of this reorientation are again of utmost importance. The concern with power and violence, in the reality of the imminent outbreak of the war, was risky, controversial and emotionally involving in itself. It became all the more so because of the bitter controversies with his closest friends and allies to which this led. These circumstances to a large extent make intelligible the difficulties Mumford experienced in finding the proper measure and balance in his new work.

In itself, the changes provoked in his work by the external situation should have meant further amplification and depth. By 1939–40, he had extended his interests in time and gone back to Seneca and especially the early Christian writers, realizing that he needed to broaden his understanding to the historical core of the self and that it had to centre on the early Christian period (MB: 415).[10] This broadening of interest coincided with a liminal period of mourning connected with the death of his second mother on 24 June 1940. A second major reorganization of his work happened around 1944 as he extended his work in time both towards the future in the direction of post-war reconstruction, and the past, farther back in time than ever before (MB: 413). This again coincided with a major event of mourning as his son Geddes went missing in combat on 13 September 1944.

The changes left a mark on the two other books of the *Renewal of Life* series. *The Condition of Man*, published in 1944, summed up his ideas and contained a first presentation of the extension of his work towards Christianity. The fourth volume of the series, *The Conduct of Life*, which was published in 1951 and finished just a month after his mother died, gave a first version of his reading of the Axial Age, a term he developed independently of Jaspers who discovered it in the immediate post-war years. However, the books were disappointing, ponderous and repetitive and failed even to approach the critical and public success of the two major books of the 1930s. This was troubling and deeply frustrating to the author who was attempting to express even more important things (MB: 414, 446, 451).

With the theoretical and methodological framework elaborated in the first section of this chapter, it is possible to venture an explanation for these difficulties. The work of a reflexive historical sociologist always advances on the thin line and delicate tension balance between autobiographically-based work and global relevance. In the dramatic, highly-charged and deeply controversial war years and with a desperate search for his voice to be heard, Mumford was not able to maintain the proper balance, the personal touch of his work was lost and it was transformed occasionally into ponderous mannerism. In order to restore balance, he needed to step back and reflect on his own past work. By the early 1950s, with three decades of work behind him, it was possible for him to do so. The disappointing reception of the final volume of the *Renewal of Life* series, *The Conduct of Life*, published in 1951, also forced him in this direction. He entered the last main period of his productive life, where reflections on his past work became the major source propelling it forward.

The first such moment was another crucial New Year resolution at the beginning of January 1953, in which he revised his strategy (MB: 454). Its central element was a combination of his new interests in the more remote past with the core, autobiographically-based interest in the city and he revised his book on cities while giving a course at the University of Pennsylvania on this topic. With it, the circle closed and his dispersed interests again focused around a coherent whole.

Though the central moving force of the work became self-reflexivity, the years 1953–5 also brought with them new sparks from much the same sources as the renewals of 1925 and the early 1930s. Thus, the 1953 and 1955 courses in Pennsylvania, one on city design and the other on ancient religion, can be compared to the role played by the Geneva courses, and the first half of 1954 was marked by an 'Indian Summer' of his marital life (MB: 454–5). In the summer of 1954 he wrote his book *Transformations of Man* in three weeks (MB: 455). Once through his first enthusiasm, he soon realized the limits of this work. It was a 'book experience' (DEIV: 47), playing a crucial role of catalyst in summing up his work up to that point and giving further momentum. The most significant impulse in this period, however, was provided by a series of reflections on his own past work and life or by philosophical exercises.

In these years, Mumford lauched two new type of activity. One was the second edition of his earlier works. He started it in 1953, with the second edition of *The Golden Day* and continued in 1955 with new editions of the *Brown Decades* and *Sticks and Stones*. In this same year, he also published a book of essays, *The Human Prospect*, and a major programmatic article, 'Restored Circulation, Renewed Life' (MR: 201–6), managing better to separate his programmatic and public involvement from the core of his written research work. In 1957, a third edition of *The Golden Day* came out with a new Preface. The other major new interest was the writing of the first draft of his autobiography in 1955–6.

All his work received a spark from his 1957 trip to Europe, which was both a repetition of and a return to the 1932 trip to Europe, which was the major catalyst for his first key book, *Technics and Civilization*. It was both an occasion of recognition, comparable to the farewell tour of a great actor (MB: 462–3) and also, precisely owing to this, a source of renewal. It was after his return that Mumford started to write his 'new' book on cities, helped by further lecture experiences, especially the December 1958 talks given in front of the Oriental Institute's symposium at the University of Chicago; the self-review of *Technics and Civilization* (Mumford 1959); and a July 1960 trip to Europe, which was ended with another major self-review on board (MB: 452).[11]

Though the 1961 book on cities contained full chapters taken over from the earlier work, it was indeed fundamentally new, as it was based on a novel vision: the insight that the birth of the city and of the human 'mega-machine' coincided and that its source was the search for ever-increasing number of victims for sacrifice (MB: 466–7). Due to the absence of possible documentation, it is simply not possible to verify or falsify fully such a thesis, but given the recent theoretical and anthropological interest in the significance of sacrifice for human history (Girard 1977, 1987, Kearney 1995, Milbank 1995), the potential fruitfulness of such an insight for future research is evident.

The City in History is widely regarded as the best book Mumford has ever written. It was a huge critical and commercial success. Mumford reached the height of his popularity and influence and, upon his return from another trip to Europe, thought that the time has come to reap the harvest of his past work (MB: 500). As he was now sixty-six, the source of inspiration came almost exclusively from reflexive exercises although becoming a grandparent in October 1962 also came just at the right moment (MB: 508). In July 1961, he started work on his autobiography but writing differently this time, less from memory and returning rather to the written sources (MB: 505). In 1962–3, he again took up the task of republishing his earlier works, adding new Prefaces.[12] In 1962, he also published a series of major, conclusive, programmatic articles which were selected for reproduction in the *Mumford Reader* carefully edited by Donald Miller in close contact with Mumford (MR vii).[13] Finally, ending the period of preparation and stocktaking, in the summer of 1963 he started work on his new project with full momentum (MB: 509).

Just as *The City in History* was a new edition of one of his two most important earlier works, *The Culture of Cities*, the new book was born out of the idea of updating *Technics and Civilization* whose second edition has just come out. As a further similarity, one of the main novelties of the book was a further retreat in history attempting to capture the origins of the myth of the machine. The new work put rituals and symbols as opposed to tool-making at the centre of the story and made much use of the two disciplines that became particularly popular at the period, anthropology and linguistics (MB: 510–11), thus advancing Foucault's recognition (OT: 378–86). However, far from being a product of generational experience, the book was based on a singular vision like all his other major works: the recognition of the similarity in pattern between the ancient and the modern megamachines, or the 'pyramid age' and modern-day Absolutism and the Industrial Revolution. It was a vision that, needless to say, provoked much controversy.

This vision was close to, and was based upon, the vision underlying *The City in History*. However, as external conditions changed with respect to the writing of the book, some of the balance was lost. There were three sets of events which on the one hand caused a retreat into himself and on the other pushed him to another arguably excessive public stand. The first was the negative reactions to his new draft autobiography, which was especially painful because of the new type of effort that had gone into them (MB: 508). Then came the 'dance of death' (Macey 1993: 415), the loss of a series of people who were very close to him. It started with the death of his father-in-law William Wittenberg in September 1964, and continued with that of Catherine Bauer in November and of his old friend Alexander Meicklejohn in January 1965 (MB: 511–12)

It was these death experiences that provided the background figuration in which the intensification of the threat of nuclear war reached Mumford, culminating in the escalation of the American war efforts in Vietnam in February 1965 (MB: 512). Since the late 1930s, Mumford had never lost his deep interest and involvement in politics, especially intensified by the threat of nuclear war. However, as a result of his anamnetic exercises, in the last part of the 1950s he managed to find a proper distinction between, and balance of, scholarship and public activities. In the mid-1960s, events again upset this balance.

Up till February 1965, he was able to work even with a furious energy despite these personal losses, but in February 1965 'he did stop writing' his book (MB: 512). Instead he wrote closed and open letters of protest to the

President and other politicians, but these failed to have any impact. He changed strategy and, when offered an award by the American Academy of Arts and Sciences, he decided to devote his speech to a condemnation of the war efforts. This act not only cost him a fever of 101 degrees, the loss of life-long friends and the condemnation of such another major public intellectual of the century as George Kennan (MB: 515), but also caused another partial derailment of his work.

As a result, the two books of the new *Myth of the Machine* series became too close to him and he became obsessed with their successful reception (MB: 530). But the work was again unbalanced in style, thus undermining the very success he craved for. Even worse, the excess of rhetoric prevented the central vision of the book from reaching its proper audience and being taken seriously. In May–June 1969, after the first volume failed to have the desired impact, he engaged in another reflexive exercise, a month-long self-review (MB: 533). This helped him to complete the second volume but it did not substantially alter its style. The book gained rather than lost in prophetic tone. It is no surprise that the reception of this work was even more lukewarm than the previous one.

Mumford drew the consequences in two ways. On the one hand, he stopped further work and, apart from publishing his autobiography and personal miscellania, he wrote no further books. Though he was already seventy-five and had some health difficulties, this is an insufficient explanation, as other reflexive historical sociologists who lived long like Elias or Voegelin kept working on their life-project practically until they died. The other consequence is a 12 December 1972 public address, delivered on the occasion of his receiving the National Book Award, the importance of which was revealed both by the care with which he prepared for it, and by the sudden way in which he came up with the eventual theme (MB: xiii–v). He identified himself as a modern day Jonah or a special kind of prophet, as somebody who fulfils his role of providing warning but who does not become enamoured with his own vision of doom (MR 365–9).

Lewis Mumford died on 26 January 1990 aged ninety-four.

Conclusion to Part I
Comparisons and contrasts

After reviewing individually the intellectual trajectories of Mumford, Elias, Borkenau and Voegelin in this book and also Weber and Foucault in my earlier book, the question is to bring out the commonalties so as to establish the type of thinking and research work that is characteristic of them.

In a sense, the Introduction and even the title of this book already prefigure the answer. The argument is that they are all reflexive historical sociologists. However, in itself, this expression is only a conceptual device. If one is to go beyond labelling, it must be filled with content.

The question of pinning down the identity of Weber, Foucault, Voegelin and the others is not new. It has created considerable perplexities for a long time. The puzzle was not only intellectual but also moral. Intellectual difficulties include the variety of academic formation and disciplinary affiliations of the work accomplished. Weber was trained in law, obtained a chair in political economy and is considered as a founding father of sociology by some, but as a historian and a political scientist, even a 'failed politician', by others. Mumford was a historian of science, architecture and technology but also a writer and a journalist. Voegelin gained a degree in political science, was considered for some time a sociologist and then a historian of political thought, and recently it has even been debated whether he was a social scientist or a mystic. The list can be continued.

However, beyond intellectual elusiveness that can stir passions in itself, there also lurk overtones of denunciation. Thus, in his own recognition, Voegelin states that

> 'I have been called every conceivable name by partisans of this or that ideology. I have in my files documents labelling me a Communist, a Fascist, a National Socialist, an old Liberal, a new Liberal, a Jew, a Catholic, a Protestant, a Platonist, a neo-Augustinian, a Thomist, and of course a Hegelian'
>
> (Voegelin, *Autobiographical Reflections* (AR): 46)

In a late interview, Foucault produced a strikingly comparable list:

I think I have in fact been situated in most of the squares on the political checkerboard, one after another and sometimes simultaneously: as anarchist, leftist, ostentatious or disguised Marxist, nihilist, explicit or secret anti-Marxist, technocrat in the service of Gaullism, new liberal, etc.

(*Foucault Reader* (FR): 383)

One could also refer to the animosity often evoked by Weber, Elias, Mumford and Borkenau.

Giving a convincing answer to the question of who these thinkers were is therefore not a trivial task. It requires a series of attempts, from different directions. Let us start from matters of situation and context.

In terms of space and time coordinates, the majority of reflexive historical sociologists belong to a group with well-circumscribed characteristics. First, there is a strong predominance of Germans. This is most likely because Germany is in the middle of Europe: that is, what is relevant is not its central position so much as its occupying a liminal position between both north and south, and east and west. This characterization receives support from two further sources. Most protagonists are from peripheral, border or liminal areas of Germany like Austria (Borkenau, Voegelin), Silesia (Elias) or outright the American East-coast immigrant community (Mumford). Furthermore, many are of German-Jewish origin. Borkenau and Mumford were both German on one side of their family and Jewish on the other, while Elias, though Jewish, considered himself a German by culture.

Even the outliers show some affinity. Thus, Foucault was French but his entire formation was dominated by German thought. Weber and Foucault also recognized publicly, in crucial moments of their life-work, a constitutive similarity between German and Jewish history which had much importance for the fate of modernity. In his 1919 Munich introductory lecture, the first academic talk he gave after the First World War in Germany, Weber not only alluded to the identification he recognized between his task and that of the ancient Jewish prophets (WB: 593–4) but also drew parallels between the two nations stating that '[l]ike the Jews we [i.e. the Germans] have been turned into a pariah people' (WB: 662). In his testament-like 1984 essay on Kant and Enlightenment, Foucault has also drawn a parallel between German Enlightenment and Jewish *Haskala*, arguing that the two not only 'belong to the same history' but also share 'a common destiny' (FR: 33).[1]

In terms of time coordinates, as has been argued in the Introduction (p. xxi), reflexive historical sociologists belong to two well-definable generations and were born in the periods of either 1895–1900 or 1920–7. Finally, a third major background coordinate concerns the sources of inspiration and those thinkers who exerted a major impact on their intellectual development. The similarities are close, even striking. Most importantly, their thought was strongly stamped by a well-defined group of philosophers. These include first and foremost Nietzsche plus Schopenhauer, Kierkegaard, Jaspers and Heidegger. These philosophers are usually labelled as existentialists. However, there are two main problems with this term.

First, it is mostly associated with Sartrean connotations which were rejected explicitly by reflexive historical sociologists. Second, the crucial issue had less to do with 'existential' matters, let alone the Sartrean 'facticity of existence' and the 'condemnation to be free', than with an interest in a philosophical life, the inseparability of matters of life and work, of personal experiences and the reflexive work of thought. It is in this sense that a close parallel can be drawn between the German philosophers listed above and those American thinkers who developed a similar type of approach, linking life and work together in a philosophical life in the similarly liminal or 'frontier' (F. Turner 1996 [1920]) situation of mid-nineteenth- century America. I am referring to people like Emerson, Whitman and Thoreau who were thinkers and formative influences for Mumford and whose strong affinity with the German thinkers listed above has been recognized by Voegelin (1995 [1928]), Hadot (1995b: 407) and even Nietzsche (Kaufmann, in Nietzsche 1974: 7–13).

A second group of thinkers, not unrelated to the first, are the so-called 'masters of suspicion', especially the two most influential 'subversives' of the century, Marx and Freud. Reflexive historical sociologists show two key common characteristics with respect to the work of these epochal figures. First, they took them seriously and accepted the challenge their work represented. This usually happened in particularly sensitive or 'liminal' moments of their own life. Second, however, except perhaps for rather short periods in their youth, hardly any of them became a convinced and dogmatic Marxist or Freudian. They all took up the questions, though obviously in varying degrees, but did not swallow the answers. In this way, they avoided the lasting effects of the kind of brainwashing that Marxism or psychoanalysis (especially and worst of all, Freudo-Marxism) represented for so many thinkers and so many young people in the twentieth century.

Obviously, a number of other thinkers could be mentioned who exerted a considerable effect on this or that reflexive historical sociologist. However, only two further names will be singled out. One goes without saying: this is Max Weber. Weber was a main, and in several cases the single most important, source and resource for most thinkers in the field. The other name is perhaps more surprising: this is Plato. Plato has been explicitly recognized by both Mumford and Voegelin as their central intellectual encounter. The reading of Plato was also crucial in Foucault's last years of lectures at the Collège de France, and it left clear marks on the interests of Borkenau and Elias.

Given that the main sources of inspiration for reflexive historical sociologists were the great dissident, shadowy, underground thinkers of the past two centuries, it comes as no surprise that they came to define themselves negatively in opposition to the mainstream intellectual and academic currents of their age. Encounters with Nietzsche, Kierkegaard or Freud came to be so significant for them because in this way they started to develop doubts whether the official school ideologies provide adequate answers to the questions they were asking, or even proper methodological tools to pursue the quest. They were often taught by the best 'schoolmen'. Elias and Voegelin were both trained by leading representatives of the neo-Kantian school, Richard Hönigswald and Hans Kelsen, while Foucault was introduced to phenomenology by Maurice Merleau-Ponty.

The modality of their reactions varied, not independently of the kind of impulse they received at school. Their dissatisfaction with contemporary academic philosophers led them to a general disillusionment with philosophy. Elias broke decisively with philosophy for his entire life, Foucault resented being called a philosopher until his last years, and Weber similarly had a strong dislike of philosophy. At one point, all thinkers studied in this book reacted by turning towards sociology, though their allegiance, especially given the similar disillusionment with academic sociology, in most cases turned out to be temporary.

The dissent turned most of them not only against philosophy but against institutionalized academic life in general. This reaction was strongest in Mumford who never finished formal education. It was also markedly present in the careers of Borkenau and Foucault, while it was sublimated into a lasting illness in the case of Weber. Voegelin also afforded himself extremely critical remarks against academia, stating that '[s]cience is flourishing today – except in the universities'; and that:

> I knew ten years ago that our universities, not only in America but in Europe, were completely rotten: brothels of opinion, no science, nothing. But I could not have predicted that five years later, in 1965, we would already have an open outbreak which recognizes that the universities are dead

(Voegelin 1980: 107, 110).[2]

However, this did not push them to a complete breach with the institutional environment. They tried to walk on the edge between the 'inside' and the 'outside', and refused to join the 'alternative sects'.[3]

But most reflexive historical sociologists went even further in drawing the consequences of their withdrawal from contemporary academic philosophy. They posed serious questions about much of the thought of the past 200 years, the 'anthropological sleep' (OT: 340–3; see also Clavel 1975: 118–26). It is important to note that their criticism was not directed against this or that modern current of thought or ideology, but what they perceived as common in all of them. Thus, they were critical of the Enlightenment and liberalism as well as of Marxism, socialism and the entire revolutionary tradition.

In this withdrawal from the dominant currents of thought of their and our age, purely intellectual and epistemological issues were in almost all cases closely related to political questions. Their thought was rooted in their life experiences (CP: xvi, OHIII: 93, DEIV: 181–2) and political events, especially the violence of the twentieth century and the predominance of totalitarian mass movements, played a large part in these experiences. However, their interest in politics and ideologies, like their withdrawal from contemporary philosophy, had unique characteristics. They refused to acknowledge a strict separation of totalitarian and non-totalitarian movements and ideologies. This was not because they would have endorsed the former, nor because they lacked a clear sense of judgement, rather because they recognized the impossibility of separating the two in any clear-cut manner (DEIV: 224, OHIII: 147, 261). They were interested in what had rendered these political ideologies possible, and here they recognized the need for an in-depth reconstruction of the movements of thought that led to the emergence of modernity. However, as opposed to many other widely-divergent attempts to identify the sources and origins of totalitarianism, they were not interested in attributing guilt. They were especially not interested in making accusations across the intellectual and political landscape and arguing that individuals like Plato, Rousseau, Hobbes, Nietzsche, Freud and Marx, or movements of thought like the Enlightenment, liberalism or positivism were 'responsible' or 'guilty' for fascism, Nazism or communism. Their interest was in contributing to understanding, especially self-understanding, and not in the setting-up of an imaginary tribunal.

However, reflexive historical sociologists eventually recognized that the reckoning about the characteristics and effects of modern currents of thought must be carried to its logical conclusion, and that this implies a reassessment of the past that goes beyond the thought of the last two centuries. In doing so, they only followed the cues of the main 'shadowy' figures of modern Western thought who had been their main reading experiences, Schopenhauer, Kierkegaard and especially Nietzsche. Their criticism was thus extended to Descartes, Bacon, Locke, Kant and Hegel, the founding figures of modern philosophy. Targeting not just this or that political ideology or epistemological school but British empiricism, French rationalism and German idealism at the same time, reflexive historical sociologists attempted to identify the problems of modern Western thought at its very roots.

The formulation of a diagnosis will be a concern for Part II. However, even at this point, it is possible to identify two main charges. The first is directed against an assumption common to Descartes, Kant and Husserl that there is a fixed self, a transcendental subject or ego that is the foundation of knowledge, and the assumed separation between this subject and the objects of knowledge to which this subject is intentionally oriented in acts of cognition. These assumptions were characterized as egology (FPP), the closed self (Voegelin 1995 [1928]), the *homo clausus* (WIS) and the 'doubles' of man (OT). The second, and related, set of assumptions connecting rationalism and transcendental idealism were the postulation of certain abstract, timeless, universal categories of thought as synthetic *a prioris* and the related positing of similarly abstract universal values as the height of human endeavours.

Reflexive historical sociologists dissented from this postulate both in an epistemological and axiological sense. Instead of abstraction and speculation, their main interest was in reality and being. This implied, first of all, a historization of those categories that were assumed as universal and given, the transcendental subject and the entire object–subject division and the categories of transcendental thought. But, beyond this critical or negative task, reflexive historical sociologists also attempted to work out the outlines of a framework to replace the dominant paradigm. This implied, first of all, a special emphasis placed on experience and the experiential basis of thought. As opposed to the reduction of experience to sense perception, the assumption common to British empiricism, French rationalism, the Kantian claim about the inchoate character of experience and thus the need for synthetic *a priori* categories in order to impose an order on them, reflexive historical sociologists argued that though experiences are events that transform the mode of being of subjects, they still possess an inherent orderliness which must be recognized and formulated through reflexion and symbolization.

Even further, directly or indirectly, they came to realize that beyond singular experiences, a search for understanding can be securely founded not on an isolated, self-enclosed monad called the subject of knowledge but on a philosophical life. It is here that a common ground can be found, outside the concerns of British empiricism, French rationalism and German idealism, between German 'existentialists', American 'pioneers' and the thought of antiquity and even the East.[4]

The field is coherent in both a positive and in a negative sense. Just as the thinkers who exerted a formative impact on its protagonists belong to a well-definable group, the approaches from which they distanced themselves are also shared. As an illustration, three thinkers will be mentioned who are diametrically opposed to reflexive historical sociology in the intellectual landscape. They are Georg Lukacs, Karl Popper and Jean-Paul Sartre.

Lukacs had the dubious honour of not only combining the heaviest jargon of Heidelberg philosophy with the ideas of Lenin and Stalin that he smuggled out of Russia, but of selling this indigestible combination as a new and improved version of Western Marxism. The trick worked quite well for decades, though not for Voegelin and Foucault who only had scorn for Lukacs, while Borkenau, in some of the most exciting pages of his history of the Communist International (Borkenau 1962 [1938]: 172–5), paints a convincing picture of the man and his ideas. Referring to an article by the Hungarian-born former Communist, Ilona Duczynska, he wrote that around 1920 Lukacs justified lying and cheating to Party members by the leadership, as 'Communist ethics make it the highest duty to accept the necessity of acting wickedly'. This was called the 'secret doctrine' of Communism and the conduct of life embodied in the doctrine was considered as the quintessence of a true communist.[5] It is nor surprising that the term 'philosophical life' is irrelevant when considering the career of Lukacs.

Though in some respects Popper could be considered as the opposite of Lukacs, they nevertheless form a fitting couple. Popper managed to fuse neo-Kantianism and neo-positivism into a seemingly natural and watertight system which offered to the incautious the advantages of both empiricism and theoretical coherence. At the same time he convinced many that those dissenting from his very specific and even quite peculiar epistemological views which focused, in a truly gnostic revaluation of values, not on truth and understanding but on falsification, that they were not just wrong in their search for knowledge, but were also committing deep moral and political errors, and were bound to become direct or indirect supporters of this or other version of totalitarianism.

The opinions of reflexive historical sociologists of Popper were also unequivocal. Voegelin in his correspondence with Strauss treated Popper as a scandal and considered his *Open Society* as an abusive travesty of Bergson.[6] Elias also had a long-standing polemics with Popper, daring to criticize the 'great man' at a faculty seminar in the early 1950s (Mennell 1992: 9, 190–1). In Elias circles, this is considered a major reason for the difficulties he later encountered in finding first a job and then broader recognition. Finally, Foucault also singled out Popper's interpretation of Plato as his negative reference point.[7]

The fundamental commonalties between Lukacs and Popper, in spite of all the divergences, become best visible through one of their best known, and certainly most infamous, books, *The Dethronement of Reason* and *The Open Society and Its Enemies*. These two books are truly appalling documents, both in their content and especially through their reception, and illustrate the depths to which thought has sunk in the middle of this century. The texts were almost contemporaneous. Popper worked on his between 1938 and 1943 and it was published in 1945. Though Lukacs's book appeared in 1954 in Hungarian, its main ideas were formulated by the end of the Second World War (Kadarkay 1991: 421–2). Both books are full of serious lapses of scholarship which, in a politically different situation, should have prohibited their very publication, not to mention their being taken seriously. Popper is not satisfied with accusing Hegel and Marx of being intellectual forerunners of the totalitarian state, but charges Plato outright with totalitarianism, in an account that not only lacks any serious attempt at understanding the thought of Plato but is full of mistranslations of crucial concepts and passages (FPP: 67–9). Lukacs, for his part, achieves a

perfect score on misjudgement, singling out as the 'irrationalist' forerunners of fascism almost all the innovative and spiritually sensitive thinkers of
the past century and a half. The list is truly impressive as it includes
Schelling, Schopenhauer, Kierkegaard, Nietzsche, Dilthey, Simmel,
Heidegger, Jaspers, Weber, Mannheim and Wittgenstein. Taken together,
the two lists contain the major formative experiences of reflexive historical
sociologists, except for the American thinkers whom Lukacs and Popper,
with characteristic 'Central European provincialism' (Cooper 1986: 21,
AR: 32), simply ignored.

It should be recalled at this point that these works by Popper and
Lukacs were not simply products of the Cold War. They had been either
published, or basically finished, by the time it broke out. They document
rather the mentality that produced the Cold War and had effects lasting
well beyond the 1950s. Furthermore, both Lukacs and Popper were
Central European intellectuals, sharing the background and to some
extent even the generational formation of reflexive historical sociologists.
It is for these reasons that the choice is not between Marxism and positivism, or between the establishment represented by Lord Popper and the
alternative of Comrade Lukacs. It is a choice between the philosophical life
and the search for understanding, or the *zetesis* and *parrhesia* of reflexive
historical sociologists, on the one hand, and the epistemological and political positions represented by Popper and Lukacs on the other.

The third name, Sartre, complements the list from another angle. If
Popper combined neo-Kantianism and neo-positivism while Lukacs mixed
the heavy German philosophical jargon with Marxism-Leninism and even
Stalinism, then Sartre interposed a similarly Bolshevik interpretation of
Marx with his own version of phenomenology and existentialism. Thus,
while Popper and Lukacs sided with one or other Cold War orthodoxy
while consistently rejecting and even denouncing all forms of innovative
thought, Sartre rather used the ideas in his own way, emptying the works
of content through trivialization and banalization. Finally, he also shared a
lack of interest in a philosophical life with Popper and Lukacs.[8]

Before moving to a more positive characterization, it is necessary to step
back and resume the argument. The difficulties encountered in past
attempts at classifying the works of reflexive historical sociologists were due
to the fact that they simply did not fit the map. They were beyond the
established dichotomies. They escaped the main dividing line between
'mainstream' and 'critical' approaches to intellectual life in this century.
They did not fit the official, secular academic 'church', but neither did
they accept membership in the established alternative sects.

These works also manifested a series of other peculiarities, jointly
showing certain characteristics that were thought to be excluding each
other. Thus, in general, a thinker is either supposed to be a lonely character, withdrawn into his/her self, pursuing in silence and isolation the
work, far from the public limelight; or s/he takes up a public role, inter-

vening in all sort of intellectual, cultural and political debates. Most reflexive historical sociologists did both at the same time. They were profoundly, even tragically lonely persons, pursuing doggedly their own work, often without any recognition for decades; but, on the other hand, they were also taking a passionate and often leading stand in major public debates of their country. Furthermore, and from a slightly different angle, a work not pursuing well-trodden disciplinary roads is usually motivated either by personal experiences or by political concerns. Thinkers driven by a personal project often explicitly set this up against political concerns, while those whose work is politically motivated often try even to erase their personality from their work. Most reflexive historical sociologists, however, pursued the two concerns together.

On still another note, the wide scope characteristic of reflexive historical sociologists is not exhausted by the fact that each of them covered practically all the different branches of the social sciences. Their interest and knowledge even extended to the natural sciences. Thus, Mumford and Voegelin both attended a technical as opposed to a liberal arts high school. Elias studied medicine and philosophy and preserved an interest in biology throughout his life. Voegelin also studied biology during his Harvard visit, and had a strong background in mathematics. After graduating in philosophy, Foucault took degrees in experimental psychology and psychopathology. Furthermore, they also demonstrated an in-depth interest in a variety of arts including literature, poetry, drama, music and paintings. This was not just an entertainment but provided a vital source of inspiration and support for their work, especially because many of them were gifted with artistic skills.

While the previous paragraphs argued that reflexive historical sociologists escaped standard classificatory schemes, the breadth and scope of their interests suggests something more. It appears as if they do not simply escape the labels usually employed, but that their work had no coherence and centre. It is fragmented, decentred, going everywhere and touching anything.

In our 'postmodern' times, such a characterization is far from being a liability but is rather considered an asset. In fact, the labelling of Foucault as a postmodern and the association of Elias and even Weber with postmodern interests and affinities is based on exactly such a perspective. This view is not unfounded, as the work of reflexive historical sociologists does have a fragmentary character. However, the postmodern labelling is still misleading. The point is not simply to assert a fundamental coherence to their work from the outside, and to propose a reading and interpretation to support this claim. But reflexive historical sociologists themselves recognized that the internal coherence and external status of their work does present a genuine problem, and they were engaged in a search for coherence and status.

This search had three targets: the underlying problem of the work, its status and its relevance.[9] Furthermore, apart from recognizing the need to reflect upon their own work in order to find its balance and coherence, and the best way to bring it to fruition, they also realized that such a task cannot be accomplished solely on one's own singular efforts, but requires the participation and the interpretive understanding of others. Identity can only be obtained through recognition (Pizzorno 1986, 1987, 1991). For intellectual endeavours, recognition is first of all related to the reception of the work. Thus, it is not surprising to discover that after dealing with the underlying problem and status of their own work, the searches by reflexive historical sociologists were closely correlated with issues of reception.

It seems as if another paradoxical result has been reached here. So far, it has been argued that reflexive historical sociologists were thinkers who obstinately persisted in their own search for understanding, outside existing disciplinary and political divisions, undeterred by the intellectual fashions of their age, performing path-breaking but untimely work. But now it is claimed that they were particularly sensitive to reception. In fact, the puzzle is even more perplexing. On the one hand, reflexive historical sociologists did indeed have an extreme confidence in their own work. It was only because of this trust in their own capacities and sense of mission that they were able to withstand neglect, misunderstanding and often violent attacks. On the other hand, despite a self-confidence that occasionally even looked excessive and close to hubris, they had serious and long periods of crisis. One could even risk the claim that their thought progressed through such crises. Even further, the two moving forces of these works and the sources of the crises were identical: they were the reflexive meditations on the work completed so far and the controversies surrounding reception.

Still, there is a way out of the puzzle. As is often the case, it can be resolved by pointing out some assumptions, the ground and perspective from which the diverse set of facts look perplexing, contradictory. The assumption here is the standard initial figuration of normal academic disciplinary work. According to this, the problem that the work addresses, its potential relevance and in an even more self-evident fashion its disciplinary credentials, are to be stated clearly at the beginning of the work. The proper assessment and evaluation of the work is then provided by peers within the discipline. For reflexive historical sociologists, however, everything was the other way around. Instead of addressing the questions usually posed within a disciplinary framework, they were engaged in a long-term personal (re)search whose exact coordinates, underlying problem, status and actual relevance could not be specified at the outset. However, far from waiting in suspense for the peer evaluation of their work, they knew how good and innovative it was. The often negative response they encountered did not make them question their belief in their work and in themselves, as usually happens with works that are either rejected or just passed over in silence, but rather it pushed them towards further attempts at formulating their ideas more clearly, to render their work accessible. To put it bluntly, they knew instinctively that, even though they still had work to do on making their own ideas clearer, the major problem was not with them but with the audience who, through some kind of blockage in thinking, was unable to comprehend their 'visions'.

This character of their works gives some clues to answering the original question: who, after all, were reflexive historical sociologists?

Starting *in medias res*, they were individuals whom, as was recognized by others already in their life, bore upon themselves the stigma of exceptionality and had a touch of genius.[10] They were often granted unusual respect by their acquaintances, even if this was often accompanied by envy, ressentiment and even hostility from others, which broke to the surface with much force especially when they made themselves vulnerable. However, far from considering their genius as a source for rent which would have made a comfortable and pleasant life possible, all of them were also characterized by an extraordinary work discipline. It is this combination that explains both the breadth and depth of their concerns and the weight of the body of work they accomplished, often under highly unfavourable circumstances.

Geniuses armed with an extreme work discipline tend to be individuals withdrawn into themselves. They are unapproachable, alien, even threatening. Most reflexive historical sociologists were indeed so recognized. Thus, they were often characterized, both by themselves and others, as mystics or ascetic monks. Still, those who knew them well recognized other qualities in them. Far from being withdrawn, unapproachable and misanthropic, they had warm, friendly and even irresistible personalities. They had good friends for whom they were ready for anything and from whom they expected, and mostly received, unconditional loyalty.

But the full depth of their personality came through best in their teaching. Besides unusual intellectual capabilities, they also received another gift: their speech had a charismatic appeal. They were formidable teachers, captivating their audience not through tricks of rhetoric but the sheer power of their personality and the truthfulness of their speech. It is through teaching that they best performed one of their central tasks which was the call for wakefulness, the attempt to shake people out of their apathy and resignation, to force them to question things that they take for granted in their environment, but which are simply unacceptable.

If they were still not fully able to accomplish this task, it was to a large extent owing to the academic and political environment of the century which rendered charismatic teaching very difficult if not outright impossible. The strongly compartmentalized disciplinarization and institutionalization of universities which was a legacy of the Prussian state and neo-Kantianism, and the later escalation of mass higher education, transformed university professors into skilled administrators in a production process. Charismatic teachers were unwilling or unable to step into the assembly line and, as a result, most of them spent much their life deprived of the opportunity of educating the kind of disciples who could have properly carried forward their work.

That the potential residing in the charismatic appeal of their speech was left unused was all the more unfortunate, indeed tragic, as they were very well aware that their main task was not simply the acknowledged purpose of higher learning, the teaching of skills and the conveying of pieces of information, but the education of the young. They were especially concerned with the provision of leadership and the education of proper leaders.

The public appeal of their work went far beyond academic concerns in other respects as well. They were public figures not only through their speech but also through their writing. This happened first of all through a modern occupation which they could still hold in high esteem, journalism. Already Weber considered that, apart from science and politics, journalism might be the third available vocation in modern societies, and for a long time he planned a sociological study of the press. Mumford and Borkenau both earned their living for much of their lives as journalists and Foucault was also recognized, by himself as by others, as a philosophical or transcendental journalist. But it was a very special kind of interest which reflexive historical sociologists had in journalism. They were not using the media to popularize and propagate their ideas. Neither did they use the opportunity to sparkle their wisdom and knowledge and to pronounce judgement on anything that came their way. Rather, they all were engaged in a special kind of investigative journalism, writing always about situations and events they personally witnessed, giving the public not just new information but new insights about the issues, and even connecting the events to the broader processes within which they took place, of which only persons with the breadth of their vision were aware.

Apart from being charismatic teachers and incisive journalists, most reflexive historical sociologists were also writers. This is visible in their almost literary style (the exception being Weber) or in their concern with reception. In a few cases (like Mumford, see MB: 155, 452; and Foucault, see Eribon 1991: 58–60), it amounted to an explicit identification with the role.

Though they had a touch of the orator, the journalist and the writer, all these characterizations still miss a fundamental element of the work and life of each reflexive historical sociologist: a passionate and genuine concern with truth. This statement requires careful interpretation and specification. They had none of the rhetoric and moral crusading with which the word 'truth' is often used today. Taking heed of Nietzsche's advice and diagnosis, they were not crusaders of the 'will to truth'. They knew the difficulties associated with truth claims but they were far from asserting that therefore the search for truth had no sense.[11] Quite the contrary, truth and reason were central signposts for their work and life. Out of respect and not out of negligence, they did not carry these words always on their lips. They passionately opposed the Cartesian reduction of the power of reason, the application of reflection and meditation to life experiences, to the use of formal principles and procedures. Last but not least, they also opposed the reduction of the search for knowledge, truth and understanding to the mechanical application of a 'scientific method'.

It was due to this genuine, passionate search for truth, understanding and knowledge that reflexive historical sociologists often, with sincere humility, emphasized or even overemphasized the non-originality of their work (Bauman 1979: 121, 124 (on Elias), DEII: 479–80, Voegelin 1970: 223), recognizing that such claims of originality with respect to methods and theories assigned to subjects as their 'author' are only modern versions of the gnostic search for a *tabula rasa*. Their work had an anchorage point different from attempts at verifying (or, even worse, falsifying), their theories. It was rather a concern with 'philosophy as a way of life' (Hadot 1995a), or 'living in truth' (Patocka 1989; see also Szakolczai 1994, 1998b). It is through this concern with truth and a philosophical life that some reflexive historical sociologists were recognized as the great men of their times and even identified as modern-day incarnation of Socrates, the thinker who was the archetype of philosophical life.

This recognition and identification, however, opens up as many problems as it solves. Though the distinction between a professor of philosophy and a philosopher has been clear enough since Schopenhauer, Thoreau, Nietzsche, Jaspers, Wittgenstein and Hadot, the retracing of reflexive historical sociology to Socrates requires some further clarification. This can be done first by a characterization of Socrates as a parrhesiast, as *per* Foucault in his last course given at the Collège de France. A parrhesiast is somebody who makes claims about which s/he has personally experienced the truth and relevance, even if such statements may be risky (Foucault 1995; Szakolczai 1998a: 179–81).

Reflexive historical sociologists were certainly parrhesiasts. They told personally acquired, dangerous truths and lived accordingly. But they were also something more. They did not simply belong to one of the four types of truth-teller identified by Foucault. They wore the marks of all four. Apart from being parrhesiasts, they were also teachers. They were sages who in some instances preferred to keep silent, who often spoke in enigmas and were in some respects even mystics. But it seems that most of all, paradoxically, they belonged to a special modern version of the fourth type. With an expression first used, in a different context and with a different evaluation, by Lawrence Scaff, they were 'anti-prophetic prophets' (Scaff 1989: 230–1).

This expression needs to be explained carefully. First of all, reflexive historical sociologists emphatically were not prophets. Prophets possess two characteristics which reflexive historical sociologists never claimed for themselves. First, a prophet shows the way, comes up with solutions to the problems of the day. Reflexive historical sociologists never fancied themselves doing that. Second, a prophet is a mouthpiece of God. The way s/he shows is not an invention, but the road indicated from above. S/he only says as a prophet what God wants him/her to say. Such claims, of course, cannot be verified by scientific means. But this does not mean that they are meaningless and as Kant and Weber knew well, only the limits of science, at least as we understand it, are reached here.

Reflexive historical sociologists, far from making claims of prophecy, rather relentlessly and vehemently attacked all forms of modern day secular prophecy. They were thus anti-prophetic. But still, they were not simply anti-prophets, as they bore several character marks close to the genuine ancient prophets. This was visible in their speech, their charisma and often even in their appearance. It was also visibly present, and with much ambivalence, in their style. Prophets not only possess the gift of eloquent truth telling, the ability to convince others through their truthful speech based on their personality and not on skilful rhetorical tricks, but also a certain 'wrath of God'. They passionately denounce injustice, immorality and lies and wage a ruthless polemic against those who overlook and perpetuate these failings. Reflexive historical sociologists were similarly capable of almost boundless anger if they felt provoked and, arguably, wasted much of their energies in polemics that only hindered a proper reception of their work.

Furthermore, there was also much similarity, though certainly not complete identity, in the central 'ideas' of the old prophets and reflexive historical sociologists. Prophets, in fact, did not have ideas but visions. It has often been claimed that the works of reflexive historical sociologists are similarly guided not simply by operational hypotheses but by global, encompassing visions. Though such claims are to a large extent correct, it is still important to make some distinction between the two types of 'visions'.

Though both prophets and reflexive historical sociologists see things that others do not perceive, they do so in a different manner. Prophets see, or claim to see, into the future. Reflexive historical sociologists see into the past, perceiving connections with the present which have escaped others. Prophets attribute the sudden illuminations they receive to God. They are selected, without any evident merit, and often much against their wish, to receive these messages. The central insights of reflexive historical sociologists, however, do not come out of the blue. They always arrive in a very specific type of moment: after a long period of passionate research, through an intense period of reflection on its direction and meaning, usually in a moment that can be considered as liminal through a figuration of factors. Thus, even if the insights cannot be 'explained', it is still possible to render an account of them. But similarly to prophetic visions, they are not hypotheses which can be tested, as the evidence that would render such a testing possible often simply does not exist. They are genuine visions about the past which can only happen to those who not only possess unique individual gifts but are also immersed deeply into a concrete body of evidence. Thus, even though these insights may not be 100 per cent correct, it is very unlikely that they are completely wrong. They could, and should, guide the research of others working on the same material. With respect to such insights, the Cartesian principle of doubt, this 'apple in the worm of modernity' (ST: 15) or the Popperian concern with falsification is simply irrelevant. In order to individuate the unique quality of such 'anti-prophetic prophetic vision', the concept 'insight' will be used throughout the book as a technical term.

There is a final reason why the term 'anti-prophetic prophet' seems to be particularly appropriate to characterize reflexive historical sociologists. The central question of reflexive historical sociology concerns the emergence and effects of the religious and philosophical rejections of the world. There is a tight connection between these promises and practices, the salvation religions and the spread of asceticism especially in the form of monasticism, and the appearance of the relatively new religious figure of the prophet. The great salvation religions were all based on prophetic utterances, and the followers of several prophets organized themselves into close, often sectarian, monastic communities. The religious rejections of the world, just as Weber argued about the 'disenchantement', can be traced back to the great prophecies. It should thus come as no surprise that the understanding of our modern condition as the secularization of these religious rejections of the world is the work of those contemporaries who, in their predisposition and the style and content of their work, are closest to the old prophets. These are the reflexive historical sociologists, or the 'anti-prophetic prophets'.

This, however, may imply a consequence and conclusion quite different from the one Weber drew. If modern-day 'disenchantement' or 'secularization' is not an inexorable consequence of the rationalization of religion, only of the religious rejections of the world, then the ultimate consequence of reflexive historical sociology may not be the completion of secularization but its termination. Indeed, the work of some of the most important reflexive anthropological sociologists like Victor Turner or René Girard is leading exactly in this direction. The pursuit of this idea, however, goes beyond the scope of this volume.

Part II
Visions of modernity

Introduction to Part II

Part I of this book, and Parts II and III of the previous volume (Szakolczai 1998a), have mapped the life trajectories of six major thinkers who can be considered as main protagonists of reflexive historical sociology. The analysis so far has been formal, in the sense of reconstructing as far as possible the decisive experiences and personal or intellectual encounter events that stamped their work, giving it shape and direction, and the changes that occurred at that basic level, due to novel encounter-experiences or intensive reflections on their own works. The aim of such a formal analysis was to restore the proper frameworks and contours of the work, assign emphases and to punctuate the dynamics of the work by letting it retrieve its own rhythm.

In this second part, the emphasis shifts from the shape of the dynamics of the works to their content. In the presentation, emphasis will be on coherence. It will be argued throughout that the works of the thinkers covered are by no means identical but form a coherent field of investigation.

Claims of coherence are central for the establishment of any new field of study. They are especially important in this case, given the programmatic intent. It is argued that, in spite of the epochal significance of his work, Parsons got many points fundamentally wrong in his synthesis of Weber and Durkheim. Most importantly, he overlooked that the most important intellectual sources of Weber, with whom he was in continuous dialogue, were Marx and Nietzsche. As a result, much of the critical effort in social theory after Parsons went into the attempt to set Marx and Nietzsche outside mainstream sociology or reintegrate them inside, failing to realize that most of what is useful in this regard had already been accomplished by Weber. Thus, the most promising directions in social theory are still contained in the works of those thinkers who read Weber before Parsons, placing a strong emphasis on his sociology of religions and being interested not in rationalization in general but in the shaping of the individual conduct of life.

At the same time, similar developments were happening with respect to Durkheim, related partly to the return to Durkheim's own sociology of religions and partly to incorporating the insights of Durkheim's main

opponents, van Gennep and Tarde and Weber's most important interlocutor, Simmel. As a result, it is possible not only to individuate reflexive
historical sociology and reflexive anthropological sociology as two particularly promising threads of social theory, but also to pose the proper
synthesis of the two as the agenda. Thus, in this way, one can argue that
Parsons correctly defined the agenda as the linking of Weber and
Durkheim but he failed to make the connection in the most fruitful way.
The reconstruction of the coherent thread of reflexive historical sociology
will be a step in this suggested direction.

This undertaking could start by reconstructing the work of individual
thinkers, along the series of characteristic backward shifts of the time horizons of their work. Alternatively, it could take the time horizon, certain
epochal ages, as the unit of analysis and collect the work of different
thinkers with respect to the early modern period, the Middle Ages and
antiquity.

In the end, none of these options were taken. The first was bound to
end in a series of monographs on individual thinkers, failing to serve the
purpose of establishing the connections between them and thus establish
the new field of reflexive historical sociology. The second option posed
different kinds of problem. It would have been difficult to restrict attention to the six thinkers covered here and, even more problematically, in
the end it would have become an interpretive exercise in the philosophy
of history.

This led to the following way of proceeding. Individual thinkers remain
the unit of analysis. The focus is on the part of their work that was closest
to the modern period, covering in most cases the sixteenth to eighteenth
centuries. In the presentation, much emphasis is placed on the actual links
between their ideas: in the case of Weber, the reliance on Nietzsche; for
Elias, Borkenau and Voegelin, the manner in which they drew inspiration
from Weber and Nietzsche. Foucault and Mumford serve as some kind of
confirmation for the general thesis. In the case of Foucault, there is a similar reliance on Nietzsche though not originally on Weber. For Mumford,
neither Nietzsche nor Weber was a major source, and yet his work fits
closely with that of the other reflexive historical sociologists. Of him, we
can say the same things that Foucault said about another major protagonist of the field, Philippe Ariès: he 'pose[d] problems that were not that
distant from Weber's', even though his work did not derive directly from it
(DEIV: 647).

Thus in the end, in a quite conventional manner, each of the chapters
will summarize the work of one thinker. However, less conventionally,
each chapter is organized around not a central concept or an idea but an
'insight' or a 'vision' of modernity. These terms are used throughout in a
strict technical sense (see Schumpeter 1954: 41–2, 561–2). They are not to
be understood in an irrational sense, as a sudden illumination coming
from the inside. But neither do they belong to the realm of rationalistic,

cognitive psychology and theory of knowledge. They are proposed as a central building block in not a cognitive but a re-cognitive theory of knowledge (using Pizzorno 1991). The sudden, illuminating character of the most important aspects of the innovative theories about the modern condition is asserted, in opposition to a merely cognitive view of the knowledge process where ideas are only representations of reality or pure hypotheses to be tested against empirical evidence. Such illuminative visions are genuine *in*-sights, the *re*-cognition of links that previously were overlooked, either because they were hidden, covered and invisible, or because they were all too familiar and taken for granted. A vision is the result of a sudden viewing of everyday reality from a novel perspective or with a fresh eye, leading to a dislocation of the entire way of looking at the world, and not just a piece of knowledge to be added to the previous stock of information. As a result, works produced on the basis of such insights have a similarly visionary character. Reflexive historical sociologists want to change the way their readers see the world around them. On the other hand, an understanding of their works requires a similar alteration of one's own vision of the world, and thus they often meet rejection or resistance on the part of those who do not want to follow this risky path.

Though these visions are not cognitive but re-cognitive, and the knowledge and experience they are based upon and imply are not additive but transformative, they are not beyond intelligibility either. There are a number of conditions that have to be met for the acquisition of such a vision/insight. These include not simply work and efforts, but the relentless, long-term, lonely pursuit of a problem that is rooted in personal life experiences. This pursuit is undergone in liminal conditions, often at both the personal and political level, along with additional encounters with thinker(s) that helps to focus the content of the insight. Last but not least, there is an element of recurrence, return, repetition, reflexivity, a rereading of these works, or often even one's own, that may provoke a breakthrough.

It is this last point that helps to close the circle by bringing together the two central terms of the approach that at first glance seem so distant, vision and reflexivity. In the current, everyday uses of the terms, vision is associated with sudden, irrational, even mystical illumination, while reflexivity is associated with abstract, philosophical speculation. However, the insights gained by reflexive historical sociologists as sociologists are neither mystical nor philosophical. They are rooted in a special type of work that combines personal experiences with the pursuit of long-term research and reflexivity both on the experiences and the results of the research. It is this type of work 'method' that is captured by the adjective 'recognitive'.

5   The Protestant spirit (Weber)

It can hardly be doubted that *The Protestant Ethic and the Spirit of Capitalism* (hereafter *The Protestant Ethic*) is the central reference point for reflexive historical sociology and of much of sociology *tout court*. Already at the time of their first publication in 1904–5, the significance of the two essays was recognized and the work has been held in the highest regard ever since. This was reconfirmed, for those who needed it, by the recent survey of the International Sociological Association members who voted it the fourth most influential sociological book of the century.

However, since first publication, the work has not only been much discussed and criticized but has been subject to attacks of special harshness and intensity. In fact, in terms of its modality, the debate surrounding *The Protestant Ethic* sits in between the controversies provoked by the *Communist Manifesto* or the *Genealogy of Morals* – works that were explicitly written as political programmes or intellectual polemics and not as scholarly treatments of their subjects – and the standard classic works in social theory. While the status and reputation of *The Protestant Ethic* is now safely established, many of its critics do not simply raise points about some of its claims but question the meaning and legitimacy of Weber's entire undertaking.

Controversy of this type alludes to a fundamental misunderstanding of one kind or another. In fact, in his 'anticritical essays', Weber charged his critics with misconstruing the entire work as they failed to identify properly the problem he was addressing (Weber 1978 [1910]: 1111, Hennis 1988).

For a number of academic and personal reasons, Weber could not do otherwise but fight his critics bitterly. However, it must be acknowledged that the clues that would have rendered a proper understanding easier were not always in place. This includes the extent to which *The Protestant Ethic* was not just half-way between Marx and Nietzsche on the one side and standard academic work on the other, but itself took inspiration and challenge from the works of these major background figures. But the most important difficulties of the work were indeed related to its underlying problem.

Weber devoted unusual efforts to the specification of this problem. The entire first essay, or 40 per cent of the total length, is entitled 'The

Problem', making even more perplexing the claim that the critics could have misunderstood it. However, Weber's response to his critics was so bitter because on his first encounter with his own work, he also recognized that something was wanting. When his publisher, Paul Siebeck asked his authorization for a full book edition in his letter of 17 July 1906, he responded that he still had to do some work on it (MWGII/5: 119). A book version of *The Protestant Ethic*, however, was never published and the essay only re-appeared in print fourteen years later, in the first volume of the *Sociology of Religions*, which was published practically at the moment Weber died. The immediate effect from the letter of the editor was not a book edition but a near relapse into illness, marking the 'dark years' of 1906–10.

The best documents of Weber's efforts at specifying the underlying problem of the essay, and of gaining a proper perspective at the work, are the four anticritical essays written between 1907 and 1910 in which he responded to his critics. These essays, together with the *Critique of Stammler* (Weber 1977 [1906]), both literally fill the gap in time between the series of essays on Protestantism (*The Protestant Ethic* and the essays on Protestant sects) and the new 'Economic Ethic' series, and mark the 'transformatory devices' (*opérateurs*) (HSII: 13, translation changed) in Weber's perspective. This is best visible in the way the 'Anticritical Last Word' actually launched or projected the 'Economic Ethic' series.

The continuation of the misunderstandings surrounding the *Protestant Ethic* is largely owing to three factors. First, authors have a tendency to erase the steps which led them to a new stage in their work, if only to forget the particularly anxiety-ridden condition of intense reflections and doubts about their own work. Thus, Weber has played down the significance of the 'anticritical essays' in a footnote to the *Protestant Ethic* and the secondary literature complied with this authorial request until Wilhelm Hennis recognized the relevance of the essays. The second problem is related to the problems of the English edition. The quality of Parsons' translation has been subjected to a series of attacks in the past decades. However, it has not been so far recognized fully that the most important problem was the very fact that it is a truncated edition of the *Sociology of Religions* (GARS). With the approval of Marianne Weber (Camic 1991: xxvii), Parsons not only combined the 1920 Preface to the *Sociology of Religions* with the two essays of *The Protestant Ethic* originally written in 1904–5 (leading to endless misreading, especially after the publisher omitted his original 'Translator's Preface'), failing to add editorial remarks even where this made the text unintelligible, but published the work exactly in the way Weber refused to permit in his lifetime.[1] *The Protestant Ethic* as a book therefore does not have a place in Weber's *oeuvre*; it is entirely the product of the translated edition. The essays in themselves are only reports from a work in progress, and can be understood properly only together with, and from the perspective of, the 'anticritical essays', the essays on the Protestant sects and the essays on the 'Economic Ethic'.

The third difficulty may be the most central and certainly is the most controversial. The formulation of the problem created so many difficulties for Weber because it was rooted in a sensitivity which was Weber's own personal gift. The underlying problem of his work was based on an insight he gained thanks to this and therefore the work was driven by a vision. This was the perception of a direct and positive link between religiosity and modern capitalism which had been overlooked before him, save for Nietzsche's related insights.

Weber objected to social scientists having visions, and he told his audience that they should go to a cinema if they needed visions. In the same way he was opposed to the great vogue of the 'pursuit of experience' (MSS: 28). But this referred to visions about the future, not insights into what is taken for granted in the present, as woven in the past. In a similar vein, he was most opposed to scholars who posed as prophets and yet he was recognized by others as possessing an unusual gift of foresight. Weber was not a methodological individualist testing hypotheses. His work can only be understood properly and continued by recognizing that it was driven by the force of insights gained about the historical roots of the present condition and by an exceptional scholarly persistence to develop the conceptual tools that enable the clear analytical formulation of these links between the events of the past and the hidden texture of the present.

The reconstructive analysis of *The Protestant Ethic* done in this chapter is at a cross-point for the entire book. On the one hand, it will situate *The Protestant Ethic* in the context of Weber's later work and of research that took this work as a starting point. On the other, this analysis will then be used to situate subsequent works that took *The Protestant Ethic* as their starting point, trying to go beyond it and complement it at the same time. Quite in the spirit of Weber's own work, it will try to show a very familiar piece of work in a light that is both unfamiliar and yet radical only in the sense of a return to original meanings.

The essays on *The Protestant Ethic*

The work does not start with the proposition of a substantive thesis, such as Protestantism being the 'source' of capitalism. Neither does it begin with the formulation of a methodological position, arguing for the primacy of an 'idealistic' over a 'materialistic' perspective. It rather points out a puzzle behind a well-known fact taken from German occupational statistics, and studied extensively by Weber's first doctoral student in Heidelberg, Martin Offenbacher: that leading businessmen are much more frequently Protestant than Catholic.

Weber points out the puzzling nature of this correlation by showing the untenability of the conventional explanations: first, that this is a consequence of emancipation from economic traditionalism due to a religious laxity of Protestantism (PE: 36–7); then the idea that this is simply a result of inherited wealth (PE: 37–9); and finally that the stronger economic involvement of Protestants was due to a link between acquisition and enjoyment (PE: 40–2). Once these explanations are discarded, the puzzle becomes visible. In modern capitalism, there is a positive link between asceticism and acquisition, while previously an interest in acquisition, money, profits, accumulation and a concern with asceticism were radically separated. This is the puzzle that sets Weber off.

It also shows directly how much Weber derived inspiration for his work from both Marx and Nietzsche and how much of its value resides in the way he managed to combine, way before the 'postmodern turn', these epochal but rightly controversial thinkers. Capitalism and acquisitiveness were central concerns for Marx but he never had any interests in asceticism. For Nietzsche, on the other hand, asceticism was a central, in a certain way even the central, concern. The third essay of the *Genealogy of Morals* is about the meaning of ascetic ideals, and it contains the diagnosis of modernity as 'distinctively ascetic planet' (Nietzsche 1967a: 117), owing to the effect of the activities of a priestly (ideal) type Nietzsche called the 'ascetic priest'. Weber's genius lay in recognizing that the links between Marx and Nietzsche open up a particularly fruitful line of investigations, going well beyond the limits of each taken individually.[2]

The first section of the first essay (Chapter One in the English version) is devoted to the identification of the puzzle. The next two address the questions of method that its treatment requires. If the underlying problem of the work can only be identified by recognizing the positive and not merely negative links Weber's work had with Marx and Nietzsche, this also holds true for its methodology. Long before Foucault (FR: 76–100), Weber had identified and used Nietzsche's genealogical method; and long before Derrida (1982), Weber's work had made implicit use of the related link between 'difference' and 'deference'.

Chapter Two is entitled 'The "Spirit" of Capitalism'. Formally, Weber follows the standard German academic conventions of the times which were transmitted to us by the Prussian state and neo-Kantianism, and starts by defining the terms used in the title, just as he would do later in *Economy and Society* and the 'Economic Ethic'. This is all the more justifiable given the unusual combinations of words he used in his titles. However, substantively, he skips or 'defers' the entire procedure (PE: 47, ES: 399, FMW: 267), thus implicitly questioning the ruling neo-Kantian orthodoxy.

Concerning the '*spirit* of capitalism', instead of starting with a definition, Weber rather claims that '[t]he attempt to give anything like a "definition" of it brings out certain difficulties which are in the very nature of this type of investigation' (PE: 47, trans., slightly modified). Then, following the methodology elaborated in the 'Objectivity' essay, he introduces the term 'historical individual'. He ends these remarks by stating that:

if we try to determine the object, the analysis and historical explanation of which we are attempting, it cannot be in the form of a
conceptual definition, but at least in the beginning only a provisional
description [*Veranschaulichung*] of what is here meant by the 'spirit' of
capitalism.

(PE: 48)

He thus defers the definition. He then proceeds to present Benjamin
Franklin through some of his writings as the document of this 'spirit', the
impersonification of the 'type'.

In his interpretation of the texts, Weber immediately makes use of his
methodological principle of studying a historical phenomenon from the
perspective of the present and the effect it produces, moving from deference
to difference. This also shows how Weber's way of proceeding is the opposite
of 'present-centred history' (Ashplant and Wilson 1988). Instead of taking
for granted, anachronistically, the problems and terminology of the present,
Weber evokes the opposite concern. The 'time is money' type of attitude
evoked in the text is all too familiar to us, so much so that its fundamental
novelty and peculiarity is overlooked. His aim is to force his readers to step
back from this familiarity and recognize how this attitude could emerge as a
difference, as 'in the country of Benjamin Franklin's birth (Massachusetts),
the "spirit of capitalism" . . . was present before the "capitalist development"'
(PE: 55). The type of moral lessons the texts present has become so
commonplace today that it is now known mostly through their caricature.
However, this hides their fundamental novelty: that they preach not a pious,
withdrawn, other-worldly type of conduct of life usually associated with
religiosity, but the proper road towards success in business.

Because in our society this capitalistic mentality has become dominant,
it looks as if this has always been the case. However, at its moment of emergence as a difference, only a small minority shared this attitude. It had to
fight its way against the perspective that was dominant then: 'Its entry on
the scene was not generally peaceful. A flood of mistrust, sometimes of
hatred, above all of moral indignation, regularly opposed itself' (PE: 69).

In specifying the actual emergence of the 'spirit' of capitalism as a difference, the genealogical method identifies two special concerns. One is
the conceptualization of this emergence as a difference through the
joining of two separate threads, while the other is to put emphasis on the
conditions under which this linking has occurred. The former is the more
straightforward of the two, and has been followed by all major figures of
reflexive historical sociology who drew inspiration from Nietzsche, such as
Foucault, Borkenau and Elias. Weber similarly emphasizes that the
methodical conduct of life and the capitalist enterprise at first developed
separately and were only eventually joined.[3]

The second concern, the specification of the conditions under which
these two separate threads were joined, presented more difficulties for

everyone, starting from Nietzsche who never managed to provide a clear hint in this regard. Nietzsche had no concept comparable to dissolution of order, transition or liminality and ultimately conceptualized emergence in terms of a struggle of opposite passions, drives or will to power which was close to a biological Darwinist vision (Nietzsche 1967a, Preface, no. 7). This perspective had an appeal for Weber and for Weber-inspired reflexive historical sociologists like Albert Hirschman, but was supplemented from two different sources. One was the Marxian idea of class struggle. Since his first writings, Weber had pointed up the fight between different social groups as one, but only one, of the central moving forces of historical change. Second, however, Weber also heroized the struggle that the early protagonists of the 'capitalist spirit' led, in the form of a fight against the forces of tradition.

This position has been central both for Weber and for the reception of his works. It also represents a major shortcoming which has not been rectified even in the *Sociology of Religions* (GARS). Identifying himself with the Protestant pioneers, Weber took for granted their self-representation as knights of a heroic struggle against the forces of the past. This prevented him from recognizing the extent to which this 'heroic struggle' was rendered possible by the prior weakening and eventual dissolution of the previous order of things, including the tragic aspect of this collapse and the extent to which this previous order of things, as Weber knew well, was not simply traditional.[4] This shortcoming was repeated in a crucial passage of the *Vorbemerkung* where, breaking his entire previous line of argument, Weber switched from the emphasis on the '*specificity* of Western "rationalism"' (PE: 26, trans. modified) to the idea that in other world religions, this type of development was 'obstructed by spiritual obstacles' (PE: 26–7). In this way, Weber remained captive of a deep-rooted, archetypal German self-image of the lonely knight, an image which was widely recognized as his own.[5]

The third section of the first essay is entitled 'Luther's concept of calling'. Weber starts again by clarifying the title and also proceeds in the same manner. He points out that beyond the familiar, contemporary, secular meaning of the term *Beruf* (calling or vocation), there hides the original religious conception, 'a task set by God' (PE: 79). This concept, however, is not to be found in the Old or New Testament, but first emerged as a difference in the translation prepared by Luther. This point is substantiated in two long footnotes on the etymology of *Beruf* that also have methodological relevance for the importance of the history of forms of thought for reflexive historical sociology (see Hennis 1988: 237–8).

The study of this shift of meaning is, however, only a methodological tool to capture the fundamental underlying change in values and attitudes, the 'valuation of routine activity in the world' as the highest duty (PE: 80). This amounts to a basic revaluation of values, and thus justifies Weber's hope that his study would be a 'modest . . . contribution to the understanding of the manner in which ideas become effective forces in history' (PE: 90). This is followed in the original edition by two pages of qualifying remarks to prevent misunderstandings, and the book was reprinted in 1920 with the addition of a footnote calling attention to these remarks, without much success. With the passage quoted above, Weber opened the way for reading his work as an 'idealist' reading of history as opposed to the 'materialist' reading of Marx, and the label stuck all too well. This was all the more so because of the lack of signposts to indicate the Nietzschean inspiration, both in the concern with the 'revaluation of values' and in the genealogical method focusing on 'effective history'.

The second essay is entitled 'The vocational ethic of ascetic Protestantism'. It addresses, after another long methodological introduction, the central substantive theme of the work, the puzzling positive link discovered between asceticism and acquisition. In any study of the emergence of capitalism, the word 'acquisition' can be assumed. The unusual word in this context is 'asceticism'. Its importance, however, is underlined by Weber in putting this into the title of the second essay and both its sections. The title of the fourth 'chapter', 'The religious foundations of inner-worldly asceticism', immediately interprets this term, by providing one of Weber's most important conceptual innovations. After a few further methodological comments, Weber goes into the first of the four Protestant denominations covered, and the one most important for his purposes, Calvinism.

The discussion starts with the dogma of predestination. A main objection of many critics was the excessive importance Weber attributed to this dogma. However, even here, Weber only kept to his methodological premise of starting with the most familiar and commonplace. Far from singling out a particular element of Calvinism that suited his preconceptions, he simply took up the element that was widely considered as its most important distinguishing feature. The novelty of the analysis lay not in the theme itself but in the manner in which it was approached. Weber's interest was not in the dogma, but in the 'psychological sanctions' which originated in it (PE: 97; see also Poggi 1983: 64).

The concern with predestination, or the need for special divine grace in order to reach salvation, did not make its appearance in Christianity only with Protestantism. The relative part played by divine grace on the one hand, and human efforts, works or merit on the other, was one of the main theological debates throughout the entire history of Christianity. How much this debate was also at the centre of Weber's interest can be seen by the original Greek terms for 'grace' and 'exercise' that he almost single-handedly rendered household words for every social theorist: *charisma* and *askesis.*

From this perspective, the Protestant emphasis on predestination moves towards charisma rather than asceticism. The question then becomes the following: how did Calvinism become associated with asceticism?

Weber suggested a solution through his emphasis on anxiety and fear, or psychological sanctions, which was again a clearly Nietzschean perspective. According to him, Calvin pushed the doctrine of predestination to its utmost logical conclusion when, with 'extreme inhumanity' [*pathetische Unmenschlichkeit*], he declared that no human merit can alter God's free decrees (PE: 104). The consequence on the personality 'was a feeling of unprecedented inner *loneliness of the single individual*' (PE: 104, emphasis restored). Significantly, it is at this point that he inserted in the 1920 edition his first reference to '[t]hat great process in the history of religions, the *disenchantment* [*Entzauberung*] of the world' (PE: 105; trans. altered). And this is also the point where he introduced Bunyan's *Pilgrim's Progress*, in order to 'see the specific results of this peculiar atmosphere' (PE: 107), the 'ideal type' text of the fourth section. This work, according to Weber, puts a 'restless and systematic struggle with life' (PE: 108) at the centre of human endeavour.[6]

Under such conditions of psychological pressure and utmost insecurity, there is a need for 'infallible' criteria to provide release from the torments. It is there that works and efforts that were ruled out earlier as having no impact on salvation return as if through the back door. Human merit cannot influence the free decision of God. However, the successful pursuit of one's calling can serve as proof of one's own status of being elect. In this way, charisma and asceticism, far from being opposed, become like different sides of the same coin.

The new valorization of works and asceticism, far from being a return to the old ways as it was alleged by Luther (PE: 115), represents rather a major innovation, as 'a more intensive form of the religious valuation of moral action than that to which Calvinism led its adherents has perhaps never existed' (PE: 115–16). This is the second and last place where Weber inserted a reference to the 'disenchantment' of the world, or 'the elimination of *magic* as a means to salvation' in the 1920 edition (PE: 117). And just as on the previous occasion, he again asserted that the Protestant position is closer to the Jewish than to the Catholic one. In both cases, the central point is the exhaustive methodical regulation of the everyday conduct of life because of the idea that life 'at every moment and in every action' has a meaning that has relevance for salvation (PE: 118). In order to distinguish the Jewish and Protestant positions, Weber turned to a short history of asceticism, especially the practice of Western monasticism. For Weber this provides the background against which the Protestant ethic, and therefore the 'spirit' of capitalism, can be understood as a difference.

The ensuing review of the history of Western monasticism and its contrast with the Puritans (PE: 118–25) takes up a strategic position in the book and, indeed, in Weber's entire life-work. It is in the middle of the longest and most important section of the longest chapter. Situated after the three introductory chapters and before the concluding chapter, this chapter runs to more than 40 per cent of the length of the entire work and contains the substance of Weber's analysis. But this account has its central role in the entire life-work, as it is at this point that the entire investigation of the 'Economic Ethic' can be fitted into *The Protestant Ethic*, as the two inserted passages on 'disenchantment' already signalled. During the fundamental reorganization of his entire project in the last months of 1910, following the 'Anticritical Last Word', Weber extended his background analysis from (Western) Christian to non-Western asceticism and to the entire range of different kinds of 'religious rejections of the world'.

The review is also central for methodological reasons, demonstrating with particular clarity the manner in which the work received its inspiration from Nietzsche, not only in its central idea but also in its method. In his historical review of Western monasticism, Weber identified in asceticism one of the separate threads that would be eventually joined in the 'spirit' of capitalism. The second thread was constituted by the techniques of rational capitalist enterprise like double-entry bookkeeping and banking. This is associated with the Florentine origins of modern capitalism and is usually given precedence. Weber, however, only mentions it in passing as he assumes it as given. This is because, according to him, the relative importance and the modality of the impact of the two sides are not equal. While accounting and banking techniques certainly provided the technical means without which modern capitalism could not have emerged, the impetus that gave the breakthrough lay elsewhere. In an expression that contains in a nutshell the central idea of Weber's entire undertaking, and whose Nietzschean origins are plain as they are a transliteration of the original title of Nietzsche's first book, *The Birth of the Tragedy out of the Spirit* [*aus dem Geiste*] *of Music* (Hennis 1988), Weber claimed that:

> [o]ne of the fundamental elements of the spirit of modern capitalism, and not only of that but of all modern culture: rational conduct [*Lebensführung*] on the basis of the *idea of calling*, was born – that is what this discussion has sought to demonstrate – from the spirit (*aus dem Geiste*) of *Christian asceticism*.[7]
>
> (PE: 180)

The short review of monastic asceticism also helps to set the record straight on two highly controversial aspects of the Weber reception. Both are related in a common case of amnesia. On the one hand, just as Weber's entire line of argument presented so far was novel and flew again and again in the face of received wisdom, though taking its starting point always from there, the emphasis on the fundamental relevance of asceticism in the genesis of modern capitalism was a novel idea. Such an idea is not present in Marx or in classics of political economy. Gibbon's assessment of the fundamentally irrational character of monasticism is only a particularly clear example of the general position. The one thinker who put asceticism at the centre of his analysis of his society, talking about the 'ascetic ideal' and the 'ascetic planet', was Nietzsche. Second, one of the recurrent criticisms of the *Protestant Ethic* was Weber's alleged neglect of monasticism. This charge goes back as far as the criticism of Brentano, and includes such important figures as Lynn White (1978: 181) and Lewis Mumford (MMI: 267). In fact, in the 1920 edition, Weber even responded to this criticism by Brentano, expressing his surprise that he was charged with having omitted the monks from his picture, while this:

> continuity is, as anyone can see, a fundamental postulate of my whole thesis: the Reformation took rational Christian asceticism and its methodical habits out of the monasteries and placed them in the service of active life in the world.
>
> (PE: 235, fn 79)[8]

The final methodological significance of this short review of Christian asceticism is that it demonstrates beyond doubt that for Weber the historical background of modernity was not 'tradition' but the institutionalization of ascetic practices in the context of the emergence of salvation religions which went back to one of the first crucial breakpoints with tradition, the axial age.

In matters of content, the central element of all Western asceticism was the bringing of order into everyday conduct. In this regard, there is no difference between medieval monasticism and Protestant asceticism or, for that matter, between Calvinists and Jesuits (PE: 118–9). The difference lies in the scope and extent of these practices. In medieval asceticism, the methodically-regulated conduct of life was only followed by monks, or as Weber would later call them, the small circle of 'religious virtuosi'. In Protestantism, asceticism became a principle for the everyday conduct of life of every single believer. Weber much liked to quote Sebastian Franck, a sixteenth-century Lutheran minister, who saw 'the significance of the Reformation in the fact that now *every* Christian had to be a monk all his life' (PE: 121; see also Weber 1978 [1910]: 1122; 1981 [1923]: 367). The consequence of Calvinism, as opposed to Lutherism, was a 'thoroughgoing Christianization of the whole everyday life [*des ganzen Daseins*]' (PE: 124, trans., modified).

However, it was a very specific aspect, and by no means the 'essence', of Christianity that has become thus secularized. Weber would later coin the expression 'religious rejections of the world' to cover this aspect. But the general idea was already clearly present at the end of the chapter:

> Christian asceticism, at first fleeing from the world into solitude, had already ruled the world which it had renounced from the monastery and through the Church. But it had, on the whole, left the naturally spontaneous character of daily life in the world untouched. Now it strode to the market-place of life, slammed the door of the monastery

behind it, and undertook to penetrate just that *everyday* routine of life with its methodicalness, to fashion it into a life in the world, but neither of nor for this world.

(PE: 154)

The last chapter, 'Asceticism and the spirit of capitalism', returns to the original question of how the two separate and even opposed threads of acquisition and asceticism became joined. Its purpose is to understand 'the connection between the fundamental religious ideas of ascetic Protestantism and the maxims of everyday economic conduct' (PE: 155, trans., modified). Much of the controversy surrounding the work was caused by the lack of clear methodological guidelines about joining the two threads. The 'form' of capitalist techniques of enterprise was filled with the 'spirit' of Protestant asceticism, and one of the aspects was not studied directly but rather assumed as evident. In order to show the joining of the threads, Weber again used a concrete text as an 'ideal type'. This time he used the *Christian Directory* of Richard Baxter, a Presbyterian minister of the seventeenth century, 'the most complete compendium of Puritan ethics' (PE: 156).[9] The book, Weber argues, epitomizes the identities and differences with the asceticism of medieval monasticism. Continuing the tradition, it preached hard manual labour as a basic ascetic technique (PE: 158). However, as opposed to monastic rules, activity was no longer promoted as an end in itself and the acquisition of wealth, if not pursued for the sake of enjoyment, became ethically valorized (PE: 163).[10] It was this displacement, this 'revaluation of values' as related to work, that has rendered capitalism possible, as:

> the religious valuation of restless, continuous, systematic work in a worldly calling, as the highest means to asceticism, and at the same time the surest and most evident proof or rebirth and genuine faith, must have been the most powerful conceivable lever for the expansion of that attitude toward life which we have here called the "spirit" of capitalism.

(PE: 172)

In this context, Weber again compares the Puritans with ancient Judaism. He argues that the idea of 'English Hebraism', if properly understood, is correct. It includes the idea that God rewards obedience even in this life, the emphasis on formal legality and the belief of belonging to the 'chosen people' (PE: 163–5).[11] But the differences were also decisive, including the 'naive acceptance of life' characteristic of Judaism and its economic ethos which was a 'pariah-capitalism' (PE: 165–6).

The last six pages (PE: 178–83) contain a summary of the basic argument. They start, in the spirit of the genealogical method, by restating the difference that Protestantism introduced into the history of asceticism. Beyond the spread and the deepening of the methodical regulation of the conduct of life, it included the creation of a 'psychological sanction' and becoming effective through the concept of 'labour as a calling' (PE: 178). The result, first observed in the Netherlands in the seventeenth century, was the striking increase in economic power. The remaining pages contain some particularly concise formulations, like the most famous and trivially Nietzschean diagnoses about the 'iron cage' or 'casing' (PE: 181; see S. Turner 1982) and the 'last men' (PE: 182), and a few remarks about the kind of work that could take its departure from here.

As is well known, Weber never took up the projects he outlined there. The 'book' of *The Protestant Ethic* thus ended on this note. However, this was not the end of the story for Weber nor for most reflexive historical sociologists. There are three series of works that can be considered as direct continuations of *The Protestant Ethic*.

First and foremost, there are the essays on the Protestant sects. Second, there are the 'anticritical essays' in which Weber responded to his early critics. Finally, there are the entire series of essays about the 'Economic Ethic', which are the authentic follow-up studies to the works on Protestantism.

The perspective of these latter essays, and especially the theoretical perspective elaborated on their basis in the *Einleitung*, the *Zwischenbetrachtung* and in the respective sections of *Economy and Society*, will be used extensively in the next section. Their subject matter, however, explodes the horizon of Part II, belonging to a comparative study of the emergence of the West and not restricted to the reconstruction of the visions of modernity. It will be revisited therefore in a follow-up study. The 'anticritical essays' were briefly introduced earlier. They were also covered extensively in Hennis (1988) and in Szakolczai (1998a). The discussion here is therefore restricted to the essays on 'Sects'.

The essays on the Protestant sects

Weber wrote the first version in 1905, directly under the impact of his visit to the United States. They therefore represent a crucial addition and further elaboration of the main themes of *The Protestant Ethic*. This is visible, first of all, both in the original title, in the new title under which they were re-published in the *Sociology of Religions* (GARS) and, finally in their position there. The original title was 'Churches and Sects', contrasting the two words Weber kept using for the characterization of the institutional difference between medieval Christianity and Catholicism on the one hand, and Protestantism on the other. The new title became 'The Protestant Sects and the Spirit of Capitalism', rhyming perfectly with the title of the first series of essays on *The Protestant Ethic*. This gives a contrast between the 'ethic' and the 'sects'. The word 'ethic' captures the individual component, the methodical and thus mechanical rationalization of the entire conduct of life, while the word 'sects' refers to the type of community that enabled and was built upon this methodical conduct as a way of life. Finally, this title is not a section heading, nor even a chapter title, but the title of one of the divisions. This is no small matter. In nearly 1,400 pages of the *Sociology of Religions*, there are only three division titles: *The Protestant Ethic* which runs for nearly 200 pages, the 'Sects' which are a mere thirty pages, and the 'Economic Ethic' that covers all the rest. The significance Weber attributed to this work could hardly have been underlined more emphatically.[12]

This did not save it, however, from the vicissitudes of a particularly sad reception. It was omitted from the Parsons edition of *The Protestant Ethic* but published in English as Chapter Twelve of the 'Weber Reader' edited by Gerth and Mills (FMW). Severed from its context, the significance of the essay was all but unnoticed (Loader and Alexander 1985: 5, fn 5), while the book version of *The Protestant Ethic* became a classic in sociology, adding fuel to allegations concerning Weber's 'idealist' thesis and the particularly misleading label of 'methodological individualism'.

Weber's account of the Protestant sects is shrouded in perplexities and paradoxes. Both versions start with a puzzle: the striking phenomenon of the intensive ecclesiastic communal life in the US which was still present during his 1904 visit. But more importantly, the entire discussion is dominated by paradoxes. Sects imply a fundamentally communal form of existence and yet they are the driving forces behind individualism. The religious life in sects is particularly marked but at the same time they are mostly vehicles for commercial undertakings, providing an assurance of the credit rating of their members and their trustworthiness in matters of business. Weber considers sects as survivals of the past, destined to disappear with the spread of 'Europeanization', 'secularization' and 'modernization' (Weber 1985 [1906]: 7, FMW: 302, 307), and yet in them he recognized a major driving force for modern capitalism. Sects are a major source for the type of democracy characteristic of America, and yet they are also primarily exclusive clubs most concerned with questions of admittance and exclusion, and restricting and maintaining their membership.[13] They also combine strong religiosity and political radicalism, while in Europe these are usually exact opposites (Weber 1985 [1906]: 10). The line could be continued.

Such a series of paradoxes indicates major underlying imbalances and excesses, posing the question of whatever could have rendered their joint emergence possible. Though not specifying either a dissolution of order or a period of transition explicitly, Weber came close to identifying such a situation when stating that '[w]e modern, religiously "unattuned" people are hard pressed to conceptualize or even simply to believe what a powerful role these religious factors had in those periods when the characters of the modern national cultures were being stamped' (Weber 1985 [1906]: 11). Such a period, as we know from *The Protestant Ethic*, Weber identified as the sixteenth and seventeenth centuries, the times when the collapse of the medieval world order created a simultaneous political, social and religious crisis. The Protestant sects gained prominence in the period because they provided an unequalled joint response to this challenge, providing their members with psychic and material security, the comfort of community and at the same time an opportunity for social mobility. In some of the most perceptive remarks of the essay, Weber argues that sect membership was most valuable not for the greatest capitalist figures, the likes of a Morgan or a Rockefeller, as '*[t]hey* stood and they stand "beyond good and evil"' anyway (FMW: 309), but for those individuals and groups who required some 'vehicles of social ascent into the circle of the entrepreneurial middle class' (FMW: 308).

This special role of the sects comes out best when compared and contrasted with those three other 'closed' or 'total' institutions with which they have been often mentioned together, both by Weber and other reflexive historical sociologists: the monastic orders, the court and the police.

As far as monasticism is concerned, the parallels are strictest and were brought out by Weber. The Protestant sects were closely modelled on the asceticism characteristic of medieval monasticism, and played the same role in the sixteenth century and onwards as the monasteries did in the centuries around the collapse of the Roman Empire. They were safe havens of peace and security among chaotic external conditions, serving as institutions of education and vehicles of upward social mobility. This parallelism is, of course, controversial as the monastic orders were among the greatest enemies of the sects. The reformers, however, committed exactly the same error as the humanists of the Renaissance by judging the entire medieval order on the basis of their decadent characteristics and thus overlooking their own descent.

As far as the court is concerned, four of the most important characteristics of 'court society', as the next chapter will show in detail, are the importance of visibility, reputation, interdependence and the 'strategification' of conduct. All these were central concerns in Weber's analysis of the sects. Just like the court, sects have an overwhelming concern with visibility. While the medieval Church could live with the idea of an 'invisible church' as the community of the elects in a state of grace, the sects had to know who the elects were and only believed the proof of their own eyes. The central currency of sects, as for court society, was 'reputation', with the only difference being that the gaining of reputation here had to be earned from scratch, and was concerned with business, not the kind of intrigues played at court. Staying with strategic games, while in the court all aspects of conduct were transformed into assets or liabilities in the complicated schemes of intrigues, in the sects conduct similarly became part of a global strategic scheme, only it was played for money and credit trustworthiness, not standing in the court ceremonies. In the closed institution of the court, everybody depended on everybody else, which ultimately broke

down the strict social dividing lines and ritual roles. In the similarly closed
sects, the interdependence of all members was especially close, as it provided help in case of need but also involved a continuous supervision of
each by all.

The parallels work out similarly with the police, an institution which was
a joint offshoot of republican concerns (the etymology of 'police' is
derived from *politeia*) and of the court. The central concern of the early
modern police was with social supervision and individual disciplining,
which covers exactly the main social functions of the sects. After all, early
modern police forces were strongest where the sects were the weakest.

The central thrust of Weber's interest, however, is directed to an aspect
of sect life that touches upon and subsumes all the characteristics mentioned so far: the voluntary character of membership which means that
individuals were admitted on the basis of personal religious qualification
only (Weber 1985 [1906]: 9); and the main consequence that admission
was granted, for example in the 'ideal-typical' case of the Baptist congregation, 'only upon the most careful "probation" and after closest inquiries
into conduct going back to early childhood' (FMW: 305).[14] This aspect was
connected to all the previous characteristics discussed. It had to do with
giving a visible proof of one's own religious qualities, while membership in
a proper congregation served as a further mark of reputation.[15] It was a
clear indication of a disciplined character and a methodically regulated,
ascetic way of life. It was also a clear sign of strategic considerations, in
accordance with the principle that 'Honesty is the best policy' (FMW: 313),
as the passing of a test was much less a matter of belief and dogma than of
ethics and the conduct of life.

Weber emphasized the specific and non-universalistic character of this
probation, its widespread existence among the sects and even argued that
'sect discipline is also analogous to monastic discipline in that it established the principle of the novitiate' (FMW: 317). This admission ritual
and testing is also a very special kind of practice, a rite of passage. This is
again best illustrated in the example of the Baptists, whose central concern,
giving their name, was a re-problematization of the main Christian 'rite of
passage', baptism. They argue that it must be a genuine test and performance, and not just a ceremonial, magic ritual performed on infants.[16]

From Parsons onward, Weber's sociology has often been called 'volun-
tarist'. This term has indeed been central to his concerns, but in a sense
radically different from Parsons and his followers, especially in the blatant
misnomer of 'methodological individualism' which was assigned to it.
Weber's interest was not in a theological question of free will or in free
individual choice and action in the sense of Homans, Boudon and Milton
Friedman. 'Voluntarism' for him implies first of all application to membership in an association and then, crucially, the passing of a test,
probation or a rite of passage. For him individualism did not mean the
trivial tautological point that only single human beings can move their legs

or exert their brains, but the extremely significant sociological idea of pinning down a type of social order in which the principle of stratification is based neither on status nor on universalistic procedures but on the nominally free choice of a community. This choice had to be argued out of deep inner conviction, and the community had to be convinced of one's own inner worth. In sum, 'this qualification through self-probation is viewed exclusively as the foundation for the social union of the congregation' (Weber 1985 [1906]: 10).

One final characteristic of this probation rite was of utmost significant for Weber and for the purposes of this book. The fundamental difference between probation in the Church and in the sects was not simply whether baptism happened in infancy or in adulthood. It was that the stage of performance in the sects was not restricted to a single ritual act, but had to become permanent. At the test of admission, the individual showed certain crucial qualities. But:

> [i]n order to hold his own in this circle, the member had to prove repeatedly that he was endowed with these qualities. They were constantly and continuously bred in him. For, like his bliss in the beyond, his whole social existence in the here and now depended upon his 'proving' himself.
>
> (FMW: 320)[17]

In the passages immediately following, Weber points out the difference between this concern and the Catholic practice of confessions.

This continuous character of the 'probing' in the sects has a crucial theoretical corollary. It implies an extremely specific type of rite of passage. Any tribal or modern rite of passage is the transition from one stage to another. Once the rite is completed, the passage is consumed and one becomes an adult, a married person, a graduate or an employee. There is no idea of performing the rite again and, in fact, there is often an explicit clause prohibiting the repetition of the act. In the case of the Protestant sects, however, it was exactly this performance and probing that had to be repeated continuously. The point was not simply that certain prohibited kind of behaviour would disqualify the status gained – this was applied to most rites of passage – but that the performance actually had positively to be repeated time and again.

This was a novel idea. Using the terminology of Turner, one could argue that this implied a – profoundly paradoxical – permanent state of liminality. This point will be discussed in depth in the Conclusion to Part II.

6   Court society (Elias)

Similarly to Weber's, the life-work of Elias was launched by an insight into the connections between the past and the present. This was the recognition of close parallels between the absolutist court and modern civil society while the two were considered in a matter-of-fact way to be opposites, like religiosity and profit-making. The proper formulation these links and of the underlying problem of his work created much difficulty both for Elias and the reception of his work. Finally, in his quest, Elias drew much inspiration from the work of Weber.

This point may meet some opposition, as it is usually assumed that Elias developed his work in opposition to Weber's. Such a position appears to receive support from the 1968 *Introduction* to *The Civilizing Process*. But that piece has been shaped by the Weber reception of the previous decades, especially the mediation of Parsons, who was at the centre of Elias's attacks. Rejecting the work of Parsons, Elias also created the impression that he wanted to re-found sociology beyond and against not only Parsons but also Durkheim and Weber. This did more harm than good to his standing in the wider sociological community. However, looked at from the 1920s and 1930s and placed in the proper perspective of the intellectual dynamics of the work, the positive and enabling links to Weber become visible.[1]

Such an idea is not at all novel. In his review of *The Civilizing Process*, Borkenau stated that the book 'recalls the best traditions of Max Weber and his school' (Borkenau 1938: 308). But Elias was by no means simply a disciple of Weber. He was taking up Weber's work not in the word but in the spirit: not as a canonical text but as a starting point for exposing his own work, where he both complemented and challenged Weber's ideas at the same time.

This is visible at the level of the central concepts, the methodology and the entire *Problemstellung* of the project.

As far as the first is concerned, four terms will be singled out as representative examples: '*habitus*', 'figuration', 'stamping' and '*homo clausus*'. *Habitus* became one of the best-known trademarks of the sociology of Elias, rectifying his long absence from English-speaking discussions owing to its omission from the English translation (Mennell 1992: 30).[2] However, it has also been used by Weber both in *The Protestant Ethic* and, with even greater emphasis, in the 'anticritical essays'. Given that the term has been widely used by the scholastics, this may not mean much. However, both Weber and Elias used the term in much the same sense and for the same purpose. Thus, for example in the third anticritical essay, Weber talks about 'the development of that *Habitus*, which I . . . named the "capitalist spirit"' (PE2: 157), implying that the 'spirit of capitalism' should be conceived of as a *habitus*. Elias in *The Court Society*, and in a crucial passage just before the concluding section of Chapter Five which is at a strategic position in the entire work, similarly states that 'the "basic personality characteristics" [*sic* in German original] or, as it is sometimes expressed, the "spirit" of court people, emerg[e] from the social figuration they form together' (CS: 113).

The passage quoted above also alludes to two further key concepts, 'figuration' and 'stamping'. The first of these was only added later, as this concept was developed in 1968 (see Chapter One of this volume). However, Weber similarly emphasized the constellation of forces out of which the 'spirit' of capitalism had emerged (PE: 93; GARS: 83).[3] The third term, 'stamp' or 'stamping' (*Gepräge* or *Prägung*) is related to the way in which the link between figuration and *habitus*, or constellation and spirit, can be conceptualized. Elias and Weber both use the term extensively. The word itself was in common usage at the time and in fact, it is contained in the long quote Elias inserted from Sombart in his original *Preface* (CS: 39). However, Weber and Elias form a concept around the word. It is not simply used in the vague sense of 'legacy' or 'influence', but refers to the modality under which certain external conditions are able to leave a lasting mark. This is not simply on certain mechanical, reflex-like forms of human behaviour, but on central aspects of personality formation as well. In fact, the specification of the exact modality of these conditions remained a central preoccupation for both Elias and Weber. The term in this sense recurs in *The Court Society* and *The Civilizing Process* (for example CP: 268–9, 517–8), and in the *Einleitung* (FMW: 268–70, 280), always at critical junctures.

The final example selected has special relevance in the sense that the similarities between the two thinkers can be demonstrated at the heart of a major objection Elias raised against Weber in the 1968 *Introduction*. At the culmination of his criticism of the dominant assumption of modern philosophy and sociology, the picture of the closed self he termed '*homo clausus*', Elias lists Descartes, Weber and Parsons as its main representatives (CP: 204–7). Using the expression 'the "self in a case"' to characterize this self-perception, he then claims that the action of this *homo clausus* or 'self in a case' was 'the starting point of the social theory of Max Weber' (CP: 207). The original word used for 'case' by Elias is *Gehäuse*. The irony of the matter is that this was exactly the term that has been translated by Parsons as 'cage' in the famous 'iron cage' (*stahlhartes Gehäuse*) metaphor. The image of the closed self therefore, far from being the taken-for-granted starting point of Weber's entire work, was its fundamental target. The aim of Weber, just as of Elias, was to reconstruct the long-term process that 'stamped' this type of personality on modern society and modern philosophy at the same time.[4]

The close parallels extend from concept formation to basic methodological concerns. The example selected, the use of 'ideal types', is again both relevant and counter-intuitive.

Another main objection of Elias to Weber concerned the use of 'ideal types', against which Elias introduces the term 'real types' (CS: 14). This was voiced in an important footnote to the original edition (CP: 526–7, fn 22). However, the target there was not directly Weber but the use Otto Hintze made of his ideas. The exact meaning and role of 'ideal types' in Weber's sociology is a tricky issue which can only be touched on briefly here. On the one hand, like Rickert, Weber considered concept formation a central methodological concern, and in opposition to a correspondence theory of knowledge took up a constructivist position which emphasized the creative role of the intellect (Weber 1949: 89–90). On the other, the aim of his historical analyses was by no means restricted to an illustration or testing of abstract concepts. Quite the contrary, his main concern was to select some very concrete, illustrative cases as representative types or examples (MSS: 50–1); a '*historical individual*' as 'a complex of elements associated in historical reality which we unite into a conceptual whole from the standpoint of their *cultural significance*, (PE: 47), corresponding to:

> the nature of the 'formation of historical concepts' which attempt for their methodological purposes not to grasp historical reality in abstract general formulae, but in concrete genetic sets of relations which are inevitably of a specifically unique and *individual* character.
> (PE: 48, GARS: 31; translation slightly modified)

Thus, at a focal starting point of all relevant chapters of *The Protestant Ethic*, there is not a definition of a particular 'ideal type' as an artificial construct but the presentation of a concrete text or even word as an example: Benjamin Franklin's *Autobiography* and other writings, Luther's word 'calling' (*Beruf*), Bunyan's *Pilgrim's Progress*, and Baxter's *Christian Directory* are all examples that are quite close to Elias's concern with 'real types'.[5]

Elias proceeds in a similar manner. *The Court Society* starts, as an illustrative example, with 'The structure of dwelling as an indicator of social structure' which is a minute description of the spatial arrangement, the Palace, in which the French courts of the sixteenth to eighteenth centuries lived. *The Civilizing Process* similarly starts, after the introductory discussion, with a history of the term *civilité* followed by the work of Erasmus as a representative text.[6]

Finally, Elias not only used concepts and methods developed by Weber, but took up the problem which he had set. At the end of the 'Anticritical Last Word' (Weber 1978 [1910]), Weber defined his interest as being concerned with the 'great process of development which lies between the highly labile late medieval developments toward capitalism and the mechanization of technology, which is so decisive for capitalism in its contemporary form' (PE2: 324, Weber 1978 [1910]: 1128). He identified as a crucial element of this process, the target of his immediate attention and the *prerequisite* for its emergence 'the creation and diffusion of the rationalist and anti-traditionalist "spirit" and the entire range of behaviour (*das ganze Menschentum*) to which in practice it was assimilated' (ibid.: 1128–9). He specified two possible projects by which such an investigation could be pursued in the most fruitful manner, a 'history of modern *science*' and a 'history of the modern *conduct of life* (*Lebensführung*)'. In both instances, he emphasized the link with the economy and made it clear that in his own work he opted for the second project. The life-work of Elias can be defined as being concerned with uncovering the exact dynamics of the 'great process of development' which led to the emergence of a type of affective behaviour that is associated with the taken-for-granted forms of modern civilized conduct of life.

Though Elias took up Weber's problem, he was interested in other non-economic aspects of the long process and posed the problem in different terms. Its exact formulation, the proper linking of personal experiences and scholarly research, caused just as much trouble to Elias as to Weber and Foucault, while the resulting absence of clear guidelines created similar difficulties for the reception of his work. Back in his Frankfurt days, he stimulated all his students to base their work on personal experiences (Seglow 1977). But it is difficult and hardly decent to make personal 'confessions' in a work of social theory, and Elias only gave brief indications to the personal aspect of the problem of his works (CP: xvi). This reluctance enabled those who lacked the power of empathy and the ability of recognition to charge Elias with the exact opposite of his intentions (for details see Mennell 1992: 228, and van Krieken 1998: 119).

While the original Prefaces to *The Court Society* and *The Civilizing Process* do provide a few crucial markers, a clear exposition and precise formulation of the entire underlying problematics of the life-work had to wait for the publication of *The Germans*. This has three components.

The first concerns personal roots. The very first sentence of the book refers to the position of Elias as an eyewitness, while the clearest statement is contained in a long footnote. Beyond general allusions, the exposition here is both autobiographical and authoritative:

Indeed, at first the problem of civilization appeared to me as a completely personal problem in connection with the great breakdown of civilized behaviour, the thrust towards barbarization, which was

something totally unexpected, quite unimaginable, taking place under
my own eyes in Germany'

(GE: 444, fn 8)[7]

The critical personal experience identified in this passage, the 'breakdown
of civilization', is also the title of Chapter Four.

The second key reference is in fact contained in the title of Chapter
Three, 'Civilization and violence'. This is much more than just one of the
chapters. It is both the original nucleus and the theoretical core of the
entire book. The first version of this essay was written during the Eichmann
trial in 1961 (Goudsblom and Mennell 1998: 113), delivered as a keynote
speech and published in German in 1981, and translated into English in
1988. The two words sitting uncomfortably together in the title highlight
the puzzling problem that lay at the heart of Elias's work and recalled the
dilemma with which *The Protestant Ethic* started, concerning the strange
positive link between acquisition and asceticism which was constitutive of
modern capitalism. The parallel and complementary character of the life-
works of Elias and Weber again becomes visible: if modern economic
society was produced by the strange bedfellows of 'acquisition' and 'asceticism', modern political society was based on the even stranger mixing of
'civilization' and 'violence'.[8]

The reconstruction of Elias's problem is completed by introducing the
third element which links the personal experience of the breakdown of civilized forms of conduct and the state monopoly of violence with the
general theoretical question of the perplexing positive link between civilization and violence. This is the ritual of duelling which is a peculiar and
bloody rite of passage (GE: 46), and the entire satisfaction-giving society
[*satisfaktionsfähige Gesellschaft*] to which it belongs.[9] This rite is of utmost
theoretical importance as it epitomizes the type of positive link between
civilization and violence whose perception was so central to Elias's work. It
was a ritual which was perfectly civilized, regulated by an etiquette in which
only gentlemen could participate, but nevertheless functionally included
the ultimate act of violence, the deliberate killing of another human being.
It also brought together in an 'ideal-typical' or 'real typical' manner the
two parts of *The Civilizing Process*, the concern with etiquette and rituals on
the one hand and violence and the state on the other. Finally, it alludes to
a fundamental difference from Weber. Weber could never lift himself
beyond the 'satisfaction-giving society'. He was engaged in duelling in his
students days (of which he carried a scar on his face) and accepted its
ethos and mentality. Together with his self-image as a tragic knight which
was also rooted deeply in German archetypal characters and myths, this
constituted one of the most important liabilities of his person and work.[10]

The argument that the puzzling coexistence of civilization and violence was the central underlying problem of Elias's work is not simply a
retrospective interpretation but is born out by the spirit and word of *The*

Court Society. Furthermore, Elias identified in it both the place and the time in which, according to him, the decisive and for us fateful joining of civilization and violence happened: it was in the courts, and in the period called 'absolutism'. Even further, he clearly specified his main insight: the court, instead of being overcome by modern bourgeois forms of conduct and rationality, in the form of a ghost (*Gespenst*) (CS: 113) exerted an impact beyond its actual lifespan and left a decisive stamp on the present (CS: 38–40).

All this, however, was far from being specified in a clear and unambiguous manner in *The Court Society*. It could not have been otherwise. His personal involvement and the difficulties of the theme, related to the extent, depth and modality of the phenomenon which Elias set out to investigate, rendered the difficulties almost intractable.[11]

A breakthrough can be identified with a single reading experience. The event and its effects can be reconstructed partly from *The Civilizing Process* and partly from the 1984 autobiographical interview.

The Civilizing Process follows the line of thought already present in *The Court Society*, and Elias had continued to work along these lines during his time in Paris. However, according to his own account, the book only got off the ground in London, when he came across books on etiquette while browsing in the British Library (RL: 53–4). The first book he picked up was Courtin's 1672 work *Nouveau traité de civilité* (New treatise on civility), but it is evident from the text of *The Civilizing Process* that the central encounter was the 'older' text of Erasmus, *De civilitate morum puerilium* ('On civility in children'). This short book does not take up a pivotal role either in the history of books on manners (the work of Baldassare Castiglione, *The Book of the Courtier*, is much more famous) or in the intellectual biography of Erasmus. However, it connects the two threads of the humanistic-philosophical concern with education and the new emphasis on civility in the courts. It was written and published at a crucial moment of transition, the 1520s, which is singled out for attention in *The Court Society* (CS: 154). It acted, both in its time and for the work of Elias, as a mediator, an important step in the 'courtization of warriors'. The text and the person of Erasmus therefore serve the role of a 'historical individual' or a 'real ideal type' in *The Civilizing Process*.

The argument can be subsumed in a simple form by recalling the 'ideal type' that Elias was using at the start of *The Court Society*, the 'structure of dwellings'. One could say, paraphrasing both Weber and Elias, that the stamp giving coherence to the figuration of the court society was formed when the 'spirit' of civility epitomized by Erasmus was inserted into the 'form' of the institutionally-closed space of the court.

The effects of the reading experience are evidenced in the enormous speed at which Elias, so slow in writing before and after, managed to get the work done. It took hardly more than six months for Elias to put together, evidently, at least the first draft of a book running up to 800 pages, so his productivity was comparable to the enormous achievements of Weber in the 1911–13 period.

The central question of the book is the same as the one posed at the beginning of *The Court Society*: 'at a certain stage in the development of European societies individuals are bound together in the form of courts and thereby given a specific stamp. What held them together and what stamped them in just this way?' (CS: 39–40). But the way in which the material is organized shows how much better a control Elias had over his problem and theme in *The Civilizing Process* than in *The Court Society*. In the latter, Elias started with the internal, almost historicist, reconstruction of 'court society' as a game on its own, centring on etiquette and ceremony, with the dynamic part, the 'sociogenesis' of court society, only coming later. *The Civilizing Process*, however, starts not with a description and analysis of court society but with the model that gave its stamp.

The lasting stamp of *The Court Society*, the successful putting of the 'spirit' into a form, was due to a specific modality of circumstances. These were the conditions under which this 'spirit' emerged, formed and was consolidated. These conditions have both a spatial and a temporal aspect.

Space: closed institution

The central importance played by spatial arrangements in Elias's sociology is shown by the methodologically and strategically-central first chapter of *The Court Society*. This was devoted to a meticulous description and structural analysis of the court as an institutionally-closed dwelling place. But it also plays a central role in three key concepts of his theorization of power: visibility, interdependence and strategic games.

Visibility

Social life in a closed spatial environment is characterized by the omnipresence of appearance, manifestations and visibility. As the same human beings inhabit the same, relatively small and closed space, they continuously meet each other and conduct all their activities in front of the eyes of the others. As a result, the visible part of the most obvious, routine aspects of everyday conduct gains a special importance. The way in which one performs the simplest 'natural' functions, eats or drinks, behaves in the bedchamber or in the toilet, blows one's nose or spits, becomes problematic and requires a mode that first of all takes into account the presence of others.

Such a pervasive mutual presence exerts a strong homogenizing tendency, a 'functional democratization' (Mennell 1992: 109, 124–5), but also a search for distinction (CS: 62) and of maintaining appearance (CS: 67). In this way, the very fact of increased visibility becomes incorporated into the self-representation and functioning of this kind of society. The 'is' is thus transformed into a 'must'. Everything had to be manifested in order to count as real. In this way, the trivial scenery of the getting-up of the king became the location of an elaborate courtly ritual (CS: 83–4). Material wealth had to be represented, especially in the form of large houses, money had to be spent and not saved (CS: 63–5). According to the *Encyclopédie* 'it was necessary to design a court "which would indicate by its appearance the rank of the person who was to live there"' (CS: 81).

Ultimately, this had a fundamental consequence for the entire structure of thought and belief systems. As far as thought was concerned, under the conditions of omnipresent visibility, truth became identified with representation.[12] As for belief, the metaphor of the Sun King was a particularly revealing image. Given the reality of court society, '[i]n power that may exist but is not visible in the appearance of the ruler the people do not believe. They must see in order to believe' (CS: 118). Under such circumstances, the concept of divine presence or *parousia,* which is so central for Christianity, loses its meaning and is transformed into a secular demand for complete transparency and constant visibility. If Weber located the source of disenchantement or 'secularization', in the 'Protestant ethic', Elias excavated a complementary source in the 'courtly ethic'.

Such a use of words is not at all strained, as Elias frequently uses terms like 'courtly ethos' or the 'estate-ethos of court people' (CS: 102), linking them to a special type of court 'rationality', and opposing it to the Weberian professional-bourgeois ethos (CS: 64, 92). The central criterion of success in such a setting is not monetary success in the marketplace, but 'confirmation of one's value or an increase in respect in the eyes of others' (CS: 75). The key words are recognition or *reputation* (CS: 137). Under such conditions, membership of the 'good society', or the opinion that others had of an individual became the 'foundation of personal identity as of social existence' (CS: 94–5).

Interdependence

A second main consequence of living in an institutionally-closed space is interdependence. This concept is one of the most widely-used trademarks of Eliasian sociology, central to his attempt at transcending the conceptual separation and contrasting the 'individual' and 'society'. In *The Court Society,* in clear allusion to the Durkheimian concept of 'social fact', he stated that the 'conditions' that are assumed to exist outside individuals in fact 'are specific forms of mutual dependence between the individuals or, to use a technical term, specific interdependences' (CS: 142). In the *The Civilizing Process,* he specified as a focal point of his interest 'the dynamics of interdependencies', identifying as two sources of these tensions the state monopolies of physical violence and the private monopolies of economic means of production and consumption. Using a vivid and powerful metaphor he argued that ' *[b]oth together form the lock joining the chain by which men are mutually bound*' (CP: 514–5; emphasis in original). And it is this same picture of interdependence that ends the 'late Preface' to *The Established and the Outsiders*: 'The whole drama was played out by the two sides as if they were puppets on a string' (EO: lii).

The original insight launching the work of Elias was a perceived similarity between court society and modern society, while his central analytical question was how such a stamp could have been left on the very fabric of modernity. The system of interdependences, the 'lock' joining the 'chain', was a prime example of such a stamp. And *The Court Society* contains a passage in which the system of interdependences described in later works is rooted specifically in the court:

> Everyone within the chains of interdependence was concerned for reasons of prestige to ensure that others performed their steps according to precept. Thus everyone automatically controlled everyone else. Any 'stepping out of line' injured and disadvantaged others. It was therefore extremely difficult if not impossible for the individual to break out
>
> (CS: 131–2)

It was such a tight-knit circle that, in spite of its seeming omnipotence, even the absolutist king was profoundly entangled in it (CS: 139–40).

Thus, the high degree of interdependence characteristic of modernity carries the 'stamp' of a special kind of 'closed institution', the court society. However, in spite of repeatedly asserting this as his position, at other times Elias seemed to forget this and considered such interdependences as being either a general law of historical development (CP: 389), the product of population growth and density (CP: 286–92), or simply of the division of labour (CP: 113).[13]

Strategic games

The third consequence of institutionally-closed space is the importance of strategy and the omnipresence of strategic games. In a court society, everything is done in front of everyone else and every person in his/her behaviour and action depends on the others. This, however, does not only mean a mechanic performance of prescribed rituals. It also implies its opposite with the constant playing of strategic interpersonal games.

The court as a place of endless intrigues is well known from both historical and literary works. Elias brought to this a precise sociological analysis and contextualization. Individuals in a court society are not simply pawns in a game or personages in a scenario written in advance. They are very much actors on their own and this is part of the problem. They continuously, literally in every single moment of their life and with everything they do or say, play a strategic game of power with and against everybody else within the court. This specifies 'court "rationality"', as opposed to 'scientific rationality' or 'bourgeois rationality', which arises from 'the calculated planning of strategy in face of the possible gain or loss of status in the incessant competition for . . . power' (CS: 93).

This has a consequence with respect to the importance of power for court society, and for the theory of power in general. Power refers to something that happens directly between human beings. Economic relations of property, or cultural relations of knowledge can mediate power and are certainly not separable from relations of power, but they are not directly relations of power. In a court society, however, direct and naked relations of power do have precedence over all other relations; they are omnipresent and pervasive.

As Elias is quick to point out, this is not because of individual qualities or the coexistence of individuals with 'an unusually strong "urge to dominate"' (CS: 93), but is a consequence of the 'figuration' of the court society. Closeness and closedness forces individuals to compete incessantly with each other. This results in a continuous state of insecurity and uncertainty, '[t]he position a person held in the court hierarchy [being] therefore extremely unstable' (CS: 90–1):

> Life in court society was not peaceful. The number of people permanently and inescapably bound to one circle was large. They pressed on each other, struggled for prestige, for their place in the hierarchy. The affairs, intrigues, conflicts over rank and favour knew no end . . . There was no security.
>
> (CS: 104)

The expression of Hobbes, *homo homini lupus*, seems more appropriate for such a setting than it is for the 'state of nature'.

We know now that '[i]t is not possible for power to be exercised without knowledge', and 'it is impossible for knowledge not to engender power' (Foucault PK: 52), but the strategic games and intrigues of the court society required a very special type of knowledge. True scientific knowledge or sober bourgeois rationality had little value in these interpersonal games. What mattered was the knowledge of how human beings behave under various circumstances, and this was helped by a specific 'art of observing' people and of 'describing' them (CS: 104–6). Under the circumstances, the type of power exercised by the central authority, and the skills required, were also of a special kind. Outstanding abilities and the provision of far-seeing leadership were not among them. The paradigmatic ruler of a court society, Louis XIV, the Sun King, was quite mediocre in terms of individual qualities (CS: 126). His talent lay in the 'art' of balancing which was the basic skill required to run the machinery of the court: 'the king "divided and ruled". But he did not only divide. What we can observe in him is an (exact assessment of the power relationships at his court and a careful balancing of the tensions within it' (CS: 120). The king

was predisposed for his role, as he was indeed characterized by an incessant curiosity about all kinds of details from the personal life of people
around him (CS: 128–9).

The question now is the general relevance of this type of exercise of
power, especially the stamp it left on modern society. Elias certainly considered that his analysis of power in terms of interdependence,
competition, balancing and even the entire figuration of the 'court society'
had a model value:

> [w]hat is observed in court society has in this sense a paradigmatic
> value. It points to a social figuration that draws the individuals forming
> it into an especially intense and specialised competition for the power
> associated with status and privilege.
>
> (CS: 93)

What remains unclear, however, is whether this 'paradigmatic value' is
restricted to understanding the dynamics, the '*order* underlying historical
changes' (CP: xv) of modern society only, or is applicable to the study of all
human societies (about this, see WIS: 71–103); and whether this conceptualization of power with its emphasis on the role of each and every
individual within the figuration as an individual actor, instead of a conception of them as mere 'subjects', and its implication for 'functional
democratization', should be valued in positive terms.

This dilemma is very similar to the one posed by, or faced, by Foucault.
It is the exact relationship between the two main images of power dominating the reality and the self-understanding of modern society. There is
the closed and total institution on the one hand and the interaction of free
individuals on the other, limited only by the freedom of others. The value
of the analyses of Elias and Foucault lies in their efforts not to ignore the
specifically-modern Western ambivalence and tension between these
aspects, which leads to a one-sided Marxist or liberal position. However, it
happened even with them, either through 'forgetfulness' or methodological 'bracketing'. It happened for example when Elias generalized
interdependence or strategic games beyond the limits of the range and
stamp of a particular institutionally-closed society, and considered it as a
general characteristic of social life (see WIS: 134ff.). It also happened
when Foucault, in the early 1970s, conceived of power as the ever-present
and omnipotent force penetrating every angle of social life, and when in
his late works he came close to an idealization of relations of power as the
strategic games of free individuals (see EST: 300).

Combining the image of the Panopticon and the court society with
power conceptualized in terms of interdependence and relations of
strategy, it is possible to coin the concept 'strategification'. This means
that, instead of conceptualizing power relations in terms of strategic games
or systems of interdependence in a general sense, it is the course of

modern Western societies that can be characterized by the increasing *trans-formation* of human relations into relations of interdependent strategic games. Human beings in most societies are not simply interdependent, playing strategic games as free agents with their fellows. Neither do they constantly play roles according to the ranks of an etiquette. Most human relations are rather between human beings who know each other in personal terms, for good or ill, and whose relationship is structured by all sorts of interlocking links such as family, kinship, friendship, neighbourhood, etc. Such relations are part of a conventional order of things whose expression, save in extraordinary circumstances, does not require visible manifestation, and where the relationship between human beings is not reduced to the either/or of dependence or strategy, domination or being dominated. The transformation of everyday human relationships into relationships of strategy and therefore mobile relations of power, is one of the basic long-term processes characterizing the emergence of modern societies. This could only have happened through the stamp left on the entire civilization by the peculiar figuration of court society that has emerged in an institutionally-closed space at a particular moment of time.

The discussion of the dimension of space will be followed by that of time. However, before we move on to this, attention must be given to one of the central aspects of living in a closed space, the psychological dimension, or the impact of living under such spatial arrangements on the psychical make-up or *habitus* of human beings.

In the formation of a *habitus* focusing on self-control, Elias sometimes places emphasis on the mere fact of visibility, the continuous presence of others and the competition and pressure that is derived from it (CP: 507–8) which results in a fear of each from all (CP: 403–4). But he also discusses the specific normative investments in visibility and invisibility, related to the internalization of shame and repugnance, that lead to the development of individual shame-frontiers or embarrassment-thresholds (CP: 497). In one expression, Elias calls these techniques of conduct the apparatuses of moulding or stamping (*Prägungsapparatur*) which is a term very close to Foucault's concept of an 'apparatus' (*dispositif*) of sexuality (Dreyfus and Rabinow 1982: 120). The end result of these processes is a special type of 'social transformation', a 'change in psychological make-up [*Habitus*] known as "civilization"', resulting in a 'total reorganization of the social fabric' (CP: 447).

Elias sometimes identifies the possibility of such in-depth psychic transformations in general characteristics of human beings, in their 'extraordinarily malleable' character (CP: 480), though he also acknowledges that the changes of the personality structure characteristic of the civilizing process happen ' without the nature of human beings changing' (CP: 212). However, his historical studies gain their full meaning and relevance if these transformation are rooted in specific spatial and temporal coordinates as conditions of possibility: in the institutionally-closed spaces analysed in this section, and in periods of transition to be analysed in the next section.

Time: periods of transition

The figuration 'court society' received its coherent stamp not simply from considerations of institutionally-closed space but also because of the special type of time period in which it was formed: a time of transition. This is emphasized at the relevant points of both *The Court Society* and *The Civilizing Process*. In the former, the first historical chapter argues that the court society emerged in the fifteenth and sixteenth centuries as a transition from one balance of forces to another (CS: 154–8). In the latter, the central problematic of the first volume, 'Civilization as a Specific Transformation of Human Behaviour', is introduced by a chapter on the Renaissance which was a period characterized by the expression '[s]ociety was "in transition"' (CP: 57). The problem of transition and transitionality took up an important place in the 'Synopsis' as well (CP: 514–8).

The court emerged in a very special period of transition. It was a period of disintegration and collapse of order (CP: 282, 513), the loss of the previous unity due to the 'waning supremacy of the Church' (CP: 491, Author's note to translation).[14] Furthermore, the court itself epitomized this period of transition, since the court of the sixteenth century was itself transitional (CS: 158). This was true in more ways than one. The medieval court had a very unique characteristic: they were peripatetic, travelling courts without fixed locations. While in most kingdoms and empires the goods were collected and brought to the centre, here the king travelled with his entire court from place to place so as to wield justice and consume his income. This practice only disappeared in the sixteenth century with the last great royal '*tour de France*' taking place in 1564–6 (Boutier *et al.* 1984).[15]

Such an emphasis on periods of transition as basic but always relative starting points of historical analysis (depending on the perspective of the problem) has central methodological implication. Elias keeps emphasizing that there are no zero points in history (CP: 480, GE 19). The task of historical sociology, with its concern with the present, is to go back in time and find the particular period of transition which, with respect to the problem posed, has particular relevance in the sense of having created the figuration that left a lasting stamp on the present. Thus, for example, it is from the perspective of the 'tendency to control the monopoly centres' that Elias talks about the period of absolutism as '[t]he first great transitional phase of this kind' (CP: 516).

A study of periods of transition and their stamping impact is all the more important because, according to Elias, from a long-term perspective '[w]e are ourselves now in the midst of such a transformation' (CP: 309). This leads to the recognition that 'our epoch is anything but a final point or pinnacle', but one of 'structurally similar transitional periods', which is 'full of unresolved tensions' and 'unconcluded processes of integration' (CP: 523). Such a self-understanding gives clear insight and helps to put things in perspective: '[p]eriods like this, periods of transition, give a particular opportunity for reflection: the older standards have been called into question but solid new ones are not yet available' (CP: 517–8). Though Elias wrote these words in the late 1930s, they are still relevant today.[16] They also reveal the tight analogy between periods of transition and liminal situations, as the words used by Elias quoted above are for all purposes identical to Turner's description of liminality.

Just as institutionally-closed space has important psychological repercussions, leaving a stamp on *habitus* or the structure of personality, so do periods of transition. Such periods are characterized by an experience of alienation in which individuals develop a feeling 'that their existence is separated from the rest of the world', leaving them uncertain about reality itself and leading them to pose 'the question of the relationship of reality and illusion'. 'This uncertainty, the doubt concerning the relation of reality and illusion, pervades the whole period' (CS: 250–2). As a result, there is the perception of a wide gap between the inside and the outside of human beings, leading to the image of the 'shell' of the 'inner self' as the only thing in whose reality one cannot doubt (CS: 253–6, CP: 206–13).[17]

If institutionally-closed space leads to pervasive visibility and the strategification of all human relationships and undermines belief, trust and innocence, the similarly pervasive feelings of doubt and uncertainty produced by periods of transition create disturbance about the counter-concepts of innocence and guilt as 'people who live in the midst of such tensions . . . are thus driven guiltlessly to incur guilt upon guilt against each other' (CP: 522). And if the psychic impact of closed institutions has been further elaborated by Foucault, the study of the psychical pressure produced by periods of transition was central to the work of Borkenau.[18]

Elias continued his argument about the psychological impact of space and time in a section entitled 'The Muting of Drives: Psychologization and Rationalization' of the 'Synopsis' (CP: 475–92). As the title indicates, this is put into the form of a dialogue with Weber.

The section starts with a quote from La Bruyère on 'life at court' which repeats the central terms and concerns of Elias's analysis: game and plan, risk and play, a life of mutual interdependence and endless strategic games, with individuals constantly forming alliances and cliques whose membership keeps changing all the time (CP: 475). Under such conditions, individuals must continuously watch everybody else and cannot avoid lapses in self-control. 'Every mistake, every careless step depresses the value of its perpetrator in courtly opinion; it may threaten his whole position at court' (CP: 476). Thus, civilized behaviour emerges as the almost natural end result of this figuration; and similar changes would follow at the level of knowledge, with the '"world picture" [*Weltbild*]' becoming less based on "wishes and fears", and more on '"experience" or "the empirical"' (CP: 478).

These short passages contain the entire theory of the civilizing process in a nutshell. The section continues with some of Elias's most concise and pertinent formulations as far as the substance and method of his argument are concerned. It locates the Weberian concern with rationalization on the horizon of *The Civilizing Process*. According to Elias, the 'historical process of rationalization' has not yet been properly analysed, as it belongs 'to a science that does not yet exist, historical psychology' (CP: 484). This is because 'rationalization' does not pertain merely to matters of thought and is neither to be associated merely with the bourgeoisie:

> What is rationalized is, primarily, the modes of conduct of certain groups of people. "Rationalization" is nothing other . . . than an expression of the direction in which the moulding of people [*Gepräge der Menschen*] in specific social figurations is changed during this period.
>
> (CP: 490)

The formulation clearly targets Weberian sociology. It is, however, valid only in so far as 'Weberian sociology' (Scaff 1984) and not Weber's sociology is concerned. This is because following the reconstruction of Hennis (1988), Weber's concern was exactly the rationalization of the conduct of life and its impact on the quality of being human. The quote of Elias given above could have been come from the beginning of the *Einleitung*, where Weber defined his aim as an:

> attempt to peel off the directive elements in the life-conduct of those social strata which have most strongly influenced the practical ethic of their respective religions. These elements have stamped the most characteristic features upon practical ethics.
>
> (FMW: 268)

One of the most important of these elements was the 'various religious or magical states that have given their psychological stamp to religions' (FMW: 279).

The section also contains a joint definition of the key methodological terms 'psychogenesis' and 'sociogenesis'. The terms are introduced to overcome the dichotomy and opposition between 'society' and 'ideas', where:

> [t]hose concerned with the history of society, like those concerned with the history of mind, perceive 'society' on the one hand and the world of 'ideas' on the other as two different formations that can be meaningfully separated . . . some say that it is society-less ideas which set society in motion, and the others that it is an idea-less society that moves 'ideas'.
>
> (CP: 484–5)[19]

Elias is concerned here only with a special aspect of mental processes:

> Civilization, and therefore rationalization, for example, is not a process within a separate sphere of 'ideas' or 'thought'. It does not involve solely changes of 'knowledge', transformations of 'ideologies', in short alterations of the *content* of consciousness, but changes in the whole human make-up [*Habitus*]
>
> (CP: 485)[20]

Elias considered 'psychologization' and 'rationalization' as processes developing together since the sixteenth century (CP: 479). However, he did not do full justice to Weber's position. Weber certainly put less emphasis on emotional factors than Elias. But psychological factors did play a central role in Weber's argument as, following Nietzsche, he emphasized psychological *sanctions* (PE: 97) and not the element of dogma in the doctrine of predestination. This was pointed out in the previous chapter.

It is true that for Weber, the primary source of anxiety lay not in a closed spatial arrangement, nor in a period of transition, but in the closure provided by a certain frame of mind, mentality or world image. The 'closed self' of the 'iron casing' of Weber was more a derivative of a 'closed mind'. However, even from the Weberian perspective, spatial arrangements and a common life had their role, which was emphasized by Weber through his study of a particular type of closed community, the sect. The sect of Weber, the court of Elias, the prison of Foucault and the monastery of Borkenau all question the liberal self-understanding of modernity as developing out of the free exchange of goods at the marketplace and of ideas in the public sphere on the one hand, and out of the heroic struggles of the free city and its citizens against the abusive nobility and the absolutist state on the other. Without denying the importance of freedom, they point out the crucial role played by closed institutions in the stamping of modernity at a critical time juncture.

Here as elsewhere, and just like another of his contemporaries, John Maynard Keynes, who completed his great work contemporaneously, Elias asks us to undergo 'a suspension of the habits of thinking with which we have grown up'.[21] Instead of conceiving of 'historical rationalization' as merely a matter of unconnected individuals getting into touch with each other and searching for 'understanding' or 'reason', '[w]hat changes is the way in which people are bonded to each other. This is why their behaviour changes, and why their consciousness and their drive-economy, and, in fact, their personality structure as a whole, change' (CP: 480). Terms like 'reason', 'ratio' or 'understanding' should not be reified, as they do not exist outside 'socio-historical change' and only express 'a particular moulding of the whole personality [*Modellierung des ganzen Seelenhaushalts*]' (ibid.).

The consequences of changes that are so deep and wide, that cover

minute details of everyday life and the very structure of personality, however, are all-encompassing: 'It is not without reason that we speak of an *age*
of absolutism. What finds expression in this change in the form of political
rule is a structural change in Western society as a whole' (CP: 266).[22] What
has happened in the West in the past also presents itself as an insur-
mountable task for the other countries of the globe as well as 'the
transformation of the whole of social existence is the basic condition of the
civilization of conduct' (CP: 462).

Conclusion: ritualization and permanent liminality

The target of Elias's work is to reconstruct the court society and analyse the
conditions of its emergence, as '[t]he moment of consolidation, the point
of social development reached at the inception of a regime . . . has a deter-
mining influence on its specific form and its subsequent fate' (CS: 146).
However, in order to assess the lasting stamp this figuration gave to
modern society, one must turn to the other end of the process and
examine the facts and reasons for its collapse.

Throughout his writings, Elias emphasizes that historical change is neither random nor predetermined but ordered (CP: xv); there is a 'strict
order of socio-historical *transformations*' (CP: 287; see also 443). This takes
the form of a 'processual succession where an event cannot come into
being if another, earlier, event has not come into being before' (ST: 1). It
even has a direction (CP: xii, 202, 517). This applies to the path the court
society followed. However, this had a puzzling and quite unique feature.
The internal dynamics of this figuration propelled two opposite kinds of
changes: rigidification, ossification and petrification on the one side and
continuous, frenetic movement on the other.

The former is due to the increasing ritualization of conduct which is
characteristic of courts of all ages. The omnipresent visibility of the court
and its valorization lead to the emergence of court etiquette. In fact,
according to Elias, in a 'court society' etiquette became an end in itself, as
'*[i]n it court society represents itself, each individual being distinguished from every
other, all together distinguishing themselves from non-members, so that each individual and the group as a whole confirm their existence as a value in itself*' (CS:
103; emphasis in original). In etiquette, every single position and possible
move is specified in advance, leaving nothing to chance and individual ini-
tiative. As a result, every act acquires a fetish character (CS: 85). While in
the time of Louis XIV, etiquette was still close to primary functions, with
the passage of time individuals became enmeshed in it and it undermined
their dignity. 'Etiquette and ceremony increasingly became . . . a ghostly
perpetuum mobile that continued to operate regardless of any direct use-
value' (CS: 86). In this way, the personal power characteristic of the court
(CS: 1) turned, by the internal logic of its development, to its opposite and
became a drive to impersonalization (CS: 139–40).

What was true in the smaller scale of court etiquette also holds true for the entire social order. In the last chapter of the work, Elias gives a socio-genetic account on the origin of the French Revolution using this type of explanation. While in the time of Louis XIV the 'Royal Mechanism', as Elias would later call it (CP: 390), was still flexible, in the time of Louis XVI 'the basic features of the structure were still the same but . . . it had become frozen' (CS: 272). This gives a paradigmatic figuration of ruling elites caught in a trap with everybody keeping watch over everyone else, and 'as every reform of the regime threatened the existing privileges and power of one elite in relation to another, no reform was possible'. The figuration became 'petrified'. To summarize, the situation outlined earlier concerning 'the development of court ceremony' is repeated on a larger scale (CS: 273).

Petrified ritualization, however, was only one of the ways in which the movement of the spirit which had closed into the figuration of court society reached its logical conclusion. The other side was its exact opposite, with frenetic activity and an ever intensifying spiral of change.

This possibility is already alluded to in the quote used above, the 'ghostly *perpetuum mobile*'. While etiquette froze the endless strategic games in the court into a fixed scenario and rank order, the strategification of society and the mentality of endless strategic games could survive and even strive outside and beyond the limits set by a court society, like a spirit lib-erated from the bottle. The stamp of court society at the heart of the present is not restricted to forms of polite conduct but extends to the cen-tral mechanism of power. This is what Elias argues in the concluding section of the Synopsis:

> Today these states in turn form analogous power balances of freely competing survival units. These states too, under the pressure of the tensions of competition that keep our whole society in a perpetual ferment of conflicts and crises, are now in their turn gradually being forced more and more clearly into mutual opposition . . . [as they] force each other in an incessant spiral to extend and strengthen their power . . . [which is bound to] embrac[e] the entire inhabited earth.
>
> (CP: 514)

Such an incessant spiral of warfare, recalling Voegelin's ideas about the concupiscence of imperial conquest in the ecumenic age (OHIV) or Mumford's concern with the modern megamachines (MMII: 266), was already present in the absolutist states, but the scope of dynastic wars was still restricted. In the twentieth century, this became extended, first in the form of world wars, and then in the mutated and muted form of economic globalization. In this latter process the fermentation of technological innovation and economic competitiveness, just as in the past, goes hand in hand with the increased legal petrification and the image of a 'blocked society' (Crozier).

These two opposite tendencies, towards freezing into ritualization on the one hand, and towards escalation into permanent fermentation on the other, help us to return to Elias's dual concerns, the puzzle between civilization and violence. They both give an interpretation and provide a theoretical framework. From the perspective of the dual dynamism of court society, the existence of two opposing tendencies is no longer puzzling. The interdependence of people living in an institutionally-closed space forces them to adopt strict forms, precise and well-enforced laws, polite manners of interaction and clear hierarchies and ranks. The pressure of incessant visibility, distinction and competition keeps the entire figuration in permanent fermentation and motion, and stimulates and unleashes energies which are bound to burst to the surface in the cracks developing in the systems of law and civility. In the figuration stamped by the 'court society', 'civility' and 'violence' are not at all opposed but are two sides of the same coin. They are interdependent outcomes of the same processes, which can ultimately be traced back to the emergence of a type of institutionally-closed space as a response to a situation of crisis and transition which has been produced by the collapse of the previously assumed system of world order.

The coexistence of these two opposing forces can be explained in an anthropological framework that at the same time provides a precise conceptualization of the situation of perpetual ferment of conflicts and crises. This in itself should come as no surprise, as rituals and ceremonies have been the central interests of anthropologists for a long time. However, as Victor Turner came to realize in the 1950s, the classical conceptualization of rituals in terms of functions and social organization proved to be deficient when measured against the actual practice of small-scale tribes (E. Turner 1985: 4–5). He had to go beyond the ingrained habits of thought, rely on his earlier education and even childhood experiences, and come up with the concept of social drama. In the language which he came to develop in the 1960s and 1970s, rituals must be understood in terms of liminality.

Liminal situations, however, whether they occur in individual initiation rites or in collective rituals, are only temporary. Once the ritual is over and the masks are taken down, the suspended conditions are terminated, the social order is restored and everybody returns home. There is no danger of a ritual of getting stale or petrified.

However, for our society and for most 'high civilizations', rituals do evoke an association of lifelessness, 'mechanized petrification' (PE: 182) and ceremonies are associated with courts as the centres of these civilizations. The court is the place in which everybody incessantly plays roles and takes part in elaborate rituals. The corollary is that courts lead a paradoxical existence because they are stuck in a permanent state of liminality.

This point and its implications, however, will be elaborated later in the Conclusion of Part II.

7   The mechanical world image (Borkenau)

Borkenau is usually considered a Marxist, a peripheral member of the Frankfurt *Institut für Sozialforschung* known as the Frankfurt School. However, this common view is open to question. His major 1934 book was indeed published in the *Institut* series. The title and some of its terminology are also unmistakably Marxist. Yet, even in this book, the sincerity of Borkenau's Marxist commitments is doubtful. The movement away from Communist orthodoxy which he started in the late 1920s was still progressing. The book is shaped partly by this shifting involvement and partly by the duty and obligation to conform to the requirements of the *Institut*. The dilemma whether Borkenau was using Marxist concepts in his book as a mere decoy, or whether the ambiguities of the book reflect his genuinely ambivalent status is probably impossible to solve and is not very relevant. He was certainly in a delicate situation in more ways than one, and attempted to make compromises. The results were mixed and no doubt contributed to the problems of reception. For Marxists, *Transition* failed to step in line with the creed and, for non-Marxists, its terminology looked prohibitive.

The book, however, becomes intelligible if placed alongside Weber. The discussion on *The Protestant Ethic* is certainly at a strategic point in the book. It is in the crucial Chapter Four, just after the background historical chapters on the concepts 'natural law', 'natural right' and 'social contract', and before the four main substantive chapters discussing Descartes, Gassendi, Hobbes and Pascal. Within the chapter, it is after the introductory section which interprets the Renaissance as being the result of the dissolution of the medieval world order, and before the third section which introduces a central concept, the 'gentry'. But Borkenau also clearly emphasized the importance of Weber for his work when he stated that Weber's thesis is an example 'of the transformations through which Marxist insights entered in non-Marxist science' (UFB: 154). This reference to Weber summarizes the ambivalence of his position. In actual words, the statement hardly even makes sense because Weber's thesis was certainly developed in opposition to the position of Marx. Yet, in spirit, Borkenau correctly guessed the genuine impact that Marx's ideas had on Weber's work.

As with Elias, Borkenau's strong reliance on Weber can be shown in the central problematic, in the method followed and in its terminology.

In terms of the problematics, Borkenau took up the other part of Weber's hint contained in the 'Anticritical Last Word' in his 1934 book, and thus either deliberately or accidentally complemented Elias's work. From the passages quoted above, Borkenau's project can be paraphrased through Weber's words as being concerned with the '*mechanization* of technology', 'the creation and diffusion of the rationalist and anti-traditionalist "spirit"', and the project of a 'history of modern science' (Weber 1978 [1910]: 1128–9).

Borkenau wanted to take up this problem in the spirit of Weber. His aim was not to write the heroic story of the birth of modern science. In fact, he was diametrically opposed to the Enlightenment's ideal of progress (UFB: 15). On the contrary, it was to go beyond the familiar, the seeming universality of the mathematical-mechanistic world image of modern natural science (ibid.: v) which seems to lie beyond questions because we live inside it (ibid.: 21) and to study the 'specific historical conditions' that led its birth (ibid.: vi). Just as Weber emphasized the spiritual component as a central part of the conditions out of which the spirit of capitalism emerged, Borkenau similarly posited the joint emergence of modern philosophy and the mathematical-mechanistic world image as his problem. He argued that modern philosophy and its anthropological assumptions were not simple corollaries of modern science but were, on the contrary, the spiritual-anthropological context out of which the modern mathematical-mechanistic world image grew.

The critical point in the emergence of the modern era, according to Borkenau, was the collapse of the medieval world order (ibid.: 95, 97, 152, 158). In contrast to Weber, Borkenau did not conceive this as the outcome of heroic struggles against the forces of tradition. On the contrary, he argued that those undergoing the changes lived them as the collapse of the order and meaning of their lives. This was accompanied by heightened feelings of anxiety, uncertainty and alienation. These feelings reached their height in the seventeenth century, which became known as a 'terrifying century' which was marked by the image of a 'terrible god', as 'no other god has ever spread such a total existential terror than the *deus absconditus* of the Puritans and the Jansenists' (ibid.: xii). In this century, as shown in the dramas of Racine, passion as such was condemned, as it could only lead 'to the abyss of irrevocable damnation' (ibid.). But at the same time, '[i]n the terrestrial inferno of this period were born those powerful thinkers who, with the same fervour as the Puritan *godlys*, posed themselves the problem of giving meaning to a terrifying life' (ibid.).

However, a 'basic fact of the human will [is] its *horror vacui*' (Nietzsche 1967a: 97). The void created by the dissolution of the medieval order was soon filled by two new types of order: the economic life of capitalism at the level of mass morality, and the order of the self or the soul at the level of upper class ethics.

Had Borkenau been a genuine Marxist when writing the book, this would have been the occasion to assert that the dying feudal mode of production had been superseded, after a period of transition, by the victorious capitalist mode of production. There is, however, nothing of the sort proposed. Far from drawing on Marx, Borkenau's argument is rather allied with Weber and Elias. As far as capitalism is concerned, he refers to Weber and his ideas on asceticism as a solution to the problem of mass morality. As to the upper classes, the direct allusion is to Dilthey but the terminology used shows a striking similarity to Elias's. He argues that with the collapse of the society of estates 'emerges the problem of how the individual, once uprooted, has to conduct himself in front of the new life' (UFB: 152).

These short passages at the start of Chapter Four contain the thesis of the book in a nutshell. Appearing in a section on Renaissance, they could be interpreted as a concern restricted to Florentine capitalism, or to 'Renaissance self-fashioning' (Greenblatt 1980). They give, however, an opportunity to resurrect the entire map that Borkenau was presenting of the broken pieces of the medieval world order.

The collapse of the medieval world order was not lived as a transition to capitalism, but as a period of uncertainty and existential terror. Far from being a necessary outcome of historical laws, modern capitalism was rather rendered possible by the kind of answers that were given to this unsettling situation. Among these, the central component, according to Borkenau, and the basis not only of capitalism but also of the modern state and the mechanistic world image, was the valorized interpretation given of this state of uncertainty.

This had two elements. The first was a general diagnosis of the situation, beyond the individual experience of anxiety. All the main religious, philosophical and political currents of thought of the period agreed about the corruptness of the age. But beyond this diagnosis of the 'situation', the most influential thinkers of the period of all persuasions, whether Calvinist or Jesuit, stoic or libertine, generalized their own experiences under the stress of acute stress and anxiety.[1] These experiences were variously described as a stark picture of 'the corruptness (*Verderbtheit*) of the world and men' (UFB: 159), the 'radical depravity of the world' (ibid.: 162; see also Borkenau [1987 [1932]: 116), the 'bad' and 'evil' character of the world that is external to the spirit (UFB: 181); the 'corruption of man', of the 'world' and of 'nature' (UFB: 196–7, 205, 253; see also Borkenau 1985 [1936]: 104). It all led to a loss of faith in the established forms of knowledge and implied not simply doubt but outright despair (UFB: 269). According to Borkenau, it was out of this spirit and not just the spirit of Christian asceticism that the entire modern world picture, beyond the spirit of capitalism, was formed. This happened because the very irrationality of a world of unlimited competition gave force to 'a given stratum to renew its life' (ibid.:162). In this way, Borkenau went further in the direction in which Weber overcame Nietzsche's rash criticism of

Christianity, though he retained more of Nietzsche's interest in the valorization of existence than Weber.

In order to present his argument, the different religious, philosophical and political segments which comprise the many pieces of the broken medieval world picture must be presented separately.

Spirituality (religion and philosophy)

In the field of religion, the collapse of world order led to the re-problematization of the main components of Christian dogma. Among this, a central place was occupied by the 'debate about the relation between the reprobation following the fall and the salvation by grace and merit' (EB: 288).[2] At stake was not simply the Protestant rejection of the institutionalized medieval solutions to these issues of confession and monasticism, but the broken link and lost balance between all the different aspects.

This is best illustrated in the polarization of views about the relative importance of grace and works for salvation. On the one hand, in the writings of Luther and especially Calvin, there was a return to the dogma of predestination and the rejection of the contribution of human efforts to salvation. On the other hand, there was a resurrection of interest in neo-Platonism and Stoicism. A new self-divinization of man coincided, just as in the axial age or in the first centuries BC, with assertions about the evil character of human nature.

However, both the religious and philosophical threads brought forward something new beyond the return to the old. As far as predestination is concerned, the utter corruption and depravity of man emphasized by Calvin went way beyond anything Paul or Augustinus would have said. The conviction of Luther and Calvin that 'the original sin corrupted man up to the last fibre' (UFB: 166) carried the possibility contained in the concept of predestination in the context of an obsession with salvation to the extreme logical conclusion. On the philosophical side, both the divinization of man characteristic of Renaissance neo-Platonists like Ficino, and the neo-Stoic presentation of the world as a hopeless place, were more excessive than the views presented by Platonists and Stoics in earlier periods.

If Calvinism and the neo-Stoicism of Lipsius had only been extreme versions of Augustinian predestination and stoic withdrawal, they would have remained extremist fringe movements, without any real effect. However, instead of complete disinvolvement and a wait for the last judgement, they went on to work in the world and to transform the world even more intensely than their predecessors. This, according to Borkenau, was the central difference between the 'old' and the 'new' Stoicism (ibid.: 181, 186). And similarly, while Calvinism was based on the one hand on a complete separation between grace and works for salvation, it found a way to connect the two in its concept of proof and the moral rigorism that ensued. Both these points would have consequences of utmost importance for the character of the emerging modern society.

While taking Weber's *The Protestant Ethic* as its starting point, Borkenau makes two objections to the work. According to him, Weber put too much emphasis on the mature seventeenth-century works of Protestantism and overlooked earlier texts. This may have contributed to his overlooking the connection between the rise of Protestantism and the dissolution of the feudal world (ibid.: 158). But Borkenau also claims that Weber over-stressed the dogma of predestination, while neglecting the concern with proof and moral rigorism. In contrast to the previous point, this does less justice to Weber's argument.

Apart from extremist religious and philosophical positions, the imbalances due to the experience of living in an age of dissolution of order also produced serious mental disturbances.[3] This led to a loss of the power and sense of judgement that was conceptualized in Christian doctrine as 'spiritual discernment' or *diacrisis*.[4] This issue was central in the early centuries AD, faded during the Middle Ages and was picked up again with particular strength by the Jesuits (Mittendorfer 1998). A passage quoted by Borkenau from Charron makes the point with particular clarity, though again couched in universalistic language: 'The errors are received in our soul by the same routes and manners as the truth. The spirit does not have the means to distinguish them and chose' (UFB: 196). And it was exactly in this period of weakening powers of discernment and judgement that spirituality became identified with extrasensory perception and miracles and was subjected to unprecedented attacks by the libertines (ibid.: 203–4).

In this book, taking the collapse of the medieval world order as the starting point of his analysis, Borkenau emphasized the uniqueness of the situation. However, all this was not very novel. The chaotic conditions of the sixteenth century were quite close to those of the first century AD which was the time of Nero and Caligula and the period in which Paul lived, and of the fifth century AD which was the time of the barbarian invasions, the collapse of the Roman Empire and the times of Augustinus. The similarities can be seen with particular clarity in the resurrection of the debate concerning Pelagianism and Gnosticism. Borkenau himself came to realize this in his later work, where the focus was shifted to the first centuries of our era and especially the collapse of the Roman Empire. The work of Pelagius would be a central theme in the book owing to the three-fold connections Borkenau envisioned 'between Pelagianism and the origins of Western civilization' (EB: 294).

Social forces

The analysis so far has been restricted to the level of religious and philosophical ideas. However, as expected Borkenau brought into the picture the Marxian concerns with class and class struggles, though in his own way. Marx considered class struggle as the engine behind the dynamics of history. In the theoretical framework of the book, which was inspired by Huizinga, class struggles, far from being external factors or independent variables, are seen as the consequences of specific types of situations of crisis, of which a collapse of the existing order of things is of special importance.

Borkenau assigned every one of the spiritual positions outlined above to a particular social group. Each of these groups is handled not only as a social class but as a segment of the broken medieval order. Additionally, it is the dynamic trajectory of these groups that is relevant, not simply their position within the social structure. This was especially because, in an age of dissolution of order and transition, the stable structural characteristics are undermined.

Unlike Weber, Borkenau assigns Calvinism not to the bourgeoisie but to the artisans and petty nobility, and therefore to social groups which were downwardly mobile, threatened by the emerging new order of large-scale production and state or political capitalism. On the other hand their main opponents, the Jesuits and the libertines, were attached to the court.

Borkenau's most important related idea was connected to his most severe blunder, the concept of the 'gentry'. It is introduced in section three of Chapter Four, at a strategic location, just after the discussion of the Weber thesis and just before the series of individual thinkers discussed which starts with Lipsius. The underlying idea is novel and brilliant, and an original development of the theory of class which is still fresh even today, advancing the ideas of Eric Olin Wright about contradictory class positions (1997). According to Borkenau, the most important philosophical ideas underpinning the modern world image were developed not simply by the bourgeoisie, but by a special intermediate or in-between class.

This class was composed of people whose standing and influence was owing to their capital, but who also enjoyed feudal privileges (UFB: 172). As a result, the social position of this group was ambivalent and dual-faceted. On the one hand, they were the highest sections of the bourgeoisie, but on the other, 'they were perhaps the only population group saved from the necessity of facing an ever more diffuse and almost unlimited competitive capitalistic struggles' (ibid.: 176). The most characteristic members of this group were the *noblesse de robe*. The group was the strongest in France and in Belgium, owing partly to the weakness of Calvinism there and partly to the incorporation of the 'rebel nobility' into the court. As a consequence, the development of capitalism there assumed a strongly '*étatist*' character.

This analysis represents one of the strongest parallels between the works of Elias, especially *The Court Society*, and Borkenau. The social group identified here by Borkenau is the same as the one Elias called 'dual front classes'. However, Borkenau committed a fatal error by calling this group 'gentry'.

The choice was unfortunate and self-defeating. In economic history, the term is reserved for a part of the land-owning class that introduced rational farming practices and thus was socially rising (Hexter 1961). It thus had the opposite meaning of Borkenau's. This has been immediately singled out by critics, not only Grossman but also Febvre who was puzzled by the term in his otherwise extremely positive evaluation (Febvre 1962 [1934]: 7). As a result, Borkenau and Elias abandoned their interest in 'in-between classes', which was a major loss for the sociology of classes.

However, though the terminology was misleading, it was not accidental and it sheds some further light on Borkenau's intellectual background. There was indeed a country where the '*noblesse de robe*' was called 'gentry' and that was Hungary. It was in the 1870s that the word was brought into Hungarian, and enjoyed a sudden, spectacular vogue, inexplicable in the context of the original meaning of the English term (Hanák 1975: 363–4). It denoted a segment of the nobility that was the main supporter of the 1848–9 independence fight against Austria, but that lost its economic and social position as a result of the abolition of serfdom in 1848. Its members had to join the state bureaucracy in order to maintain their living standards. As a result, they had divided loyalties or 'two souls': they were loyal supporters of the existing order, but at the same time they also wanted to be a radical opposition. It was out of this situation that Borkenau developed his concept.

Borkenau argued that the gentry emerged only in countries where the development of capitalism could not be based on a strong spirit of capitalism promoted by Calvinism and therefore it became problematic. This problematicity had an intellectual and a political angle. Intellectually, the most important developments of modern philosophy, according to Borkenau, took place in non-Calvinist countries and among members of the gentry.

These thinkers, however, were also strongly involved in politics. The main opponents of the gentry were the court and its spiritual supporters, the Jesuits. This entailed the strong involvement of philosophers and intellectuals in political intrigues and secret clubs.[5]

Though not neglecting the political angle, the central focus of the book was the emergence of the modern world image. In this, Borkenau attributes a major role to four thinkers; Lipsius, Descartes, Gassendi and Pascal.[6]

Lipsius

Justus Lipsius was the main figure of neo-stoicism which, along with Dilthey, Borkenau considered as the first modern philosophy. On the basis of his interpretation, neo-stoicism could be called a secular version of Calvinism. Like Calvin, and in contrast to the classical Stoics, Lipsius did not simply consider the world as radically corrupt but argued that the body was doing positive harm to the soul (UFB: 184–5). Under the impact of passions, man is inexorably driven to egoism (ibid.: 188–9). The central virtues of the stoic sage thus became not simply wisdom and judgement, but outright constancy and the 'indiscriminate' resistance to all passions. The stoic had to fit himself into the world, but only to transform it by opposition to it. His attitude was a variant of 'inner-worldly asceticism', in the service of what could be called a 'philosophical rejection of the world'.

Instead of the psychological sanction of predestination and its proofs, Lipsius recommended a very different kind of sanction by the purification of passions through the actions of the magistrates.

In a particularly striking characterization, Borkenau claims that the 'moral norms of acting without any affects (*affektlosen Handelns*) as developed by Lipsius . . . are constitutive elements of a capitalistic art of living (*Lebenskunst*)' (ibid.: 190). The withdrawal and pure rationality of the sage, however, were not conducive to the development of a mass morality and thus, according to Borkenau, Lipsius had little effect.[7]

Descartes

By far the longest chapter of the book is devoted to Descartes. This is clearly the centrepiece of Borkenau's analysis as, according to him, it was Descartes who laid down the philosophical basis of the modern mathematical-mechanistic world image. Within the limits of this chapter, it is impossible to do full justice to the argument and therefore only a few relevant points will be presented.

The way in which Borkenau went beyond the traditional method of the history of ideas is best illustrated in this chapter. The treatment of Descartes is both experiential and biographical. According to Borkenau, as a son of a councillor of the Parliament in Rennes and a grandson of a *lieutenant général du présidial* in Poitiers, Descartes was a figure of the 'gentry' *par excellence* (ibid.: 269–70). But he was also a son of his age.

The fundamental background experience of Descartes was the same as the neo-stoic and Calvinist experience of alienation (ibid.: 298–9) or the 'alienness between world and soul' (*die Fremdheit von Welt und Seele*) (ibid.: 302). The link between man and nature, between the body and the soul, had been severed. However, Descartes gave himself the task of reconstructing this link, a task which was radically different from that of Lipsius or Calvin. He was able to do so thanks to a personality trait and intellectual hubris which, taking cues from Voegelin (OHIV: 48, 57, 260; see also Chapter 8, below) and like his basic life-experience that was characteristic of the age, could be described as 'gnostic'. He was convinced that he was the most intelligent of men (UFB: 272).

It was on the basis of these feelings and convictions that he started his quest. It was special as it was a search for the key to knowledge. In this quest, he made acquaintance with hermetic intellectual circles, including the Rosicrucians (ibid.: 281), but was troubled by persistent feelings of anxiety and doubt (ibid.: 282).

This was the context of his famous dreams. For Borkenau, this episode is not just a piece of intellectual curiosity but is of the utmost theoretical importance. The dreams, and especially the interpretation Descartes gave them, were not simply a dramatization of his discovery but had the character of a profound mystic experience. They convinced him that he was on the right track, and that his search for the truth through the otherwise 'Luciferian' road of doubt had a divine approbation.

The consequence was a radical revaluation of the experience of alienation which was rooted in the dissolution of the established order of things. The externality of man to nature or nature to man, and the radical separation between the soul and the body, were experienced as tragic and fateful, and provoked profound pessimism, However, it was here that Descartes discovered, or rather posited, a source of optimism. It is true that nature is external to man and the body is external to the soul. But these external, sensible, given things also follow certain fixed regularities and have their natural laws. It is exactly these external regularities that provide the key for man's own self-understanding. The 'optimistic turn' of Descartes 'derives from his conviction that the laws constitutive of an alien nature, external to man, nevertheless in the last analysis realize the proper essence of man' (UFB: 307). Thus, the experience of extraneity and alienation were far from being the tragic events they were supposed to be and were in fact the sources of the real, 'scientific' self-understanding of man. Therefore the road of self-doubt, far from leading to damnation, is rather the key to truth and to salvation through true knowledge. In this way, Descartes accomplished a genuine revaluation of values.

Thus in a case of literal *deus ex machina*, the paradoxes of the stoics were solved. As both the growth of human knowledge and the knowledge of God are unlimited, 'we may arrive at the extravagance of wishing to be God' (UFB: 326–7); and even though God could not be directly, internally experienced, this can be deduced intellectually (ibid.: 330–1). In this way, Borkenau found in Descartes's philosophy the point where the normative and causal conceptualizations of natural law became identical. Ultimately, Descartes's philosophy was based on a faith which was a faith 'in the possibility of finding the way of happiness through knowledge only' (ibid.: 382). In the language of Voegelin, this could be called a modern gnostic position.

Gassendi

Out of the four thinkers discussed in Chapters Five to Eight which is the main body of the book, Gassendi is the least known, particularly in comparison with Descartes, Hobbes and Pascal. Yet, this chapter has a central place in the composition of the book. Contrary to Descartes's boundless faith in the powers of the intellect (especially his own), Gassendi presents sceptical arguments on its fallibility. In emphasizing the importance of 'criterion', he also returns, beyond problem-solving and explanation, to the fundamental issues of discernment and judgement.[8] Far from questioning intellectual efforts, he rather emphasizes the importance of the freedom of research, as opposed to the emphasis which Descartes placed on official recognition.

Finally, in spite of the closeness in substance between the arguments of Lipsius and Gassendi, the differences are even more fundamental:

asceticism for the stoics has the meaning of a heroistic-pessimistic ethics that wants to impose itself on the world, while for the sceptics it is only a renunciation of the transformation of the world as a price for the conquest of the modest happiness of individual sages.

(UFB: 435)

In opposition to the hubris involved in the posture of the transformation of the world, whether in the form of Calvinistic or stoic inner-worldly asceticism, or Cartesian intellectualism, the final word of Gassendi is modesty (ibid.: 436).

Pascal

The book ends with a discussion of the fourth main thinker covered, Pascal, but without a proper conclusion. There was a very good reason for this, as will soon become apparent, although it no doubt only further contributed to the difficulties of reception. Though such an importance attributed to Pascal seems strange and out of place in social thought, Borkenau is not alone with his emphasis. The penultimate part of the *History of Political Ideas*, entitled 'Last Orientation', is closed with a long chapter on Nietzsche and Pascal. Foucault, on the other hand, starts the original Preface of his first main book, *Histoire de la Folie*, with quotes from Pascal and Dostoevsky. These names indeed belong inextricably together. As Voegelin shows in detail, Nietzsche considered Pascal to be one of his most important sources (Voegelin 1996: 129–32), while Dostoevsky was Nietzsche's last main reading experience (Kaufmann 1974: 340, fn 2). One could even venture to say that it was reading Dostoevsky that prevented Nietzsche from reading Kierkegaard, which was something he promised several times to Brandes in his last sane year (Kaufmann, in Nietzsche 1968: 52–3, fn 48). Thus, Pascal can be identified as a major 'second-order' background figure of reflexive historical sociology, beyond thinkers like Nietzsche or Kierkegaard, and providing a connection in the concern with philosophy and Christianity as a way of life.

The experiential basis of Pascal's thought is the same as that of the other thinkers. His world image was also dominated by the vision of *homo homini lupus* (UFB: 558) and he shared the conviction of the 'acute sense of impotence of man' (ibid.). Under such conditions, he agreed that the control and reduction of passions was the most important decision that human beings should make (ibid.: 551). In fact, his vision can be ranked among the most pessimistic of the age, with the novelty of his thought being 'the disappearance of all optimistic elements' and the conviction in the absurdity of human life (ibid.: 558). But his concrete suggestions were contrary to the ideas of Descartes and ran parallel to the views of Gassendi, with the main difference being that intellectual scepticism was replaced by conversion to faith (ibid.: 550).

For Pascal, the central issue is not the powers or failure of the intellect but feelings or sentiments (ibid.: 551). Salvation comes through emotions (ibid.: 555–6), as 'Pascal's God is not the god of Cartesian demonstration, neither that of the Judaic–Islamic "promise". It is, rather, a God of salvation through the heart. "God is sensible to heart, not to reason"' (ibid.: 553). In this way, Pascal returns to the 'God of grace' but gives an interpretation radically different from Calvin's.

The contrast is also visible in the central instrument of salvation, which for Pascal is humility (ibid.: 556). This mirrors Gassendi's concern with modesty and is in contrast to the hubris characteristic both of Calvin and Descartes. Pascal's way of opposing emotions to Cartesian reason, emphasized by Borkenau, is also comparable to the way Elias set aristocratic romanticism and the courtly ethos against one another (CS: 102). His strongest words are reserved for the libertines, whose rejection of all higher aspirations he called an 'imbestialization' of man, based on a 'Luciferian revolt' (UFB: 556–7).

Though his unstated personal sympathies come clearly out of the text, Borkenau thought that the solution suggested by Pascal and the neostoics was impracticable and without any real effect. However, in the last words of the chapter and after more than 550 pages, his personal conviction shone through. He claimed that it is 'historicism', the:

> only fundamental progress that was completed in philosophy with respect to Pascal that would indicate, with the help of dialectics, the way out of contradictions: changing life, instead of just reinterpreting or complaining about it in thought only.
>
> (ibid.: 559)

The choice of words was again questionable, particularly the term 'historicism', referring arguably to Dilthey, Nietzsche and Weber who were Borkenau's main sources. But the meaning of the sentence, in the context of the entire argument of the book and situated in a chapter on Pascal, is quite clear. With it, Borkenau completed his critical analysis and rejection of not just the word but the spirit of Marxism and the emphasis in the eleventh Feuerbach thesis on the transformation of the world. Borkenau singled out and criticized this idea as central in the 'inner-worldly asceticism' of Lipsius and Calvin. He furthermore identified it in the thought of Descartes and then presented Gassendi's work as its antithesis. It is only at this point, however, in the last words of the chapter on Pascal, that Borkenau came up with a positive suggestion: it is not the world that must be changed, but one's own life. The cryptic closing sentence of the section, and of the entire book, arguably gains its meaning in the context of the key concept of Pascal's thought, which is conversion.[9]

8   The gnostic revolt (Voegelin)

Voegelin's vision concerning the gnostic character of modernity is not a common currency in contemporary social thought. However, sociologists ignore the thesis at their peril as it is arguably the most significant further elaboration of Weber's major theoretical and diagnostic concept, or the 'religious rejections of the world'.

The phrase is contained in the title of the *Zwischenbetrachtung* that is now widely regarded as both personally and theoretically the most important work of Weber. This was the essay he kept correcting on his death-bed, the second and last major theoretical summary statement of the 'Economic Ethic' (WEWR) and the closing piece of the first volume of *Sociology of Religions* (GARS). Furthermore, it was his only work where Weber included the word 'theory' in the title. Even more significantly, this term was not used in the 1915 *Archiv* publication title and only finally appeared in the 1920 version.

In spite of the interest which the essay received after publication and in the last few decades, this particular phrase has arguably not received proper recognition. Much has been written on Weber's theses about rationalization and secularization, but it has rarely been recognized that Weber's central insight was not simply that the rationalization process can be rooted in the secularization of a major world religion, from Hebrew prophecy through medieval monasticism and Puritan inner-worldly asceticism, but that the process was to be connected to the secularization of the religious *rejections* of the world. It was exactly this point that was taken up by Voegelin in *Political Religions*, followed by his study on the medieval sectarian movement, and gained its full recognition in his insight on modernity as a gnostic revolt.

Of all thinkers discussed in this book, the debts Voegelin had to Weber are both the most evident and most controversial. They are evident because Voegelin repeatedly returned to Weber at crucial moments of his career, and he stressed the role which Weber had had in his intellectual formation in *Autobiographical Reflections*. But the links are also controversial, and are often reduced to the criticism voiced against Weber in the *New Science of Politics*. Thus, the argument put forward in the first paragraph also works in the other direction. Voegelin's entire life-work needs to be rooted in the work of Weber; and have the concept of the 'religious rejections of the world' as its starting point for a proper assessment of its worth.

Given the explicit discussion of Weber's work by Voegelin and the reconstruction of the ongoing dialogue he had with Weber throughout his life in Chapter Three, the discussion here will be restricted to the direction in which Voegelin's work diverged from Weber's. Four of these departures are of special importance.

The first is the grounding of the historical investigation as a starting point, in an experience of dissolution of order. Voegelin here proceeds similarly to the other reflexive historical sociologists who reflect on their own fundamental common life experiences, which centred round the collapse of the entire socio-political order into which they were born due to the First World War. The difference in Voegelin's approach is of both degree and kind. While the collapse of the medieval world order is often only taken as a background of investigation, Voegelin took this situation more seriously and elaborated in considerable theoretical detail. From *History of Political Ideas* via *The New Science of Politics* to *Order and History*, the starting point of the main divisions of his historical investigations are always rooted in a situation of crisis and disintegration. In *The New Science of Politics*, after claiming that political science as founded by Plato was born out of the crisis of the *polis*, he goes on to make the point in general terms: 'In an hour of crisis, when the order of a society flounders and dis-integrates, the fundamental problems of political existence in history are more apt to come into view than in periods of comparative stability' (NSP: 1–2). He also placed the accents differently because he considered the dissolution of order as fundamentally spiritual in nature (HPI: 69–84; OHIV: 114–7).

The second direction is also widely shared and, to a large extent, is also related to differences in experiential background. Partly because of his upbringing and partly through the reading experience of Marx, Weber focused his investigation around the economy while most other reflexive historical sociologists studied political phenomena and ideas. Again just as in the previous case, the novel angle that Voegelin brought to this matter was by drawing attention to the intimate links that exist between politics and spirituality. Even here, Voegelin followed the spirit of Weber to a considerable extent. Just as Weber started with the unlikely, counter-intuitive connection between religion and business, Voegelin recognized that throughout human history, politics and spirituality were intimately con-nected. Additionally, they were far from being separated under conditions of modernity, as it is shown by their interpenetration in political revolutions, one of the most important phenomena of modernity whose analysis took up a central place in Voegelin's work. Though Voegelin even here followed the example and method of Weber, he also went beyond a major limitation.

While Weber recognized the spiritual character of both the modern capitalist economy and modern revolutionary politics, he failed to recognize the spiritual impulse behind the 'ordinary' business of politics and came to assume, following an interpretation of Nietzsche's 'will to power' (Mommsen 1984), that violence, warfare and *Realpolitik* is a fundamental character of human existence.[1]

Third, Voegelin did not simply take up Weber's project in *The Protestant Ethic* in order to continue or complement it, but based his work on a synthesis of all Weber's major related writings to a far greater extent than any other reflexive historical sociologist. He placed an emphasis on the essay on Protestant sects and on the conceptualization of the psychological aspect of religious experiences as in the *Einleitung*, but particularly on the central concern of the *Zwischenbetrachtung* or the 'religious rejections of the world' which led to his diagnosis of the modern gnosis.

Voegelin's ideas about Gnosticism and his diagnosis of modernity as a 'gnostic age' or a 'gnostic revolt' are among the best known and most debated aspects of his work. The controversies surrounding the concept in a sense only reflect the explicitly polemical purpose it originally served. However, as often happens these polemics do more harm than good to Voegelin's fundamental insight. With his recognition of the affinities between modernity and Gnosticism, Voegelin managed to give an experiential basis to Weber's concept of the 'religious rejections of the world' which further wedged the gap between Christianity on the one side and *ressentiment* and the hostility to life on the other, which had been mistakenly and untenably identified by Nietzsche.

The fourth major direction in which Voegelin took off from the work of Weber is certainly the most important and also the one in which he went farthest. Not satisfied with providing an original diagnosis of modernity or a study of the processes that led to the emergence of modern capitalism in a comparative perspective, he also formulated a philosophy of his own. He not only went back to the original works of Plato and Aristotle, but put the existential tension with the divine that was still present in their works at the centre of all philosophical undertaking.

At this point the competence of a sociologist, even a reflexive historical sociologists, ends and Voegelin's work moves beyond the field. One could argue that therefore most of Voegelin's mature work should lie outside the scope of this book. However, things are not quite that simple. This is partly because, as shown in Chapter Three, Voegelin's meditations often extended from reflections on Weber, including the concept of *metaxy* which was perhaps Voegelin's single most important term. It is also partly because this term, in spite of all differences, is closely related to Victor Turner's concept 'liminality' which also had fundamental spiritual connotations. And finally, it was because Voegelin's critical and reconstructive work, the diagnosis of the various kinds of the 'religious rejections of the world' and the return to the ground were also intimately connected. Thus, even though no attempt will be made in the following to resurrect the central components of Voegelin's philosophy, it will not be possible to operate with clear-cut divisions between the different facets of his work as they were closely connected.

People of God

Voegelin's approach to the problem of the revolution and the key to his diagnosis of modern Gnosticism, is contained in the chapter of *History of Political Ideas* called 'The People of God'. He certainly considered this section as central to the work. Given its close links to *Political Religions*, it was probably among the first sections completed.[2] At any rate, by May 1941, the first draft of the section was certainly ready. More importantly, this was the section he sent to Strauss at his request for publication in *Social Research*. Though Strauss was smart enough to spot that the text was part of a larger manuscript, much more significantly he committed a major editorial blunder by failing to recognize the importance of the analysis offered. Had the text been published in 1942, it would have ranked with and preceded the works of Arendt (1958 [1951]), Cohn (1970 [1957]), Löwith (1949) and Talmon (1986 [1952]) as a classic on the origins of totalitarian movements and ideologies. Though it remained unpublished for more than half a century, the significance of the work was also recognized in the literature on Voegelin. Allusions to the manuscript were often made in the secondary literature, and a German translation was published in 1994.

The remarks of Strauss notwithstanding, the section has a self-contained structure of its own. Furthermore, in this very structure, the presence of Weber shines through more than anywhere else in Voegelin's works. The entire task is an innovative pursuit of Weber's concerns. It performs the task formulated at the end of *The Protestant Ethic* of tracing the 'historical development [of rational asceticism] from the medieval beginnings' (PE: 183) for the case of heretic sects. It is present in the section titles, in the clearly Weberian terminology such as the typological opposites 'institution and movement' and 'church and sect' and the concern with 'the social structure of the movement'.[3] It is also visible in the discussion on the text *A Glimpse of Sion's Glory*, a Puritan pamphlet from 1649, which Voegelin selected for illustrating the sense that 'practically all of the main features [of the revolutionary sect] are assembled that have made their appearance in one or the other period of the movements' (HPIV: 147). Thus, there are exactly the 'ideal-type' in the Weberian sense. (PE: 47–8).

The section, finally, is also the place where it is possible to capture the spark or actual reading experience that inflamed Voegelin's interest in Gnosticism. In his autobiographical recollections, Voegelin connected this interest to Hans Urs von Balthasar's 1937 book *Apocalypse of the German Soul*. However, in the new version of this section, the discussion of the 'Free

Spirits' which was written probably in autumn 1949, Voegelin does not mention Balthasar's work, but rather discusses extensively another book published in 1947, Wilhelm Fränger's *Hieronymus Bosch*. Given that we have to do with a manuscript, it is most probable that the text was written shortly after the reading experience.

The close link is confirmed by the internal evidence of the text. First, the new, extended interpretive meaning of Gnosticism makes its entry in the discussion of the 'free spirit' heresy which was appended to the text in its new version. This is precisely the sect whose ideas were painted by Bosch, according to the interpretation offered by Fränger. But indirectly, the paintings also offer a clue to the reason why the book had such a major impact on Voegelin. The title of the left panel of the triptych which represents creation is called 'Garden of Eden'. Voegelin's introductory section entitled 'The Spiritual Disintegration' and containing a striking analysis of the collapse of the *polis* and the rise of a 'definitely apolitical attitude' (HPI: 69) among philosophers after Socrates, closes with a section on 'The Garden of Epicurus'. The description of the Epicurean 'calculus of pleasure' (HPI: 83) closely resembles the analysis of the Bosch painting, while the ending of the Introduction which evokes the 'mild, friendly, unobtrusive, psychologically shrewd and slightly parasitic society of frightened little men in the garden' which is 'a fitting symbol of the end of Hellas' (HPI: 84) cannot but recall the 'last men' of Nietzsche which was also evoked by Weber in the closing pages of *The Protestant Ethic*.[4] If we add Voegelin's idea that Nietzsche was the last person with whom the Renaissance closed (HPIV: 214), we can see how the reading of Fränger's interpretation of Bosch could have had the character of an illumination for Voegelin by connecting the collapse of the *polis,* the Middle Ages and the times of Nietzsche in a single line of meaning.

The final remark about the section is related to the issue of the gnostic character of modernity and addresses the question of the puzzling, out-of-chronological order status of the section within the work. It seems that throughout the manuscript, Voegelin was struggling with reconciling the incompatibilities he perceived between Protestantism and modernity. While Weber claimed that it is specifically the 'modern' capitalism that was rooted in the Protestant ethic, Voegelin rather perceived the central character of Protestantism as highly problematic.[5] While writing the *History of Political Ideas*, he was speaking from inside modernity, and this led him to argue that the central character of Protestantism was not modern but medieval. With the vision of gnostic modernity, however, all this changed and Protestantism was recognized as being modern *and* gnostic.

This leads to the question of Voegelin's account on the emergence of modernity in *History of Political Ideas*. The account given will have to be provisional, as the analysis must be restricted to the published volumes.

Voegelin on modernity in the *History of Political Ideas*

Voegelin defined modernity through the *History of Political Ideas* in a straightforward and consistent way. This definition had a negative and a positive character. Negatively, the emergence of modernity was due to the breakdown of the medieval world order: 'modernity (if we can attach any meaning to the term at all) is a historical process, extending over centuries, in which the medieval, spiritual-temporal order of Western mankind gradually dissolves' (HPV: 183; see also HPIV: 88).

Voegelin's positive definition is again straightforward as he repeatedly identifies modernity with the rise of the national state (HPIV: 88; HPV: 181). In fact, up to the insight on Gnosticism, the titles of the last chapters or volume of the work were supposed to be about the 'national state'.

In the text, however, the exact characterization of modernity presented a more complex problem for Voegelin than such a straightforward characterization would indicate. This is obvious in his claims about the multiple origins of modernity and in the actual position of the sections on the transition to modernity within the manuscript. Voegelin argues that modernity was 'twice born', in Machiavelli, More and Erasmus, in 1516; and in the Reformation with its breakthrough of 1517 (HPIV: 88).[6] In a clear allusion to Weber, he claims that in the past, emphasis has been placed excessively on the second birth. This is problematical not only because of the relative neglect of the first birth but also because this second birth is in fact fundamentally non-modern because it is a resurrection of medieval sectarianism. In fact, its 'modernity' lies only in the spread and wider respectability of these views, which are inherently non-modern and medieval. It is this assessment that would be reversed in the later idea that would characterize the entire modernity as gnostic, rather than the sectarian movements as medieval remnants.

However, when composing the manuscript, Voegelin had problems placing the sections on the transition to modernity within his work. This is best shown with the section 'People of God' which is the discussion of medieval heretic sects and is situated between the twin origins of modernity, Machiavelli, Erasmus and More on the one hand and Luther and Calvin on the other. This ambivalence is repeated with the section entitled 'The Problem of Modernity', which is not placed at the beginning of a major part but at the start of Chapter Five entitled 'Man in History and Nature' (in HPV). This chapter discusses astrology, cosmology and mathematics and is placed after the section on the Reformation, Hooker and Vitoria and before the section on Bodin.[7] It is this section that heads off with a discussion on 'Mediterranean modernity' (HPV: 181–4). This term is used in the *History of Political Ideas* to distinguish between the modernity of Machiavelli and the medieval sectarian roots of Luther and the Reformation. However, in his later work, Voegelin rather used the expression 'Mediterranean tradition' (NSP: 133, 187–8) as a contrast to the modern growth of gnosticism

These hesitations are the indications that Voegelin only found the equilibrium of the third thread within his project, the diagnosis of modernity, with the recognition of the parallels between modernity and gnosticism.

This hypothesis gains further support from the way Voegelin discussed Erasmus and Bodin who were two of the most important thinkers of the sixteenth century.

Erasmus

Of the three authors Voegelin connected to the year 1516, Erasmus was evidently the least important for him. This is illustrated by the fact that both the Machiavelli and the More sections appeared in print in 1951. However, for the purposes of this book his ideas on Erasmus have a peculiar importance, owing partly to the parallels it offers with Elias, Huizinga and others, and partly to the specific angle of the analysis offered.

Voegelin argues that the thought of Erasmus can be rendered intelligible against the background of the breakdown of Christianity and, in fact, his general comments about this breakdown are located in the introductory section of the chapter on Erasmus which came immediately after the chapter on Machiavelli. The main targets of the wrath and ridicule of Erasmus are the Church and the scholastics. These were the two institutions which were central to the intellectual-spiritual part of the medieval world order, and their weakening had a central role in its collapse. In his criticism and his intentions, Voegelin argues that Erasmus was right. His call for reform was a sincere attempt to overcome corruption of the 'tricks of human ratiocination . . . the definitions of scholastics and the power of some bishops' (HPIV: 95), and to return to the words of the Scripture and the life of Jesus and the apostles. However, he committed an error of interpretation by failing to distinguish between the contemporary corrupt state of the Church and the university and their original purpose and thus he took up a general, indiscriminate critical attitude against institutions in general.[8] Additionally, he exacerbated this error of interpretation by a serious error of judgement in dismissing the entire ecclesiastic and scholastic traditions and thus 'tak[ing] it for granted that such return [to true Christianity] requires the destruction of Christian intellectual civilization' (ibid.: 96).[9] This was because he failed to understand the civilizing function of systematic analysis of the 'complex and explosive spiritual forces' contained in the New Testament and combined an 'almost unbelievable historical *naiveté*' with the 'hubris of the intellectual'. In this way, Erasmus became a paradigmatic case of 'modern' intellectuals in that 'he was fundamentally right in his emotional revolt but totally wrong in his intellectual response (ibid.: 96–7).[10]

The central work of Erasmus, published in 1516 which was the year when both *The Prince* and *Utopia* were finished, is *The Education of the*

Christian Prince.[11] Thus, at the same time that More gave a twist to Platonic ideas by developing his concept of Utopia, Erasmus returned to Plato and the concept of the philosopher king but gave it a Christian touch.

However, according to Voegelin it is precisely here that the most serious problems with Erasmus appear. Having dismissed the entire intellectual culture and institutional structure of Christianity, Erasmus had to posit his argument on matters of the heart, emotions and their control on the one hand, and on deeds on the other. Thus he identified Christianity with a particular 'philosophical' way of life. His 'Christian Prince', therefore, is really an 'Ascetic Prince' as Voegelin argues even with his section title. Additionally, Erasmus established a string of identities. He claimed that Jesus was really a philosopher (ibid.: 92–3), posed 'virtuous asceticism' as the ideal form of conduct (ibid.: 99–100), and thus tightly identified Christianity with asceticism (ibid.: 100), asceticism with philosophy and philosophy with Christianity (ibid.: 92–3). Thus, Erasmus's position could be considered as a version of Pelagianism but tainted with an Oriental touch (ibid.: 98).

Bodin

Of the many enigmas Voegelin's life-work poses, Bodin's case is among the most striking. On the one hand, he repeatedly talked of Bodin in the highest possible terms (AR: 112–3, AN: 195–6), mentioning him together with Aristotle and Thomas Aquinas as the three most important political theorists (HPI: 232), and claiming that he was a crucial link from Plato to Vico and Schelling (HPV: 214). In fact, combining these two claims, it would come out that Bodin is unrivalled in importance for Voegelin, as his is the only name mentioned both in the group of the greatest theoretical minds who managed to build systems, and in the group of those thinkers that he listed among the greatest mystical or spiritual thinkers of political thought. However, on the other hand, Voegelin not only never finished his long-planned book on Bodin but hardly ever mentioned him in his published work (for an exception, see AN: 195–7).

In the rest of this section, an attempt will be made to solve this puzzle. It will largely rely on the general problem of the place of Gnosticism in Voegelin's work.

In his analysis, Voegelin is first of all stressing that the fundamental experiential basis of Bodin's work is given by the collapse of the medieval order, and especially the conditions of the religious and civil wars he lived through. In searching for the answer, Bodin turned to the nation state and developed the theory of sovereignty. This shows the fundamentally modern and not medieval character of his thought. However, in contrast to Hobbes, for example, he did not think that this solution had to be sought in a secular setting, but kept the religious or spiritual component in the search for political order and argued that only a 'true religion' would find a solution to the difficulties.

This aspect of Bodin's work is much less known than his ideas about sovereignty or the influence of climate on national character, but it was close to the heart of Voegelin's interest and takes up a central part in the section. The presentation of Bodin's related ideas highlights the close affinity with some of Voegelin's key concerns. Thus, Bodin had an interest in conceiving history as a history of religious experiences (HPV: 189), focusing on the order of the soul (ibid.: 196) and on the concepts of *conversio* and *epistrophé* (ibid.: 188, 198–9). He argued that 'true religion is nothing but the intention (*conversio*) of a purified mind toward the true god' (ibid.: 188). Along the lines of Dionysius Areopagita, he also developed a four-fold hierarchical classification of human types according to their spiritual endowments, starting from the 'spiritually dead' up to the 'prophetic saint' (ibid.: 200–2).

The central interest of Voegelin, however, concerned Bodin's ideas about the connection between the political and the spiritual. Far from trying to separate worldly activities from spiritual matters, Bodin's main concern was to relate the two, as for him a 'polity cannot be considered truly happy unless there is room in it for contemplation, and a man cannot be considered happy unless his contemplation is that of a man in society' (ibid.: 195). Thus, relying again on the analogy of Weber, one could argue that at the same time that 'inner-worldly asceticism' became a driving force behind modern capitalism through the Protestant ethic, in the writings of Bodin, there also appeared an 'inner-worldly mysticism'.

This was necessary, apart from the intrinsic human need for mystic experiences assumed by Bodin, because a purely secular approach does not pay enough attention to the spiritual forces that reside in man. Bodin's wrath is especially directed against those who deny the existence of evil, as 'unbelief with regard to evil is the conclusive symptom of insensitiveness toward spiritual good; lack of discrimination with regard to evil is rooted in lack of discrimination with regard to good' (ibid.: 206). It is due to an awareness of the existence of evil and the explosive nature of spiritual forces that Bodin preaches tolerance with respect to all historical religions, as all these contain 'the core of "true religion"' (ibid.: 205). However, in them this is 'veiled by the historically and geographically conditioned varieties of symbols' (ibid.: 205). The task Bodin perceives for himself is therefore to work towards the establishment of this true religion.

Students familiar with Voegelin's later work would immediately perceive that this idea qualifies Bodin as a gnostic. And, indeed, this is the way Voegelin actually analyses and classifies Bodin. The opening chapter of Bodin's *Methodus*, which contains his fundamental concepts, is elusive. Though the definitions are clear, their theoretical implications were not specified, 'mak[ing] us profoundly regret that Bodin did not communicate more of the Gnostic speculation that apparently formed the background for his brief, esoteric definitions' (ibid.: 220). In the following pages, Voegelin further claims that Bodin's anthropology has a gnostic origin, that the imagery of his work resembles steps from a gnostic hierarchy and that his concept of right reason (*recta ratio*) is a 'gnostic aeon' (ibid.: 201–2). The subsection concludes by stating that Bodin's activism has its source in a gnostic faith that evil can be overcome by an intellectual operation (ibid.: 203).

Were this not enough, the last two subsections of the chapter which are devoted to Bodin's ideas on the spatial and temporal order of history, contain further judgements which sound like especially weighty accusations in light of Voegelin's later work. As far as spatial order is concerned, Bodin's ideas are closely modelled on Plato and the novelty lies not in the elements but in their combination. In his celebrated theory about the influence of climatic factors on personality characteristics, he singled out three main types: the wise, the prudent and the strong (ibid.: 228). Here he was simply following Plato, but the novelty lay in the emphasis he placed on the second type, the 'prudent', which he called a middle or mixed type, being a combination of both wisdom and strength, the 'truly political' type and thus *prudentia* being 'the characteristic of true rulership' (ibid.: 228). The conduct of politics is thus not a matter for a philosopher, which is again in contrast to Erasmus. From here, however, Bodin not only universalized Plato when discussing the nation state by enlarging 'Plato's theory of the polis to a theory of the world-republic' (ibid.: 229) but he also placed France and especially its central region, 'Celtic France', into the position of the centre or the *omphalos* of the world. According to Voegelin:

> This is the first instance, on a grand scale, of the appearance of a national mission, discovered and propagated by a thinker who thus becomes the intellectual apostle of his nation to mankind. The mixture of contemplation and action that may result in the prudence of the statesman has dangerous consequences in a realm that should be reserved to contemplation, foreshadowing the disaster of intellectual imperialism in the period of Enlightenment and after.
>
> (HPV: 231–2)

On the subject of temporal order, Voegelin's criticism is similarly trenchant. Bodin starts by attacking the two main political myths of his times, the Danielic prophecy of four monarchies and the myth of the 'Golden Age'. Bodin easily deconstructs these myths, which have become emptied and disenchanted. However, as a consequence of his attacks:

> Bodin ignores Christian sacred history as a source of meaning for the process of mankind in history; he eliminates all remnants of eschatological speculation from profane history; what is left is an empirical structure of history governed by the law of eternal return.
>
> (HPV: 233)

This led him further to divide world history into three periods, each lasting for 2,000 years, which were a 'sequence of religious, political and technological ages, corresponding to the faculties of the soul' (ibid.: 234). This periodization, as Voegelin remarks, anticipates the ideas of Turgot and Comte, although Joachim is conspicuously absent from this section. With this periodization and after the elimination of the eschatological elements,

> Bodin returns to an immanent meaning of history. The return is pregnant with implications for the future. . . . Through this transfer of meaning from the transcendental to the immanent plane, empirical history is apt to acquire the qualities of sacred history
>
> (HPV: 235–6)

Though this tendency is still checked in Bodin owing to his mystical culture, the possibility thus opens up under Comte for 'the later Positivistic speculation on history which injects the peculiar flavour of a perverted, medieval sectarianism into the modern intellectual climate' (ibid.: 236).

This leaves two conclusions. First, Voegelin found the signs of future derailment in the thinker he esteemed highest: in the appearance of Gnosticism, the intellectual support for the imperialist wars of national states, and the immanentization of history. Second, it is also clear that in this section, Gnosticism still had no negative connotation for Voegelin. Quite the contrary, it even had a positive flavour and was related to his appreciation of 'inner-worldly mysticism'.[12]

For a proper assessment of the significance of these facts, a number of further comments must be made which concern publication plans. The essay on Bodin was one of the three articles for whose publication Voegelin secured a commitment from Macmillan in March 1949, and it was to be published in the *Review of Politics*. But in contrast to the articles on Marx and Machiavelli which appeared on schedule in 1950 and 1951, the Bodin essay never appeared. However, Voegelin had prepared a much shorter version of the essay for publication, and this was published by the editors as a *Variorum* (HPV: 7–8). This article follows the previous text very closely, except for the fact that all segments of Voegelin's remarks on the gnostic speculation on which Bodin's work was based, and the sections devoted to Bodin's ideas on the spatial and temporal order of history, are completely missing. The paper ends with a section entitled 'Ascent to God' (HPIV: 250) which reasserts the attitude of 'inner-worldly mysticism' or, using Voegelin's own terminology, 'spiritual realism', and has an evident and quite polemical identification with Bodin's own position.

This fact helps to explain better the excessively polemical tone that characterized Voegelin's diagnosis of modernity as gnostic from the beginning. It was not just a diagnosis about the spiritual illnesses and derailments of modernity. As the crucial section on Bodin makes clear, Voegelin's own position of 'inner-worldly mysticism' had a strong affinity with Gnosticism. The problem looming large beyond the emotional charges and polemics about Gnosticism was therefore a task of self-overcoming.[13]

Gnostic modernity

Voegelin's vision of modern Gnosticism will be presented in four steps which provide a successive elaboration of the idea. Each was connected with a particularly significant occasion: the Walgreen lectures leading to his first American book (NSP); the article 'Gnostic Politics' which was his first piece written and published in German for fourteen years (Voegelin 1952); his Munich inaugural lecture (SPG); and the *Introduction* to the *The Ecumenic Age* that presents his mature philosophy of history.

Emphasis will be put on the last piece whereas the previous one will only be used to introduce the argument.

The New Science of Politics

In *The New Science of Politics* the emergence of Gnosticism is presented in the context of the eschatological expectations that characterized Christianity in the first centuries (NSP: 107–8). The reconciliation of chiliastic tendencies with the existence of a Church was the great work of Augustinus (ibid.: 109). Until that point, 'Gnostic heresy was the great opponent of Christianity' (ibid.: 126). Though the movement went underground for a number of centuries, it re-emerged with full force in the work of the Joachim of Fiore (ibid.: 110–3) who was a breakaway Cistercian monk. He was the first in a long line of thinkers who attempted the immanentization of the transcendent by bringing down Heaven into Earth. The central argument of the book is that we have to 'recognize the essence of modernity as the growth of gnosticism' (ibid.: 126) and that Puritanism, positivism, national socialism and communism can all be considered as modern versions of the ancient gnosis.

According to Voegelin, this would also answer the main ambivalence of modernity, which is 'the question how a civilization can advance and decline at the same time' (ibid.: 129) and this was his interpretation of modern progress. The price of this progress is the death of the spirit (ibid.: 131) which is all the less acceptable as such a combination of 'advance and decline' cannot last forever (ibid.: 132). This point will be re-examined in the conclusion to Part II, when the concept 'permanent liminality' is considered.

'Gnostic Politics'

The article 'Gnostic Politics' has certainly not received the attention it deserves. The importance of the paper is shown first by its language. This was the first piece Voegelin wrote and published in German for fourteen years, a point he emphasized in a letter to Strauss (FPP: 92). It is also demonstrated by an overview of its content. The seventeen-page article goes through in outline some of the central points covered in *The New Science of Politics*, 'The People of God' (HPIV:131–214), his published short articles on Bakunin, Marx and positivism and other parts of the *History of Political Ideas* manuscript (in FER). If *The New Science of Politics* was a reflection on the work done so far, then it was a reflection on the reflections or a third-order phenomenon. With slight exaggeration, it could be called Voegelin's *Zwischenbetrachtung,* as it was a concise summary of the central points of his past work and a personal manifesto.

The article defines the central insight motivating his work. Even though the facts concerning Gnosticism are well-known, 'what is less known even today is their decisive influence on the development of modern politics' (Voegelin 1952: 301–2).[14] This impact is invisible because it is simply taken for granted in its secularized version, and there is a lack of distance and available conceptual tools to analyse it. Thus, the fundamental methodological question is the development of the conceptual tools that can render visible the gnostic character of modern politics.[15] In the article, however, only allusions are given to classical philosophy and Christian thought, which are the two main sets of tools Voegelin considered adequate for the tasks. He even gives an explanation. As in the period of mass democracy reason has lost its authority, the fight against gnostic politics cannot be led by simply intellectual means but requires recurrence to the use of force (ibid.: 302, 317).

But what is Voegelin talking about exactly? In the article, he uses the expression 'the gnostic' so often that one gains the uneasy impression as if it were a label, a fetish or a stigma. The reasons why Voegelin would be called a 'gnostic anti-gnostic' are evident here. However, Voegelin does provide a definition and an analysis of his term. A 'gnostic' is somebody who is sick in his spirit (ibid.: 304, 305). This sickness can be characterized by the term *ressentiment* (ibid.: 308) but also by a general rejection of reality which leads to the chimerical idea of altering nature and of replacing reality with a dream-world.[16] This characterization allows him to provide two final descriptions of gnosticism: a philosophico-theological one in which gnosticism is 'the pathological attempt to translate a transcendental realm of perfection into an immanent historical reality' (ibid.: 316); and a socio-political one that sees the essence of gnosticism not simply as a call for revolution and for a revaluation of values but as an attempt to transform the revolution into a permanent state. In one of the most striking passages of the article, he traces the origin of this idea back to the French liberals Dunoyer and Charles Comte (ibid.: 312; see also FER: 179–81).

This definition of gnosticism allows Voegelin to diagnose the gnostic character not only of the totalitarian states and movements, but of the modern condition in general. Even here, Voegelin is not creating a straw man. Far from identifying totalitarianism with modernity, he merely refuses to separate the two completely.[17] He claims that just as the puritan radicalism of the seventeenth century was a sign and symptom of the corruption Christian society had undergone, 'positivism, communism and national socialism are man-eating flowers of a corrupt liberal society' (Voegelin 1952: 310).

Science, politics and Gnosticism

The Munich inaugural lecture, apart from elaborating the argument about Marx, Nietzsche, Hegel and Heidegger especially concerning the gnostic 'prohibition of posing the question' (*das Verbot der Fragestellung*) (SPG: 21), added three main points of clarification. First, Voegelin listed his predecessors who had recognized the gnostic character of modernity, going back as far as the 1835 work of F. C. Baur (SPG: 3–5).

He also gave a much more comprehensive analysis of the experiential basis of Gnosticism. The heart of gnosis consists of a cosmology and an anthropology. Creation is the work of a demiurge and is fundamentally flawed. As a result, the spirit is imprisoned in matter and is thrown into an alien and evil world. The task is to escape the world unscathed. The work of salvation is through knowledge, and every individual should carry this work on him or herself.

According to Voegelin, this symbolizes a genuine experience of alienation: the chaotic age of the ecumenic empires, the continuous warfare and conquests when the world was experienced as a hostile, alien, evil place and where it seemed impossible to find a home in the world (ibid.: 8–9).

Finally, Voegelin also gave an indication about the way out. Just as eight years previously, he did not consider the situation hopeless. The emphasis, however, was now different. It was not on the institutional structures of democracies. It was rather a call for each and every human being to resist the spiritual disorder and civilizational crisis of the age, avoid the folly and to live a life of order in accordance with the truth of the soul (ibid.: 21–2).

The Ecumenic Age

At the time when he delivered his Munich inaugural lecture, Voegelin was working on the planned fourth volume of *Order and History* which was provisionally entitled 'Empire and Christianity'. This volume was never finished in this form. However, he did provide a comprehensive and conclusive, though short, presentation of his views on both ancient and modern Gnosticism, in *The Ecumenic Age*, the published fourth volume.[18]

Though no special chapter is devoted to it, the discussion on Gnosticism appears in three prominent places in the book: in the middle of the *Introduction* (OHIV: 17–27) and at the end of two of the arguably most important chapters of the book, 'Conquest and Exodus' and 'The Pauline

Vision of the Resurrected' (ibid.: 234–8, 267–71). Furthermore, the introductory comments on the theme of Gnosticism are striking in all three cases. Voegelin starts not simply with representatives of an ancient or modern gnostic sect or current, but by claiming that the most important sources of our intellectual tradition contain the seeds of Gnosticism. Thus, gnostic ideas can be traced back to the opening sections of the Gospel of John 'when the author lets the cosmogonic "word" of creation blend into the revelatory "word" spoken to man from the Beyond by the "I am"' (ibid.: 18). Similarly, 'certain problems that became acute in Gnosticism were latently present even in Plato's work' (ibid.: 234). Finally, '[t]here is the original discrepancy in Paul's interpretation between the hard core of truth, as I have called it, and the not-so-hard fringe of ambiguities and metastatic expectations', referring especially to the expectation of the immediate 'Second Coming' (ibid.: 267–8). The problem is therefore not simply whether we can talk about the reappearance of Gnosticism in a modern context, but the reasons why the dangers of Gnosticism appear together with the most important figures and values of our intellectual tradition.

In generic or 'phenotypical' terms, Voegelin introduces Gnosticism as a certain imbalance of the 'beyond' and the 'beginning'. The 'beyond' stands for the immediate experience of the divine ground, the 'presence' in the movements of the soul, and its symbolization requires:

> the revelatory language of consciousness . . . the language of seeking, searching, and questioning, of ignorance and knowledge concerning the divine ground, of futility, absurdity, anxiety, and alienation of existence, of being moved to seek and question, of being drawn toward the ground, of turning around, or return, illumination, and rebirth
>
> (OHIV: 17–18)

The presence of 'beginning', however, is not direct, is mediated and 'requires the mythical language of a creator-god or Demiurge, of a divine force that creates, sustains, and preserves the order of things' (ibid.: 18). The gnostic deformation occurs when the two languages are blended and used indiscriminately. This happens when an intense experience of the 'beyond' in the consciousness is carried further in the same movement of the soul to encompass the beginning as well: 'In the construction of Gnostic systems, the immediate experience of divine presence in the mode of the Beyond is speculatively expanded to comprehend a knowledge of the Beginning that is accessible only in the mode of mediated experience' (ibid.: 19). This emphasis on 'speculation' is the reason why Gnosticism is always associated with a specifically intellectual 'hubris' that Voegelin calls the 'egophanic revolt' (ibid.: 48, 57, 260). Such a literal, speculative interpretation of the beginning, however, in a second step is accompanied by a similarly speculative deformation of the 'beyond', where 'a consciousness of the movement toward the Beyond . . . becomes an obsessive illumination, blinding a man for the contextual structure of reality' (ibid.: 20), and leading to the illusion that the 'beyond', the realm of transcendence, can be fully implemented and made a principle of worldly, cosmic existence. Thus, Gnosticism is always closely associated with apocalyptic currents of thought and social movements or, turning to a modern and secular equivalent language, positivistic and evolutionary scientism always appears together with political, social and technological utopias.

The question now is to understand the emergence and influence of Gnosticism, especially the reasons why it happened 'precisely at the time when the consciousness of a pneumatic Beyond becomes intensely luminous' (ibid.: 18) both in Christianity and in philosophy.[19] For a full explanation, however, it is necessary to move from the generic to the genetic level and focus on the exact conditions of emergence of these ambivalent experiences of the 'beyond'.

The fundamental experiential basis of gnostic thought is a particularly intense and one-dimensional awareness of the negative aspects of the beyond, alienation, anxiety and despair. The experiences are products of isolation but they also contribute to a further individualization. They lead to excessive intellectual speculation, the search for a purely mental and verbal solution to existential troubles, and then to the gathering of mass support in the revolt against the order of reality through the appeal of apocalyptic visions and utopian systems in which all the ills of human existence would be suddenly and completely obliterated. As far as negative feelings are concerned, Voegelin is especially stressing the experience of alienation: 'The imaginative game of liberation derives its momentum from an intensely experienced alienation and an equally intense revolt against it; Gnostic thinkers, both ancient and modern, are the great psychologists of alienation, carriers of the Promethean revolt' (ibid.: 19).[20]

The presence of similar experiences on a massive scale which is a precondition of the influence and success of gnostic ideas, however, assumes a special type of historical situation with experience of the collapse of traditions and the conventional order of things. The life span of historical Gnosticism was tied to one such time period, that lasted from the empire of Alexander the Great to the end of the Roman Empire or, as Voegelin would call it, the 'Ecumenic Age' which was 'a time of imperial expansion' in which the 'futility of existence' (ibid.: 19) was particularly strongly felt. Because the age of imperial conquests attempted to extend its 'concupiscence of power and knowledge' (ibid.: 313) to the entire world, these experiences were widely shared, and gnostic thought cannot be reduced to a particular religion and region. On the contrary, its main characteristic was an ethnic and religious syncretism. However, according to Voegelin, it was Hebrew prophecy that gave it its most important stamp (ibid.: 25–7).

Given the controversial reception of his ideas in *The New Science of*

Politics, Voegelin was careful here with his terminology. In his analysis of Hegel's 'egophanic deformation of history' (OHIV: 262–6), for example, the term 'gnostic' is not even used. However, it is also clear that he maintained his idea about the generic as opposed to the merely historical use of the term Gnosticism and its applicability to the modern period. In this respect he made a distinction between 'the essential core and the variable part of a Gnostic system' (ibid.: 20). The former is defined as 'the enterprise of returning the pneuma in man from its state of alienation in the cosmos to the divine pneuma of the Beyond through action based on knowledge' (ibid.: 20). As ancient and modern examples, he mentions the Valentinian psychodramas and the speculations about the phases of history in the works of Schelling and Hegel (ibid.: 20–1). The only difference is that the imagery of ancient Gnostics which is rooted in the 'more spectacular Egyptian, Syrian, and Anatolian varieties' (ibid.: 21) is replaced by the opening lines of the Gospel of St John.[21] There is, however, a further difference between ancient and modern gnostics in the orientations of the realization of their ideal and this difference has contributed much to the lack of recognition of the tight links between them. While the early Gnostics 'attempt to escape from the *metaxy* by splitting its poles into the hypostases of this world and the Beyond, the modern apocalyptic-Gnostic movements attempt to abolish the *metaxy* by transforming the Beyond into this world' (ibid.: 237–8).[22] In Weberian language, one could say that while the ancient Gnostics stayed within a pure acosmic religious rejection of the world, the modern Gnostics secularized this religious rejection of the world and made it into a principle of inner-worldly conduct.

Returning to the ideas of Bodin, just as the denial of the existence of evil, which is so characteristic of certain modern forms of thought, can be considered as a sign of its acute presence, the vehement denial of the relevance of the vision connecting the ancient Gnostics to their modern variants is an indication of the resistance to take the diagnosis seriously and work on the remedy. Voegelin considers the return of gnostic ideas and the deformation of experiential insights into philosophical and religious dogmas as symptoms of a deep civilizational and spiritual disorder.[23] Voegelin closes the substantive argument of the *Introduction*, the piece that he himself identified as presenting the core of his philosophy of history and justifying his entire undertaking, with the following sentences:

> In our time, the inherited symbolisms of ecumenic humanity are disintegrating, because the deforming doctrinalisation has become socially stronger than the experiential insights it was originally meant to protect. The return from symbols which have lost their meaning to the experiences which constitute meaning is so generally recognizable as the problem of the present that specific references are unnecessary. The great obstacle to this return is the massive block of accumulated

symbols, secondary and tertiary, which eclipses the reality of man's existence in the Metaxy.

(NSP: 58)

However, in spite of the strengths of the analysis, the last page of the *Introduction* leaves two questions open. The promise made in its closing sentence that '[t]he next and last volume entitled *In Search of Order* will study the contemporary problems which have motivated the search for order in history' (ibid.: 58), was not fulfilled, in the same way that the original Volume Four, to study ancient Gnosis in detail, was never written. Though Voegelin kept working on this volume in the remaining decade of his life, and the fruits of his work appeared in a posthumous volume, the book contained the summary of his philosophical meditations and not the analysis of 'contemporary problems' as has been promised.

The final problem is related to the last words of the substantive argument quoted above, 'the reality of man's existence in the *metaxy*'. This idea occupies a central place not only in this piece but in Voegelin's entire work. However, Voegelin's ideas about the *metaxy* are open to two quite different interpretations. According to one, the *metaxy* or tension towards the divine is a permanent possibility of human existence which cannot be eliminated without grave consequences. This implies either the rejection of the world and the exclusive pursuit of other-worldly salvation or the immanentization of the 'beyond' and the denial of divine presence. These two alternatives, by their very opposition, closely suppose and produce each other. According to the other interpretation, human life is or should be permanently in the state of tension that is assumed by the *metaxy*. Such an existence, however, can only be maintained in the long run by religious virtuosi. This idea also begs the question of when and how the state of tension or *metaxy* appears. Because Voegelin assumes the permanence of *metaxy*, he fails to discuss the problems of its appearance similarly as he did with the emergence of Gnosticism.

However, the presence of the divine in human communities was hardly ever assumed as permanent. This presence was connected to specific occasions, times and places. Thus, the function of religious practices which contained paradigmatic value in the universal practice of pilgrimage (Dupront 1987) was to evoke or suddenly be aware of this 'presence'. Staying with the example, the idea of staying permanently in a state of *metaxy* evokes Bunyan's metaphor of life as a permanent pilgrimage. But if pilgrimage becomes permanent, it has every chance of becoming degraded into mass tourism.

In the terminology used in this book, Voegelin ends up conceiving of human existence as being in a permanently liminal state by claiming *metaxy* as permanent. This idea and its implications will be re-examined in the conclusion to Part II.

9 The new megamachine (Mumford)

When six major thinkers are analysed together, in an attempt to establish common points, it is inevitable that injustice is done to the singularities of the thought of each as they are forced into the Procrustean bed of a common problematic. This is bound to happen all the more if the aim is programmatic, with the establishment of an entire field of enquiry, reflexive historical sociology. However, there is remarkable convergence in their ideas, as the exceptions are restricted to one or two thinkers and are mostly minor.

Nevertheless, in one or other respects, each thinker shows characteristics that are radically different from all the others which make him an 'outlier' in that particular dimension. Thus, Elias is the only one of the six who never attributed much significance in his work to religious factors. Voegelin, on the other hand, is alone not simply in going outside the limits of academic sociology but also in developing an interest in philosophy and 'religion', which focused especially on their interconnections and thus moved beyond the 'taboo' of keeping religion and science separate. Borkenau is the only one who is not generally considered a master thinker and who did not generate a devoted group of followers. Still, arguably Lewis Mumford is an 'outlier' in more dimensions that any of the other thinkers discussed.

Starting with the most obvious, Mumford as an American is the only non-European, or even non-continental, even though he had a strong German-Jewish background. He is also the one not to have his formal academic papers in order. He never completed his studies, let alone acquired a doctorate, and he practically never had a full-time academic appointment. These formal characteristics left a trace on his writings. More than a social scientist, he considered himself a writer and shunned the need for special expertise, proudly proclaiming himself a generalist which risked the charge of being a dilettante.

Finally and most relevant, his central vision of modernity came not at the start or the middle phase of his career but in the context of his last major self-reflexive exercises when he shifted the focus of his interest back to antiquity.

For these reasons, the discussion of Mumford's vision will be particular in two senses. First, while in the other chapters the presentation of the later thought of the respective thinkers which dealt with more remote historical periods was reserved to a further volume, here it will be impossible fully to proceed in this way. This peculiarity creates fewer problems than it seems. Mumford is not completely unique as, even in the case of Voegelin, the study of Gnosticism had to move back beyond the sixteenth to eighteenth centuries. As Mumford perceived links between antiquity and modernity as opposed to the Middle Ages, his visions of modernity and the West will be quite different. Second, the direct connection with the other thinkers analysed is weak so that much more attention will be devoted to high-lighting indirect parallels.

Mumford's vision of modernity has two components. The first is the insight proper which is the perception of close links between our own age and the ancient civilizations of the Near East belonging, in his terminology, to the 'pyramid age'. These characteristics are encompassed in the term 'mega-machine'. The second part is an interpretation of the conditions of this vision. It is the identification of a myth that blurred our sight and rendered the perception of such links impossible. This is the 'myth of the machine', the idea that the ultimate consequences of the 'machine' are beneficial and that therefore we have to accept the march of the 'megamachine' as inevitable.

Mumford only gained this vision in the late 1950s at a later stage in his work, when he was working on the new edition of his 1938 book *The Culture of Cities* which eventually became *The City in History* (MMI: 11). Significantly, it had not been experienced when preparing the new edition of *Technics and Civilization,* even though he recognized the resemblance between the 'brutal conditions' of the 'industrial age' and the age of pyramids in his first book (SU: 116). As he self-critically admitted in 1959, this was because he was still under the impact of the 'myth of the machine' (Mumford 1959: 534–5). This myth was so powerful because it was based on an assumption hidden by the very meaning of the word 'machine' based on the idea that it comprises only tools and utensils. However, as Mumford now recognized, the 'machine age' originates 'at the very outset in the organization of an archetypal machine composed of human parts' (MMI: 11; see also CH: 34, 66). In this way, Mumford was then able to identify the 'megamachine', and indeed to redefine our concept of the 'machine' itself.

The conventional view on which the 'myth of the machine' was based had two interdependent components. On the one hand, the machine was defined as a tool, and on the other, tool-making was identified as the central characteristic of humankind. At the end of several decades of research, Mumford was able to go beyond both. On the latter he claimed in *Transformations of Man* that 'man' was primarily not a tool-making animal but a being whose primary activity was the making of symbols, dramas and rituals (TM: 19–21; see also MMI: 4–6).

Mumford was not alone in redefining 'man' from an animal tool-making into a symbol-making animal. He shared this discovery with many of the contemporary protagonists of the 'linguistic turn' though he reached the conclusion on his own. His great discovery, however, concerned the other component of the 'myth of the machine'. About a decade later, he recognized that tools are not the central components even of the machine. It is rather organization (MMI: 188). The archetypal machine was not a simple or a complex tool, but was an organization composed of human parts. According to Mumford, '[t]his machine escaped notice and so naturally remained unnamed until our own day' (MMI: 188). Combining the two insights, and taking a cue from Mumford's crucial 1930 article 'The Drama of the Machines', one could argue that the archetype of the machine is a frozen ritual in which the performance of each individual player has been meticulously prescribed in order to reach a uniformity of motion and to maximize useful output.[1]

It must be emphasized that Mumford considered this a genuine discovery and not just the use of a metaphor. He was a foremost historian of technology, and this vision came to him after spending almost four decades in the field he helped to establish, while in the process of rethinking his twin projects of histories of technology and the city. Far from coming up with a definition that would suit his purposes, he could easily refer to the classic definition of Franz Reuleaux and show that it fitted his particular case (MMI: 191). What is at stake is a fundamental reorientation of our entire conceptual apparatus and worldview: the idea that the machine originally was not an objective tool which human beings could use upon its invention, but that it was rather fundamentally composed *of* human beings. Mumford does not want to offer us a useful hypothesis or a conceptual tool; he wants to change the way in which we see the world around us. His histories of the city and of technology are exercises in self-understanding (Mumford 1959: 529).

This 'invisible machine' or the 'megamachine' has two major components, the 'labour machine' and the 'military machine' (MMI: 188). These two machines developed together and indeed assume each other. The military machine is performing the negative activities of destruction, while the labour machine performs the related positive activities of construction (ibid.: 191). The constructive part is profoundly ambivalent. It is always based on the destruction of existing human communities and organic patterns which had been developed through long time periods in symbiosis with the environment, and implies their replacement with mechanical types that only the machine is capable of producing. The labour machine and the military machine therefore assume each other, which renders the otherwise difficult assessment of priorities and origins irrelevant (ibid.: 192).

The comparison of the ancient and modern megamachines, however, is a primary and overwhelming concern for Mumford. Both volumes of *The Myth of the Machine* are full of direct parallels drawn between the past and the present. Furthermore, these comparisons were couched in an extremely polemical style that had a major impact on the reception of the books. It also brings out some parallels with the other reflexive historical sociologists that have broad implications.

Three of the visions discussed in Part II date from the early period of their author. *The Court Society* was Elias's *Habilitation* thesis and the basis of his first book, *The Civilizing Process*; *Transition* was the first book of Borkenau; while *The Protestant Ethic* was the first major work of Weber that is sociological in its focus. All three authors were in their thirties at the time. Though these works had no major problems in terms of style and rhetoric, their message proved to be almost indigestible to their audience, who stuck to the conventional views questioned by these visions. The visions of Foucault, Voegelin and Mumford, however, date from their mid to late period when they were at least in their mid-forties, established and at least relatively famous. However, it is exactly these visions and the work based on them that were formulated in an extremely passionate, rhetorical way and whose reception was disturbed not simply by matters of comprehension but also by resistance to style.

In fact excesses did much harm to the book. not only in matters of style which was in itself no small matter, but also directly in matters of content. Due to his urge to denounce the modern myth of the machine, Mumford forgot even the starting point of his entire investigation, which was the idea that the modern world emerged as a response to the collapse of the medieval world order. When comparing the eventual answers of the two megamachines, it slipped his mind that both were responses to the same kind of problem.

This is all the more surprising because all the elements were present in his writings that would have enabled him to extend the argument used for the sixteenth and sixteenth centuries to the earlier period. He gave vivid accounts of the collapse of order for all three time periods (MMI: 206–7, CH: 343, 415–9). He used a terminology for the conditions characterizing the emergence of the megamachine, including expressions like anxiety, paranoia, trauma and pathology (MMI: 218–22), which were the exact terms used by Voegelin and Borkenau to identify a 'dark age' or a period of spiritual disintegration in a generic-typical sense. Yet, Mumford stayed here at the level of psychologization.

There may have been a further reason why Mumford did not give full consideration to the conditions of emergence in his comparisons of the two megamachines. This was because machines not only imply self-movement in the sense of an automatism, but as answers they also have their own power of imposing themselves on their environment and generating an automatic 'self-sustained' growth and progress. The 'machines' analysed by Mumford, the armies, factories, prisons and monasteries have a tendency to impose and perpetuate their answers, even when the chaotic conditions that called for their emergence in the first instance are no longer there. In other words, apart from the parallel conditions between the ancient and modern situations that gave rise to the megamachines, there was also a direct lineage of transmission from antiquity to modernity (MMI: 189).

Mumford focused especially on the institutions of the army and the monastery (MMI: 191–2, 215–16) which 'survive' today in the businessman and the city. The most important of the two, he claimed here, was the army: '*Through the army, in fact, the standard model of the megamachine was transmitted from culture to culture*' (MMI: 192), with no major modification, except 'in the perfection of its discipline and its engines of assault' (MMI: 216). In this way, like Foucault, he identified in the military machine a fourth ideal or archetype of legitimate power.

This solution, however, has the slight problem that, in spite of his previous assertions concerning the equal weight of the military and labour machines, Mumford revealed a preference for giving priority both in matters of origins and descent to the former over the latter. This may have contributed to the polemical style of his book. This in turn, both in its form and substance and its emphasis on questions of war, could have been influenced by his strong involvement in nuclear politics and then in the protest against the Vietnam war. It also went against the importance he attributed to the construction of pyramids, as this activity was clearly cultic and not even indirectly military in its aim.

The second line of descent went through the monastery. For Mumford, this was of secondary importance, providing some missing components and helping to increase the efficiency of the megamachine (MMI: 263). It also implied a curious paradox as in this way, the perfecting and full legitimation of the megamachine was completed by an axial religion, Christianity, which came into being in precise opposition to the megamachine. Mumford further argues, much anticipating Foucault in *Discipline and Punish*, that the central innovation of the monastery was its ability to reconstruct the machine on a small-scale voluntary basis, by adding to the megamachine 'precisely the one element that [it] was lacking: a commitment to moral values and social purposes that transcended the established forms of civilization' (MMI: 263). Here Mumford identified, just as Weber, Borkenau and Foucault did, the archetype of the peculiarly modern 'paradoxical' machine: the machine that is composed not simply of human beings whose discipline and regularity is forced, but of one with a difference and with a soul.

However, just like the others, Mumford was not able fully to draw conclusions from his insight and devote a full study to the monastery. This may well have been due to the excessive importance he attributed to the Benedictine Order. His discussion of the early centuries of monasticism is just as cursory as Voegelin's, which forced him into errors such as the assumption that the duty of daily work originated only with them. The most important oversight this produced for his purposes, however, was related to two of the crucial aspects of the line of descent and transmission: the military and Eastern roots of early monasticism.

As is well known, the first form of the withdrawal from civilized urban life out of which monasticism grew was the solitary life in the desert by hermits. The first monastery, in the sense of a collecting together of hermits, was the work of Pachomius near Thebes in upper Egypt. Pachomius was a former soldier, a retired sergeant of the Roman army (EB: 332). Even more significantly, his operation was not at all minor as he ended up housing and in a way 'employing' seven thousand monks and nuns in his monasteries (Waddell 1987 [1934]: 7). He was not the only soldier among the most important figures of early monasticism. One could also mention St Martin, the founder of Gallic monasticism, which would become central to the foundation of Irish monasticism through the mediation of Wales. He was a military tribune and thus a higher-ranking officer than Pachomius (EB: 343). In fact, this pushes Borkenau into making a comment about the 'not surprising' role of soldiers in shaping monasticism even as late as the times of Ignatius of Loyola, due to the fact that ['t]he military and the monastic discipline have something in common' (EB: 342–3).

Furthermore, monasticism is closely linked to the megamachine through not only the military past of its major founding figures but also their Eastern roots. In light of Mumford's argument it gains significance that the main founders of monasticism were from the mainlands of the megamachine. Pachomius, as was pointed out above, was Egyptian while Cassian who was the author of *Institutions*, the first textbook on monastic conduct, had Mesopotamian origins. Irish monasticism was also greatly assisted in the fifth and sixth centuries by an influx of Eastern monks.

The tight links between military and monastic discipline bring Mumford's vision close to Foucault's. The Eastern origins of the megamachine and monasticism, and the strong involvement of science (especially mathematics and astronomy) in the performances of the megamachine, also establish tight links between Mumford's work and Voegelin's vision on the link between modernity and Gnosticism. The starting sentence of one of the most important chapters of the book could well have been written by Voegelin: 'Kingship deliberately sought by means of the megamachine to bring the powers and glories of Heaven within human reach' (MMI: 212; see also 283). This should come as no surprise as the work of the Chicago Oriental school, especially of Henri Frankfort, was a major source for both thinkers. Furthermore, in all respects, whether related to monasticism, army discipline, science, the mechanical-scientific world image, or even the concern with traumas, paranoia and anxiety, the links between Borkenau and Mumford are perhaps the closest. Adding only one further example, at the start of *Technics and Civilization* Mumford defines the questioning of the modern scientific world picture and the combination of mathematical and physical sciences with technology as his aim.[2] It is more surprising and even controversial to claim, however, that Mumford and Weber were also very close in their fundamental insights.

Mumford repeatedly criticized Weber's *The Protestant Ethic*, calling its thesis erroneous and anachronistic (MMI: 272, 275; CH: 257), especially in his alleged omission of the monastic sources of Protestant asceticism. However, Mumford is clearly wrong here. He should have consulted Weber in the original instead of relying on the common wisdom of the Weber reception, because the missing background reference is present in Weber's work, as was shown in detail above. Instead of conceiving their works as opposites, Mumford's works on monasticism, and on the megamachine in general, can be considered as belonging to those kinds of background studies to the *Protestant Ethic* that Weber never managed to undertake. This also applies to the sense of the concern with the 'mechanization of technology' also quoted above (Weber 1978 [1910]: 1128–9). Indeed, using a medical-epidemiological analogy, the monastery could be defined as the 'carrier' of the 'spirit' of the megamachine which it 'transmitted' to Europe. While in the medieval period, its spread was contained in extent and kind, it ended up 'contaminating' the entire culture after the collapse of the medieval world order.

The works of Mumford and Weber also complement each other in another respect, but in an opposite temporal sequence. This concerns the history of the city. While it was one of the two main dimensions in Mumford's work, it also has its importance for Weber. It was the subject of one of his most enigmatic writings, the manuscript fragment on the 'City' which was written during the crucial 1911–13 period. Though its inclusion in *Economy and Society* has been questioned in the past, and the manuscript was published in English in a separate volume, Marianne Weber's editorial work in this respect has been vindicated. As Hiroshi Orihara (1994) has shown through careful philological work, the manuscript was indeed intended as the last chapter of *Economy and Society*. Weber's work, however, is only concerned with the origins of the Western city and stops at the threshold of the modern age. It is at this point that Mumford supplements Weber in the direction not only of the distant past but also the present.

Such ideas are not even that opposed, as Mumford held Weber's work in high respect. At least, he listed his name as one of the few outstanding exceptions, together with his three long-time favourites, Geddes, Kropotkin and Ebenezer Howard, who was able to come to a full understanding of the city (CH1 606; see also SL: 151).

At this point, after presenting Mumford's vision of the megamachine, we have not only reached finally the early-modern period which is the central focus of Part II of this book, but also identified his special contribution to the discussion regarding the modern city. The other reflexive historical sociologists identified particular social groups that had a special contribution to the rise of modernity, like the sects, the 'gentry' or the dual-front classes. Some of them, like Foucault, occasionally paid close attention to questions of space and the urban landscape, whilst others, most notably Elias, were explicitly critical of existing approaches as giving too much attention to the city and bourgeois rationality. Mumford, however, added the direct treatment of the new urban space emerging with the sixteenth century to the panorama.

The baroque city

Mumford starts his chapter on 'The structure of baroque power' with a short section on 'Medieval dissolution' (CH: 344–5), but much of the previous and the following sections are also devoted to a detailed description of the facts and reasons for this collapse. Mumford does not agree with the Renaissance perspective of the Middle Ages as a period of darkness, though he also steers clear of an idealization of the past. Agreeing with Huizinga and contrary to the conventional self-presentation of the Renaissance, he interprets it not as a period of progress but as being born out of the profound demoralization of medieval institutions (CH: 346).

In Mumford's view, there is a clear-cut break between the medieval and the baroque cities, and indeed between the two broad world pictures in which the city was one, albeit central, component. The two compose two fundamentally different systems, circles or constellations (ibid.: 347). The decisive moment of transition between the two constellations was the sixteenth century (ibid.: 344). While medieval survivals persisted up to the eighteenth century, the contours of the new order had become clearly visible by the seventeenth century (ibid.: 345).

The new urban pattern can be arranged on three main dimensions: a new type of economy or 'mercantilist capitalism'; a new type of political order or 'centralized despotism or oligarchy' in the form of a 'national state'; and a new form of thought which derived from 'mechanistic physics' (ibid.: 345). These three dimensions correspond to the three main pictures that exist about the city: the idea that the city is fundamentally an economic entity and oriented to commerce, as propagated by Pirenne (1925) in his classic work; that the city is linked to kingship, empire and warfare which was the view of Frankfort; and the Simmelian vision emphasizing the particular mentality that derives from living in a large city. Mumford emphasized the special character that each aspect of the city gained during the baroque period, and particularly their interaction.

Economics: traffic and communication

Of the three components, Mumford ranks the economic aspect the least important. This is partly because he is polemical about the view of Pirenne on the primacy accorded to commerce among the functions of the city, but also because he criticized Weber and Marx for the excessive importance which he believed they attributed to the economic factor. Thus, far from attributing a central role to commerce in the foundation of cities, Mumford considers commerce and capitalism as outright alien from, and hostile to, city life. With a telling metaphor, he talks about the 'egg of the capitalist cuckoo' in the 'nest' of medieval city (CH: 411). This is because liquid capital indeed acts as a 'chemical solvent' (ibid.: 413) on the frameworks and contents of city life: 'capitalism, by its very nature, undermined local autonomy as well as local self-sufficiency, and it introduced an element of instability, indeed of active corrosion into existing cities' (ibid.: 416).

Though Mumford again explicitly formulates his ideas directly opposed to Weber's, it is striking how close they are even here. Mumford, like Weber, starts with the thesis popularized by Sombart about 'modern capitalism'. According to this, capitalism is a universal characteristic of human culture and not specifically modern. What needs to be explained is not its singular emergence in the sixteenth century but the reasons why an activity that previously was severely restricted and at best tolerated, suddenly became not just accepted, but the norm.

Mumford even follows Weber in looking for the answer. The reasons for this drastic change must be searched for in religion. The major 'innovations of capitalism' which emerged and were consolidated between the thirteenth and the eighteenth centuries were 'transferred from religion to business' (ibid.: 414). It is for this reason that the 'new commercial spirit' had a dualistic nature: 'speculative adventure and audacious expansion' on the one hand with the drive for acquisition and profit-making that were the universal features of capitalism in all societies; but also an 'emphasis on the regular and the calculable' on the other hand, which was driven by an unprecedented emphasis on abstraction (ibid.: 421).

The effects of this new 'spirit' and the commercial expansion that followed it, however, were not at all abstract but left very visible imprints on the framework of the city. In opposition to the tendency that treats the movement of goods and people as an analogy of the movement of money and credit in an abstract way, Mumford underlines that a central aspect of the new constellation was the unprecedented importance attributed to traffic and transport. The fight concerning the use of city streets by wheeled vehicles is not just a matter for our century, it was started in the sixteenth century. Yet, despite all resistance, 'the new spirit in society was on the side of rapid transportation' (ibid.: 368) and other city functions became progressively neglected. It is for this reason that the avenue became the 'most important symbol' of the baroque city (ibid.: 367). However, here as elsewhere, this 'spirit' was also supported strongly by, if not originated in, military concerns (ibid.: 387). As a consequence and using the appropriate military–religious analogy, Mumford argues that 'the city was sacrificed to the traffic' (ibid.: 391).

The concern with speed and transport went together with an interest in visibility. Baroque power was not simply about speed, transport and discipline, but also about the display of force and splendour (ibid.: 386–90). In the police utopias of the period, splendour played a major role as it was closely related to force and vigour and special attention was also paid to problems of communication (PPC: 79). Both concerns were jointly manifested in the new master plan of the big cities, with the asterisk type of city plan where all the big avenues started from a central square and radiated towards the periphery. Because of this characteristic, 'one can take in a baroque town almost at a glance' (CH: 390). It directly served military purposes as the artillery could easily shoot through all the main streets from a central point (ibid.: 388). But it also served ceremonial purposes, and the model of this type of plan was the royal hunting park (ibid.: 389).[3]

Politics: court and palace

If Mumford's account of the origins of modern mercantile capitalism was close to Weber's, then his account of baroque politics rhymes with Elias's, down to minute details. This should not be surprising, as Elias started his book by an architectural description of the dwelling place of the court, the palace. Being a lifetime historian of cities and a critic of architecture, Mumford was bound to be struck by the way in which the palace gave a stamp to the entire city. In fact, the starting sentence of the related chapter of his book could be considered as a resumé of Elias's work which had been applied to the city itself: 'Baroque city building, in the formal sense, was an embodiment of the prevalent drama and ritual that shaped itself in the court: in effect, a collective embellishment of the ways and gestures of the palace' (CH: 375).[4]

According to Mumford, the court was a world in itself, though it was a peculiar looking-glass world where 'all the harsh realities of life were shown in a diminishing glass, and all its frivolities magnified' (ibid.: 375). Though the Goffmanesque vision of the court as a total institution is still shared by both Elias and Mumford, the passage also indicates the point where the two thinkers part. Mumford was not satisfied with the sociological reconstruction of the court and the genealogical assessment of its impact on the present, and added his own personal evaluative angle.

There was also another main divergence on the origins of the baroque city. Mumford moved back towards Weber and put the emphasis on religious roots. According to him, the new city can be understood as the 'analytical decomposition of the Church' (ibid.: 372). Each of the former functions of church ceremonies acquired an independent role as an institution. However, though the functions of the Church became parcelled up in the baroque city, even the central motivating idea of the Church has been preserved in the secular disguise of the 'new divinity' of the Court. Mumford quotes from a panegyric of Breton: 'Oh, the gallant life of the Court, where so many are the choices of contentment, as if on earth it were the Paradise of the World' (ibid.: 376).[5]

In its structural description and analysis of court life, Mumford's account again closely mirrors Elias's. It can even be arranged under the three section titles of visibility, interdependence and strategic games. A central characteristic of court life which was transmitted to the entire baroque city is a pervasive concern with visibility. This applied to the plan of the city as well as social life in general: '[t]o be "seen", to be "recognized", to be "accepted" were the supreme social duties, indeed the work of a whole life-time' (ibid.: 377).

The court was also the place for the permanent playing of intrigues and strategic games. The accents of Mumford, however, were slightly different owing to his diagnostic angle. Elias wanted to reconstruct the rationality of court life from the inside, whereas Mumford moves to the outside and, while not denying its internal coherence and especially its lasting impact on modernity, also shows the substantive 'irrationality' of this formal 'rationality'. For Mumford, the pervasive involvement in intrigues was not simply the rational outcome of a specific figuration, but was the inherently perverse consequence of a parasitic lifestyle. The court was composed of individuals who were not just idle, but were in a certain way forced to be idle. They were not simply entertaining themselves to have a good time but, partly by the ceremonialization of all aspects of life, they were forced to do so as 'the very distractions of the court became duties' (ibid.: 377). The result was a 'pervasive tedium' which was comparable to the 'labours of consumption', the royal 'boredom of satiety' of the Egyptian pharaoh (MMI: 206) or the modern assembly plant. According to Mumford, '[f]rom the moment the Prince's eyes opened to the last moment when his mistress left his bedchamber, he was, so to say, on the assembly line' (CH: 376). The parallels between the court society and modernity are just as strict for Mumford as they were for Elias:

> As in so many other departments of life the baroque court here anticipated the ritual and the psychal reaction of the twentieth century metropolis. A similar grind: a similar boredom: a similar attempt to take refuge in "distractions" from the tyrannical oppression that had become routine and from the routine that had become an overwhelming oppression.
>
> (ibid.: 377)

The utopian dreams and the drudgery of everyday routine assume themselves (SU: 196–7), while the 'idea of abolishing all work' is 'only a slave's dream' (MMI: 242).

It is this extreme boredom which dominates the everyday life that was transformed into an endless ritual and that explains further the strategification characteristic of the court. The plots, while being complex in their set-up and deadly serious in outcome, were often simple-minded, childish and more typical of the behaviour of schoolboys kept under too strict control than of that expected of serious diplomats and courtiers. Using a term developed by Elemér Hankiss (1982) to describe the 'court society' *par excellence* that was the 'existing socialism' of East Europe, these kinds of arrangements had an infantilizing effect on the personality structure.

Finally, though he does not use the concept 'interdependence', Mumford also addresses this aspect. The constant presence in the same environment and the participation in the same rituals and plots make human beings very much aware of each other in matters of power and sexuality. The combination of repetitive public rituals and the escape into privacy led to a 'dilation of the senses' (CH: 385) and an escalation of sexual activities which 'transformed full-blown love-making from a seasonal to a year-round occupation' (ibid.: 384). In diagnosing this fact and its massive after-effects, Mumford is quoting Rilke: 'Have you ever seen, when men acted or let themselves go in the direction of pleasure, relaxation or enjoyment that they came by any pleasant results?' (ibid.: 379).[6]

On the other hand, these rituals were also bound to transform all human relations into relationships of power. In these mechanized rituals, every single member of the court ended up becoming entangled which led to the 'paradox of power' that, after a time, even the absolutist ruler will not be that different from its humblest servant with both becoming 'cogs, caught in the same mechanism' (ibid.: 391).[7] This insight pushed Mumford with giving a similar account about the fall of the court to that Elias gave in his final chapter of *The Court Society* on the socio-genesis of the French Revolution. On the one hand, the mechanic court rituals became mere shells which were no longer able to generate support and legitimacy. On the other, while the large opens spaces and the splendour of the baroque city were supposed to magnify royal power, '[t]hese long avenues serve as a diminishing glass: in the long perspectives of Versailles or St. Petersburg, the central human figure, King or Czar, became ever smaller and soon reached his political vanishing point' (CH: 391).

Mentality: abstraction and mechanism

Of the three main dimensions of the new urban pattern, Mumford assigns the greatest role to the intellectual dimension. This is also obvious in the passage where he connects the army and the monastery, which are the two main archetypal sources of the new urban complex, directly to the third of the three dimensions listed (CH: 345).

The new mentality has the two main components of abstraction and mechanism. The three abstractions of money, time and space dominate this mentality.[8] In the economy, the emphasis shifted from the exchange of concrete goods at a concrete location to the abstract market, or from the marketplace to market economy (ibid.: 410–14). In this context, Mumford hints at the twin processes of the monetarization of government and the militarization of capitalism (ibid.: 363–4). This is accompanied by a new concept of space, with an emphasis on continuity, measurability and order, and where space is associated with motion and time (ibid.: 364).

The new mentality of abstraction was socially significant as it did just not remain on paper (just like the utopias: see SU: 233) but was closely related to the new developments in science and technology (CH: 365). Like Elias, Borkenau and Foucault, Mumford considered Descartes not simply as a philosopher but as the figure of this new mentality *par excellence*, and he called attention to the fact that he was also a scientist, a mathematician and a soldier (ibid.: 395).

The different aspects of abstraction and mechanism were closely inter-related and thus left a marked stamp: '[t]he abstractions of money, spatial perspective, and mechanical time provided the enclosing frame of the new life' (ibid.: 365). The problem, as Mumford keeps repeating, is neither abstraction itself nor mechanism nor the machine, but resides in its social effect. This leads to a situation where abstraction and mechanism begin to dominate forms of thinking, so one witnesses 'a society of abstraction' or an' age of abstractions' (ibid.: 367). This leads to a reductionist perspective on experience which accepts only whatever can be seen and measured and denies the reality of all those aspects of human existence that escape its grid. It is this mentality, and not abstraction, science, mechanism or tech-nology, that is bound to have disastrous consequences (ibid.: 366).

The economic, political and intellectual aspects of the new city life were closely related. Their interdependence can be captured in the three levels of the origins of this city, its structure and its effects.

As far as origins are concerned, the new urban complex is rooted in two 'archetypal' institutions, the army and the monastery (CH: 345), which are the same two institutions that became the main transmitters of the mega-machine. Thus, to make the parallels between Mumford and Elias complete, one could argue that the court and its stamping the image of the baroque city was the basis of the modern megamachine. These two insti-tutions shape the central characteristics of all three dimensions of the new urban complex though, even here, Mumford gives priority to the mental aspects.

As far as the general structure of the baroque age is concerned, the links between the three aspects discussed above can be demonstrated at the level of the institutional framework and the ruling mentality. On the first, Mumford quotes a striking passage from Palladio who was a main architect of the period, and then makes an even more stunning commentary:

> The palace: the exchequer: the prison: the mad-house – what four buildings could more completely sum up the new order or better sym-bolize the main features of its political life. These were the dominants. Between them stretched the blankly repetitive façades; and behind those façades the forgotten and denied parts of life somehow went on.
> (CH: 395)

These sentences, which sum up Mumford's storyline, also demonstrate with particular clarity the close links that exist between his vision and those of Weber, Elias and Foucault.

On the second point, the economic, political and social institutions dominating everyday life share a common vision and mentality which combines belief in infinity, eternity and universality: 'baroque planners tacitly assumed that their order was eternal' (ibid.: 393). This conceit was possible because of the 'assumptions – and superstitions – of unqualified power' (ibid.: 402).

Using Mumford's later terminology, both concerns can be summed up in a single expression, as the megamachine and the myth of the machine.

Finally, Mumford continues with the effects of the court up to the present day. He is motivated by the same concern as all other reflexive historical sociologists, and the story he tells matters not simply to understand the past, but also to realize the extent to which aspects of our past still hold a sway over the present. He even agrees with the others that the area where these effects are most pervasive is the self itself.

Just as his criticism was not targeting 'science' or 'technology' as such, but only the extension of a mechanical mentality into a wholesale world picture, he similarly recognized the dual facetedness of the court and its baroque cult of power, which contrasted the polishing of manners to the new type of despotism it promoted. The problem was that both effects prevailed and survived the court that engendered them (ibid.: 382). The modes of conduct characteristic of the court spread into the entire population, through the impact of various elites, and not only in the seventeenth and eighteenth centuries. In the footsteps of de Tocqueville, Mumford argues that in many respects such as conscription, the French Revolution only reinforced dictatorial trends: it was '[t]hrough the very workings of democracy [that] baroque absolutism tightened its hold upon society' (ibid.: 400). For Mumford, the opposites of the liberal and Marxist perspectives are two sides of the same coin. Just as capitalism and the military establishment developed hand in hand and not in opposition, the same holds true for centralized power and democracy: '[I]f tyranny is a consequence of democratic confusion and ineptitude, it is equally true that democratic vulgarization is an inevitable result of the final stage of tyranny: depersonalized efficiency' (ibid.: 391). As a particularly apt example, Mumford likes to refer to the way marketing and advertising are now assumed to be natural, though it is only a sign that '[w]e have now exchanged autonomy for automation' (SL: 23–4).

The most lasting link between baroque power and modernity, however, lies in the formation of the individual. The mentalities of abstraction and mechanism shaped not only the way human beings related to each other but also towards themselves. If the walls of the closed institutions only encircle a small fragment of the population today, it should not give us much relief, as the mentalities are carried over into everyday conduct:

> [t]his myth of the untrammelled individual was in fact the democrati-
> zation of the baroque conception of the despotic Prince: now every
> enterprising man sought to be a despot in his own right: emotional
> despots like the romantic poets; practical despots like the businessmen
>
> (CH: 448)

The self-conceited individualistic cogs of the modern megamachine, and
the many modern day Oedipuses springing up from the pages of Cocteau's
Infernal Machine, who are driven by the conviction that 'nothing can ever
happen to me', are 'doubly degraded because they have no consciousness
of their own degradation' (MMI: 183). The parallels with Weber and
Foucault, the 'specialists without a heart' and the emancipated liberals, are
so strict and evident that they do not require further elaboration.

Mumford is not a modern day Rousseau who is dreaming of returning
to an age before cities and civilization. He was born in New York City and
throughout his long life, he preserved a love for the city, but especially 'his'
city, or at least the one in which he was brought up. But he was all too well
aware of the immense ambiguities which have accompanied the city since
its emergence, especially in the present day. The city and civilization, organized warfare and religion which were both born out of sacrifice and the
myth of the machine, and mechanized rituals have all formed tight knots
around themselves since their joint emergence. Since its emergence, the
city was an asylum in both senses of the word: it was a safe haven and a
place of escape and refuge, but also a prison with a closed, closely-con-
trolled, chaotic, crowded and artificial environment. This ambivalence has
also been increasingly magnified in the modern city with every new
epochal turn: the 'crystallization of chaos' reigning in the modern cities
since the nineteenth century (Mumford 1946 [1938]: 7); the state of permanent war that emerged after the Second World War when 'the
megamachines of the United States and Soviet Russia instead of being dis-
mantled as a regrettable temporary wartime necessity were elevated into
permanent institutions' (MMII: 266); and finally the communication revolution that fully realized the 'potentials' of the city (or anti-city?)
developments started in the sixteenth century (MMI: 175, 187). One only
has to refer to Simmel's famous characterization of life in a metropolis to
realize that city life always had a vibrant, hectic, active but reflexive, spiritual but mundane, and thus also liminal, character. It always required the
countryside as its counterpoise – a source of stability to balance its
excesses, a place of vacation, refuge and escape – just as it was a safe haven
in another sense for the countryside. The current stage of globalization
breaks down this pattern and, whether it is called a global village or a
megapolis, it implies a permanent state of liminality and is thus life-hostile
and world-rejecting for Mumford as well as for Nietzsche, Weber, Voegelin
and Foucault.

10 Disciplinary society (Foucault)

In contrast to the three thinkers discussed in the previous chapters, Foucault's work did not start under the aegis of Weber and did not develop in a continuous dialogue with his works. For various reasons, Weber's work was not very well known in France until the 1980's. It was all but ignored both by the Durkheimian school in sociology and by the *Annales* school in history. Furthermore, after the Second World War his works were championed by Raymond Aron, and that gave a very specific intellectual and even political–ideological connotation to his ideas. Yet, the procedure followed previously can be applied even in mapping Foucault's work, and this would not only conform to its spirit but even to his words, as he acknowledged it (Foucault 1983: 14).

Foucault's work has such a close elective affinity with Weber's because they shared much of their main reading experiences. Foucault did not read Nietzsche through Weber, but in the last years of his life recognized the similarity in the way their approaches developed independently on the basis of an ongoing dialogue with Nietzsche. Even further, Foucault shared with Weber a further reading experience in Kierkegaard.[1] Thus, in spite of living sixty years after Weber, Foucault could be said to have embarked independently on a parallel life project.

As a best indication, Foucault's life-work can be compared to Weber's central concerns along the lines pursued in the previous chapters. Just as Elias and Borkenau took up the project outlined by Weber at the end of the 'Anticritical Last Word', Foucault's trajectory can also be interpreted in a similar manner. In his last years Foucault repeatedly stated that the central underlying problem of his historical investigations was the link between subjectivity and truth. This can be compared to Weber's interest in the history of the conduct of life and modern science.

The parallels extend even to the ambivalent presence of a third main dimension in their historical work, which was the question of power. Foucault specified it as the third main axis of his work in his last two conclusive statements, the *Introduction* to *The Use of Pleasure* and the 'What Is Enlightenment?' essay. However, whenever the question was brought up of the underlying problem giving unity to his work, and not simply the classification of the work he had completed, at least after 1981 he always left power out and mentioned only truth and subjectivity.[2] He occasionally added that he was only interested in the study of power to the extent that it was concerned with questions of power exerted on the subject through the force of a discourse claiming to be true. For Weber, power was similarly an omnipresent concern. His classificatory scheme about the three pure types of legitimate authority is arguably the best known and most used part of his work. Similarly, the *Vorbemerkung* specified the fateful force of modern capitalism as his central concern (PE: 20–7). And yet he never completed or even considered a study of the emergence of power in the manner of conventional political histories, nor even in the manner of such neo-classical works as those of Giddens (1981), Mann (1986) or Skocpol (1979).

However, even though the main axes of their work were the same because of their common roots in Nietzsche, they went in opposite directions. Foucault, as Borkenau did and Elias planned to do, started with histories of modern science. Weber, however, started with a genealogy of the modern methodical conduct of life, and never explicitly studied the rise of modern science.[3] However from the very start, Foucault also shared a basic interest in the question of subjectivity, or the methodical and reflected conduct of life, and thus his work can be arranged along the forms of dissent from the work of Weber used in the previous cases.

Situating Foucault

One of the main dimensions of dissent concerns the particular social group singled out for attention. Weber put the middle classes or the 'sober bourgeois' as a type at the centre of interest as the 'carrier' of the 'spirit' of capitalism (PE: 23–4). In contrast to this, Elias brought in the importance of the court nobility, Borkenau sharpened the analysis by his dynamical in-between class, while Foucault provided a new angle by his focus on social exclusion and marginalization.

His interest in techniques of exclusion and marginalization has often been interpreted as an attempt to be more radical than Marx himself and to be a champion of the marginals among the marginals. However, once he realized the possibility of such a line of reception, Foucault was quick to dissociate himself from this image and stated that he was no 'melancholic historian' or teller of sad tales (DEIII: 257; PPC: 111). He certainly entertained sympathy and empathy for the lot of the weak and downtrodden, and took part in political activity supporting and not simply representing but often silencing their voice. Even in the last unpublished part of his work he emphasized that *parrhesia*, or frankness of speech as a political right, was connected in Greece to the power of the weakest.[4] But his interest in exclusion and marginalization also had an important theoretical motivation, though not from a Marxist but from a phenomenological–hermeneutical perspective. According to this viewpoint, it is from the margins, the gaps or the cracks that it is possible to gain a clear perspective on the central characteristics of the way power was exercised and human beings were shaped in modern societies, and the assumed is rendered visible. Put another way, in his work in contrast to his political activity as a citizen, Foucault was interested in marginality in so far as marginal situations were at one and the same time liminal.[5]

In fact, in this respect, Foucault's concern was not that different from most of the other reflexive historical sociologists. These works are complementary not simply in the sense of covering the entire spectrum of social classes. On the contrary, they are also complementary in putting the emphasis on specific social groups which at one time or another, whether at the upper or lower end of the spectrum, entered a liminal situation and thus could become the 'carrier' of the 'spirit' of modernity.[6] This holds true for Elias on the 'dual-front classes', Borkenau on the 'gentry', and the interest in sects shared by Weber and Voegelin. All were fundamental according to them to carrying the 'spirit' (or the 'spiritual virus'?) of capitalism and modernity.

This is not simply an interpretation of Foucault's work, but is in tune with his own self-assessment, which was contained in a series of attempts at reflecting upon the course of his own work which characterized his interest during the later 1970s and the early 1980s. In these, a central term used for his work was 'experience'. On different but always significant occasions, he applied it both to his concrete lines of investigation and to a general systematic description of the work as a whole. The best known examples are the 'What Is Enlightenment?' essay and the versions of the *Preface* to the *History of Sexuality* series, particularly the 'Intended Preface' included in the *Foucault Reader,* which was even more characteristic than the version which was eventually published. But perhaps the first such occasions were the major 1979 Stanford lectures (PPC: 57–85).

Foucault started by characterizing his work in contrast to the Frankfurt School: 'It may be wise not to take as a whole the rationalization of society or of culture, but to analyze this process in several fields, each of them grounded in a fundamental experience: madness, illness, death, crime, sexuality, etc.' (ibid.: 59). At the end of the first of the two lectures, he resumed his argument by stating that the problem of the links between experience, knowledge and power is the problem that had preoccupied his work since his first book. He finished with two questions:

> Our civilization has developed the most complex system of knowledge, the most sophisticated structures of power: what has this kind of knowledge, this type of power made of us? In what way are those fundamental experiences of madness, suffering, death, crime, individuality connected, even if we are not aware of it, with knowledge and

with power? I am sure I'll never get the answer; but that does not mean that we don't have to ask the question.

(PPC: 71).

While intended as a resumé of his entire past work, this formulation can be read as a shift in Foucault's concern with marginality and liminality. Liminal situations and experiences not only provide a privileged perspective for gaining access to what otherwise remains taken for granted in structures of power and knowledge, but the very formation of these structures assumes fluid conditions of real world large-scale liminality. This is how Foucault came to recognize that major socio-political events and discontinuit' in the systems of thought can be connected without ignoring the materiality of discourse and reducing thought to the role of representing reality. This recognition came at the end of his work, as 'the most general things are those that appear last' (PPC: 257), in the concept of 'problematization'. Throughout his earlier works, Foucault refused to root changes in the institutional and discursive treatment of fundamental life experiences to socio-political events like the French Revolution or the consolidation of the absolutist state. His basic approach was to take changes of thought seriously, first in isolation. The development of the concept 'problematization' enabled him to link changes in thought back to global events without giving up his position on the possibility of analysing discontinuities in thought in their own terms.

However, apart from the question of visibility, the problems posed by marginal individuals, social groups and basic life experiences, provide a further angle towards understanding the modern condition which is the fundamental task of reflexive historical sociology. This is because modern societies seem to have specific problems with marginal and liminal situations. The most peculiar character of the modern institutional order is that, from its perspective, marginality and liminality are not simply close but are all but identical.

One has to be very careful about the formulation of this problem, and the joint treatment of marginality and fundamental life experiences in the spirit of Foucault's work helps to avoid derailment. The problem with modernity is not the mere fact that there are individuals or groups in marginal situations. There have always been, and will always be, inequalities of power and wealth. In an even more trivial way, illness, madness, crime and death can never be eliminated as they are constant features of existence, and are part of the reality of the human condition. The specificity of modern societies lies not simply in the very existence of marginal and liminal situations, but in the fact that they have become so problematic and the manner in which this has happened.

The dilemma, of course, is not a result of sensitivity towards the fate of the suffering, or a concern with social justice. It is a feature of modern culture that is neither unique nor general, and goes back to Christianity and even to Jewish prophecy (Zeitlin 1994). At the opposite end of the spectrum, the problem is not simply that at an absolute level, the modern age can be characterized by more suffering, poverty and oppression than other time periods of history. Such comparisons are impossible to make, and in another sense only push real problems to an imaginary and ideological level which ends up in a self-flagellation and self-hatred (because of a sense of guilt so characteristic of modern intellectuals) that has become impossible to handle. The specific feature of modernity is rather the wide gap wedged in these societies between the utopian dreams of the solution of *all* problems related to *both* marginal and liminal experiences on the one hand, and the peculiar modality in which the stubborn survival of these characteristics is handled on the other.

A crucial feature of modern thought is its utopian character, and the strong tendency, not simply to create imaginary and ideal worlds in fantasy, but to move towards their implementation in actual reality. In diagnosing this characteristic, Foucault's concern and terminology closely parallels that of Voegelin, Mumford and Koselleck.

This leads up to the second point, that marginal situations and fundamental life experiences are lived differently under the conditions of modernity than in any other kind of society. They share at least three unique features. First, they have become hidden, denied, silenced and repressed. As this is a central point in Foucault's work, and for many reflexive historical sociologists, it has to be elaborated in some detail.

The 'marginalization of liminality'

In the areas of poverty there were a series of attempts, from the sixteenth century onwards, at separating and eliminating beggars, vagabonds, and the poor in general from society, chasing them out of public spaces and rendering them therefore invisible and seemingly non-existent.[7] As part of the same process, those who for various reasons could not care for themselves or be cared for by family members became similarly enclosed in the 'Great Confinement'. Foucault argues that in this process, for a long time, the poor, the sick or petty offenders (those threatening public order and not law, and handled by the police and not the courts) were handled in the same way. No distinction was made between marginal and liminal situations as from the perspective of the 'same', they all looked 'other'.

When such distinctions were made around the late eighteenth century, this coincided with a shift in the locus of utopias from the well-ordered police state to a society from which all fundamental life experiences were to be eliminated. On the treatment of the sick, their separation and the scientific classification of diseases went together with the utopian dream of the full elimination of all sickness (BC: 31–2). In a similar manner, the entire economy of punishment was reorganized, replacing the public spectacle of the scaffold with more hidden ways of punishment. The story can be continued with the case of sexual pleasures. This may sound surprising, as according to received wisdom, Foucault 'deconstructed' the idea of sexual repression. However, such an interpretation and even Foucault's position must be taken with a pinch of salt. Sexual behaviour most certainly became increasingly problematic in the eighteenth and nineteenth centuries. There also were certainly attempts to eliminate, minimize, reduce and push this fundamental life experience into the dark. The point of Foucault was on the one hand to criticize a certain kind of 'Freudo-Marxism' which had become an almost common-sense wisdom in French intellectual circles at that time, and on the other to argue that this official outlawing of sexuality went hand in hand with an explosion of discourse on sexuality. This produced all sorts of 'perversions' (HSI: 47).

One could continue with a theme that Foucault touched upon in the first and last period of his work, and which was surrounded either by silence or noisy criticism, the issue of spirituality. Spiritual experiences, or sudden encounters with the 'beyond', are universal and appear in all cultures. They are closely linked to the fundamental, similarly universal (Dupront 1987), liminal practice of pilgrimage (Turner and Turner 1978). For a long time the attitude of modern philosophy and science to such experiences was to ignore them or to treat them as psychopathological phenomena. The fundamental importance of the philosophies of such people as William James and Karl Jaspers lies in a return to the question of 'religious experiences'.[8] The handling of individuals with religious sensitivity and spiritual experiences as examples of psychopathology shows a basic affinity: between the modern mechanistic-mathematical world image and totalitarianism, not science and despotism. Science has nothing to do with spiritual experiences. Science is based on experiments. It assumes repetition, regularity and universal laws and it cannot take up a position concerning the existence or non-existence of the irruption of the divine into the realm of human beings. The truth-claims and authenticity of singular human experiences cannot be tested by scientific means. This may be considered a triviality, and has certainly been argued extensively by Kant, who attempted to separate religion from both science and morality.[9] However, what requires understanding and has been central to Weber-inspired sociology, is the reason it has become so important for some circles of Enlightenment-inspired thought to argue that science does indeed refute religion or spirituality.

Finally, and in an even more evidently paradoxical way, an enclosing and silencing has happened with respect to the two single most basic and least dispensable life experiences, the emergence and disappearance of life, birth and death. On the one hand, this implied a hospitalization of these two events, which at a certain moment of time almost became complete; on the other, it amounted to a situation where death became 'forbidden' (Ariès 1974) or 'inverted' (Ariès 1977). Part of this can be attributed to rational factors, like the presence of competent medical personnel, or the risks and costs of providing adequate care at home. Another part is owing to psychological factors like increasing sensibility or lower thresholds of tolerance for pain and suffering. However, given the importance and inevitability of these events for the human condition, the evident troubles which these natural phenomena cause in modern societies indicates more fundamental causes which must be brought to the surface and tackled directly.

The 'liminalization of marginality'

These attempts at a silencing, denial or elimination of the fundamental experiences of human existence can be termed as the 'marginalization of liminality'. This, however, is only one aspect of the paradoxical modern mentality with respect to marginality and liminality. The second, inverse process can be called the 'liminalization of marginality' or the re-valorization of marginal, outcast status as the only 'authentic' or 'genuine' human condition. Among the 'alternative' political sects and movement, this involves the redefinition of marginal individuals and groups as the 'true carriers' of revolution and progress. This goes back at least to Marx and his championing of the proletariat. Since then, all 'truly' revolutionary movements have been desperately searching for new and new 'marginal' groups who could be proclaimed and thus launched into the vanguard. This applied at various times to Russian workers in contrast to the Western workers who have lost the 'revolutionary zeal', the peasants of China, students or different movements from the Third World.

All these ideas and movements share a number of common features. They are never satisfied with redressing real grievances or injustices, but always press for an 'alchemic' transformation of a marginal status into a liminal one and making the outcast into a leader and vanguard (Horvath 1998). In itself, this seems an unlikely idea and can seem just the naive dream of a handful of utopians. However, this dream was dangerous enough as it did have a genuine basis in the real-world liminal situation. The actual 'revolutionary potential' was provided by social groups who did not share a 'liminal' potential in the sense of possessing a particular 'destiny' to guide mankind into a bright future. On the contrary, they were going through a genuine process of marginalization owing to the impact of modern capitalism on previously accepted forms of life, and thus entering a liminal situation with no hope in sight.

The formation of marginal and liminal identities

The third aspect of the modern mentality concerns the formation of lasting identities around marginal and liminal conditions. This may be even more puzzling than the previous two, but it is also the most relevant for the present. The first aspect, the disciplinary dream of 'marginalizing the liminal' is in certain respects in retreat. There is a definite, though not unopposed, move away from practices of hospitalization and confinement, and it certainly no longer makes sense to talk about sexual repression. The second aspect, the revolutionary dream of the 'liminalization of the marginal', seems to have lost its political effectiveness though not its emotional appeal. However, the third aspect is still gaining momentum and the 'politics of identity' are only the tip of the iceberg. Even more importantly, the identities that are today used and formed in the loudest and most assertive manner are often based on previous marginal and excluded or forced positions.[10]

In Foucault's work, there has indeed been a shift in relative focus from the first concern, through a temporary flirtation with second, to the third. Thus, his first books were about techniques of confinement, silencing, enclosing and repression. Starting with *Discipline and Punish* and especially the *History of Sexuality* series and related works, the emphasis shifted to the 'positive' aspects of power. However, this shift was only in emphasis, as the formation of lasting identities and subject positions around techniques of exclusion or disciplining was always at the heart of Foucault's interest.

The persistent concern Foucault had, with the positive formation of a permanent identity around a marginal and liminal situation and its character, can be best illustrated with an episode that turned up at crucial moments of his trajectory. It concerns a practice employed by a French psychiatrist, Leuret, around 1840. He put patients believed to be simulating madness under a strong cold shower. After a while, he asked them whether they were mad. In case of a negative response, he continued the 'therapy' until they finally admitted that they were mad. At that moment, Leuret considered the patient cured.

The story fascinated Foucault for about two decades, though for a long time he was evidently not able to give a proper account of what was going on. He may have encountered the story while writing *Histoire de la folie*. Yet it is not contained in the book, but appears in a short piece published in October 1963 (DEI: 270–1). The date is significant as, at that time, Foucault accomplished one of the most important reorganizations of both his professional and private life. He abandoned the planned continuation of his genealogy of madness, and turned to literary criticism and the analysis of discourses that eventually culminated in *The Order of Things*. The publication could be interpreted as an attempt to leave at least a trace of the problem that kept bothering him and that he was not able to solve.[11] At any rate, his short comments characterize the exchange as a dialogue of the deaf, then fit the story in the line of argument of the piece, which was related to the material substance of water. In late 1977, he had Leuret's text 'The moral treatment of madness' published with a very short introduction entitled 'The scaffold of truth'. In it he interpreted the text in the language of *Discipline and Punish*. Finally, the story was taken up again in autumn 1980 as the starting point of his American lectures (Foucault 1993: 200–1, EST: 175–6). The date is again significant as it indicates that the return of the story can be connected to Foucault's major self-reflexive exercises of summer 1980 (Foucault 1994). It coincided with the abandonment of the attempt to specify his approach to power as lying at the heart of his work, in favour of specifying instead his problem around subjectivity and truth.

At this point, Foucault was also able to give an interpretation of the story in its own terms. In contrast to 1963, he compares it with performative speech act and not with psychoanalysis. In the verbal recognition of one's own madness, '[t]he affirmation destroys in the speaking subject the reality that made the same affirmation true'. This poses the following question: 'What conception of truth of discourse and of subjectivity is taken for granted in this strange and yet widespread practice?' (EST: 176). Here Foucault was finally able to formulate properly the question underlying his work. The full answer to this, and related, questions is given by his turn towards antiquity. This can be compared with Weber, whose successful formulation of the underlying problem of *The Protestant Ethic* in the 'Anticritical Last Word' led to the 'Economic Ethic' project. Within the limits of this book, however, attention will be restricted to the perspective Foucault gained concerning his previous writings.

Though Foucault could not yet formulate his question fully, the formation of a positive, permanent identity around a simultaneously marginal and liminal position had been present in his works since the first books. Thus, in *Histoire de la folie*, his interest was not restricted to discourses about madness but focused on the formation and labelling of individuals as mad, plus the formation of the identity, or indeed nonidentity, of the 'mad subject'. In *The Birth of the Clinic*, he similarly analysed the experience of illness, while in *Discipline and Punish* he showed in detail how the modern method of punishment was not oriented simply towards the punishment of crimes, but towards the construction of the criminal as a special kind of subject.

This perspective on identity formation adds a further angle to the previous discussion on the peculiar problematicity of marginality and liminality under modern conditions. As Victor Turner argued in his pathbreaking paper, the structures of human experiences can be analysed as rites of passage (V. Turner 1985: 226). These have a tripartite and sequential structure, consisting of the phase of separation, the liminal period proper, and the phase of reaggregation (see V. Turner 1969: 94–5). In the case of illness, for example the three phases are the infection and latency, the illness proper and the period of convalescence. In the case of death, these are the agony of dying, the death and the mourning by those affected. Liminal experiences, save for the experience of death, do not 'objectify' the individuals in the sense of giving them a definite identity.

Quite the contrary, such an idea does not make sense, as liminal periods are by definition only temporary and not permanent. However, such identities are constructed in modern societies.[12] Thus, we can add the further paradox of the construction of permanent identities out of temporary liminal conditions to the puzzling problems discussed previously of the marginalization of liminality and the liminalization of marginality. As an example, in the case of illness, this was laid bare by Thomas Mann in his *The Magic Mountain* where he captured a society whose members are stuck in a permanent state of sickness and made it a powerful metaphor. This was a state which, in his Nietzschean vision, was a prelude to the Great War of 1914–18.[13]

Matters become further complicated when the static legalistic dichotomies of good or bad and right or wrong are joined to the triadic, processual form of liminality. A liminal situation is defined as being outside order, so it can also thus easily move outside the law. In other words, liminal experiences always border on the transgressive. By definition this is most evident in the case of crime, which explains why criminality gains a paradigmatic status under conditions of modernity, starting from detective stories and leading up to *Discipline and Punish*. However sexuality, madness and even illness can also become transgressive. In this case, the question concerns the manner in which a permanent negative identity is built up around certain kinds of transgressive acts.

Even more general and tricky complications emerge when the dichotomy of the true and false is joined to liminal experiences. This is a more general case as it can be applied to any fundamental experience, even those that do not transgress any laws. It is also trickier because the application of the adjective 'true' to a liminal experience implies a set of thorny dilemmas. The first issue to be settled is whether 'truth' refers to the experience itself or to the individual or the group undergoing the experience. In either case, further complications are bound to appear. If 'truth' refers to the experience, the trouble is that all liminal experiences are singular dislocations of order for the individual or community concerned, and therefore their 'truth content' cannot be assessed, because of the dissolution of the very reference point. It is certainly true that Weber went through a serious illness that impeded his activities in much of his working life and that Nietzsche went mad. But there is no consensus, and probably never will be, concerning the actual character of their illnesses. The further idea that it could be possible to describe what their 'true experience' of illness and madness was certainly seems ludicrous, though both experiences were most relevant to the work of these thinkers. This yields the result that 'truth' in the sense of an objective, scientific truth cannot be established with respect to basic human life experiences. The truth of an experience can only lie in the way it is lived, remembered and told (if at all).

We do not get further if we try to pin down the 'truth' of an experience to the individual undergoing the experience. On the contrary, the results

are even weaker, and the complication is again due to the legalistic terminology applied beyond its scope. Rites of passage are performed in
order to produce a change in the mode of being of the individuals and
communities undergoing them. Experiences are thus transformative. It
therefore makes no sense to talk about the 'true' identity of the individual before and after the experience. In a biological sense the human
being, of course, remains the same before and after undergoing an experience. Furthermore, no legal system could function without maintaining
the fiction of the persistence of legal subjectivity.[14] However, this has
nothing to do with the 'truth' of the individual self. No individual is completely changed by a single life experience, be it spiritual, sexual or
health-related. But neither is s/he the same afterwards. The very idea of
the 'true self' as a fixed entity which is beyond the narrative story of the
experience-events one has undergone is therefore a denial of the reality
of the human condition.[15]

The fiction of the 'true self', however, has its own effectiveness under
modern conditions, and is comparable to the utopian longing for the elimination of basic human life experiences. The identity of the 'true self' is
incompatible with the sequential rhythm of liminal processes, but is com-
patible with their short-circuiting in the form of a paradoxical 'permanent
liminality'. In this sense, the fiction of the 'true self' corresponds to the formation of marginal identities around liminal experiences which are
considered transgressive. This issue, together with related other considerations of 'permanent liminality', will be discussed in the concluding
section of the book.

In the next section, a presentation will be given of Foucault's 'vision' of
modernity. It will focus first on his best known work, *Discipline and Punish*,
and then reconstruct the changes this vision underwent from the mid-
1970s onwards.

The 'disciplinary society'

The most powerful, though quite controversial and problematic, formulation of Foucault's vision of modernity is contained in *Discipline and Punish*.
The insight was the outcome of two experiences, his personal experience
during his visit to the prison of Attica and his experience of reading
Bentham's *Panopticon*. These two encounters not only gave focus to
Foucault's current work on punitive institutions, but clarified and summarized, at least for the time being, the various segments of the work which
he had completed so far. The links between *Discipline and Punish, Histoire
de la folie* and *Birth of the Clinic* were especially close.

The content of the vision first becomes obvious in the formal organization of the book. It has no Preface or Introduction, but starts *in media res*
with the two contrasting pictures of the public execution of Damiens for
regicide in 1757 and a timetable containing some of the rules set up for

young prisoners eighty years later, which extended to the first five pages of the book.[16] Foucault used the technique in his earlier works, though not to such an extent. The original editions of both *Histoire de la folie* and *Birth of the Clinic* had a *Preface*. *Birth of the Clinic* starts with two short paragraphs which contrast the treatment of hysteria in the mid-eighteenth century, which today sounds simply bizarre, with the familiar anatomical description of lesion a century later. Chapter One of *Histoire de la folie* similarly begins with the contrasting images of the emptying of the leper towns at the end of the Middle Ages and the 'ship of fools' which was a new object of the Renaissance, and an image that could have been taken from Huizinga. Furthermore, the technique bears a resemblance to Weber's 1904–5 concept of ideal types as historical individuals. But Foucault's way of proceeding is not identical with Weber's, and this difference is most obvious in this book.[17] These pages provide more than an interpretive illustration. They appeal not only to the intellect but also to the emotions, purposefully provoking shocking effects. They are dramatizations or performances. All performance is a sort of 'rite of passage' which is aimed at a cathartic, transformative effect.[18] These vivid images indicate that Foucault does not simply want to convince his reader, but to captivate, change and transform. Furthermore, he wants to do so not by ideological and manipulative arguments. If stylistic devices are used in the book, they are deployed in the sense of performance and not of rhetoric. The aim is to render the experiences that underlie and motivate the book accessible for the reader, giving coherence to its vision.

The opening scenes provide an ideal–typical contrast between past and present practices, between the Middle Ages and modernity. The execution of Damiens is in 1757 but it could have happened hundreds of years earlier, as the practice remained unchanged from the early Middle Ages. The scenes lie beyond good and evil, as the question of which mode of punishment is preferable is not decided in the book and could not be decided given the equally undesirable character of both methods. In fact, the point is that such a choice does not make any sense whatsoever, as the two methods have never been offered as options. One simply replaced the other. Between the two, there seems to lie an abyss.

The two scenes are shocking not simply in their internal content or through their contrast, but by the links they have with the present and our self-image and 'identity' as modern subjects. The Middle Ages is our own past, yet it is hardly possible to recognize the practice described as part of our 'tradition'. The discontinuity and break seems to be complete. On the other hand, the image of the prison timetable is shocking because of the evident continuity with the present. The modernity of the method cannot be denied and yet we do not want to recognize ourselves in it either. The scene evokes the return of another 'dead spirit', another 'repressed' part of our past. It is less shocking in its imagery, but more unsettling, because of the lack of an abyss separating us from it and thus preserving our self-image.

The first pages of the book are not the only examples of the use of the technique of contrasting images. It recurs at the beginning of the most important sections of the book, introducing and marking them at the same time. Part Three entitled 'Discipline', arguably the most important and certainly the most widely-read section of the book, contrasts the ideal figure of the soldier from the early seventeenth century with that of the late eighteenth century. The former was 'someone who could be recognized from afar', as he bore 'signs' and 'marks': the signs of his 'strength and 'courage', and the marks of his 'pride' (DP: 135). The latter, however, was someone produced almost custom-made, as by then it had been realized that 'out of a formless clay, an inapt body, the machine required can be constructed' (ibid.). The allusion to the 'machine' was not accidental. In the following page Foucault refers to La Mettrie who was one of the favorite early materialists of Marx, and his book *L'homme-machine*, or 'Man-the-Machine', claiming that the:

> great book of 'Man-the-Machine' was written simultaneously on two registers. The first was the anatomico-metaphysical register which Descartes wrote the first pages and which the physicians and philosophers continued. The second was the technico-political register which was constituted by a whole set of regulations and empirical and calculated methods relating to the army, the school and the hospital for controlling or correcting the operations of the body.
>
> (DP: 136; trans., slightly modified).

The same technique is repeated at the start of the second chapter of the fourth and last part of the book. This contains Foucault's central argument with respect to the function of the prison, which according to him was not to reintegrate the offender into society but rather to fabricate the delinquent itself (ibid.: 278). The chapter starts with medieval images which survived into the early nineteenth century, and which were equally as vivid as the stunning introductory pictures of torture and execution, though in a different manner. This is the carnevalesque scene provoked by the chain gang. The last chain gang, which left Paris on 19 July 1836, still had 'the dimension of a public spectacle' as it was watched by over 100,000 people (ibid.: 258). A central feature of the spectacle was the ambiguous character of the interaction between the convicts and the crowd, who were 'alternating insults, threats, words of encouragement, blows, signs of hate or complicity' (ibid.). Occasionally the police had to work hard to prevent the outbreak of serious disorder. According to Foucault,

> [i]n this festival of the departing convicts, there was something of the rites of the scapegoat that is struck as it is chased away, something of the festival of fools, in which the reversal of roles is practised . . . the play of truth and infamy, the procession of notoriety and shame,

invective against the guilty who have been unmasked and, on the other hand, the joyous avowal of crimes. . . . In every town it passed through, the chain-gang brought its festival with it; it was a saturnalia of punishment, a penalty turned into a privilege.[19]

(DP: 259, 261)

It was this festival that had been replaced by the next year, in a change as sudden in time as the striking contrast between the images, by 'a machine that had been very meticulously designed: a carriage conceived as a moving prison, a mobile equivalent of the Panopticon' (ibid.: 263). In this, separated by a corridor, the convicts were divided into two rows consisting of six cells which were separated by solid walls but facing each other. Foucault provides the rationale by a quote from a contemporary journal, dated 15 June 1837: in this way, '[w]hatever the length of the journey, all would be brought to their destination without having been able to perceive one another or to speak to one another' (ibid.). The disparity between this picture, where the convicts could not even see each other, and the previous carnevalesque scenes in which they were in continuous interaction even with the crowd, could not have been greater.

These scenes, and the additional imagery evoked throughout the book, illuminate and can be rendered intelligible by the previous considerations about marginality and liminality. The vivid imagery surrounding the chain-gangs makes it especially clear that a crime was never considered as a singular isolated act, but as an event that challenged or broke the established order of things, and thus brought the entire community potentially to the brink of disorder. It thus created a liminal situation which had to be addressed by similar liminal carnevalesque rituals. Under such conditions, the results of the 'civilizing process' were suspended and the convicts were often executed in a fashion recalling the violence and cruelty of the most barbarous atrocities of the Germanic invasions of the fifth and sixth centuries.

It was these ambivalent, joyous and horrible rituals, where Nietzsche's *Gay Science* encountered Artaud's 'theatre of cruelty' (Brustein 1970), that were replaced around the *Sattelzeit* of 1800 (Koselleck 1985) by different kinds of arrangement. These can be characterized in two main ways, by their manner of proceeding and by the 'output' they produced. As regards the former, the central element was the replacement of the rituals, with the focus on individual performances at their culmination point and with their closing by collective celebrations at the phase of reaggregation, with regularized, predictable, calculated, repetitive, machine-like procedures and operations.[20]

Concerning the other aspect of the process, its main 'output', Foucault returned to the body–soul terminology at the end of the first chapter, in interpreting the first set of contrasting images. In passages which have since became famous, he described the book on the one hand as a 'history of the modern soul' (DP: 23), or a ' genealogy of the modern "soul"' (ibid.: 29). He described it on the other hand as belonging variously to the 'history of the body' (ibid.: 25): of the 'political investment of the body' (ibid.: 25), the individual body, the bodies of individuals subjected to different kind of punitive regimes, and also of the 'body politic'. It was redefined as 'a set of material elements and techniques that serve as weapons, relays, communication routes and supports for the power and knowledge relations that invest human bodies and subjugate them by turning them into objects of knowledge' (ibid.: 28).

The histories of the soul and the body are connected. This 'soul' has a 'historical reality' (ibid.: 29). Contrasting it with the soul of Christian theology, Foucault claims that it is born 'out of methods of punishment, supervision and constraint' (ibid.). In contrast to Marx, this material reality, however, is not an occasion for celebration for him:

> The man described for us, whom we are invited to free, is already in himself the effect of a subjection much more profound than himself. A 'soul' inhabits him and brings him to existence, which is itself a factor in the mastery that power exercises over the body. The soul is the effect and instrument of a political anatomy; the soul is the prison of the body.
>
> (DP: 30)

Foucault had his own reasons for using the terminology of the soul. It was a clear allusion to Descartes and the body–soul dualism, with which Foucault had an account to settle which went back to his university studies and his first thesis plan. However, in a terminology that is closer both to contemporary social theory and to Foucault's later work and interests, the term 'soul' should be substituted with 'self' or 'identity'.[21]

These two points of the replacement of both repulsive and attractive liminal scenes with social regulation and the shaping of the self, coming immediately with the first interpretation of the striking images, contain Foucault's central concerns in the entire book in a nutshell. They furthermore illustrate its method. In a certain way, the book is nothing but an extended elaboration and interpretation of a few basic almost 'archetypal' contrasting 'ideal' pictures. It follows a tight structure which combines scholarly presentation and argument with an almost theatrical script. The pictures are followed by long sections in which the related historical and archival evidence is presented. They are closed, especially in Parts Three and Four, by broad, often sweeping, general comments which transmit and further characterize Foucault's vision. Thus, the introductory section to Part Three ends by repeating the assertions of the first chapter that 'the man of modern humanism was born' out of 'trifles', a 'meticulous observation of detail, and at the same time a political awareness of these small things' (ibid.: 141).

The chapter itself is concluded by the famous, slogan-like statement about politics being the continuation of war. More exactly, Foucault states that:

> [i]t may be that war as strategy is a continuation of politics. But it must not be forgotten that 'politics' has been conceived as the continuation, if not exactly and directly of war, at least of the military model as a fundamental means of preventing civil disorder.
>
>   (DP: 168; trans., slightly modified)

This military model as a dream of the ideal society is then contrasted with the utopias of jurists and philosophers. It depicts the vision of nationalized discipline, a state administration that resembles a huge machine and thus will be able to withstand the trials of time, gaining power forever and escaping an eventual decline and fall which is the fate of even the mightiest of empires. Thus:

> [w]hile jurists or philosophers were seeking in the pact a primal model for the construction or reconstruction of the social body, the soldiers and with them the technicians of discipline were elaborating procedures for the individual and collective coercion of bodies.
>
>   (ibid.: 169)

The concluding paragraphs of the next chapter restate the point about positive as opposed to negative power and the actual 'fabrication' of the individual by the 'specific technology of power' called 'discipline' (ibid.: 194).

The central part of the book is the next chapter entitled 'Panopticism', which contains the most comprehensive presentation of Foucault's vision. The chapter is organized around the presentation of his great negative reading experience of the period, Bentham's *Panopticon*. It is introduced by another 'contrasting image', of the measures taken against plague around the end of the seventeenth century. In this way, an additional medical-epidemiological dimension is added to the legal-philosophical and military-mechanistic models. This allows Foucault to return to his former works and to compare the technique of exclusion and confinement characteristic of the leper houses and the asylums and hospitals built on them with the disciplinary mechanisms and techniques deployed in the case of a plague. He can thus introduce the 'Panopticon' as an at once programmatic and ideal representation of modern power, which relies on a combination of both models.

The image of the 'Panopticon' – the central inspection tower surrounded by a circle of cells in which the inmates were separated from each others by walls but remained fully visible for the guards who remained invisible in their tower – has by now become so well known in social theory that its detailed presentation seems superfluous. The picture simply captivated Foucault's imagination and, during an informal May 1975 seminar in Berkeley (DEIII: 464), he claimed outright that '[i]n Bentham I have found the Columbus of politics' (DEIII: 466). This was because Bentham compressed in a simple architectural design the major aspects characterizing the exercise of power in modern societies. These are the omnipresence of visibility (DP: 200–1), the integration of external pressures with self-control through the almost automatic functioning of consciousness (ibid.: 201–2), the closing of the functioning of the system by catching the supervisors themselves in the same system of automatic controls (ibid.: 203, 207) and the application of the disciplinary model to the whole scope of everyday activities instead of reducing them to special circumstances only.[22] The latter happened in the case of the plague (ibid.: 205).[23]

Though the work had the character of a dream or a vision, the central idea was not at all utopian:

> the Panopticon must not be understood as a dream building: it is the diagram of a mechanism of power reduced to its ideal form . . . it is in fact a figure of political technology that may and must be detached from any specific use.
>
> (DP: 205)

Bentham's dream thus had a programmatic aspect: 'It programmes, at the level of an elementary and easily transferable mechanism, the basic functioning of a society penetrated through and through with disciplinary mechanisms' (ibid.: 209).[24]

This claim has a methodological and a substantive corollary. Methodologically, paraphrasing Foucault's words in a Weberian terminology, with this model he left the contrasting images of the 'ideal types' understood as 'historical individuals' and gained access to a 'pure type' of political power. Thus, according to this, the three pure types of legitimate authority should be complemented with a fourth type, disciplinary power.

The latter is explicitly stated by Foucault, and in fact by Bentham himself: the Panopticon should not simply be a model prison, but a 'magical' way to solve at once all problems of social life (ibid.: 207). It is for this reason that Foucault can close the chapter with the following question: 'Is it surprising that prisons resemble factories, schools, barracks, hospitals, which all resemble prisons?' (ibid.: 228).

This question appears at a crucial strategic place in the book. In this way, at the end of the chapter and the entire part that was most general in its scope and thus most distant from the particular theme of punitive rationality and the prison, Foucault suddenly returned to the specific theme of the book. But it also poses another set of basic questions: do prisons really play such a central role in modern societies? Are they paradigmatic for the exercise of power in modern societies or, for that matter, for the experience of life under conditions of modernity in general? And if so, then why?

These questions go to the heart of the message and the problems of the book. On the one hand, Foucault did indeed think that the prison filled such a paradigmatic role. Though later he would regret the style he used in the book, he stood by the central thrust of this vision. But, on the other hand, it is also clear that this vision can only be understood in a metaphorical sense. Modern society as such is not a prison. There is a difference between its totalitarian and non-totalitarian versions. Having lived in Poland in 1958–9, Foucault had first-hand experience of the reality of 'existing socialism', and in his political activities he remained an uncompromising opponent of all Soviet-type regimes. And yet he also recognized basic similarities across different modern systems. On the inner jacket of the first edition of *Histoire de la folie* Foucault presents himself as 'somebody who has been astonished', and who:

> having frequented [in France] the psychiatric hospitals (from the side where the doors opened), having been acquainted in Sweden with the socialised happiness (from the side where the doors no longer opened), in Poland with the socialist misery and the courage it requires, in Germany, not too far from Altona, with the new fortresses of German wealth, and having returned to France as an academic, made [the author] reflect, with a little bit of seriousness, what is an asylum.[25]
>
> (HF: quote on jacket of original edition)

Before going into a detailed interpretation, it is important to call attention to the stylistic devices used by Foucault in presenting his version of the vision of the 'iron cage'. In *Discipline and Punish*, he is not asserting the identity of prisons, hospitals, schools and so on, only posing a question about their surprising resemblance. In the jacket of *Histoire de la folie*, similarly, far from identifying the various countries and locations where he lived in his 'years of pilgrimage', he is only alluding, half-seriously, to the strange commonalties he experienced beyond the evident variety and difference. Any literal interpretation of Foucault's vision, in which he identifies modern society with a prison, is therefore simply nonsensical.[26]

With this *caveat*, I would suggest an interpretation along the lines of liminality and marginality which continues the argument proposed in the previous section. This would put the emphasis on a combination of two factors: the case of the prison both illustrates with particular clarity the set of problems that gave rise to the emergence of modern society and highlights the main character of the answers given.

On the former, the general context is provided by the idea that the problematization of punishment was part of a broad process, the rise of modernity in which all the liminal aspects of human existence became particularly problematic. This went together with a transformation undergone by the concept and reality of the everyday. Weber is again instructive in this context. One of the organizing cleavages of Weber's entire work was the contrast between the ordinary or the everyday (*alltagliche*) and the extraordinary (*außeralltagliche*).[27] Furthermore, this was particularly central for Weber's conceptualization of economic action, as Weber defined the field of the economy as being extended in modernity to the entire range of everyday activities. It was exactly here that the link between the 'Protestant ethic' and the 'spirit' of capitalism lay. Foucault also recognized the contrast between the everyday redefined as economic activity and the 'out-of-ordinary' or 'liminal':

> For the life and the time of man are not by nature labour, but pleasure, restlessness, merry-making, rest, needs, accidents, desires, violent acts, robberies, etc. And this quite explosive, momentary and discontinuous energy must be transformed by capital into labour-power which is continuous and constantly offered in the market.[28]
>
> (Foucault 1973: 61)

It is due to this overwhelming presence of the new meaning and reality of the 'everyday', and the novel emphasis on conformity, that the links between the 'liminal' and the 'marginal' became particularly tight. All temporary liminal situations were transformed into permanent marginal identities through the intertwining of 'liminal' conditions with the binary divisions of true and false, good and bad, right and wrong. In this type of development, the field of punishment, punitive rationality and criminal justice played a leading role. Thus, as a first step, we may conclude that liminality suddenly became problematic from the perspective of a new emphasis on the regular and the everyday.

However, the argument can be taken still further. As a second step, and continuing with Elias, the importance attributed to the regular everyday conduct of life can be attributed on its own to a problematization of the everyday. And third, following Elias, Borkenau, Mumford and especially Voegelin, we arrive at the problem of the collapse of the medieval world order, or a situation of large-scale real-world liminality. This leads to the conclusion that modern societies have so much difficulty in handling the phenomenon of temporary liminality that they scapegoat liminal conditions into a permanent state of marginal identity. This is because modern society is a type of society that emerged out of a situation of long-lasting and large-scale liminal crisis, which renders even routine everyday behaviour particularly problematic.

On the other hand, there was also something paradigmatic in the concrete response of the prison itself. The main solution found to the problem of the religious and civil wars of the sixteenth century was the strengthening of individual and social discipline, and the regularization of individual conduct and collective affairs, which were crystallized in the emergence of a new political entity, the absolutist state, and a new field of social reality, the economy. The two aspects were connected with the new 'discipline' of political economy, which was an expression that would have made no sense to Aristotle. In this respect, the prison has a special place, as it was an attempt to apply the methods used to alleviate the general problem of overall liminality with particular strength and attention to the special case of those individuals who fell outside the scope of their first application. Thus, the prison represented 'second order' social disciplining, where the actual techniques and programmes were appearing with particular clarity. This also means, however, that once punishment became so paradigmatic, something of its original meaning and purpose was lost.

This was an interpretation of *Discipline and Punish* based on Foucault's later works and the ideas of other reflexive historical sociologists. But it is also close to what Foucault actually said retrospectively about this book. Thus, in his last related interview, he claimed that his work and involvement in prisons was 'an enterprise of "problematization"', rooted in the fact that, paraphrasing Nietzsche, 'our societies no longer know what it is to punish', and the task he therefore set to himself was to pose the question of 'how to think today what a punishment should be' (DEIV: 688, 691–2). The reaching of that position, however, took several years for Foucault. During that time he was constantly reflecting on his approach to the study of the exercise of power, and further clarifying, even altering significantly, his vision of modernity, without ever rejecting it completely.

An aside which Foucault gave at the start of the fourth lecture of 1980 is particularly instructive in this regard. He claimed there that the aim of his theoretical work was neither to create a coherent system nor to establish a position to which he would stay firm. Rather, 'my problem, or the only kind of theoretical work I feel capable, would be to leave, in the clearest possible manner, the traces of the movements by which I am no longer at the place where I have just been.' In this series of passages, every displacement modifies the interpretation of the previous readings, though it does not alter the shape of the entire curve. His work cannot be read as a permanent building, only 'a trace of development, a trace of permanent displacements.' Thus, in the analogy of negative theology, he can be called a 'negative theoretician'.[29]

A central element of this quest was to figure out what, if anything, was the positive driving force behind this attempt at a standardization, normalization and disciplining. In the following, the main steps of this quest will be examined briefly, in the only possible way such an intellectual quest or *zetesis* can be resumed: in strict chronological order.

Foucault's reflections on power

Foucault is often considered as a foremost contemporary theorist of power. Though such views are certainly plausible, they fail to give justice to the thoroughly problematic place the study of power takes up in Foucault's entire work.

The concern with power has its own lifecycle within Foucault's entire trajectory. Up to 1971, Foucault hardly ever used the term in his works. Then suddenly, from 1971 onwards, he redefined all his past works as being concerned fundamentally with nothing other than power, and in 1975–6 he published two books which have since gained a classic status in social theory. For Foucault, however, the matter was not put to rest, and in the following years he kept working on the refinement of his conceptual tools. This lasted until 1980–1 when he came up with a reassessment of his entire work, claiming that at its centre was not the question of power but the link between subjectivity and truth.

This led to the paradoxical situation that just when Foucault became an international celebrity owing to his books on power, he stopped being interested in its study. The point was driven home with considerable force, and no doubt with explicit polemical intent, in his October 1981 lecture delivered at the University of Southern California, where he told the audience of several thousand who expected him to lecture on power that this theme had not even been the central target of his work in the past.

Still, understandably, Foucault was continually asked for clarification about his position on power. His numerous interviews contain a wealth of further material on the theme. However, as he repeatedly made it clear, by that time he had not worked on questions of power, politics and contemporary or even early modern society for a long time, therefore his remarks cannot be taken at face value as 'authoritative' or containing definite improvements over the earlier pronouncements. The problem is only rendered more difficult by the fact that much of the earlier material, especially in the Collège de France lectures, is still unpublished.

In the following, an attempt will be made to reconstruct the path of Foucault's reflections on the study of power, making reference to those lectures which are available on tape in the Foucault Archives.

The 'Archimedean point' on which the development of Foucault's ideas on power can be anchored is not the completion or the publication date of *Discipline and Punish*, but the moment in which the vision-experience of disciplinary society happened. This was his visit to the prison at Attica on 21 April 1972. The experience came at the culmination of an intense personal involvement in the 'prison movement' which had started on 1 February 1971, coupled with work done on penal institutions since August 1971. In fact, the context was even more specific. In contrast to his work on asylums and hospitals, he lacked personal experience with prisons and had therefore for a long time faced considerable difficulties in getting his work started or even preparing his lectures. The experience happened just after his first, quite painful course on prisons finished at the Collège de France.

The visit to Attica distanced him from his earlier view of power: 'Until then I envisioned exclusion from society as a sort of general function, a bit abstract, and I tried to plot that function as in some way constitutive of society'. Now he asks the reverse question: as prison is too complex to be used just as a mechanism of exclusion, what is its positive function in a modern capitalist society? (DEII: 528, Foucault 1974: 156).

Much of Foucault's conceptualization of power up to the mid 1970s was an interpretation of this experience, a long footnote to his visit to Attica. The focus was given to him by his major reading experience of Bentham's *Panopticon*. This led him to the vision of modern power being mechanical, and focusing on the disciplining of individual bodies, who all thus became parts, like cogs, in a vast, anonymous and autonomous machine. He saw this machine as first of all a military machine. This posed the question of why a military machine could play such a major role for social organization, and led Foucault in December 1972 (DEI: 42) to the idea that civil war is indeed the model for the exercise of social power.

This outcome of his speculations on his experience illuminates both the sharpness of Foucault's thinking and the limits of his approach in the 1970s. He reached the same conclusion as Borkenau, Voegelin, Koselleck and Oestreich by recognizing the collapse of the medieval world order and the ensuing permanent civil and religious warfare in the situation of the sixteenth century as the conditions out of which the modern political and social order was born. However, in spite of all his historical interests and erudition, this recognition was not an insight gained about history, but a retrospective speculation based on his personal experience of the functioning of a modern prison. Because of this, the historical specificity of the prison machine and its character as an answer to a concrete problem were inaccessible to him at that moment. He therefore had to interpret the experience as inescapable, omnipresent, diabolic which was a genuine *Infernal Machine* .

On the other hand, by distancing himself from it, this experience made apparent his earlier assumed conceptualization of power in terms of techniques of exclusion, or the legal model of sovereignty, the emphasis on discursive or other rules, and on binary divisions.

The first modification in Foucault's conceptualization of power was a shift from discipline to the norm, from an anatomic-military model to a psychiatric-medical model. This was more of a return than a novel turn, as it moved Foucault back to concerns that had preoccupied him since writing *Histoire de la folie*. Psychiatry always had a special place in his work on prisons: from his first interviews of the period (DE95) to the seminars devoted to penal psychiatry from 1971 to 1975; the special concern about the psychiatric wing in Attica (DEII: 527); the two years of courses in 1974 and 1975 devoted to questions of psychiatry just after his courses about the prison book; his claim that his only direct personal background with prisons was his work as a prison psychiatrist (TS: 12). This psychiatric-medical angle was incorporated into *Discipline and Punish*, for example in the emphasis on norms, the diagnosis of the 'normalizing society' which was used almost interchangeably with the diagnosis of the 'disciplinary society', and in the epidemiological model of plague control where Foucault located the historical source of the Panopticon.[30]

However, the two angles of psychiatry and medicine do not provide identical perspectives. They looked the same only from the perspective of Foucault's work on prisons and discipline. This identity would become increasingly questioned once Foucault finished *Discipline and Punish* and gained some distance from his manuscript. In fact, well before the publication date, Foucault had started to develop second thoughts about the conceptualization of power contained there, and by autumn 1975, he was ready to start all over again (Szakolczai 1998a: 236).

This happened after another major experience in the US, the May 1975 trip to Death Valley which was much publicized and interpreted out of context by James Miller (1993). Though not *the* turning point in Foucault's life, it was an important experience which was liminal in many ways. He was far from home, in the middle of a desert, under the impact of LSD, and this decisively dislocated him from his earlier conceptualization of power but without giving a decisive new focus.

The following years would see Foucault going through a series of attempts at reflecting on his past work and developing new directions; mental fireworks which were both impressive and disconcerting.[31] At the start of his 1976 Collège de France lectures, he declared his past five years' work fragmentary and clearly indicated the problems that this represented for him (PK: 78). He was planning a book on war, which was in line with his metaphor of the military machine, but at the same time he wanted to use the 1976 lectures to distance himself from his earlier idea of politics being the continuation of war by other means. He was also reflecting on the proper conceptualization of the link between the individual and the social body, and argued that 'the political significance of the problem of sex is due to the fact that sex is located at the point of intersection of the discipline of the body and the control of the population' (PK: 125).

It was this connection that the first volume of the *History of Sexuality* series was supposed to put at the centre of his conceptualization of power. The book contains some of the most striking diagnostic formulations of Foucault, about Western man being a 'confessing animal' (HSI: 59), on the 'threshold of modernity', being defined as the point where 'the life of the species is wagered on its own political strategies' (ibid.: 143), or on 'normalizing society', which is 'the historical outcome of a technology of power centred on life' (ibid.: 144). However, by the time this book was published, Foucault had moved on. Far from becoming the definitive methodological statement for an entire series of volumes, it documents a short and passing moment in the development of his thought, which was rendered timeless by its reception. At any rate, the books that were supposed to come in quick succession in his sabbatical year on the basis of these methodological reflections did not arrive.

When Foucault returned to lecture at the Collège de France in January 1978 after the gap of a sabbatical year, he faced the expectation and promise of both others and himself of completing the series of books on *The History of Sexuality* and delivering the final word on his views on power. The first lectures of the course were clear enough in terms of the distance from his earlier works. While a few years earlier Foucault had contrasted his own view of power with the legal-philosophical model, and discipline with sovereignty, now he talked of the sovereignty–discipline–security series.[32]

This should not be understood as a straightforward temporal sequence. The technologies of security do not replace law and discipline, but only make them function even more efficiently. As an example, he adds to his earlier 'ideal types', the exclusion of lepers for sovereignty and the plague for disciplinary power, the case of chicken pox illustrating the new technologies. The issue is no longer to impose a discipline but to address the following questions: how many people are attacked, at what age and with what effects; what are the rates of mortality, what is the probability and risk of death? The corresponding technique is neither exclusion nor quarantine but medical campaigns. Thus, the shaping of 'docile bodies' was complemented (though not replaced) with other kinds of normalizing processes, targeting not an inept body to be moulded and drilled but a population with its own natural characteristics, situated in a particular '*milieu*'. The question to be posed and the stake of the lectures therefore, was the following: is this a sign of a general transformation? Can it be said that in our societies, the general economy of power is about to be based on matters of security? In other words, the question is whether one can talk about a society of security/insurance.[33]

This opened up another dimension, which had its own effects, and some ideas even returned in Foucault's later views (DE325). However, the first lectures of 1978 lack the precision, coherence and persuasive power usually characterizing Foucault. They are more symptoms of a search turned anxious than signs of a new path. However, the fourth lecture suddenly shifted the focus. Foucault was again born out of his ashes and this time he launched the new concept 'governmentality' (DE239).

This event is clearly rooted in a new reading experience, that of *L'homme devant la mort* by Philippe Ariès, another major reflexive historical sociologists. Even the word itself incorporates a tribute to Ariès and his histories of mentalities. The concept 'government', however, is Foucault's own. With it, Foucault shifted his interest again from the 'body' back to the 'soul'. In this way the concerns of the first three lectures suddenly gained a proper focus:

> Accordingly, we need to see things not in terms of the replacement of
> a society of sovereignty by a disciplinary society and the subsequent

replacement of a disciplinary society by a society of government; in reality one has a triangle, sovereignty-discipline-government, which has as its primary target the population and as its essential mechanism the apparatuses of security.

(Foucault 1991: 102)

As a result, Foucault gave a new title to the course; instead of the loose list of terms 'Security, Territory and Population' contained in the original title, he decided it should be 'a history of "governmentality"' (ibid.).

The new concept also enabled Foucault to reach a stable resting point in a number of aspects of his long quest. With it, Foucault's interest in pinning down the specifically modern way of linking individuals to larger entities acquired a stable footing. According to him, the concern with government simultaneously connected a number of issues: the government of oneself, of the soul, of children and even of the state (ibid.: 87). Furthermore, it helped him to locate this problem of government in the 'crisis' of the sixteenth century. This was an event that he would soon call 'a general crisis of the pastorate' (EST: 68) and that, using his last terminology, could be termed as a general 'problematization' of government. It is also here that the state of civil war as the 'model' of modern power, which was only a speculative concept in the early 1970s, gained historical reality in the religious and civil wars of the sixteenth century.[34]

Finally, this allowed Foucault to sharpen his diagnosis of modernity. The neologism 'governmentality' means three things. First, as an analytical concept it refers to the ensemble of the form of power introduced earlier, which is centred on the government of populations through apparatuses of security. But it is also a diagnostic tool in two senses. It allows us to pin down a specific 'tendency' characteristic of the West: 'the pre-eminence over all other forms (sovereignty, discipline, etc.) of this type of power which may be termed government' (Foucault 1991: 102–3). Last but not least, it also identifies the main locus of this type of power, which is the state. Foucault offers this diagnosis not to return to a 'theory of state' and of the 'essence' of the state but rather to complete its demythologization which had been started by Cassirer:

maybe, after all, the state is no more than a composite reality and a mythicized abstraction, whose importance is a lot more limited than many of us think. Maybe what is really important for our modernity – that is, for our present – is not so much the *étatisation* of society, as the 'governmentalization' of the state.

(Foucault 1991: 103)

Though Foucault emphatically is not discarding his earlier work, the displacements are clear. The somewhat cryptic 'will to discipline', and the mad desire to remould society on the model of the army, are replaced not simply by a 'will to govern' but in a general problematization of government. The 'microphysics of power' is complemented by an explicit analysis of the state. The links are close, as the fifth lecture of 1978 makes clear. In analysing the etymology of the term 'government', Foucault argues that in the fourteenth and fifteenth centuries, the use of the term was restricted to individuals and groups. It was part of a Christian vocabulary which related to pastoral power and the direction of consciousness, and the terminology had pre-Christian roots. The political meaning of 'government of men' belongs to the sixteenth century. In this way, Foucault has reached the same conclusion as Elias, who argued that the crisis of the sixteenth century was a general 'problematization' of the everyday conduct of life. It was as a response to that crisis that the joint concerns of the reason of state and the early modern police apparatus developed. They were two ways to translate pastoral power into a secular context.[35]

This idea, however, recalls not only Elias but also Weber, concerning the link between rationality at the state level and the everyday conduct of life (see also Gorski 1993), and the idea of conceiving of the modern state as a 'secularized' version of a type of power characteristic of the Church. Indeed, it is at this moment that Foucault developed a deep interest in Weber. Without a detailed study of Foucault's notes, it is difficult to identify the moment of the reading experience. The encounter with Weber was part of an ongoing process. When working on the first volume of *The History of Sexuality*, Foucault perused *The Protestant Ethic*.[36] However, in the 1978 course, there are still minimal signs of Weber, and the round-table discussion of 20 May 1978 referred to above also does not yet indicate a profound impact. In the 1979 course, however, the presence of Weber is much more marked. One can therefore provisionally assign the Weber reading experience to the second part of 1978.

This is all the more probable as this was a period of heavy reading for Foucault and a sign of the intensity of his quest. In 1976–7, he produced more book reviews than in the entire previous decade. This activity stopped after his review of the work of Ariès. One reading of the period, however, was especially significant concerning his encounter with Weber: the systematic reading of the novels of Thomas Mann.[37]

In his chronology Defert states that Foucault started a 'systematic re-reading' of Thomas Mann in November 1978 (DEI: 55). The copy of *The Magic Mountain* owned by Foucault was printed on 10 July 1978, while that of *Buddenbrooks* was printed on 20 January 1979. The links between Weber and Thomas Mann are very close, and were recently discussed by Harvey Goldman (1988, 1992). As the titles of these books already indicate, these links revolve around the self, power and death, issues that were also central for Foucault, and especially so around that time. For years, he reflected on his approach to the study of power, and he was just about to reorganize his entire work around the questions of self and subjectivity when in July

1978, he went through a near-death experience when he was hit by a car close to his home in Paris. The circle can be closed by referring again to Ariès. The Ariès reading experience was because of a book about death. The related neologism 'governmentality' would soon be used inter-changeably with the term 'governmental rationality' which is clearly Weberian. Finally, the comments made in his February 1984 obituary of Ariès, saying that Ariès developed concerns close to Weber but without knowing his works, may be taken as an autobiographical allusion and as referring to this moment of Foucault's work. Thus, it seems safe to argue that the reading of Thomas Mann could have been the 'catalyst' for Foucault in his Weber reading experience.[38]

Foucault was not alone in suddenly reading Weber with a fresh eye. This very moment generally marks the birth of the Weber renaissance, beyond the neo-Marxian 'antithesis' to the Parsonian–functionalist 'thesis'.[39] Tenbruck originally published his path-breaking article in 1975 (see Tenbruck 1980) and Hennis also started his new interest in Weber in the late 1970s (see Hennis 1988). Hirschman published his book in 1977, while Oestreich's work also gained currency in the 1970s. Though most of these developments were independent, the ideas eventually circulated together (Kalberg 1979), and most of the authors listed above were soon commented upon in the literature on Foucault (Gordon 1980: 247, 1986: 84–5, 1991: 12–14, 17–18; Pasquino 1985: 98–100). Unfortunately, they would soon be eclipsed by other, much less relevant names, in the general frenzy to label and misread Foucault as a 'post-modern' or 'post-structuralist'.[40]

Foucault's new Weber reading experience is obvious in both the termi-nology and the theme of his next 1979 course. As a synonym of 'governmentality', he uses terms like 'governmental reason' or 'govern-mental rationality', while in his Stanford lectures he talked about 'political rationality' (PPC: 85), with even clearer allusions to Weber. As far as the theme is concerned, a good part of the course dealt with the 'ordoliberal' school of German economists who counted Weber among their main sources of inspiration.

It was the last lecture of the course that took up the current state of Foucault's conceptualization of power and documented the shift com-pared to his 1978 position. The first main change concerns the general attitude with respect to power. His earlier combative and diagnostic atti-tude towards the specific omnipresence of power in Western societies is replaced by a more stoic attitude that the exercise of power is inescapable. It pointed towards his eventual definition of power in terms of govern-ment, as the conduct of conduct and as ever-present strategic games. Though the loss of the ballast of rhetoric is a welcome development, and the statement in itself is not objectionable, this is the first sign of a loss of diagnostic precision in Foucault's work.

The second main point concerns a three-fold periodization of the his-tory of governmental reason. According to this, the Middle Ages can be characterized as government by truth, while from the sixteenth century onwards this was replaced with government by reason. This is further divided into two sub-periods: government according to the 'rationality' of those who govern, or the sovereign, which is characteristic of reason of state; and government according to the 'rationality' of the governed, which is characteristic of liberalism.

The first lecture of 1980 represented a drastic reversal with respect to this model and in Foucault's entire conceptualization of power.[41] This extends to both the central methodological tools and the overall framework of his approach. Concerning the first, it was at this moment that Foucault claimed to go beyond the term 'power–knowledge' which was central for his works in the 1970s. He claimed in the first hour of the lecture that there had been two major displacements in his analysis of power. The first happened when he replaced the concept 'dominant ideology', alluding possibly to his interventions of 1971–2, with 'power–knowledge'. The second was at this point, when he gave a 'positive and more differentiated content' to the terms 'power' and 'knowledge' by replacing 'power–knowledge' with 'government by truth'. For the specification of power in terms of 'government', he referred to the lectures of the previous two years. The elaboration of knowledge (*savoir*) would be done in the course of this year.

However, even though Foucault assumed here a smooth passage from 1978–9 to 1980, there was a significant displacement. While in the last lecture of 1979, government by truth was part of the history of governmental rationality, now the terms were reversed. It was government by rationality that became a stage in the broad history of the 'government by truth' or the 'government of individuals by their verity', as he had called it in the Stanford lectures (PPC: 71).

With this, the main contours of Foucault's last work and the central underlying problem of his work since the early 1950s were drawn. It was dominated by the return from questions of power to the more all-encompassing question of the modern forms of subjectivity. This was accompanied by a basic reorganization of the time horizon of his work from the early modern period back to early Christianity and then, in a series of shifts, back to Greco-Roman antiquity. Thus, both in his main theme and in his time horizon, Foucault's work became distanced from his vision of power and modernity contained in *Discipline and Punish*, and the other writings of the late 1970s which exerted such a wide appeal. This in a certain way represented a problem, as the links between his more mature thought and the earlier works were not evidently visible.

His last major testament-like overviews of his work, 'What Is Enlightenment?' and the *Introduction* to *The Use of Pleasure*, made it clear that there was no question of an overall retreat. If anything, these pieces are a bit too cosmetic and make the dynamics of the work appear smoother than it actually was, as Foucault himself acknowledged occasionally (TS: 15).

Furthermore, he kept reflecting on the question of power. He was forced to do so by the repeated demands of interviewers who, in this case, genuinely represented the public at large who wanted further clarification. The most important results of these reflections are contained in the essay 'The Subject and Power', the 'Afterword' to Dreyfus and Rabinow (1982) and a 20 January 1984 interview entitled 'The Ethics of the Concern for Self as a Practice of Freedom' (EST: 281–301). These pieces are invaluable in so far as they contain Foucault's last position on the question of power. They also show with particular clarity how Foucault's position, his conceptualization of the exercise of power as 'a way in which certain actions modify others' (Foucault 1982: 219), 'a mode of action upon the actions of others' (ibid.: 221) or 'a relationship in which one person tries to control the conduct of the other' (EST: 292), came close to Weber's. In these pieces, he also made a clear distinction between power and domination.

Without engaging himself in a ritual of self-flagellation, Foucault makes clearly self-critical remarks. He states that these terms are usually quite badly defined and that he was not sure either whether he used the words properly when he first started to be interested in the question of power. 'Now I have a clearer sense of the problem. It seems to me that we must distinguish between power relations understood as strategic games between liberties . . . and the states of domination that people ordinarily call "power"' (EST: 299). This latter he defined earlier as 'a general structure of power' which presents 'in a massive and universalizing form, at the level of the whole social body, the locking together of power relations with relations of strategy and the results proceeding from their interaction' (Foucault 1982: 226). In 'situations or states of domination . . . the power relations, instead of being mobile . . . remain blocked, frozen' (EST: 283). In sum, his final conceptualization of power has three main axes: the ever mobile strategic relations of power aiming to control the conduct of others; the states of domination that represent the immobilization of these strategic games into permanent, fixed positions; and the 'technologies of government', understood in the broad sense of all instruments that render it possible to act upon the conduct of others, and including 'not only the way institutions are governed but also the way one governs one's wife and children' (EST: 299), which are situated in between these two.

However, they also point out a major dilemma in Foucault's earlier 'vision' of power in modernity. This is best shown in the new definition of 'governmentality' contained in the same 20 January 1984 interview. According to this, '"governmentality" implies the relationship of the self to itself', and it covers 'the whole range of practices that . . . individuals in their freedom can use in dealing with each other' (ibid.: 300). In this way, the diagnostic intent behind the earlier concept is gone. Power for Foucault remains omnipresent and inevitable, but only in the sense of free strategic games in the social body. He even argues that the specificity of the West lies precisely in the number and variety of such strategic power games and the resulting desire to control others: 'the freer people are with respect to each other, the more they want to control each other's conduct. The more open the game, the more appealing and fascinating it becomes' (ibid.). The sharpness of Foucault's new insight is in contrast to his evident approval of this development, or at least his lack of ability to gain perspective and distance with respect to this trend. It also poses the question of the exact experiential basis of this oversight and lack of precision.

This can be found in two different instances which reinforce each other. On the one hand, Foucault had not done any work on contemporary problems of power and governmentality since the late 1970s. He occasionally expressed his regret about this development and was planning to return to this type of work, but it never got off the ground before his death. This lack of involvement in the form of actual research about the theme led to a certain deterioration of diagnostic vision and intention, concerning the specific type of power characteristic of modern societies.

At the same time, another kind of experiential basis gained increasing prominence for both his life and his thought. This refers to the kind of homosexual practices to which he was introduced in his first 1975 visit to California. For him, for various reasons, this represented a kind of liberation from a certain pressure. This was first visible in *The History of Sexuality, Volume One*, in the passage on 'bodies and pleasures' (HS1: 157), which is the only positive note to be found in an otherwise quite grim book. It is this language, which recurs in interviews that he gave around the theme of homosexual practices later (for example see DEIV: 737–9) together with terms like strategic games and role reversals, that would be the language of power in his last efforts at a conceptualization.

Thus, with the 'Panoptic society' and the free strategic games of individuals in search of pleasures without name or identity (DEIV: 331), we get the two quite opposing visions which Foucault had of power and modernity, which highlight both the values and the limits of his approach. In themselves, both visions are based on genuine 'limit experiences', but they can only be accepted as limits and not as models of the exercise of power in modernity. They are torn between the extremes of pain and pleasure and thus, paradoxically, reinforce the language of the utilitarian paradigm to which he was rightly most opposed.[42] The crucial issue now is the explicit and systematic contrasting of these visions. This was something Foucault could not or did not want to do, but for which he laid down the groundwork.

Conclusion to Part II
Modernity as permanent liminality

The six thinkers discussed in the previous chapters were powerful and original minds, who in most cases had not only influential ideas but also a larger-than-life personality. They cannot be said to have shared a single vision of modernity. However, whether they started their work by directly drawing inspiration from Weber or not, many of their most important ideas and central aspects of their vision, are remarkably similar. The main thrust of their historical work can be arranged in four main dimensions. Three of them are substantive. They concern the historicity of forms of subjectivity, knowledge, and closed institutions. The fourth is methodological and is concerned with the history of forms of thought including discourse, concepts and words.

Reflexive historical sociologists are certainly not historians of political events in the classical sense, though neither are they social historians nor historians of institutional structures or economic processes. They are rather historians of forms. It is for this reason that historians proper so often find their work objectionable, or that they are often classified as 'structuralist'. They are interested in singling out for study those forms and modalities of individual and social life that are either handled as trivial and self-evident or justified as universal. This is because their purpose is to go beyond the taken for granted of modernity. For them it is precisely at that level, and not in some kind or other affirmations of 'post-modernity', that the roots of main problems of contemporary life can be exposed.

It is for this reason that in their methodology the history of thought, concepts and even words takes such central importance. Changes in forms of life, experience and thinking are always accompanied by new types of verbal expressions, the invention of new symbols or the assigning of new meaning to old words. While a history of ideas that tries to trace streams of unbroken meaning across history can be charged with neglecting real events and people, by giving a proper attention to the historicity of words the aim here is to restore reality in the sense of the reality of changes, events and experiences. At one point or another, almost all reflexive historical sociologists explicitly defined their project as an attempt to historicize the universal categories of Kant.

The histories of thought, symbols and words are the main methodological tools used by reflexive historical sociologists in their investigations. These studies, however, are not just antiquarian histories, attempts to systematize and upgrade the field of the history of ideas, or sophisticated etymologies pursued for their own sake. They are parts of a coherent quest or *zetesis*; they are driven by passionate involvement in their times and in attempts to get to the bottom of contemporary problems; they are drawn by a vision. It is this vision, which is based on personal and reading experiences and the reflections resulting from them, that guides the historical work of these thinkers. Conversely, it is these historical works that give support and solidity to these visions and help to substantiate and clarify them by giving them coherence and analytical power.

Through their visions and their works, reflexive historical sociologists gained insights on the specificity of modern societies, especially in the three elements of modernity that are especially difficult to see because of their extreme closeness to us, our values and even our very being. These are knowledge, technology and science; individuality, subjectivity and personal identity; and the power generated by institutionally-closed space and regulated time. Reflexive historical sociologists were pioneers in the field of the history of technology and science well before its current fashionability. Most of them either started, or planned to start, their work precisely in this dimension, by raising questions about science, the central value of modernity which seemed to be the most evident, universal and reigning beyond question. However, none of them were engaged in the rhetorical excesses that today seem to question the very value of this undertaking.

However, whether or not they actually pursued studies in the history of science and technology, at one point all reflexive historical sociologists turned towards a theme that could be called the central concern of their work. This was the history of forms of subjectivity, individuality and personality; the order of the self or the soul. If knowledge is the most cherished 'external' value of modernity, the mode of being of the individual subject, or the identity of the self, is the most evidently taken for granted aspect of our being. It can be called the most cherished 'internal' value of modernity. The individual subject, with its responsibilities and choices, is the starting and end point, the foundation and the centre of modern economics, law, philosophy and political science. It is also at the centre of the critical attacks of sociologists and Marxists who put their emphasis on the collectivity and argue that the individual is only an ideological representation.

Reflexive historical sociologists are not interested in normative criticism. Their questions are different. They accept that the individual subject, with self-management based on his/her desires and interest, has become the foundation of the modern world. They rather pose the question of the specificity of a type of social order in which this could happen;

the reconstruction of the conditions that gave rise to its emergence; the mapping of the historicity of the very forms and techniques that rendered possible such individualization and subjectivation, the shaping and construction of personal identity.

In trying to pin down the exact conditions out of which the long-term process of the forming and shaping of the self was born, all reflexive historical sociologists came to assign a special role to a special type of institutional arrangement. It has to do with a kind of power which, on a face value, seems most contrary to the values of freedom and individual choice associated with the modern form of the self, because it has to do with institutionally-closed space and regulated time. Using the terminology of Erving Goffman, they could be called 'closed' or 'total' institutions (Goffman 1961). In the works of reflexive historical sociologists, two special types of closed institutions played a key role. These were the court, the central organ of imperial power, the moving force of the military megamachine, and the monastery which at least originally was the staunchest opponent of warfare and centralized power. The latter was the animating spirit of the other, peaceful version of the megamachine, the labour machine, and also of the ancient medieval and modern sects and sectarianism with which monasteries were closely associated for most of their history.

The special characteristics of these institutions are important not just by themselves, but in connection with the two other major themes of the histories of knowledge and subjectivity. They were instrumental both in shaping subjectivity, resulting in a regularized, rationalized and reflected everyday life conduct of individuals, and in the history of knowledge. A full study of these connections can only be done after a detailed discussion of the later works of the individual reflexive historical sociologists, which focus on the ancient roots of closed institutions and techniques of self. It belongs therefore to a future volume. At this point, an attempt will be made only to summarize and interpret the links between their visions of modernity.

As was discussed extensively in the previous chapters, one of the main clarifications that the other reflexive historical sociologists brought to the work of Weber concerned the exact conditions in which the line of development Weber traced to *The Protestant Ethic* can be rooted. Contrary to Weber's heroization of a struggle waged against the forces of tradition, they all drew attention to the particular situation of the sixteenth and seventeenth centuries, which they defined as the collapse of the medieval world order, and conceptualized as the dissolution of the conventional order of things. They interpreted the rise of Protestantism as one answer to this problem. They widened the circle by considering other answers, but preserved a coherent conceptual framework by treating all of them as answers to this specific problem of dissolution of order. They placed considerable emphasis on the way the problem was actually formulated at the time, in contradiction to restricting attention to the formulation of the problem by the investigator himself. (This was the central focus of Weber because of the partial hold the neo-Kantian methodology had on him.) They all developed various concepts to capture the link between the conditions of emergence and the lasting effects, which had been posed as a central dilemma by Nietzsche's *Genealogy of Morals*, without coming up with a satisfactory answer.

In the following, I will argue that such a framework can be found in the work of anthropologists, especially in the concept of 'liminality' as developed by Victor Turner and of 'mimetic crisis' as developed by René Girard. Turner's work was based on the earlier work of Arnold van Gennep, and Girard's work on Gabriel Tarde.

First, it is necessary to extend the concept of 'liminality' from its narrow meaning as the middle phase in rites of passage into a general concept. This can be done without losing conceptual vigour and precision. It will be argued that this concept is potentially one of the most general and useful terms of social science, and is comparable to the familiar concepts of structure, order and institution. The central point is that the binary oppositions between order and disorder, structured and unstructured situations, should be replaced by a tripartite and processual model. This model would identify a type that could be distinguished both from a regular normal state of order and from the total lack of structure and order that the conceptual opposites of order such as chaos and disorder usually imply, in a temporary, suspended, transitory, in-between situation.

However, for developing it into a proper conceptual tool, a few further clarifications are required. Most importantly, a concept developed in small-scale ritual settings must be extended into a real-world large-scale liminality (see Eisenstadt 1995: 317ff). This implies two fundamental changes to the original conceptualization. In a rite of passage, social order is purposely but temporarily suspended, and this very same order is solemnly reasserted at the end of the performance. In the case of real-world liminality, the previously taken-for-granted order of things has actually collapsed. It cannot therefore simply be restored. This means that the central task in a real-world large-scale liminal situation is an actual search for order, with all the existential anxiety this entails.

Furthermore, even staged liminal situations are dangerous, as the temporary suspension of stable structures opens up the forces of darkness and unleashes the energies of the subconscious. Thus, such rites are only performed in the presence of 'guardians' of order or 'masters of ceremonies' who possess the very special, indeed 'charismatic' expertise of being able to keep such rituals under control. In real-world large-scale liminal situations, however, the collapsing order also undercuts the authority of those individuals who could act as such 'guardians' or 'masters'. In their absence, and in the frightening presence of the dissolution of all stable frameworks, no effective control is put against the dark forces that are liberated in the 'situation'. Under such circumstances, the liminal conditions are far from being restricted to a temporary suspension of order, and enter an escalating spiral of violence.

This can be understood by complementing Turner's ideas by René Girard's reflections on the 'mimetics of desire' (Girard 1978, Livingston 1992). According to Girard, the imitation of the desire of others is a standard feature of human existence. People desire things not simply because of the inherent qualities of objects or their innate preferences, but because others desire them as well. Such imitations of desire are contagious, and can escalate into massive violence unless checked. The collapse of the established order of things described above can be interpreted as exactly the kind of crisis situation that leads to an escalation of 'mimetic violence'.

This conceptual framework is applicable not only to the conditions of the sixteenth and seventeenth centuries, but to earlier periods on which the later work of reflexive historical sociologists came to focus, like the collapse of the world of antiquity, or the 'axial age' and the ensuing 'ecumenic age'. The three main dimensions discussed above, the problematization of truth and knowledge, the search for order in the 'inside' of the self or in the regularization of the life-conduct of individuals which is characteristic of the 'axial religions and philosophies', and the interest in 'closed institutions', can all be conceived as answers to the general problem of the violent escalation of a 'mimetics of desire' under conditions of real-world large-scale liminality.

The sociological question at this point concerns the reasons for the effectiveness of some of these responses. This brings out a central feature of the various different works of reflexive historical sociologists. The series of responses to the liminal crisis in which they rooted modernity shares a fundamental common characteristic. They were all cases where temporary liminal conditions became permanent. Thus, one may argue that the effective long-term solution to large-scale real-world liminal situations is to make such liminal conditions permanent. This would insulate social 'order', in a paradoxical but apparently effective way, against further possibilities of a liminal crisis.

This requires the introduction of the new concept of 'permanent liminality'.

The concept is introduced with due acknowledgement of the fact that it is inherently paradoxical, if not a contradiction in terms. Liminality is defined as a temporary situation. Turner is very clear when introducing the concept that one cannot talk of a liminal 'state' because the word implies a fixity that is not characteristic of liminal situations.[1] Yet he also points out one exception which is of particular significance to this book. According to him, it appears that:

> with the increasing specialization of society and culture, with progressive complexity in the social division of labour, what was in tribal

society principally a set of transitional qualities 'betwixt and between' defined states of culture and society has become itself an institutionalized state.

(V. Turner 1969: 107)[2]

As an example, he provides an 'ideal typical' sentence in inverted commas which could be a direct quote from Bunyan's *Pilgrim's Progress,* which according to Weber (PE: 107) is by far the most widely read book in the entire literature of Puritanism: 'The Christian is a stranger to the world, a pilgrim, a traveller, with no place to rest his head'. In commenting, he claims that '[t]ransition has here become a permanent condition. Nowhere has this institutionalization of liminality been more clearly marked and defined than in the monastic and mendicant states in the great world religions' (V. Turner 1969: 107). The crude Durkheimian sociology implied in the sentences is certainly not tenable, but by singling out the importance of monastic orders, Turner is right on target again.

In a certain way, the task of continuing the work of reflexive historical sociologists who dealt with antiquity and the early Middle Ages is to give a better explanation for the significance of monastic orders than Turner's allusions, and replace 'specialization' and the 'division of labour' with 'dissolution of order' as the anchorage point of historical change. Within the limits of this book, however, attention will be restricted to a conceptualization of the different *types* of permanent liminal conditions that are central both for the genesis of modernity and for an understanding of its peculiar functioning.

This can be done using the three different types of permanent liminal situation which correspond to the three phases of the rites of passage. These are the phases of separation, the liminal period proper and reaggregation (see for example V. Turner 1969: 94–5). Liminality becomes a permanent condition when any of the phases in this sequence becomes frozen, as if a film stopped at a particular frame. This can happen both with individuals undergoing an 'initiation rite' and with groups who are participating in a collective ritual, 'a social drama'.

If freezing happens in the first phase, then the individuals or groups of human beings involved will be permanently stuck in rites of separation. As solitary hermits or a community of monks, they will continuously perform the type of ascetic exercises, the regular deprivations from shelter, food and clothing and the complete abstention from sexual activity that characterized individuals preparing for the performance of an initiation ritual in their entire life. They will also live a meticulously-regulated everyday life under the guidance of their supervisors, who wield over them a complete power, and they will have no possibility of opposition or appeal. On the other hand, however, members of the group will live a very warm community life, which is a genuine form of *communitas* in the Turnerian terminology.

Such a characterization, taken from the related anthropological writings of Turner and van Gennep, indeed gives an accurate description of monastic orders. For example, monks indeed address each other as 'brothers'. Monasteries are therefore permanently liminal in the sense of forever performing rites of separation and playing the preliminaries of a performance which will only be given in the next world. This explains the Weberian 'paradox of all rational ascetism, which in an identical manner has made monks of all ages stumble . . . that rational asceticism itself has created the very wealth it rejected' (Weber FMW: 332).

It is also possible, however, that individuals or groups are stuck forever in the second phase of the rites of passage. Turner does not give any example. However, the conditions of the discovery of his other crucial concept, 'social drama', can be considered as an indirect indication. Edith Turner (1985: 4–5) told the story that, back in the 1950s, he encountered exceptional difficulties in trying to put together the theoretical framework of his Ph.D. thesis. His supervisors insisted that he treat rituals as manifestations of social organization, following the rigid Durkheimian functionalism of the day, but he was unable to abstract from the vivid liveliness of the actual performances which to him seemed to be at the centre of the message. He only managed to solve this dilemma by coming up with the conceptualization of actual ritual performances as social dramas, and using the imagery of actual stage performances that dominated his childhood experiences.

Victor Turner often argued that theatre performances are a closer analogy to actual rituals than the terminology of functionalist anthropology. This is because the latter takes for granted an understanding of rituals as being purely ceremonial, with the rehearsing of a fixed scenario written in an etiquette, and not the actual performance of real human beings. In other words, functionalist anthropology wanted to understand simple rituals from the perspective of a ritual where liminality has already become a permanent condition.

The middle phase of a ritual is the actual performance or the 'staging' of the ritual. In such performances, individuals all play certain roles. In order to mark the distance from their everyday activities, performers often wear masks. On their own, these masks render all sort of role reversals possible, including even the most funny and most unlikely of such reversals, the reversal of sex roles (Bateson 1958 [1936]). These roles are partly well defined by custom, but are also partly free, and leave all sorts of improvisations possible. Those who play these roles are genuinely 'playing', as these role are not permanent and are different from everyday roles and 'identities'.

The question is what happens in the hypothetical situation where such a ritual becomes permanent; when individuals become stuck with their roles, which they must play from now onwards for the rest of their lives. Most evidently, the 'play' character of the ritual disappears. Individuals keep repeating the same roles, movements and gestures all over again which, after a time, becomes extremely boring. The word 'play' implies fun, but nothing is more boring than to be forced to play continuously. At the same time, playing will not just become a bore, but also deadly serious. Individuals are required to identify with the roles they are supposed to play all the time, all their lives, and their role will *become* their life. Furthermore, the mechanical performance becomes permanent, which means that the 'actors' remain continuously in the presence of each other. Everything becomes transparent and visible to everyone else; human beings become interdependent due to the conditions of living in a stage. In the end, the differences between 'life' and 'stage' disappear and it seems that life itself is nothing but performance on a stage.

Particularly perceptive observers, from Shakespeare to Goffman, have indeed come up with such a characterization of their times. However, from the previous chapters, it should have also become clear which specific institution was the archetypal carrier of the 'virus' of this type of permanent liminality, transmitting it to modern society where it thrives and spreads beyond all bounds under these particularly fertile conditions. It was the court. The above description, created by rendering the middle stage of a ritual permanent, rhymes exactly with the sociological analysis of a court society given by Elias. The typical character of the court in this respect is so evident that even the terms used in the description given above, like 'ceremony' or 'etiquette', are associated with the court.

If courts are permanently stuck in the middle phase of a ritual, it does not mean that they bear no relationship to the permanent rehearsal of the rites of separation. Indeed, they are built rather on one of its features, the absolute separation between the rulers and the ruled. As is well known, the position of ruler was by no means universally catered for in small-scale societies. The enormous gulf between the ruler and the ruled only appeared once their separation became permanent, and was embodied and represented in the form of the court.

The approach of Elias not only identifies the court as a place of permanent liminality, but even helps to pin down the play which is endlessly staged there. Elias talks about the 'courtization of warriors'. Taking the argument a step further, the court is definitely suited to the pacification of warfare, as its games are nothing but warfare played by other means.

This can help to further clarify the values and the limits of Foucault's vision of power and modernity. I have already argued that even though civil war was not the foundation of social order, this was the actual situation of the sixteenth and seventeenth centuries, which is where the emergence of modernity can be rooted. Similarly, politics as such is not the continuation of war. However, the type of politics characteristic of the courts and court societies in the seventeenth and eighteenth centuries can indeed be conceived as a 'pacified' version of warfare, with the strategic games of personal competition and rivalries substituting for the real mortal combats of warfare.

Permanent performance, however, is not only reserved for courts. It is also possible for single individuals to act as if they were continuously performing an initiation ritual. This fits exactly the manner in which Weber described membership in Protestant sects in America, where, he argued, sect members not only had to pass a demanding scrutiny in order to be admitted, but had to prove themselves repeatedly and positively and not just avoiding negative acts (FMW: 320; see also page 121 of this volume). Weber already considered this as a metaphor for the modern condition, and calling it 'permanently liminal' only adds analytical precision to his vision.

The third possibility, where the ritual is frozen in its third and last phase, seems to be the most unlikely of the three. The stage of preparation can be played endlessly while the performance is postponed forever. One can also imagine situations in which it is the performance that is being staged endlessly, and all the actors become pinned down or identified by their roles.[3] But the idea of the players remaining wandering endlessly in a state of frenzied suspension once the performance is over, seems less believable. And yet, this is exactly the theme of Homer's *Odyssey* which is one of the most important pieces of literature of all times. This epic poem is thought to represents the 'genesis' of individualism, and was selected by James Joyce as an archetype for the modern condition. If *The Protestant Ethic* was the discharge of the tension generated by medieval monasticism, then the *Ulysses* of Joyce represents the wanderings of the modern subject, worn out by the duty of permanent performance. Thus disenchanted, *The Magic Mountain* is replaced by the *Endgame*. As always, the process became visible at its *limes*, in this case the Western margins of Europe.

The collectivist example for the third kind of permanent liminality can be found in Soviet-type Bolshevism which is another periphery of modernity.[4] The communist regimes in Europe and Asia were all established under one very special kind of condition: the end of a world war. If all wars are liminal situations in which the cycle of mimetic violence escalates beyond measure, then the closing stages of a world war, and especially the process of reconstruction that starts after such massive warfare, can be conceived of as a rite of reaggregation. This is the moment to assess guilt and mete out punishment, but also to heal wounds, look towards the future and thus actively forget what has happened just recently. The singular specificity of communist regimes, however, was to play continuously on the sentiments of suffering, revenge and hatred, prevent the settling down of the negative emotions, stir up the worst in human feelings by submitting a population that had already suffered beyond measure in a world war first to an endless civil war and then to a period of forced and unintelligible terror. As has been recognized everywhere since 1989, but as was also experienced daily in the countries of then-existing socialism since 1948, communism was a regime in which the Second World War never ended.

This argument about 'permanent liminality' opens up many possibilities for the interpretive understanding of modernity. Only one will be sketched here. This concerns a question that took up a central place in the vision of modernity of many, though not all, reflexive historical sociologists This was the question of 'America'. Weber and Foucault both felt a particular attraction towards some characteristics of 'America', though both were also quite aware of the other side. The special characteristics of the American experience were a main theme in the first works of Mumford and Voegelin.[5]

This should not be surprising, as 'America' is certainly the case of permanent liminality *par excellence.* It is a country created by those who made the 'great passage' through the ocean, thus severing themselves from their past and traditions, and it was further built on the experience of the 'frontier' moving always further to the West (Mumford GD: 20–39; F. Turner 1996 [1920]).

The description of 'America' as a country in a permanent state of liminality restores what is captivating in it without hiding away all that is outrageous and repulsive. Even more importantly, it also explains why the image of 'America', as propagated around the world in films, TV series and commercials, proves to be so irresistible and contagious. It is also outrageously absurd, as there is no other country in the world that is less imitable than the United States. The experience of the United States cannot be repeated, unless some kind of United Nations dictatorship manages to organize a worldwide game of musical chairs in which all people of the world are forced to leave their homes permanently.

Furthermore, there are clear signs that the days of the last of the great modern experiments are also numbered. The historical and contemporary descents and parallels are clear enough. The American experiment is the third great social experiment of the century, comparable only to the Nazi and Bolshevik experiments. The analogies are tight, especially with the latter. Both these experiments were based on a revolutionary experience of which they were close, often even theatrically conscious, replays: the English revolution of 1640–9 with its special emphasis on its Puritan stream, and the French revolution of 1789–98 with its special emphasis on its Jacobin stream. Stretching the parallels further, both second editions followed their model by almost exactly 130 years. Finally, to end on another temporal non-accidental coincidence, the American Revolution which was the second phase of the first type, and the French Revolution which was the first phase of the second type, were contemporaries.

Though such parallels may seem stretched, unfair and rhetorical, they serve a purpose. This is to point out the fundamental similarities, beyond the evident differences, among these events and these experiments which at first glance seem so different, or even diametrically opposed. Following the terminology of Eisenstadt (1998), there are 'multiple modernities', of which the various types of fundamentalism are a variant, and these can be rooted in the various revolutions.

The drawing of such parallels does not even serve the purpose of eliminating all differences. It rather follows the Nietzschean way of posing the question: instead of asking, 'How could anything originate out of its opposite?' (Nietzsche 1966, no. 2), we should rather ask about the common roots of seeming opposites.

In the case of the revolutions and ideologies discussed above, the answer is simple and can be put in straightforward Weberian terminology, using the title of his single most important work, the *Zwischenbetrachtung*. The common roots of these diverse phenomena can be traced to the various 'religious rejections of the world' that emerged as a response to the real-world large-scale liminal crisis of the 'ecumenic age'. This expression was the Weberian formulation of Nietzsche's diagnosis of the 'revaluation of all values'. Other reflexive historical sociologists gave further precision to the term, adding the 'philosophical rejections of the world' to the 'religious rejections of the world' and calling attention to its various gnostic, apocalyptic and utopian components.

From this perspective, a new, though also very old and 'radically' Weberian, meaning can be given to the old secularization thesis. There is indeed such a thesis in the works of Weber. This, however, is not about the necessary decline of all religion with the progress of 'rationality'. It rather asserts that it is the religious *rejections* of the world that are being secularized. This happens precisely in the manner that these religious and philosophical rejections of the world take up an increasingly inner-worldly character, and transform this world into their world (hostile) image, losing all other worldly relevance and appeal in the process. It is this strange, paradoxical process, where the formerly other-worldly ideals lose their transcendent character and become immanentist utopias, that was characterized by Voegelin as a gnostic revolt and by Foucault as Panopticism.

This utopian and eschatological mentality has become incorporated into the everyday reality of a world that has entered a phase of permanent liminality. It may be countered by the reality and truth of events, experiences and with the mystery of being that can never be exhaustively closed in formulae and structures. Thus, with anything that acts as a brake to the spinning wheel of permanent liminality (a genuine Infernal Machine): by being linked to concrete human beings and other living beings in their concrete lived settings; and by institutional arrangements that incorporate in themselves the wisdom of tradition, the recognition of the impossibility of capturing the fleeting quality – and therefore eternal value – of being in abstract speculations or in individual dreams and desires whose 'deep truth' lies in mimetic triangles of desire on the one hand, and in frozen, procedurally oriented, legal-bureaucratic institutional arrangements on the other. These arrangements are only the complements of permanent liminality, curtailing its excesses but also rendering its ever more unchecked progress possible.

This dissolution of meaning in human life and the melting of all that is solid into thin air has been singled out for attention and analysed for decades, if not centuries. For many, this was a development to be saluted and promoted. However, more than anywhere else, it is in this attitude – whether proclaimed by the prophets of modernity, post-modernity, liberalism or socialism – that the 'betrayal of the clerks' can be located and diagnosed as nihilism. Human life is not possible and worth living without some degree of stability, meaning and a sense of home. Liminality is indeed a source of renewal, a restoration of meaning and the pouring of fresh wine into old bottles. But if there are no proper 'bottles', the fermenting power is diluted and lost. If everything is continuously changing, then things always remain the same. Liminality is a source of excitement and variety and a shakeup from the dull routines of everyday life, but nothing is more boring than a permanent state of liminality, where even the hope of escaping the routine is lost. Individuals are forced to invent more and more sophisticated and ultimately perverse forms of entertainment in a mad search after experience, in the wish to surpass in excitement the boredom of the hectic existence in a permanent state of liminality.[6]

One of the central and most controversial contentions of Foucault was the claim in the very last sentence of *The Will to Know* that the most diabolic trick of the mechanisms that were characterized here as permanently liminal, was 'in having us believe that our "liberation" is in the balance' (HSI 159). Perhaps nowhere is this more evident than in one of the most powerful words today, 'identity'. Identification is a way to tie an individual to a role, a position and a place in the machine by force of his/her own being and emotional involvement. It may be therefore a most blatant method of indoctrination, and it has been analysed as such by Foucault. However, identification may also be a way to tie oneself to a stable role model, and thus a way out of the spinning wheel of permanent liminality (Mittendorfer 1998). 'Identity' may also be a way to assert being, and the reality and truth of the events and experiences that formed that being. Arguably, it is this concern that animates much of the passionate current involvement in concerns with identity.

Identity cannot be proposed as a slogan to end permanent liminality. Its dangers are only too evident. Yet, it is vital to take the current quest for identity seriously. This is sign of a promising quest for the truth and reality of events and experiences, beyond the trivial and misleading identification with media-produced role models and the alleged 'truths' of one's self related to gender, sexuality, race, ethnicity, nationality, occupation and so on. It is a search for meaning and for the mystery of being.

Conclusion

This book started by drawing attention to the strong but not self-evident links between theoretical sociology and history. This has characterized the discipline since the classic work of Weber, and goes even further back to the main background figures; Marx, Nietzsche, Saint-Simon and Comte.

Through the main works of six major social theorists, it was demonstrated in detail why this is the case. Any theoretical effort requires a step back from one's immediate surroundings, a distancing from the taken for granted and a questioning of the familiar. Such an ability to see the habitual in a sudden new light and to wonder at the everyday and familiar has been the central experience of philosophy since its start. Indeed, it is the centre of any spiritual experience.

However, sociology as a discipline emerged with the conviction that under the new conditions of 'industrial' society and in 'new times' (*Neuzeit*), this approach is not sufficient for understanding what is going on. It was not always clear in the past what this exactly involved; and it is far from being clear even today. It involved a wholesale rejection of philosophy, religion and spirituality; claims for a completely new and perfectly scientific study of society; a radical break between modernity and all the other 'traditional' types of society; and a questioning of any substance behind the concept 'human nature'. Such exaggerations, though in themselves unacceptable, share a core insight that the difference of modernity cannot be denied, even if it is not a complete break from all that came before.

The fact of this difference poses a major question of method. The classical philosophical and spiritual position starts from one's mundane, concrete, trivial, everyday setting, and reaches, through distancing, reflexion and meditation, to the true, valid, general, eternal, and transcendent. The emergence of modernity introduces a third element. The relationship between the mundane and the holy, the empirical and the transcendent, the shallow and the profound becomes disturbed. Is the boring routine of trivial day-to-day existence a part of the human condition or is it an attribute of modernity? Do the theoretical categories gained through a process of abstraction and generalization on the basis of this experience have general validity and relevance, or are they solely related to the idiosyncrasies, or even idiocies, of modern life?

The triangle sketched above cannot be studied either by the most detailed empirical investigation or by the most profound and sophisticated theoretical analysis. In the language of mathematics, one cannot solve a problem of three unknowns with only two equations. There is need for a third external reference point. This is one of the reasons why the most incisive social theorists of modernity turned towards the past, while others turned to anthropological evidence and methods.

There is, however, another reason why history has a special relevance for social theory. The immediate past of modernity does not simply provide a reference point as a contrast, but directly gives information about the characteristics of modernity in its process of emergence. It is for these combined reasons that reflexive historical sociologists have not simply theories, but visions of modernity. It is through their historical studies, and their works on the courts, sects, disciplinary institutions, philosophical and religious theories of the sixteenth to eighteenth centuries that they gained profound insights into the character of modern societies, and that they were able to wonder on the present and see it in an unexpected light.

It is also at this point that reflexive historical sociologists encounter the reflexive anthropological sociologists. While the former have the substantive advantage of using their historical material not simply as a reflexive reference point for modernity but as a key to its very mechanisms, the latter have a methodological advantage because their study of non-modern, non-Western societies enables them to recognize universal patterns of human existence outside the conventional scope of European history of the last 500 years. This is why the works of Mauss, Bateson, Girard, Goffman and especially Victor Turner and his concept 'liminality' provide the conceptual tools both for mapping the dynamics of individual life-works, and for identifying the characteristic dynamics of modernity as a permanent liminality.

This would suggest that the most promising approach to follow lies in an integration of reflexive historical sociology and reflexive anthropological sociology. This would realize fully the potential recognized by Parsons in the integration not simply of the works of Weber and Durkheim, but of the entire field generated by their most important mature works.

However, it is exactly at this point that reflexive historical sociologists come up with another surprise. Their books on the early modern period were prepared with the explicit promise of providing a better understanding of modernity. However, once these works were completed, all of them took a further backward step in history, to the early Middle Ages or even antiquity, instead of returning to the present. This happened because of a fundamental reorientation of the central concern of their work, from the problem of modernity to the question of the West. This reorientation represented a break with their earlier published work, but in all cases it was also a return to their earliest and most profound interests.

In an age of globalization, which equates to the spread for better or worse of Western culture to the entire planet, an interest in these works does not require a detailed justification. This is why the reconstruction of these 'visions of modernity' must be supplemented by a study of their 'visions of the West'.

Notes

1 Norbert Elias

1 Elias was very close to his mother, while his father – another recurrent motif of the period – wanted him to realize all the dreams he had not succeeded in. On the other hand, compared with Weber or Mumford, Elias was not particularly attached to some members of his extended family.

2 By the 1890s, Nietzsche of course had became fashionable, compared with his earlier neglect. However, he was certainly not read in the sense of the project Elias engaged upon which was a 'sociological historization of Freud'.

3 It should be emphasized here that Buber and Nietzsche were the main figures, apart from Marx and Freud, having an effect on the type of Zionist youth circles Elias took part in, and not just among a larger group of thinkers who exerted some 'influence'.

4 As the work of Pierre Hadot (1993), who had such a major impact on Foucault's last period, made clear again, the term 'conversion' was used in philosophy before it was taken up in a religious setting. To drive the analogy further, Hadot's work also resurrected the concept of 'philosophical exercises': exactly the type of creative technique which was much used by Elias (Schröter 1997: 236–46).

5 See the end of *The Protestant Ethic*, but especially the 'Anticritical Last Word'. This was also taken up by Robert Merton. It should be added here that, strangely enough, Parsons and Elias could easily have met in Heidelberg because Parsons spent the 1925–6 academic year there, and went back to defend his thesis in July 1927.

6 For more details, see Szakolczai (1997).

7 For Nietzsche, untimeliness meant a distance from the current intellectual fashions, leading to an isolation and a lack of understanding and recognition; but it also meant a profound timeliness in the sense of going to the heart of current problems which would be recognized by later readers. In this sense, the analogy between the way in which Nietzsche wrote *The Birth of Tragedy* during the Franco-Prussian war (Nietzsche 1967b: 17) and the alleged 'untimeliness' of the *Civilizing Process* with the Second World War (see for example the view of Edmund Leach, as quoted in Mennell 1992: 228), is striking. On Elias's views concerning 'untimeliness', see *Reflections on a Life*, pp.75–6.

8 It is very important to emphasize that the point is by no means to accuse Elias of narcissism and an excessive search for glory and fame. On the contrary Elias, like Weber and Foucault, was only interested in his voice being heard and his work being continued (RL: 38, 73). However, it is true that with this work Elias, like Weber or Foucault, had a very high ambition which was much greater than a simple search for fame: he wanted to change the way in which

people see themselves and the world around them. Or, in the words of Stephen Mennell, he did not simply want to form a school in sociology, rather change the whole discipline itself (Mennell 1992: 251–2).

9 During his Leicester period, Elias had a recurrent dream-nightmare in which he was not able to get through to his interlocutor on the telephone (Mennell 1992: 23, RL: 73–4).

10 For further details, see Szakolczai (1998a: 132–8, 206–17). The envy Elias felt towards Borkenau, which was recognized by Papcke when Elias talked about the ease with which Borkenau was able to write quickly and yet perceptively (Papcke, 1991: 136), should also be situated here, and helps to explain the silence of Elias towards Borkenau in his recollections.

11 This is close to both Weber's self-characterization and the definition of a parrhesiast which was the way Foucault saw himself. It is also close to Weber's characterization as an 'antiprophetic prophet' (see Szakolczai 1998a: 165, 179–86).

12 As a consequence, he considered this book as his most successful one (Schröter 1997).

13 The conflict came to the surface in a *Preface* Elias wrote to a book on community (Elias 1974).

14 It may well be that the accounts of Stephen Mennell and Michael Schröter, the main English and German translators and commentators on Elias, diverge on the translation process because Mennell's involvement started in 1971–2 when Elias was very depressed, while Schröter's was in 1977 when Elias was again in high spirits.

15 One should be careful here, though. Lewis Mumford, who like Elias was reputed to possess an extraordinary memory, remarked how surprised he was about the many mistakes he found in his own autobiographical writings, once he checked his recollections against written evidence (Mumford, SL).

16 It is quite embarrassing that Mumford often published the same material three times; once in the autobiography, and twice in his collected miscellanea.

17 Though only published officially in German in 1986 and in English in 1987, it had already appeared in 1984 as a working paper in Bielefeld.

18 This idea again closely mirrors Lewis Mumford's last interests. However, Mumford, who was arguably in a much better state of health and certainly younger, as he was still in his seventies, decided not to commit himself to another long-term project. The parallels with Voegelin's and Borkenau's interests in symbols are also evident.

19 Elias was very conscious about possible problems of reputation owing to slips in work done in old age (Schröter 1997: 236).

20 Just around that time, in quick succession, he had disputes with some of his main personal and intellectual friends and supporters. These included Stephen Mennell who had expressed some doubts related to the new project (this happened in September 1985; see Mennell 1996); Johan Goudsblom over allegations of plagiarism (around 1988; see Mennell 1996); and Godfried van Benthem van den Berg over the 1985 Dutch book publication of the essay on time, from which the new Preface which had been judged superfluous by the editors was left out (personal communication).

2 Franz Borkenau

1 Valeria Russo, personal communication.

2 See Jay (1973: 306, fn45). This was supported by Dennis Wrong (personal communication).

3 The effects of their efforts, however, were quite different. Bell succeeded in getting EB published. The book, however, was little reviewed and had very

little impact (for a perceptive review, see Grew 1982). As a result, the planned publication of *Transition* never got off the ground. In Italy, however, the interest in Borkenau was more substantial. It led to the emergence of important secondary literature that looked upon Borkenau's work in a promising light, alongside Foucault and Koselleck (see the writings of Marramao, Negri, Russo and Schiera).

4 Given that Voegelin was only nineteen days younger than Borkenau, and he had also lived in Vienna since the age of ten, they shared a series of external formative influences. For example the book *The Last Days Of Mankind* by Karl Kraus, the noted journalistic and critic, is singled out for attention as a special document of the age both in Voegelin's *Autobiography* (AR: 18), and in Lowenthal's obituary on Borkenau (1957: 57).

5 His father broke with him because of his radical views (Tashjean 1962: 6).

6 Borkenau had taken part in some discussions around the mid 1920s (Russo 1981: 296, fn13).

7 According to Lowenthal, this chapter was not part of the original manuscript (Russo 1981: 297–8, fn15).

8 As if this were not enough, the correspondence between Horkheimer and Grossman was full with 'extremely pungent, bitter judgements' on Borkenau in the period (Russo 1985: 114, fn7), like the claims that he was '"dangerous"' and '"intolerably renegade"' (Russo 1981: 298, fn16). This characterization gains its intended sinister meaning if we add that the adjective 'renegade' was used by Lenin against his former idol, Karl Kautsky, after his support for the German war efforts in 1914. The interest of Grossman became particularly obsessive and he returned, like the murderer to the location of his crime, to the theme of Borkenau even in 1945. By then the sixty-four year old economic historian, who had so far only published works on Sismondi, Marx and the question of capitalist development and was considered as the 'embodiment of the Central European academic: proper, meticulous, and gentlemanly' (Jay 1973: 17), came to complete a manuscript on the alien theme of Descartes' *Geometry* , in which he argued for the need to put the book in the context of a history of machinery which would go back to the thirteenth century (Russo 1987: 184, fn5). However, one place where Grossman did not or could not return was the *Zeitschrift* which was the actual scene of the deed. Though he joined the *Institut* as an assistant of Grünberg in 1926 (Wiggershaus 1994: 29–30), published the first monograph in the book series of which Borkenau's was the fourth, and wrote an article in the very first issue of the *Zeitschrift*, he never appeared there again. Finally, even when a new print of the book was produced thirty-seven years later, two unauthorised versions which were published in Hamburg and Frankfurt included the criticism of Grossman as a 'red tail'. The standard practice of book publishing in communist countries was to let 'unorthodox' works appear only with a long Preface or Postface in which the correct orthodox position which was highly critical of the work was stated. This was called the 'red tail'.

9 One of Grossman's main charges concerned a lack of erudition. However, a short glance at the book, and a slight attention to the conditions in which it was published, are sufficient to show how outrageous this claim was. Borkenau took meticulous care in referencing his argument, going into such excesses as to make notes specifically in case a particular Preface to a book did not contain page numbers (UFB: 406, fn 54). In the 1930s, especially on the continent, it was not at all general practice to prepare an index for academic books. Nevertheless, the book appeared with a detailed and precise index, situated before rather than after the text. Given the reserve Horkheimer showed toward the book in his Preface, it is unlikely that this was part of general publication strategy. Borkenau's true scholarship comes out all the more strongly given that he prepared the book for publication as a refugee in Paris.

10 According to Elias, the theme of Italian fascism was much discussed among German intellectuals in the early 1930s (Korte 1997: 119, quoting a letter written in 1982). Borkenau himself published an article on this theme in the *Archiv* in 1933.

11 This was mostly thanks to the efforts of Lawrence Henderson at Harvard, who steered Talcott Parsons to write on Pareto at exactly the same time (Camic 1991: xxxiv). Aron also published his first essays on Pareto in 1936–7 (Campbell 1986: 287).

12 In the first years of the Nazi regime, it was a common practice of exiles to use pseudonyms. It was done, among others, by Horkheimer, Adorno and Benjamin. However, in this volume it was not practiced by the other contributors.

13 Strangely enough, Orwell had considerable difficulties in publishing this review, which led to his break with his old association with the established left-wing periodical *New Statesman* (Orwell 1968, I: 279–81).

14 At that moment Borkenau was just thirty-seven years old. In his work on Ndembu ritual, Victor Turner mentions as a common belief that 'diviners' are initiated into their vocation between the ages of thirty-five and forty. This starts with an illness, after which the initiand had to go through a ritual where '[t]owards the end of the performance he must kill a cock by biting through its neck' (V. Turner 1975: 289). This is close to Nietzsche's peak experience in Sils Maria, '6000 feet beyond man and time' (Nietzsche 1967a: 295), as described in the section 'On the vision and the riddle' in the *Zarathustra*, where the nauseating sickness was overcome by biting off the head of a snake (Nietzsche 1954: 271). Furthermore, one of the symbols used by Turner in his best-known article to characterize the experience of a rite of passage was the 'snake symbolism (for the snake appears to die, but only to shed its old skin and appear in a new one)' (V. Turner 1967: 199). The same symbolism was used in one of the most famous aphorisms of Nietzsche: '*Shedding one's skin*: The snake that cannot shed its skin perishes. So do the spirits who are prevented from changing their opinions: they cease to be spirit' (Nietzsche 1954: 92). Given this, it is intriguing to observe that Nietzsche was turning thirty-seven when he had his experience; Max Weber was thirty-seven when he read Nietzsche's posthumous *Will to Power* at the end of a long period of illness; and Borkenau was also the same age when, after his illness in Panama, he read *The Civilizing Process*.

15 It should be noted that just as Borkenau's 1934 book positively advanced many of the ideas Foucault put forward in a certainly more rigorous and systematic way, in 1966 Foucault was most negatively critical of exactly these figures of Western Marxism. In 1967–9, he was engaged in a major debate with Sartre and during the same period when visiting Budapest, he refused to pay the conventional visit to Lukacs (DEI: 28). They also had a common opponent in Lucien Goldmann, who spoke up against Foucault during his famous 1969 talk 'What Is an Author?' (DEI: 812–8) and who took up Borkenau's theme. He even went so far as to borrow the title of his 1955 book *The Hidden God* 'without ever so much as mentioning Borkenau', though 'go[ing] over the same ground in rather more pedestrian fashion, and in the end com[ing] up with the identical conclusion' (Lichtheim 1967: 269). Furthermore, it was precisely the work of Borkenau that made it evident that it is quite misleading to call Lukacs as a 'Western Marxist' as opposed to the 'Stalinist East', as it was Lukacs and his essay on 'History and Class Consciousness' who made Russian Bolshevism acceptable in the West (Borkenau 1962: 172–5). Until that point there had been no serious intellectual or mass support for Bolshevism outside Russia. Finally, Negri's first article introducing Borkenau to Italy was severely attacked by Massimo Cacciari (Negri 1978: 139, fn 1) currently mayor of Venice and then a young Communist philosopher but the same person who would be among the first to attack Foucault in Italy (see DEIV: 833).

16 Many of these pieces were published as leading articles in *Merkur*, considered then as a main German-language periodical. Interestingly, one of his most significant analyses 'The Zhdanov crisis' was published just two months before Voegelin's 'Gnostic Politics' which was the first work he published in German since his 1938 exile.

3 Eric Voegelin

1 This can be contrasted with the case of Martin Buber, for whom Kant's idea of synthetic *a priori* provided a solution for anxiety about space and time (Buber 1967: 12).

2 It was on the basis of a similar recollection, which happened on a Sunday afternoon walk, that Huizinga had the insight about the 'waning of the Middle Ages' (Huizinga 1968: 272–3). To make the parallel even closer, just as Huizinga's experience helped him to gain an insight that the dissolution of the medieval order was the source and not product of the Renaissance, Voegelin's recollection was also connected to the anxiety he then experienced about the precocious dissolution of the last few rows of the parade (AN: 39).

3 Grünberg is mentioned by Voegelin as the third popular lecturer at the Law Faculty at that time (AR: 3) and, according to Lami (1993), he taught Voegelin. Given that Grünberg brought Borkenau to the Frankfurt Institut in the 1920s and that Borkenau only finished his studies in Leipzig in 1924, it is quite probable that during autumn 1919, Voegelin and Borkenau sat together in the lectures of Grünberg at Vienna University.

4 The encounter with the thought of India, which happened way before contemporary fads, was a central experience for Schopenhauer, Nietzsche, Weber and Huizinga. In fact, together with the 'frontier thought' of Emerson, Whitman and Thoreau (Mumford 1968, Hadot 1995b, F. Turner 1996 [1920]), it was a major source for the return to philosophy as a way of life as opposed to an exclusive concern with doctrine and propositions.

5 This is all the more appropriate as in characterizing the importance Weber exerted on the post-war generation, Wagner made use of the letter Voegelin wrote him about this matter. See note 87 for more details.

6 Eduard Meyer's reflections on the work of the historian gave occasion for one of Weber's methodological writings. He was a source of inspiration for both Toynbee and Spengler.

7 Curiously, Voegelin was just able to catch those aspects of the American intellectual scene, such as commonsense philosophy, pragmatism and institutional economics, that would soon be obliterated because of the successive waves of 'Germanization' of the American academic life and especially the influence of neo-Kantianism. It is of much symbolic interest that in precisely the years when Voegelin had his study travels in America, Parsons who was only a year younger travelled to Europe and brought home to the States a predilection for exactly the kind of 'heavy' German methodological and theoretical baggage that Voegelin got rid of there.

8 The conference paper of Caringella remained unpublished. It was summarized by Geoffrey Price in the first few pages of Frederick Lawrence's contribution to the published volume (Lawrence 1997: 35, fn 1).

9 As a point of interest, at that moment Elias was still in Heidelberg as a *Habilitation* student of Alfred Weber whose course on the sociology of culture Voegelin attended. As it was the first time it was delivered (AR: 15), Elias must also have been present in the audience.

10 In 1930, Voegelin entered into correspondence with Leopold von Weise and Marianne Weber on, among other things, the extent to which Weber had read

Nietzsche and Kierkegaard (Voegelin 1995: 48–60). Evidently, it took more than five years for Marianne Weber to answer the question concerning the link between Weber's illness and the possible reading of Kierkegaard's *Sickness unto Death* and even then she started her letter without any formalities (not even an address like 'Dear Mr' or 'Dr') and with the following sentence 'The question for me is very difficult to answer' (ibid.: 59).

11 Caringella identified this occasion as the background for the first anamnetic exercises of 1943 (see Lawrence 1996: 37). However, he put the emphasis on the output, not on the engendering source.

12 Voegelin published a major review of this book in 1931. At around the same time, Schmitt's work was also a reading experience for Borkenau.

13 The fate of these books again stands in close parallel to those of the works by Elias and Borkenau which were written at the same time. One could only speculate how far the history of sociology would have been different had Weber become a 'founding father' not solely through Parsons, but also through the way Elias, Borkenau and Voegelin further developed his ideas. The potential for sociology in Voegelin's 1936 and 1938 books has even been recognized, as the *American Sociological Review* published reviews of both works by different authors, in 1937 and 1941 (Price 1994: 111). In fact, the latter was evidently the only review published of the book at the time.

There is, however, one good example of the possible impact. Shortly after his arrival in the States, Voegelin sent a complimentary copy to Thomas Mann who read the book and sent back an appreciative letter (letter of 18 December 1938, in Voegelin Archives, Hoover Institute, Stanford, box 24, file 11. In the following, I will refer to Archival material only by box and file number). At around the same time Elias also sent him a copy of *The Civilizing Process* which he read with similar interest. It is of quite some interest that he was therefore in the rare position of being familiar with these two outstanding books, which were destined for long oblivion because of the exile of their authors and the destruction of the book stock owing to bombing. The attention will leave its traces. Mann would soon work on his *Dr Faustus*. In a letter of 21 March 1949 to Löwith upon reading the book, Voegelin states that he wished that a professional historian or sociologist would understand as much of the 'dynamics of spiritual decay' as the novelist (box 24, file 4). To close the circle, Voegelin owned a copy of *The Civilizing Process*, in both its 1939 and 1968 editions (I am grateful for Dr. Helmut Klumpjan, University of Erlangen, for this information) though it seems that he never referred to it in print.

14 It must be emphasized that the idea is not based on the Freudian concept of the 'return of the repressed' though it is obviously related. The term 'repression', whether explicitly intended or just implied, would be very misleading anyway.

15 They are published as volumes nineteen through to twenty-six of *The Collected Works of Eric Voegelin*. The publication proceeds with a speed that in some respects is exemplary. The first two volumes were published in 1997, the next four in 1998 and the final volumes are planned for summer 1999. But in other respects it poses serious problems about the editorial work on what was done, and what was not. A full critical analysis goes beyond the scope of this book though some related comments will be presented when appropriate.

16 For example they claim that 'the conception of the "History" remained fundamentally unchanged from the start' (Hollweck and Sandoz 1997: 16). As will be argued in detail, this is untenable. (When I finished the manuscript, I was not yet able to consult the Introduction of Gebhardt to HPVII.)

17 The general neglect of Weber's work in American Voegelin scholarship is a serious liability of this literature. This may well be caused by the extreme departmentalization of North American academic life, which leads to the

classification of Weber as a sociologist and Voegelin as a political theorist, and by the long domination of the Parsonian interpretation of Weber's work.

18 See Skinner (1978), Tully (1988). See also the important work done on Weber by Wilhelm Hennis (1988, 1991, 1994) and Lawrence Scaff (1984, 1989); on Durkheim by Robert Alun Jones (1986, 1991); and on Parsons by Charles Camic (1989, 1991, 1992).

19 The last anamnetic experiment is entitled 'First Emigration' and ends with the following sentence: 'What had happened only dawned on me several weeks later when I first went to school in Vienna' (AN: 51).

20 The same passage was contained in his October 1949 Guggenheim application material (box 15, file 25).

21 Like Elias and Foucault, Voegelin went where the 'spirit' led him.

22 For example see the 1942–3 correspondence between Voegelin and Leo Strauss, which related to the publication of 'The People of God' (FPP: 5–15) and between Voegelin and Waldemar Gurian, editor of the *Review of Politics*, about the publication of 'Siger de Brabant' (Opitz 1996: 175).

23 For details, see the official correspondence with Louisiana State University (box 23, file 27).

24 The assumption of an opposition between sudden experiences and insights on the one hand, and a long process of intense work on the other, is another of the methodological shortcomings of the editors. In fact, in the case of Voegelin and the other thinkers discussed in this volume, the sudden insights were rendered possible against a background of decades of hard work, and came in special liminal conditions. Their 'experiences' and 'visions' thus did not come out of the blue but they did happen. They were events.

25 Campbel P. Hodges, President of LSU to Voegelin, 20 August 1943 (box 23, file 27).

26 On the joint importance of these two names for Voegelin, see the typescript of the 16 March 1984 Lonergan Symposium, University of Santa Clara (box 85, file 12, p.12).

27 In the key 1977 'late Preface' to *Anamnesis*, Voegelin claimed that '[m]y own horizon was strongly formed and informed by the restoration of the German language through Stefan George and his circle' (AN: 5).

28 See for example. letters of 14 June, 18 July and 17 August 1944 (box 11, file 7).

29 This indeed became Voegelin's final word on the Middle Ages. These volumes would not be touched anymore except for the section on sects.

30 When pressed by Webb, Voegelin dated the experience as occurring about two months before Hiroshima (Webb 1981: 6, fn 6). In a letter to Hermann Broch, the author of *Sleepwalkers*, Voegelin, like Max Scheler, diagnosed the age as a series of 'free-floating hate-waves' where activity is futile, and one has to wait until all this passes by (Voegelin to Hermann Broch, 30 March 1945, box 8, file 42). Chapter one of 'The Last Orientation' which leads up to the Schelling chapter, has the following postscript: 'This chapter was finished six weeks before the atom-bomb was dropped on Hiroshima – the date that has brought us one step nearer to the point where reality and comic-strip become indistinguishable' (HPVII: 151).

31 This very much recalls Elias's idea concerning 'involvement and detachment' which was conceived in the same post-war situation and published in 1954 in the *British Journal of Sociology*. This was the only major article Elias published in the thirty years that elapsed between the first and second editions of *The Civilizing Process*.

32 Voegelin to Karl Loewenstein, 23 August 1942 (box 23, file 23).

33 In fact, even here, the trajectory would be not only linear but also circular. As we shall see, around 1966 at the time of writing *Anamnesis*, there would

be a return to the more 'mystic' and less 'Christian' or 'philosophical' Voegelin.

34 Letter of 13 June 1946 to Voegelin (box 23, file 27.)

35 Voegelin to Kurt H. Wolff, 14 March 1949 (box 42, file 15).

36 Though the correspondence with Strauss was conducted in German, these sentences were written in English.

37 See Voegelin to Engel-Janosi, 7 December 1948 (Hollweck and Sandoz 1997: 29–30) and also P. J. Vatikiotis to Geoffrey Price, 13 July 1994. I am thankful to Geoffrey Price and Pat Vatikiotis for permission to use this letter.

38 Voegelin to Gurian, 22 February 1949 (box 15, file 27).

39 Voegelin to Gurian, 22 April 1949 (box 15, file 27), Voegelin to Gurwitsch, 16 April 1949 (box 15, file 28).

40 'Goethe's Utopia', 29 April 1949 radio talk (box 62, file 31).

41 Voegelin to Gurwitsch, 27 August 1949 (Opitz, 1994a: 131).

42 Voegelin to Henry A. Moe, 8 October 1949 (box 15, file 25).

43 Ibid.

44 P. J. Vatikiotis to Geoffrey Price, 13 July 1994.

45 Voegelin to Alois Dempf, 20 November 1949 (box 10, file 4).

46 A detailed analysis will be done in Chapter Eight.

47 Voegelin to Gurian, 6 December 1949 (box 15, file 27).

48 Voegelin to Kerwin, 20 February 1950 (box 63, file 11).

49 Voegelin to Moe, 17 April 1950 (box 15, file 25). This in itself contradicts the claim that 'from the very beginning' Voegelin was engaged 'in writing a systematic work' (Hollweck and Sandoz 1997: 16).

50 See Opitz 1994a: 131; Voegelin to Dempf, 20 February 1950 (box 10, file 4); Voegelin to Eduard Baumgarten, 10 July 1951 (box 7, file 17).

51 "Notes on T.S. Eliot's *Four Quartets*", c.1950 (box 63, file 1). As Voegelin often took cues from his friends, one may wonder whether this one originated from an 8 March 1950 letter of Gregor Sebba (box 35, file 4).

52 These events have also parallels with Voegelin's first university semester, which was another moment of personal and political liminality

53 'Impressions about his trip to Vienna' (box 63, file 3).

54 Voegelin to Henry A. Moe, 18 May 1951 (box 15, file 25).

55 Voegelin characterized his colleague and friend Heberle, who taught Weber at the LSU Sociology Department, as a 'solid positivist'; see Voegelin to Eduard Baumgarten, 21 April 1952 (box 7, file 17). His 14 March 1949 letter to Kurt H. Wolff also contained scathing remarks about the profession of sociology (box 42, file 15).

56 Kelsen recognized himself as a target and took exception to being labelled as a gnostic. This led to an exchange of letters, including a 120 page review by Kelsen (Sattler 1997).

57 Sebba (1981: 431) and Opitz (1993: 110) both recognized the difference between two Webers.

58 Voegelin to Eduard Baumgarten, 10 July 1951 (box 7, file 17); see also Opitz 1994b: 138. Baumgarten was a relative of Max Weber who inherited the remains of Weber's library and correspondence after the deaths of Marianne Weber (1954) and Alfred Weber (1958). Baumgarten and Voegelin had known each other in the 1930s, resumed correspondence in 1950 and were in contact after Voegelin's return to Germany.

59 All this has become known only as the result of the last decades of Weber scholarship and is still surrounded by major controversies (see Schluchter 1989). The edition produced by Marianne Weber in 1921–2 failed to pay attention to this peculiar character of the work. Voegelin thus could not have been aware of the full situation related to *Economy and Society*, though on the basis of Marianne Weber's *Biography* he certainly knew about the original textbook

character of *Economy and Society*. However, the posthumous editors of his manuscript certainly should have known better.

The parallels even extend to external conditions of the two world wars. Given the joint internal and external conditions, both Weber and Voegelin grew increasingly polemical in their style and conduct. For Weber, the years 1911–13 were the years of his famous 'controversies' (WB 431–48). In the case of Voegelin, the same discharge of tension can be seen in the increasingly polemical tone of his letters and, in contrast to Weber, even in published works.

60 This was in spite of the support he received in Baton Rouge. His crucial 17 April 1950 letter to Moe contains the following passage: 'I do not have to explain what dangers work in comparative isolation is exposed – dangers which are only insufficiently countered by an extensive correspondence with my friends in the profession' (box 15, file 25).

61 On the links between illness and thought, see Ellenberger (1970), Greco (1998), and Szakolczai (1998a, chapter 6). This is all the more relevant as, just like Weber and Foucault, Voegelin's life was his work and his work was his life. On 'recognition', see especially the work of Alessandro Pizzorno (Pizzorno 1986, 1987, 1991, Greco, Della Porta and Szakolczai forthcoming).

62 As has been emphasized throughout this book, the concern about reception for Elias, Foucault, Mumford and Voegelin was largely due to the contrast between the relative isolation of the authors, and the significance of their works and their vision, of which they were convinced.

63 Voegelin to Paeschke, 28 October 1951 (box 25, file 11).

64 Voegelin to Eduard Baumgarten, 21 April 1952 (box 7, file 17).

65 The reopening of Volume One of *History of Political Ideas* marks the definite break with this project. Retrospectively, in December 1954 (see Voegelin to Moe, 16 December 1954 (box 15, file 25), Voegelin would speak of four years of work done on the first volumes of *Order and History*. This would put the start of this work sometime in 1951.

66 The last chapter of Mumford's *Pentagon of Power* ends with a section 'if the sleepers awaken' (MMII: 409).

67 Voegelin to Gurian, 16 November 1952 (box 15, file 27).

68 Elizabeth de Waal, an acquaintance of Voegelin's from Vienna, was much disturbed by the style of this article; see Price 1997.

69 This correspondence is published in Voegelin *et al.* (1993). Great thinkers are just as prone as any other human being to consign the distressful memory of past controversies to oblivion. Max Weber did not even want to hear about the 'anticritical' essays, thus misleading generations of scholars about their importance. Voegelin similarly forgot about this entire exchange until Helmut Wagner showed him the letters after the American publication of *Anamnesis*. Upon receiving the copies, he wrote back claiming that 'I had completely forgotten this correspondence.' (Voegelin to Helmut R. Wagner, 14 February 1978 (box 39, file 21; misclassified); see also Sebba (1981: 431).

70 Voegelin to John H. Hallowell, 28 January 1953 (box 16, file 3).

71 Voegelin to G. Niemeyer, 11 April 1953 (box 27, file 13).

72 Voegelin to G. Mure, 28 April 1953 (box 63, file 11).

73 The criticism voiced here, like that concerning his earlier assessment of Popper, is against not content but style. Voegelin's points against Locke are well taken, especially on what concerns the question of a philosophical life. But the style undercuts these points and is therefore twice counter-productive.

74 The letters suggest that even within these three volumes, like Elias and Foucault, Voegelin worked backwards. The major part of Volume Three was completed in 1946–7. The central thrust of work on Volume Two was done during 1949–51. The new version of Volume One was started some time in late 1951 and was finished during the summer of 1955 when 150 new manuscript

pages were completed on Israel. See Voegelin to Eduard Baumgarten, 10 January 1956 (box 7, file 17).

75 This is not always easy to trace as the editors do not apply the general practice of putting editorial remarks in square brackets.

76 It is not accidental that Voegelin never sent sections of this part of the manuscript for review. His general lack of interest in de Tocqueville, a thinker with whom his outlook shows much affinity, is perplexing. The omission of Rousseau is even more striking. It is not conceivable to write a history of political thought without discussing his works in detail. In fact, according to the 1941 plans, Rousseau would have had a central role in the discussion of modernity (Opitz 1996: 181). One could argue that the moment the project lost any resemblance to a book on the history of political ideas was when the Rousseau chapter was dropped. Tentatively, one could further argue that this happened in the summer of 1945 and that the place of Rousseau was taken up by Schelling.

77 One should not even be surprised at such coincidences. The attribution of liminality is not arbitrary but rather follows the course of human life and of nature: the rites of passage that accompany one's upbringing and academic life, like appointments, publications and promotions; the periods of travel and vacation that break the everyday work routine; and the cycle of seasons with which such breaks are associated. The 'father' of liminality, Arnold van Gennep, published huge volumes on the folklore of France and organized the rites collected around two principles: the linearity of the individual life course and the cyclical pattern of nature.

78 Such claims are not restricted to late recollections, but are present for example in both the October 1949 and December 1954 work plans which Voegelin sent with his application to the Guggenheim Foundation. For example in the latter he claimed that '[i]n the course of a closer study of sources and monographic literature, the original plan had to be abandoned' (box 15, file 25).

79 In support of the editors, it must be acknowledged that the dilemma whether a life-project is continuous and linear or whether it develops through crises is not restricted to the life-work of Voegelin. Exactly the same issue is posed repeatedly with the works of Weber and Foucault. Some of those who were either closest to, or were the most knowledgeable interpreters of these thinkers, like Marianne Weber, Wolfgang Schluchter, Daniel Defert or Colin Cordon, also argue for such a continuity in those cases. These positions are often formulated explicitly against criticisms that charge Weber and Foucault with having 'crises' in their works. However, the terms of this debate are badly posed. A crisis in thought does not count against a thinker, especially a modern thinker, but is the sign of genuine worth. Weber, Foucault and Voegelin should not be 'defended' on the basis of the fundamental continuity of their thought, but it is the conventional position valorizing such a continuity of a thought that should be exposed and criticized. This position, I would argue, is the 'prejudice of humanism' that cannot even conceive of transformative experiences, spirituality, *conversio*, metanoia or *periagoge*. The terms of the tables should therefore be turned. It is the thought of those thinkers who have never undergone a crisis, like Parsons, Habermas and Luhmann that remains shallow, in spite of their undeniable merits.

80 Voegelin to Moe, 27 December 1955 (box 15, file 25).

81 At almost the same time, in July 1964, Foucault was giving his famous lecture on Marx, Nietzsche and Freud in a conference organized about the new French edition of Nietzsche's works (DE46). Weber became a 'reading experience' for Foucault only about fifteen years later. One could argue that this 1964 omission greatly hindered Foucault's intellectual trajectory.

82 See box 72, file 3.
83 This was a central issue in the 1994 Voegelin conference. See Gebhardt (1997) and Lawrence (1997).
84 Voegelin to Heilman, 19 June 1966 (box 17, file 9).
85 This is in contrast to the published German Preface where, in spite of commonalties, the name of Heraclitus is absent and attention is restricted to Plato (Voegelin 1980: 38–9).
86 Plotinus was the best known neo-Platonist of the first centuries AD, while Dionysius Areopagita was considered as the main transmitter of Eastern Gnosticism to the West, as Voegelin himself acknowledges (HPIV: 151–7).
87 In a letter to Wagner who was then working on his biography of Schutz, Voegelin stated that 'Max Weber and Bergson were indeed dominant figures in the 1920's, after Weber's "massive work" has come out', and added that 'Max Weber was so important that, as soon as I was habilitated in 1929, I gave a Max Weber Seminar in which Schutz also participated' (Voegelin to Helmut R. Wagner, 25 January 1975 (box 39, file 21).
88 The process can be followed through the reports Voegelin was required to write at the end of each year (box 3, file 23).
89 Given Foucault's strong interest in both the Enlightenment and revolution in the second part of the 1970s, it is most likely that he encountered this work in one of his many visits to the United States. Had he looked through the book, he must have been struck by the fact that this work, published in the same year as *Discipline and Punish*, also made Bentham, precisely through the *Panopticon*, into one of its main negative heroes (FER: 59–60, fn-s 23 and 24, and 67–8, fn 39).

4 Lewis Mumford

1 He also felt it important to make a remark on the way traditional children's games were passed on from one generation to another on the streets without the intervention of adults (SL: 94–5). All this, of course, implied the absence of television, the frequent presence of family members other than the nuclear family, and the security of playing in the streets. It was light years away from the current mainstream options of suffocating parental supervision and care, and absentee working parents.
2 The symptoms closely resemble Weber's illness. Mumford even recognized that the illness 'saved' him as otherwise he would not have had the strength to escape his situation.
3 It is true that he was appointed as a full professor at Stanford in 1942 and taught there for two years. However, the reason he accepted this post shows that he was not a teacher-technician, as he considered that his 'mission there was to give "the young the vision and discipline they will need to lift themselves out of the muck and chaos that their easy-going elders have created"' (MB: 408).
4 The language Mumford used in his autobiography in describing his own experience was taken from Erikson's famous work *Young Man Luther*.
5 Interestingly enough, it was *The Dial* that became the 'vehicle' that introduced Thomas Mann to America around the same time (Heilbut 1996: 358–9, 393).
6 Had he accepted the post, he could have read Borkenau's review on Elias some fifteen years later.
7 Both these characterizations are contained in private notes written on the same day, 8 December 1925 (MB: 230, fn 38).
8 This work also had a major impact on Weber. It is at least intriguing that Weber's crucial 5 May 1908 letter (MWGII/ 5: 557), written after his reading of *Ecce Homo* and in a period of intense meditation and self-reflexion on his own 'passage' in the middle of life, was addressed to Vossler.

9 The parallels with Weber are again striking. Weber had an intimate relationship with Mina Tobler in 1911–14, when writing the first drafts of *Economy and Society* and 'The Economic Ethic of World Religions'; and with Else Jaffé in 1916–20, when finishing the works for publication.

10 Such a shift again has close parallels with Foucault's intellectual trajectory around 1978–82, though arguably, the priorities of Foucault were reverse as he preferred Seneca to the Christian fathers.

11 At this point, the parallels come out with Voegelin who similarly gave the lectures on which his *New Science of Politics*, a work which had a similar place and role in his oeuvre to the one *The Transformations of Man* had in Mumford's, was based at the University of Chicago in 1951. At that time and during the writing of *Israel and Revelation*, Voegelin also considered contacts with the Oriental Institute as being of utmost importance in checking his ideas with the best experts.

12 As the late Prefaces Nietzsche wrote to his books in 1886–7 demonstrate, such an activity can be considered as a sign of philosophical exercises. For more details, see Szakolczai (1998a: 38–9, 61–76).

13 See 'The Case against "Modern Architecture"', MR: 72–83 (originally published in April 1962); ' The Future of the City: Part 1 – The Disappearing City', MR: 108–112 (originally published in October 1962); 'The Future of the City: Part 2 – Yesterday's City of Tomorrow', MR: 176–183 (originally published in November 1962); 'Home Remedies for Urban Cancer', MR: 184–200 (originally published in December 1962).

Conclusion to Part I: comparisons and contrasts

1 Similar parallels between the German and Jewish fate and concern with 'fate' have been drawn by Borkenau (EB: 267) and Voegelin (HPII: 45–6).

2 These remarks also are most interesting because they reveal a profound affinity of attitudes, beyond all differences, with respect to 1968 between Voegelin, Foucault, Elias and Mumford. They all recognized the genuine problem of sensitivity and spirituality animating the student movement, though sooner or later they were all horrified to find out that the old and defunct ideologies and false prophets took over its 'spiritual direction'. Here as elsewhere, the thinking of Maurice Clavel, one of Foucault's closest friends, represents an important bridge between the concerns of Foucault and Voegelin.

3 Most of them spent a short spell under the influence of Marxism. This amounted to a few months for Voegelin, a few years for Foucault and perhaps Mumford, and a full decade for Borkenau. As a result, Borkenau suffered more serious scars, not so much in his way of thinking as in the difficulties he encountered when trying to break out of the ghetto into which he closed himself.

4 One could also add here a distinct group of East-Central European thinkers like the Czech Jan Patocka, the Hungarians István Bibó and Béla Hamvas, the Romanian Constantin Noica and the Pole Julius Domanski. For more details, see Szakolczai (1994, forthcoming).

5 Borkenau compared this attitude to Nechaiev's (Borkenau 1962 [1939]: 173, see also pp. 24–7). Nechaiev was an anarchist student who in the 1860s accused a fellow revolutionary of being a spy and secured his execution. He revealed afterwards that he only invented the story in order to cement the cohesion and community of the group through participation in a common crime. Voegelin (FER: 228) also identified Nechaiev as a representative figure of the frame of mind leading to Russian Bolshevism.

6 This was all the less acceptable for them as Bergson's *Two Sources* was one of their major reading experiences. This is well known about Voegelin, but

Borkenau also mentions this book in his manuscript (EB: 278, fn 13; and, in fact, this is the only non-specialist book referred to in the important chapter 'The Gods of the Ancient Germans'). One could further argue that Bergson's work, published first in 1932, was also read by Elias who arrived in Paris in 1933 and may have derived inspiration for his ideas concerning the 'open self' from there. Finally, Foucault was lecturing for years at the Collège de France in the same room where Bergson kept his famous lectures.

7 See the seventh lecture of 1983, 16 February 1983 (Foucault Archives tape C 68 (09)).
8 This was at the heart of Foucault's long-lasting hostility to Sartre (FR: 374).
9 For more details, see Szakolczai (1998a: 83–6).
10 Concerning Weber and Foucault, see Szakolczai (1998a: 89, 193); about Voegelin, the well–known historian Engel-Janosi stated that he is 'I believe the only one among us who can be described as almost a real genius' (Webb 1981: 53, fn 1).
11 The diverse statements of Foucault on the fiction and truth character of his work amount to a difficult puzzle. Last words, however, carry much weight and two of his very last publications are entitled 'The Care of Truth', while his last course at the Collège de France was entitled 'The Courage of the Truth'.

Introduction to Part II

I am grateful for Dennis Smith for returning my attention to the work of Schumpeter.

5 The Protestant spirit (Weber)

1 Thus, on page twenty-seven the text refers to 'two older essays' that are 'placed at the beginning'. These, of course, are the *Protestant Ethic* essays that in English consist of the entire book.
2 In fact, this goes back to idea of diagnosing 'capitalism' as the 'fate' of the modern condition (see Käsler 1988: 66).
3 For a particularly clear reference, see PE: 65.
4 Weber could not have read the work of Huizinga on the collapse of the medieval world order as it was published in 1919 but only in Dutch. It was a work that broke away from centuries of interpretation about the link between the Middle Ages and the Renaissance and became a main source for later reflexive historical sociologists.
5 Borkenau and Voegelin both would provide an important excavation of this image of the German past, which has been assumed by Weber.
6 This again recalls Nietzsche and his concern with the 'hostility towards life'.
7 The genealogical method traces emergence to the joining of separate threads. It does not assume a single source of origin.
8 In fact, Brentano also had a similar crossing of sword with Marx about a similarly mistaken charge of omission (see the Preface by Engels to the fourth edition of *Capital* in Marx 1976: 118–20). In one sense, however, Weber himself was partly responsible for this general oversight, through the antagonism he set up between traditionalism and Reformation. Monasticism and asceticism do not fit the dichotomy between tradition and 'modernity'.
9 This book is exactly the kind of manual about how to live everyday life that was used by Elias in *The Civilizing Process* and by Foucault in the last volumes of *The History of Sexuality*.
10 As a particularly clear example of activity-oriented other-worldly asceticism, the desert fathers were reputed to burn the fruits of their work each year (Waddell 1987 [1934]: 232).

11 In this context, it is particularly intriguing that Weber planned a piece on the Book of Job; see PE: 164 and Schluchter (1989).

12 To think of an alternative, he could have easily given a joint title to the essays on 'Protestantism'. For an analysis of the difference in the two versions of the 'Sects', see Loader and Alexander (1985).

13 Foucault and Voegelin would both single out this predilection for admittance and exclusion in their diagnoses of modernity (see especially *Histoire de la folie* and 'The People of God').

14 It was also archetypical in the sense of the first '"believer's church"' (FMW: 313–4).

15 Weber provides further examples of secular 'badges' that are replacing in a 'modern', 'secular' context the 'label' of religious affiliation here (FMW: 307–8).

16 The debates around the institutionalization of infant baptism were extensively discussed in Foucault's 1980 Collège de France lectures. See lectures of 6, 13 and 20 February 1980 (C 62 (5), (6) and (7), Foucault Archives).

17 The concern with 'breeding traits', repeatedly used in this page, is again a clearly Nietzsche-inspired idea in Weber.

6 Court society (Elias)

1 This is also true with respect to Durkheim. Célestin Bouglé, one of Durkheim's closest associates, is acknowledged in the original Preface to *The Civilizing Process*, and the work has many Durkheimian traits. There are probably too many such traits, given the sometimes excessive reliance on demographic factors like population growth in the account on the origins of modern society.

2 To a considerable extent, this is owing to the efforts of Bourdieu, who has made it clear recently that his concept of *habitus* was influenced by the work of Elias.

3 Elias and Mumford also used the same concept (CP: 472; CH: 347, 566).

4 This does not mean that Weber's position was without ambiguity. Weber was indeed struggling with the neo-Kantian position which he found a powerful challenge and was not always able to go beyond. However, his concern was not with 'action' as an absolute beginning, but with action as a difference. This comes out by tracing his 'theory of action' back to its engendering source which was his comparative historical studies of the world religions and especially the attention paid to the 'extraordinary' character of magical and religious behaviour (ES: 399–401).

5 The point is not to assume a complete identity between the position of Weber and Elias. It is rather that the criticism Elias voiced in the 1950s and 1960s against Weber was more against the interpretation of Weber characteristic of the then-dominant structural–functionalist school.

6 The works of Foucault give a similar impression. All his main institutional analyses start with a powerful image or text which is more presentative than representative, whether it is the 'ship of fools' (HF: 18–24), the treatment of hysteria by Pomme (BC: ix) or the execution of Damiens (DP: 3–6).

7 On the unexpected changes brought about first by the First World War and then the Nazi takeover, see also RL: 13–14, 51–2. Elias is also clear that it was only in Frankfurt, after 1932, and not in Heidelberg, that he first became aware of a real threat (RL: 43).

8 About this, see also Foucault, DE280.

9 It is worth noting that in his 1975 Collège de France lectures Foucault also assigned an important role to the German idea of 'giving satisfaction' in the history of confession (CF75: 159–60).

10 It is of considerable interest that the works of Elias and Borkenau have a complementary character even here. If Elias provided a 'genealogy' of duelling (in GE), then Borkenau complemented it with his 'genealogy' of the lonely knight as the tragic hero of German mythology (in EB). Voegelin also studied this point (see HPII: 45–6).

11 These difficulties posed special problems of method for Elias. If only to underline the elusive character of these changes, which were so all-encompassing that they included the routine everyday conduct of life and so pervasive that they extended to the formation of personality, Elias emphasized that the investigation had to pay attention to the modality of changes. This includes concern with the 'tone' and the 'manner of seeing' characteristic of the writings of the period (CP: 57) and with the 'tempo' characteristic of the particular time (CP: 457). Such concerns usually are of interest not for the social sciences but the humanities.

12 Elias's approach provides a way to interpret Foucault's concern with representation in *The Order of Things* by pointing out a certain kind of 'material' or 'experiential' basis of this new form of thought. In fact, the painting *Las Meninas* by Velasquez analysed by Foucault (OF: 3–16), also served as the basis for Elias's own Introduction to *Involvement and Detachment,* his main methodological work (ID: lii–lxviii). Even further, the front covers of both books reproduce the painting.

13 In fact, the example that comes closest to reproducing a court society in a contemporary setting is also the symbol of (post)modernity: the television. It starts from its internal organization, through the images it projects especially in the sitcom, its genre *par excellence,* up to its reproduction of the 'sun-kings' in the persons of the media moguls. This has happened just when it was thought that the spread of large organizations would render the type of the great individual capitalist a phenomenon of the past.

14 The crucial importance Huizinga exerted on Elias in this respect has been recognized (Blok 1979: 171–4; van Krieken 1998: 24–5).

15 It may be worthwhile noting that in English it was precisely this journey that was called 'progress' in the fifteenth century.

16 This all the more so as he repeated this claim in *The Germans* where he defined the present moment as a 'turning point' (GE: 20).

17 Elias, just like Borkenau, also connected the rise of modern individualism to the collapse of the medieval world order (Borkenau, 1985 [1936]: 98, 105; 1987 [1932]: 111–12; CP: 310).

18 See especially the chapter 'Primal Crime and "Social Paranoia" in the Dark Ages' (EB: 381–91), where Borkenau poses the question of 'whether it makes sense to speak of a paranoiac age' (EB: 388). Like Foucault, he advanced ideas that would be presented years later by the 'anti-psychiatrists'.

19 Foucault stated the same thing in almost the same words:

> What I react against is the fact that there is a breach between social history and the history of ideas. Social historians are supposed to describe how people act without thinking and historians of ideas are supposed to describe how people think without acting. Everybody both acts and thinks. The way people act or react is linked to a way of thinking and of course, thinking is related to tradition.
>
> (TS: 14)

20 Foucault made the same separation between knowledge content (*connaissance*) and knowledge form (*savoir*) in *The Order of Things*.

21 In the Preface to his *General Theory* which was published in 1936 and for which he anticipated problems of reception, Keynes argues that '[t]he difficulty lies, not in the new ideas, but in escaping from the old ones, which

ramify, for those brought up as most of us have been, into every corner of our minds' (Keynes 1964: viii).

22 This passage was also quoted by Oestreich, in his important chapter on early modern police (Oestreich 1982: 164, fn 24). This reference is all the more relevant as the early modern police had a key role in spreading court manners in the social body.

7 The mechanical world image (Borkenau)

1 I use the term 'situation' throughout the book in a strict technical sense and using the terminology of Jaspers (1951 [1931]: 9–35) and Gadamer (1975: 268–9).
2 The quote is from Borkenau's later work. However, far from stretching the argument, this only points out the parallels with earlier periods that he only recognized later.
3 About this, see Huizinga (1990 [1924]: 226–31).
4 This concept was central for Foucault's 1980 lectures at the Collège de France (see lecture of 26 March 1980, C 62 (12), Foucault Archives) and also for Koselleck (see 1988: 103–4, fn 15).
5 Other reflexive historical sociologists like Koselleck (1988) and Ariès (1975) would also attribute an important role to secrecy in the emergence of the modern political and intellectual landscape.
6 A main chapter of the book is devoted to the ideas of Hobbes. However, as Borkenau himself argues that in Hobbes's case he largely relied on the existing secondary literature as it was satisfactory (UFB; viii), and as this chapter is not closely related to the purposes of this book, it will not be covered here.
7 It is at this point that Gerhard Oestreich, who otherwise recognized the value of Borkenau's work (1982: 32), challenges this interpretation by showing that the neo-stoic ideas were taken up and developed in another setting concerned with modern military discipline.
8 This also shows how much Borkenau's work grew out of the spirit of Weber. While methodologists in sociology and philosophy kept arguing for decades about the 'positivism' of Weber's methodological writings, it is only recently that Wilhelm Hennis (1991) recognized that Weber's main task was the education of judgement.
9 This would also reinforce the links between Borkenau and the more recent rediscovery of 'philosophy as a way of life' in the works of Hadot and Foucault where the concern with 'conversion' took up a central place (see Hadot (1993: 173–182) and Foucault's lectures of 13 and 20 February 1980 (C 62 (6) and (7)). Mumford and Voegelin also ended very important writings on a similar note. Voegelin used the symbol of the exodus from Babylon (AN: 140; see also NSP: 23), while Mumford claimed that 'the gates of the technocratic prison will open automatically . . . as soon as we choose to walk out' (MMII: 435). On conversion, see also Pizzorno (1987, 1991).

8 The gnostic revolt (Voegelin)

1 For a criticism of Weber's position, see Mittendorfer (1998).
2 One of the major problems of the edition of the *History of Political Ideas* is the almost complete lack of dating of the texts in the editorial sections. This is all the more regrettable as it is not possible to understand the dynamics of Voegelin's thinking without knowledge of the exact chronological order. It is also regrettable because there are extant works, notably the writings of Opitz, that provide some attempts at dating and place special emphasis on 'The People of God' section and the question of gnosticism.

3   This conceptual opposition has become a central organizing principle of Troeltsch's great book *The Social Teaching of the Christian Churches*. However, in the first footnote of the 1920 version of his essay on sects, Weber clearly laid down his claim for originality. Given that this was indeed the title of his 1906 essay, there can be little doubts that he was right.

4   The parallels of this description of the crisis of the Hellenic world with the present, and in particular with Weber's diagnosis of disenchantement, are explicitly discussed by Moulakis in his editorial Introduction (HPI: 55).

5   In fact, as it was shown above, in his essays on sects Weber had stumbled into the same puzzle. The Puritan sects of New England were the prime examples of the 'spirit' of modern capitalism and yet, according to Weber, they were being swept away by the tide of modern 'Europeanization'.

6   This claim is probably untenable. I would argue that 1516 was the culmination of liminal suspense and 1517 the discharge. As Voegelin would later argue, modernity starts with the Reformation (NSP: 134).

7   This arrangement is, however, the work of the editors. In the Table of Contents contained in the *Archives*, this section comes after the section on Spinoza.

8   According to Mittendorfer (1998), this attitude had a major impact on the works of Nietzsche and even Weber.

9   This seems to contrast strikingly with the ideas of Elias, according to whom Erasmus took up a paradigmatic role in the modern civilizing process. The contradiction, however, is only apparent. Erasmus could only have become the founder of civilization in the modern secular sense of the term because he indeed closed the chapter of the medieval Christian meaning of the term. Thus, from their perspectives, both Elias and Voegelin were right.

10 This will indeed be the way in which Voegelin would characterize, in his best moments, the most important modern 'Gnostics' like Comte, Marx and Nietzsche. However, in his less clear moments, he would charge them with consciously and with full awareness promoting ideas which they knew were false and corrupt.

11 Erasmus's *Civility* book written for children and analysed by Elias is in a direct line of descent from this work. Furthermore, Castiglione's work *The Book of the Courtier*, arguably the most important contemporary textbook on manners and civility, was also written in between 1513 and 1518 (Whitfield 1974: vi). It is thus almost contemporaneous with *The Prince*.

12 This is also apparent in a few casual references to Gnosticism in the earlier parts of the work (see for example HPI: 177, 236).

13 To return again to parallels, Voegelin's struggle against Gnosticism has thus exactly the same character as Nietzsche's diagnosis of nihilism or Weber's struggle with rationality. Nietzsche stated repeatedly that it takes a 'nihilist' to diagnose nihilism and that only a decadent being can perceive the decadence of the age. Though far from identifying himself with these claims, Nietzsche was trying rather to overcome his own nihilism and decadence in a tragically limited, unsatisfactory and unsuccessful way. Weber similarly struggled against the different forms of 'rationalism' in music, science, the conduct of life, etc., by the most rational means. At the same time he was thoroughly unhappy with the progress of 'rationality' and enjoying tremendously the inherent failure of the full rationalization of music. Needless to say, any simple assertion that therefore Nietzsche was a nihilist, Weber a rationalist and Voegelin a Gnostic is not simply erroneous and untenable, but represents a lack of ability to comprehend the quest and the *zetesis* characteristic of the life-works of these towering intellectual and spiritual figures. Even the statement of the previous sentence was made with personal reservations, bearing in mind the evocative power of language and done only to avoid the possibility of gross misinterpretation.

14 In order to avoid misunderstandings: with respect to this point, the new discov-

eries of the Nag Hammadi library are irrelevant. They may be crucial on matters of content but are not decisive in an insight that is focusing on formal-structural similarities. The material then available was sufficient to make the connection.

15 Such a search for distance and conceptual tools, because of the recognition that they were lacking, was also at the centre of the undertakings of Foucault (see especially HSII: 4–6) and Elias (see especially ID).

16 The term is usually associated with Nietzsche. However, Voegelin points out that Hooker and Hobbes had used it to characterize the Puritans.

17 This is all but identical to Foucault's reference (1982: 209) to the problem of totalitarianism in his conclusive 1981 statement on power.

18 For a similar interpretation of *The Ecumenic Age*, see Price (1999). For a detailed account on the link between ancient and modern Gnosticism, see Rossbach (forthcoming).

19 Though putting the emphasis on the New Testament and on classical philosophy, Voegelin traces back this process in both cases to the prophets, especially Jeremiah and to the Presocratics, especially Heraclitus.

20 The image of Prometheus was on the cover page of Nietzsche's first book, *The Birth of Tragedy*, and was evoked in the Preface of Marx's dissertation on Democritus. It also took up a prominent place in Voegelin's 1945 discussion of Schelling (see Chapter Three of this volume).

21 About this, see also Voegelin (1971: 368).

22 The *metaxy* is defined by Voegelin as an 'In-Between reality' (OHIV: 185), the in-between of God and man (AN: 128), the 'domain of human knowledge' (OHIV: 184).

23 This is covered in the rest of the *Introduction* (OHIV: 36–57).

9 The new megamachine (Mumford)

1 Mumford's idea is close to Foucault's argument contrasting the 'accumulation of men' to the the the 'accumulation of capital' (DP: 220–1).

2 One of the chapters of *The Pentagon of Power* is also entitled 'The Mechanized World Picture'. See also MB: 417.

3 The parallels with Foucault's Panopticon are evident. Even more important, however, are the close links with Foucault's lasting interest in the 'gaze' and with his characterization of the period as the 'classical age'.

4 Thus, in a paradoxical way, Mumford who was the historian of cities, supports and even explains Elias's thesis about the primacy of the court over the city in the genesis of modernity.

5 This recalls Voegelin's characterization of the modern immanentization of transcendence.

6 One could refer to the same effect of another main diagnostician of modernity in that Thomas Mann also identified lust and desire with self-abandonment, release and ultimately with death (1999 [1924]: 496, 533–4). This point in itself invalidates the entire concocted thesis of Heilbut (1996).

7 The close coexistence of these two concerns recalls Foucault's concern with politics and sex and even gives it an interpretation.

8 Though Mumford is not referring to Simmel's *Philosophy of Money*, only to his article on 'Metropolis', his considerations bring out the interdependence between these two key works of Simmel.

10 Disciplinary society (Foucault)

1 This has been argued in detail in Szakolczai (1998a: 115–21, 201–2). While the importance of Nietzsche for sociology has been increasingly recognized,

Kierkegaard is still all but ignored. However, he was certainly one of the most important background figures in the history of sociological thought and is comparable to the other three 'masters of suspicion', Marx, Nietzsche and Freud. Apart from Weber and Foucault, he exerted a major impact not only on Simmel, Mannheim, Voegelin and Victor Turner but also on two philosophers who were themselves influential for sociology, Lukacs and Jaspers. The set of names has three characteristics. First, within their generations, it is difficult to collect eight other names that equal the standing and influence of the group listed above for social thought, and this substantiates the claim about the importance of Kierkegaard. Second, the group is not just a loose list of names, but almost all can be arranged in a single chain of lineage. Weber was 'introduced' to Kierkegaard and Nietzsche by Simmel. In turn, he developed close intellectual ties with Lukacs and especially Jaspers who were the main figures of his Sunday circle, and this was arguably due to the close intellectual affinity they shared at that time because of their interest in Kierkegaard and Nietzsche. Lukacs and Jaspers respectively then introduced Mannheim and Voegelin to Kierkegaard. Finally, for almost all thinkers mentioned, the link to Kierkegaard became somehow forgotten or arguably even actively repressed. Their impact on Weber and Foucault has been practically ignored so far, not least because they never mentioned him directly. Mannheim named Kierkegaard as the single most important intellectual force in his formation and in his generation in his first major public talk while he was still resident in Hungary. However, his later references to his intellectual lineage do not include Kierkegaard. Voegelin similarly ignored Kierkegaard in his *Autobiographical Recollections* and his importance was only brought forward by the persistent questioning of Webb. Finally, though Kierkegaard was a major reading experience for Turner, this came to be forgotten for long decades and only became widely known through the Prologue Edith Turner wrote to the second set of his collected essays (see E. Turner, 1992: xii).

2 For the most important examples, see the first Collège de France lecture of 1981 (Lecture of 6 January 1981, C 63 (1), Foucault Archives), Foucault 1982: 208, PPC: 48, and EST: 281.

3 This was taken up, independently of Elias or Borkenau, by Robert Merton, but not independently from the Parsonian interpretation.

4 See for example, the lecture of 26 January 1983 (C 68 (4)).

5 The close link between liminality and marginality has been repeatedly emphasized by Victor Turner (1967: 96–7, 1969: 110).

6 In fact, one of the main problems of Marx was owing precisely to his failure to recognize the importance of liminal or in-between social position (Marx 1981: 1025). The working class carried a revolutionary potential only in so far as it was in not simply a marginal but also a liminal situation. This, however, only persisted for a very short time, and started the desperate search among Marxists for all kind of social groups that shared the joint marginal and liminal character and thus could be projected into the revolutionary 'vanguard'.

7 This is in line with Elias's assessment of the mentality of a 'court society': whatever is not seen, is not believed in or is believed to be non-existent.

8 Interestingly enough, both James and Jaspers departed originally from the perspective of psychopathology. These works by James and Jaspers proved to be central first for Weber and then for Voegelin. Foucault also had a university degree in psychopathology.

9 However, it could be argued that through a proper conceptualization of experience and relying on the way Turner solved Dilthey's problem through his concept of liminality, it is possible to establish links between the two rather than their complete separation (see V. Turner 1982: 12–18, 1985).

10 Paradoxically, this is not at all restricted to radical ideologies and movements. One of the most central neo-liberal slogans is the reference to the 'taxpayer' who is invoked as the undisputed highest authority in matters of state budget and spending, and indeed fits perfectly the bill. Taxation was one of the first and most contested monopolies of the central state power. In fact, the right of *not* paying taxes was one of the most highly cherished and sought after privileges in medieval and early modern times and this 'right' has a main role in the history that leads to the much cherished contemporary concept of rights. Invoking the 'taxpayer', who was constrained through long centuries into paying his dues, as the supreme authority in matters of state spending is therefore a strange idea indeed.

11 For more details concerning this interpretation, see Szakolczai (1998a: 213–6).

12 It is for this reason that in *The Birth of the Clinic* and *Raymond Roussel*, Foucault makes such close connections between death and the modern concern of the scientific study of individuals.

13 The titles of the most significant chapters of the last part of the book pin down the stages of this build-up of a liminal crisis: 'The Great Dumbness', 'The Great Nervousness' and finally 'The Thunderbolt'.

14 Complication can emerge even here, though. One could refer to recent cases of individuals on Death Row who have undergone transformative religious experiences and thus become different kinds of ethical subjects.

15 For narrative and identity, see Somers and Gibson (1994), and V. Turner (1985: 224).

16 In fact, as if to underline the importance of images, the Illustrations of the book, which are inserted in the middle of the English edition, were set at the start of the original French edition.

17 Foucault's well known remarks distancing his interest in 'programmes, techniques and apparatuses' (DEIV: 28) from Weber's interest in ideal types cannot be taken at face value. At the time when these remarks were made, on 20 May 1978, Foucault had not yet studied Weber extensively. In fact, these remarks could well have been part of the 'transformatory devices' that turned Foucault towards Weber.

18 In fact, 'performance' provides the third element, apart from experience and rite of passage, in the conceptual framework that Turner developed in the last period of his work.

19 As these scenes illustrate, the 'powers of the weak' were as important a characteristic of carnivals and rituals for Foucault as they were for Victor Turner (see Turner, 1969: 102, 108ff; also Pizzorno 1987: 39–40). This was also a persistent concern which returned in Foucault's last Collège de France lectures on *parrhesia*. Foucault made the point that discourse of the weak against the strong in matters of injustice was also called *parrhesia* (see also Rabinow 1997). It may not be accidental that Foucault's description here, and his general interest in rituals, mirrors Turner's. Foucault owned a copy of the 1972 French edition of *The Drums of Affliction*.

20 The initial phase also has its place in the argument as, originally, the prison performed a 'rite of separation' by detaining individuals until trial. This also helps to clarify the limits and validity of Foucault's vision with the prison as the metaphor of modernity.

21 For further details, see Szakolczai (1994).

22 This is literally the meaning of the title as 'pan-opticon' means 'all-visibility'. It was certainly not lost on Foucault that the discovery of the sine law of refraction, which was one of the most important scientific discovery of Descartes, was related to optics (Clarke 1980: 173–6), and that the *Discourse on Method* was originally written as a Preface to his three scientific essays, *Optics, Geometry and Meteorology* (Descartes 1985: 109–10).

23 In spite of the obvious differences, there are also striking analogies between these ideas and Elias's description of a 'court society'.

24 About this, see also PK: 164, and Gordon (1980: 245–50).

25 The importance of this early self-description has been recognized by Colin Gordon who starts his Introduction to the second volume of the English language collected works of Foucault by referring to these words (Gordon 1999).

26 The device is comparable to Nietzsche's dramatization of his main ideas such as the eternal return or the will to power in the *Zarathustra,* or the oft-forgotten but significant detail that the 'death of god' is proclaimed by a madman in the marketplace (Nietzsche 1974, no. 125).

27 See especially the introductory pages of the 'Sociology of Religion' in *Economy and Society.* These pages are the links between ES and WEWR concerning the genesis of Weber's work; while theoretically central for understanding the links between Weber's theoretization of action and power, the link between them is provided by the concept 'charisma'.

28 See lecture of 28 March 1973 (Foucault 1979: 61).

29 See lecture of 30 January 1980 (C 62 (4)).

30 See lecture of 28 March 1973 (Foucault 1979).

31 Commenting on HSI, Didier Eribon claimed that '[I]t is, perhaps, the one [book] in which Foucault, writing with astounding economy, "kept thought moving" the most' (Eribon 1991: 275). I would only add that this was rather characteristic of the entire period of the late 1970s. This is best illustrated in the fact that, between 1975 and 1980, Foucault never gave a course about its original title. By the time he was due to deliver such a course, his thoughts had already moved on.

32 See lecture of 11 January 1978 (C 64(1)). For an important and detailed discussion of the 1978–9 lectures, see Gordon (1991).

33 Thus, Foucault pre-dated the ideas of Beck (1992) by about a decade.

34 The most important formulation of this idea of conceiving of social power in the form of warfare occurs in the major June 1976 interview given to Fontana and Pasquino. It was again posed in the form of questions: 'Who wages war against whom? . . . Is it a war of all against all? What is the role of the army and the military institutions in this civil society where permanent war is waged?' (PK: 123) Foucault posed these questions against those who kept talking about class struggle, failing to realize that they thus placed themselves inside a discourse of warfare. The main importance of the quote for the purposes of this book, however, is the reference to a 'permanent war' because of its closeness to the image of 'permanent liminality'.

35 Most of the main issues discussed in the 1978 course would be taken up again and elaborated in the October 1979 Stanford lectures (PPC: 58–85).

36 Personal communication from Daniel Defert. Foucault owned a copy of the French edition of *The Protestant Ethic,* printed on 12 March 1976. It is extensively marked.

37 This was evidently also the period in which he read Goffman. At least, he owned a copy of the French version of Goffman's *Asylums,* printed on 10 November 1978.

38 A further aspect of interest is that Foucault's joint encounter with Max Weber and Thomas Mann happened in the context of the events in Iran. Foucault took a passionate interest in the events (Salvatore 1997) and wrote a series of journalistic pieces which encountered a particularly hostile response. This was to a large extent due to a new concept Foucault experimented with in these articles: 'political spirituality'. This fits into a persistent concern Foucault had with the question of the 'revolution', where his Kant reading experience played a major role. Far from being a temporary concern, Foucault kept to his interest in ques-

tions of spirituality in his Collège de France lectures. In an important 20 January 1984 interview, he defined 'spirituality' provisionally as 'the subject's attainment of a certain mode of being and the transformations that the subject must carry out on itself to attain this mode of being' (EST: 294).

39 It is, however, by no means a synthesis of the two extreme perspectives. In fact, the Hegelian conceptual framework is inapplicable, as the main figures of the Weber renaissance ignored both. This can be understood rather from a hermeneutical perspective of a return and restoration of meaning.

40 This situation is ironic in more ways than one. It was just at the moment when the Weber reception finally got rid of the thick layers of misinterpretation that Foucault encountered Weber, paving the way for a proper reading of his work together with the retrieved relevance of Weber. The misinterpretation had been perpetuated by both the mainstream structural-functionalists who followed Parsons and the critical theorists who followed the Frankfurt School. However, very soon afterwards and in spite of the hints provided by Gordon, Pasquino, Pizzorno, Rabinow and Veyne, the Foucault reception got bogged down in the meaningless 'post-modernism versus Enlightenment project' debate. The new trenches were dug on the ruins of the previous ideological lines, which had been very conducive to the lasting misreading of Weber.

41 See lecture of 9 January 1980 (C 62 (1)).

42 Foucault called *Discipline and Punish* the 'book on the pains' (DEI: 42) just as he called *The Order of Things* the 'book on the signs' (DEI: 25), in an attempt to go beyond the utilitarian-liberal paradigm. However, from mid-1975, 'pleasures' become a central part of his own vocabulary, evidently failing to diagnose that the specific character of power in our contemporary society, which is precisely the kind of mechanized happiness he perceived in his aside in the inner jacket of his first major book, is to connect the exercise of power to pleasure and not to pain. He succeeded in singling out identity formation mechanisms and the force of desire as being part of the power game and not a source of 'resistance', whatever that may mean. He failed to do the same with bodily pleasures.

Conclusion to Part II: modernity as permanent liminality

1 Elias similarly argues against 'process-reduction' [*Zustandreduktion*] (see WIS: 112–13, Mennell 1992: 253–4).

2 For his use of the term 'permanent liminality', see also Turner (1992: 146).

3 In fact, this may shed light on the strange fact that the etymological source of the word 'person' is the Etruscan term for 'mask' (see Mauss 1985).

4 The following interpretation will draw heavily on the work of Agnes Horvath (1997, 1998). See also Bauman (1992) and Wydra (forthcoming), who applied the concept 'liminality' to the case of East-Central Europe.

5 As a particularly striking parallel, Chapter One of Mumford's third book and arguably his first major work *The Golden Day* is entitled 'The Origins of the American Mind', while the first book of Voegelin is entitled *On the Form of the American Mind*.

6 'Machines. Smash a man to atoms if they got him caught. Rule the world today. His machineries are pegging away too. Like these, got out of hand: fermenting. Working away, tearing away' (Joyce 1961 [1922]: 118).

Bibliography

Albrow, M. (1990) 'Norbert Elias (1897–1990): A Memoir', *International Sociology* 5, 4: 371–2.

Arendt, H. (1958 [1951]) *Origins of Totalitarianism*, New York: Harcourt.

Ariès, P. (1974) *Western Attitudes toward Death*, Baltimore: Johns Hopkins University Press.

—— (1975) *Centuries of Childhood*, Harmondsworth: Penguin.

—— (1977) *L'homme devant la mort*, Paris: Seuil.

—— (1993) *Essais de mémoire, 1943–1983*, Paris: Seuil.

Arjomand, S. A. (1999) 'Theory for the New Century in International Sociology', *Perspectives* 21, 2: 3–6.

Aschheim, S. E. (1992) *The Nietzsche Legacy in Germany, 1890–1990*, Berkeley: University of California Press.

Ashplant, T. G. and Wilson, A. (1988) 'Present-Centred History and the Problem of Historical Knowledge', *Historical Journal* 31, 2: 253–74.

Bader, W. B. (1966) *Austria Between East and West*, Stanford: Stanford University Press.

Bateson, G. (1958 [1936]) *Naven*, Stanford: Stanford University Press.

—— (1972) *Steps to an Ecology of the Mind*, New York: Ballantine.

Bauman, Z. (1979) 'The Phenomenon of Norbert Elias', *Sociology* 13, 1: 117–25.

—— (1992) 'The Polish Predicament: A Model in Search of Class Interests', *Telos*, 82: 113–30.

—— (1997) *Postmodernity and Its Discontents*, Cambridge: Polity.

Baumgarten, E. (1964) *Max Weber: Werk und Person*, Tübingen: J. C. B. Mohr.

Beck, U. (1992) *Risk Society*, London: Sage.

Blok, A. (1979) 'Hinter Kulissen', in P. Gleichmann, J. Goudsblom and H. Korte (eds), *Materialien zu Norbert Elias' Zivilisationstheorie*, Frankfurt: Suhrkamp.

Borkenau, F. (1936) *Pareto*, London: Chapman and Hall.

—— (1937) *The Spanish Cockpit: An Eye-Witness Account of the Political and Social Conflicts of the Spanish Civil War*, London: Faber and Faber.

—— (1938) Book review of Norbert Elias, *Ueber den Prozess der Zivilisation*, vol. 1, *Sociological Review* 30, 3: 308–11.

—— (1939) Book review of Norbert Elias, *Ueber den Prozess der Zivilization*, vol. 2, *Sociological Review* 31, 4: 450–52.

—— (1962 [1938]) *World Communism: A History of the Communist International*, Ann Arbor: University of Michigan Press.

—— (1985 [1936]) 'L'origine della filosofia e della scienze moderne, *La Politica* 1, 2: 95–109.

—— (1987 [1932]) 'The Sociology of the Mechanistic World-Picture', *Science in Context* 1, 1: 109–27.

Bottomore, T. and Goode, P. (eds) (1978) *Austro-Marxism*, Oxford: Clarendon.

Boutier, J., Dewerpe, A., and Nordman, D. (1984) *Un tour de France royal*, Paris: Aubier.

Brenan, G. (1974) *Personal Record 1920–1972*, London: Jonathan Cape.

Brustein, R. (1970) *The Theatre of Revolt*, London: Methuen.

Buber, M. (1967) 'Autobiographical Fragments', in P. A. Schilpp and M. Friedman (eds), *The Philosophy of Martin Buber*, La Salle: Open Court.

Calhoun, C. (1992) 'Sociology, Other Disciplines, and the Project of a General Understanding of Social Life', in T. C. Halliday and M. Janowitz (eds), *Sociology and Its Publics*, Chicago: University of Chicago Press.

Camic, C. (1989) 'Structure after 50 Years: The Anatomy of a Charter', *American Journal of Sociology* 95, 1: 38–107.

—— (1991) 'Introduction: Talcott Parsons before The Structure of Social Action', in T. Parsons, *The Early Essays*, Chicago: University of Chicago Press.

—— (1992) 'Reputation and Predecessor Selection: Parsons and the Institutionalists', *American Sociological Review* 57, 4: 421–45.

Cassirer, E. (1946) *The Myth of the State*, New Haven: Yale University Press.

Chignola, S. (1991) 'E. Voegelin – C. Schmitt: un carteggio inedito, lettere (1931–1955)', *Filosofia Politica* 5, 1: 141–51.

—— (1997) 'The Practice of Limitation: Political Form and Legal Science in the Early Writings of Eric Voegelin', paper presented at the Second International Conference on the work of Eric Voegelin, 3–6 July 1997, Manchester.

Clarke, D. M. (1980) *Descartes' Philosophy of Science*, Manchester: Manchester University Press.

Clavel, M. (1975) *Ce que je crois*, Paris: Grasset.

Cohn, N. (1970 [1957]) *The Pursuit of the Millenium*, London: Paladin.

—— (1993) *Cosmos, Chaos and the World to Come: The Ancient Roots of Apocalyptic Faith*, New Haven: Yale University Press.

Connell, R. W. (1997) 'Why Is Classical Theory Classical?', *American Journal of Sociology* 102, 6: 1511–57.

Cooper, B. (1986) *The Political Theory of Eric Voegelin*, Lewinston, New York: Edwin Mellen Press.

Crozier, M. (1970) *La société bloquée*, Paris: Seuil.

Derrida, J. (1982 [1968]) *Margins of Philosophy*, Chicago: University of Chicago Press.

Descartes, R. (1985) *The Philosophical Writings of Descartes*, Cambridge: Cambridge University Press.

Domanski, J. (1996) *La philosophie, théorie ou manière de vivre?*, Freiburg: Editions Universitaires Freiburg.

Dreyfus, H. L. and Rabinow, P. (1982) *Michel Foucault: Beyond Structuralism and Hermeneutics*, Chicago: University of Chicago Press.

Dupront, A. (1987) *Du sacré: Croisades et pèlerinages*, Paris: Gallimard.

Eisenstadt, S. N. (1963) *The Political Systems of Empires*, Glencoe: Free Press.

—— (ed.) (1986) *The Origins and Diversity of Axial Age Civilisations*, New York: State University of New York Press.

—— (1995) *Power, Trust and Meaning*, Chicago: University of Chicago Press.

—— (1998) 'Multiple Modernities in an Age of Globalisation', manuscript.

Elias, N. (1974) 'Foreword – Towards a Theory of Communities', in C. Bell and H. Newby (eds), *The Sociology of Community*, London: Frank Cass.

—— (1985) '*Theory, Culture and Society*, interview with Norbert Elias', manuscript.

—— (1987a) 'The Changing Balance of Power between the Sexes – A Process-Sociological Study: The Example of the Ancient Roman State', *Theory, Culture and Society* 4, 2–3: 287–317.

—— (1987b) 'The Retreat of Sociologists into the Present', *Theory, Culture and Society* 4, 2–3: 223–47.

—— (1997) 'Towards a Theory of Social Processes', *British Journal of Sociology* 48, 3: 355–83.

Ellenberger, H. F. (1970) *The Discovery of the Unconscious*, New York: Basic Books.

Eribon, D. (1991) *Michel Foucault*, Cambridge, Mass: Harvard University Press.

—— (1994) *Michel Foucault et ses contemporains*, Paris: Fayard.

Erikson, E. H. (1958) *Young Man Luther*, New York: W. W. Norton.

Febvre, L. (1962 [1934]) 'Fondations économiques, superstructure philosophique: une synthèse', in *Pour une histoire à part entière*, Paris: S.E.V.P.E.N.

Foucault, M. (1974) 'Michel Foucault on Attica: An Interview', *Telos* 10: 154–161.

—— (1979) 'Power and Norm: Notes', in, M. Morris and P. Patton (eds), *Power, Truth, Strategy*, Sydney: Feral Publications.

—— (1982) 'The Subject and Power', in H. L. Dreyfus and P. Rabinow (eds), *Michel Foucault: Beyond Structuralism and Hermeneutics*, Chicago: University of Chicago Press.

—— (1983) 'A propos de Nietzsche, Habermas, Arendt, MacPherson', April 1983 conversation at Berkeley, Foucault Archives, D 250 (8).

—— (1986 [1963]) *Death and the Labyrinth: The World of Raymond Roussel*, New York: Doubleday.

—— (1991) 'Governmentality', in G. Burchell, C. Gordon and P. Miller, (eds), *The Foucault Effect: Studies in Governmentality*, London: Harvester Wheatsheaf.

—— (1993) 'About the Beginning of the Hermeneutics of the Self', *Political Theory* 21, 2: 198–227.

—— (1994) 'Foucault, Michel, 1926–', in G. Gutting (ed.) *The Cambridge Companion to Foucault*, Cambridge: Cambridge University Press.

—— (1995) *Discorso e verità nella Grecia antica*, Firenze: Donzelli.

Fränger, W. (1947) *Das Tausendjährige Reich*, Coburg: Winkler.

Frankfort, H. (1978 [1948]) *Kingship and the Gods*, Chicago: University of Chicago Press.

Frankfort, H. *et al.* (1949 [1946]) *Before Philosophy*, Harmondsworth: Penguin.

Gadamer, H.-G. (1975) *Truth and Method*, London: Sheed and Ward.

Gebhardt, J. (1982) 'Toward the Process of Universal Mankind: The Formation of Voegelin's Philosophy of History', in E. Sandoz (ed.) *Eric Voegelin's Thought: A Critical Appraisal*, Durham, N.C.: Duke University Press.

—— (1997) 'The Vocation of the Scholar', in S. A. McKnight and G. L. Price (eds), *International and Interdisciplinary Perspectives on Eric Voegelin*, Columbia: University of Missouri Press.

Giddens, A. (1981) *A Contemporary Critique of Historical Materialism*, London: Macmillan.

Girard, R. (1977 [1972]) *Violence and the Sacred*, Baltimore: Johns Hopkins University Press.

—— (1978) *Double Business Bound*, Baltimore: Johns Hopkins University Press.

—— (1987 [1978]) *Things Hidden since the Foundation of the World*, London: Athlone.

Gleichmann, P. R. *et al.* (eds) (1977) *Human Figurations: Essays for Norbert Elias*, Amsterdam: Amsterdams Sociologisch Tijdschrift.

Goffman, E. (1961) *Asylums*, New York: Doubleday.

Goldman, H. (1988) *Max Weber and Thomas Mann: Calling and the Shaping of the Self*, Berkeley: University of California Press.

—— (1992) *Politics, Death and the Devil: Self and Power in Max Weber and Thomas Mann*, Berkeley: University of California Press.

Gordon, C. (1980) 'Afterword', in M. Foucault, *Power/Knowledge*, Sussex: Harvester.

—— (1986) 'Question, Ethos, Event: Foucault on Kant and Enlightenment', *Economy and Society* 15, 1: 75–85.

—— (1987) 'The Soul of the Citizen: Max Weber and Michel Foucault on Rationality and Government', in S. Lash and S. Whimster (eds), *Max Weber, Rationality and Modernity*, London: Allen Lane.

—— (1991) 'Introduction' in G. Burchell, C. Gordon and P. Miller (eds), *The Foucault Effect: Studies in Governmentality*, London: Harvester Wheatsheaf.

—— (1999) 'Editor's Introduction', in *Power*, vol. 3 of *The Essential Works of Michel Foucault*, New York: New Press.

Gorski, P. S. (1993) 'The Protestant Ethic Revisited: Disciplinary Revolution and State Formation in Holland and Prussia', *American Journal of Sociology* 99, 2: 265–316.

Goudsblom, J. (1977) 'Responses to Norbert Elias's Work in England, Germany, the Netherlands and France', in P. R. Gleichman *et al.* (eds), *Human Figurations: Essays for Norbert Elias*, Amsterdam: Amsterdams Sociologisch Tijdschrift.

Gouldner, A. (1971) *The Coming Crisis of Sociology*, London: Heinemann.

Greco, M. (1998) *Illness as a Work of Thought: A Foucauldian Perspective on Psychosomatics*, London: Routledge.

Greco, M., della Porta, D., and Szakolczai, A. (eds) (forthcoming) *Identità, riconoscimento e scambio*, Bari: Laterza.

Greenblatt, S. (1980) *Renaissance Self-Fashioning*, Chicago: University of Chicago Press.

Grew, R. (1982) Book Review of Franz Borkenau, *End and Beginning*, *American Historical Review* 87, 5: 1352–3.

Grossman, H. (1987 [1935]) 'The Social Foundations of Mechanistic Philosophy and Manufacture', *Science in Context* 1, 1: 129–80.

Hackeschmidt, J. (1997) *Von Kurt Blumenfeld zu Norbert Elias*, Hamburg: Europäische Verlagsanstalt.

Hadot, P. (1993) *Exercices spirituels et philosophie antique*, Paris: Institut d'études Augustiniennes.

—— (1995a) *Philosophy as a Way of Life*, ed. A. Davidson, Cambridge: Cambridge University Press.

—— (1995b) *Qu'est-ce que la philosophie antique?* Paris: Gallimard.

Hamvas, B. (1993) *Patmosz I–II*, Szombathely: Eletünk.

Hanák, P. (1975) *Magyarország a Monarchiában*, Budapest: Gondolat.

Hankiss, E. (1982) *Diagnózisok*, Budapest: Magvető.

Havard, W. C. (1978) 'Voegelin's Changing Conception of History and Consciousness', in S. A. McKnight (ed.) *Eric Voegelin's Search for Order in History*, Baton Rouge: Louisana State University Press.

Hawthorne, G. (1987 [1976]) *Enlightenment and Despair: A History of Social Theory*, Cambridge: Cambridge University Press.

Heilbut, A. (1996) *Thomas Mann: Eros and Literature*, London: Macmillan.

Heilman, R. (1996) 'Reminiscences', *Southern Review* 32, 149–67.

Hennis, W. (1988) *Max Weber: Essays in Reconstruction*, London: Allen and Unwin.

—— (1991) 'The pitiless "sobriety of judgement": Max Weber between Carl Menger and Gustav von Schmoller – the academic politics of value freedom', *History of the Human Sciences* 4, 1: 27–59.

—— (1994) 'The Meaning of "*Wertfreiheit*": On the Background and Motives of Max Weber's "Postulate"', *Sociological Theory* 12, 2: 113–25.

Hexter, J. H. (1961) 'Storm Over the Gentry', in *Reappraisals in History*, Chicago: University of Chicago Press.

Hintze, O. (1975) *The Historical Essays of Otto Hintze*, ed. F. Gilbert, New York: Oxford University Press.

Hirschman, A. O. (1959) *The Strategy of Economic Development*, New Haven: Yale University Press.

—— (1977) *The Passions and the Interests*, Princeton: Princeton University Press.

—— (1991) *The Rhetoric of Reaction: Perversity, Futility, Jeopardy*, Cambridge, Mass.: Harvard University Press.

Hochgeschwender, M. (1997) 'Freedom in Offensive: The Congress for Cultural Freedom and the Germans', paper presented at the workshop 'Between Propaganda and Cultural Hegemony', 10 June 1997, Florence.

Hollweck, T. A. and Caringella, P. (1990) 'Editors' Introduction', in E. Voegelin, *What Is History? and Other Late Unpublished Writings*, Baton Rouge: Louisiana State University Press.

Hollweck, T. A. and Sandoz, E. (1997) 'General Introduction to the Series', in E. Voegelin, *Hellenism, Rome and Early Christianity*, vol. 1 of *History of Political Ideas*, Columbia: University of Missouri Press.

Horváth, A. (1997) 'The Political Psychology of Trickster-Clown: An Analytical Experiment around Communism as a Myth', Florence: EUI Working Papers SPS no. 97/5.

—— (1998) 'Tricking into the Position of the Outcast', *Political Psychology* 19, 2: 331–47.

Huizinga, J. (1936) *In the Shadow of Tomorrow: A Diagnosis of the Spiritual Distemper of our Time*, London: Heinemann.

—— (1955) *Homo Ludens: A Study of the Play Element in Culture*, Boston: Beacon Press.

—— (1968) *Dutch Civilisation in the Seventeenth Century and Other Essays*, London: Collins.

—— (1990 [1924]) *The Waning of the Middle Ages*, Harmondsworth: Penguin.

Iser, W. (1978) *The Act of Reading*, Baltimore: Johns Hopkins University Press.

James, W. (1902) *Varieties of Religious Experience*, London: Longman Green.

Janik, A. and Toulmin, S. (1973) *Wittgenstein's Vienna*, New York: Simon and Schuster.

Jaspers, K. (1951 [1931]) *Man in the Modern Age*, London: Routledge.

—— (1953 [1949]) *The Origin and Goal of History*, New Haven: Yale University Press.

Jay, M. (1973) *The Dialectical Imagination: A History of the Frankfurt School and the Institute for Social Research*, London: Heinemann.

Johnston, W. M. (1972) *The Austrian Mind: An Intellectual and Social History*, Berkeley: University of California Press.

Jones, R. A. (1986) 'Durkheim, Frazer and Smith: The Role of Analogies and Exemplars in the Development of Durkheim's Sociology of Religion', *American Journal of Sociology* 92, 3: 596–627.

—— (1991) 'La Genèse du Système: The Origins of Durkheim's Sociology of

Religion', in W. M. Calder (ed.) *The Cambridge Ritualists Reconsidered*, Atlanta, Ga.: Scholars Press.

Jones, W. D. (1992) 'Toward a Theory of Totalitarianism: Franz Borkenau's *Pareto*', *Journal of the History of Ideas* 53, 3: 455–66.

Joyce, J. (1961 [1922]) *Ulysses*, New York: Vintage.

Kadarkay , A. (1991) *Georg Lukacs: Life, Thought and Politics*, Oxford: Blackwell.

Kalberg, S. (1979) 'The Search for Thematic Orientations in a Fragmented Oeuvre: The Discussion of Max Weber in Recent German Sociological Literature', *Sociology* 13, 1: 127–39.

Käsler, D. (1988) *Max Weber: An Introduction to his Life and Work*, Cambridge: Polity.

Kaufmann, W. (1974) *Nietzsche: Philosopher, Psychologist, Antichrist*, New York: Vintage.

Kearney, R. (1995) 'Myths and Scapegoats: The Case of René Girard', *Theory, Culture and Society* 12, 4: 1–14.

Keynes, J. M. (1964 [1936]) *The General Theory of Employment, Interest and Money*, New York: Harcourt.

Kierkegaard, S. (1954) *Fear and Trembling/The Sickness Unto Death*, New York: Doubleday.

Kilminster, R. (1993) 'Norbert Elias and Karl Mannheim: Closeness and Distance', *Theory, Culture and Society* 10, 3: 81–113.

Korte, H. (1997) *Über Norbert Elias*, Opladen: Leske and Budrich.

Koselleck, R. (1985) *Futures Past: On the Semantics of Historical Time*, Cambridge, Mass.: MIT Press.

—— (1988 [1959]) *Critique and Crisis*, Oxford: Berg.

—— (1989) 'Linguistic Change and the History of Events', *Journal of Modern History* 61, 4: 649–66.

Lami, G. F. (1993) *Introduzione a Eric Voegelin*, Milano: Giuffrè.

Laqueur, W. (1972) *A History of Zionism*, New York: Holt.

—— (1978) *Die Deutsche Jugendbewegung*, Cologne: Verlag Wissenschaftlich und Politik.

Lawrence, F. G. (1997) 'The Problem of Eric Voegelin, Mystic Philosopher and Scientist', in S. A. McKnight and G. L. Price (eds) *International and Interdisciplinary Perspectives on Eric Voegelin*, Columbia: University of Missouri Press.

Lichtheim, G. (1967) *The Concept of Ideology and Other Essays*, New York: Vintage.

Livingston, P. (1992) *Models of Desire*, Baltimore: Johns Hopkins University Press.

Loader, C. and Alexander, J. L. (1985) 'Max Weber on Churches and Sects in North America', *Sociological Theory* 3, 1: 1–6.

Lowenthal, R. (1957) 'In memoriam Franz Borkenau', *Der Monat* 9, 106: 57–60.

Löwith, K. (1949) *Meaning in History*, Chicago: University of Chicago Press.

McDonald, T. J. (ed.) (1996) *The Historic Turn in the Human Sciences*, Ann Arbor: University of Michigan Press.

Macey, D. (1993) *The Lives of Michel Foucault*, London: Hutchinson.

Mann, M. (1986) *The Sources of Social Power*, vol. 1, Cambridge: Cambridge University Press.

Mann, T. (1999 [1924]) *The Magic Mountain*, London: Vintage.

Mannheim, K. (1953) *Essays on the Sociology of Knowledge*, London: Routledge.

—— (1982) *Structures of Thinking*, eds D. Kettler, V. Meja, and N. Stehr, London: Routledge.

Marramao, G. (1984) 'Introduction', in F. Borkenau, *La transizione dall'immagine feudale all'immagine borghese del mondo*, Bologna: Il Mulino.

Marx, K. (1976) *Capital, Volume One*, Harmondsworth: Penguin.

—— (1981) *Capital, Volume Three*, Harmondsworth: Penguin.

Mauss, M. (1985 [1938]) 'A Category of the Human Mind: The Notion of Person; The Notion of Self', in M. Carrithers, S. Collins and S. Lukes (eds.) *The Category of the Person: Anthropology, Philosophy, History*, Cambridge: Cambridge University Press.

Menczer, B. (1950) 'Karl Kraus and the Struggle against the Modern Gnostics', *Dublin Review*, 32–52.

Mennell, S. (1992) *Norbert Elias: An Introduction*, Oxford: Blackwell.

—— (1994) 'The Formation of We-Images: A Process Theory', in C. Calhoun (ed.) *Social Theory and the Politics of Identity*, Oxford: Blackwell.

—— (1996) 'Elias and the counter-ego', manuscript.

Milbank, J. (1995) 'Stories of Sacrifice: From Wellhausen to Girard', *Theory, Culture and Society* 12, 4: 15–46.

Miller, J. (1993) *The Passion of Michel Foucault*, New York: Simon and Schuster.

Mittendorfer, K. (1998) 'Founding Moments of Western Moral Experience', Florence: EUI Working Papers SPS no. 98/3.

Mommsen, W. (1984) *Max Weber and German Politics, 1890–1920*, Chicago: University of Chicago Press.

Mumford, L. (1946 [1938]) *The Culture of Cities*, London: Secker and Warburg.

—— (1952) *The Conduct of Life*, London: Secker and Warburg.

—— (1959) 'An Appraisal of Lewis Mumford's *Technics and Civilization* (1934)', *Daedalus* 3: 527–36.

Negri, A. (1978) 'Manifattura e ideologia', in F. Borkenau, H. Grossman and A. Negri, *Manifattura, società borghese, ideologia*, ed. P. Schiera, Roma: Savelli.

Nietzsche, F. (1954) *The Viking Portable Nietzsche*, ed. W. Kaufmann, New York: Penguin.

—— (1966) *Beyond Good and Evil*, New York: Vintage.

—— (1967a) *On the Genealogy of Morals/Ecce Homo*, New York: Vintage.

—— (1967b) *The Birth of Tragedy*, New York: Vintage.

—— (1968) *The Will to Power*, ed. W. Kaufmann, New York: Vintage.

—— (1974) *The Gay Science*, New York: Vintage.

Noica, C. (1993) *Sei malattie dello spirito contemporaneo*, Bologna: Il Mulino.

Oestreich, G. (1982) *Neostoicism and the early modern state*, Cambridge: Cambridge University Press.

Opitz, P. J. (1992) '"La nuova scienze politica": Lo sfondo biografico e teoretico di un classico', *Filosofia Politica* 6, 1: 67–77.

—— (1993) 'Max Weber e Eric Voegelin', *Filosofia Politica* 7, 1: 109–27.

—— (1994a) '"The People of God": Eine Forschungsnotiz zur Datierung des Textes', in E. Voegelin, *Das Volk Gottes*, Munich: Wilhelm Fink Verlag.

—— (1994b) 'Erste Spurensicherung: Zur Genesis und Gestalt von Eric Voegelins "History of Political Ideas"', in E. Voegelin, *Das Volk Gottes*, Munich: Wilhelm Fink Verlag.

—— (1996) 'Eric Voegelins Nietzsche – Eine Forschungsnotiz', *Nietzsche-Studien* 25, 172–90.

—— (1997) 'Le prime traccie: genesi e struttura della "History of Political Ideas" di Eric Voegelin', in G. F. Lami and G. Franchi (eds) *La scienza dell'ordine*, Rome: Pellicani.

Orihara, H. (1994) 'Eine Grundlegung zur Rekonstruktion von Max Webers "Wirtschaft und Gesellschaft"', *Kölner Zeitschrift für Soziologie und Sozialpsychologie* 46, 1: 103–21.

Orwell, G. (1968) *Collected Essays, Journalism and Letters,* 4 vols, London: Secker and Warburg.

Papcke, S. (1991) *Gesellschaftdiagnosen,* Frankfurt: Campus Verlag.

Pasquino, P. (1986) 'Michel Foucault 1926–84: The Will to Knowledge', *Economy and Society* 15, 1: 97–101.

Patocka, J. (1977) 'Wars of the 20th Century and the 20th century as War', *Telos,* 30: 116–26.

—— (1981) *Essais hérétiques sur la philosophie de l'histoire,* Paris: Verdier.

—— (1983) *Platon et l'Europe,* Paris: Verdier.

—— (1989) *Philosophy and Selected Writings,* ed. E. Kohák, Chicago: University of Chicago Press.

Petropulos, W. (1997) 'Eric Voegelin and German Sociology', Occasional Paper no. 50, Department of Sociology, University of Manchester.

Pirenne, H. (1925) *Medieval Cities,* Princeton: Princeton University Press.

—— (1939) *Mohammed and Charlemagne,* London: Allen and Unwin.

Pizzorno, A. (1986) 'Some Other Kinds of Otherness: a Critique of "Rational Choice" Theories,' in A. Foxley, M. S. McPherson and G. O'Donnell (eds), *Development, Democracy and the Art of Trespassing: Essays in Honor of Albert O. Hirschmann,* Notre Dame: University of Notre Dame Press.

—— (1987) 'Politics Unbound', in C. S. Maier (ed.) *Changing Boundaries of the Political,* Cambridge: Cambridge University Press.

—— (1991) 'On the Individualistic Theory of Social Order' in P. Bourdieu and J. S. Coleman (eds) *Social Theory for a Changing Society,* Boulder: Westview Press.

Poggi, G. (1983) *Calvinism and the Capitalist Spirit: Max Weber's Protestant Ethic,* London: Macmillan.

Poirier, M. W. (1997) 'Voegelin – A Voice of the Cold War Era? A Comment on a Eugene Webb Review', *Voegelin Research News* 3, 5 (vax2.concordia.ca/~vorenews).

Price, G. L. (1994) 'Eric Voegelin: A Classified Bibliography', *Bulletin of the John Rylands University Library of Manchester* 76, 2: 1–180.

—— (1997) 'The Language of Political Diagnosis: Voegelin's Portrayal of Social Decline', *Voegelin Research News* 3, 5 (vax2.concordia.ca/~vorenews).

—— (1999) 'The Epiphany of Universal Humanity', in G. A. Hughes (ed.) *Eric Voegelin and Religious Experience,* Lanham, Md.: Rowman and Littlefield.

Purcell, B. (1996) *The Drama of Mankind,* New York: Lang.

Rabinow, P. (1997) 'Editor's Introduction' in *Ethics: Subjectivity and Truth,* vol. 1 of *The Essential Works of Michel Foucault,* New York: New Press.

Rabinow, P. and Sullivan, W. M. (eds) (1987) *Interpretive Social Science,* Berkeley: University of California Press.

Rinken, S. (forthcoming) *The AIDS Crisis and the Modern Self: Biographical Self-Construction in the Awareness of Finitude,* Dordrecht: Kluwer.

Ritzer, G. (ed.) (1992) *Metatheorizing,* Newbury Park, Calif.: Sage.

Rossbach, S. (forthcoming) *Gnostic Wars,* Edinburgh: Edinburgh University Press.

Russo, V. E. (1981) 'Profilo di Franz Borkenau', *Rivista di filosofia* 20: 291–316.

—— (1985) 'Franz Borkenau e l'origine del moderno', *La Politica* 1, 2: 110–14.

—— (1987) 'Henryk Grossman and Franz Borkenau: A Bio-Bibliography', *Science in Context* 1, 1: 181–91.

Salvatore, A. (1997) *Islam and the Political Discourse of Modernity,* Reading: Ithaca Press.

Sandoz, E. (1981) *The Voegelinian Revolution: A Biographical Introduction,* Baton Rouge: Louisiana State University Press.

Sattler, M. (1997) 'The Controversy between Hans Kelsen and Eric Voegelin on The New Science of Politics', paper presented at the Second International Conference on the work of Eric Voegelin, 3–6 July 1997, Manchester.

Scaff, L. (1984) 'Weber before Weberian Sociology', *British Journal of Sociology* 35, 2: 190–215.

—— (1989) *Fleeing the Iron Cage,* Berkeley: University of California Press.

Schumpeter, J. A. (1954) *History of Economic Analysis,* New York: Oxford University Press.

Schluchter, W. (1989) *Rationalism, Religion and Domination: A Weberian Perspective,* Berkeley: University of California Press.

—— (1996) *Paradoxes of Modernity: Culture and Conduct in the Theory of Max Weber,* Stanford: Stanford University Press.

Schorske, C. E. (1961) *Fin–de–siècle Vienna: Politics and Culture,* London: Weidenfeld and Nicholson.

Schröter, M. (1997) *Erfahrungen mit Norbert Elias,* Frankfurt: Suhrkamp.

Sebba, G. (1981) 'Introduction to Documentary Appendix', in P. J. Opitz and G. Sebba (eds) *The Philosophy of Order,* Stuttgart: Klett-Cotta.

—— (1982) 'Prelude and Variations on the Theme of Eric Voegelin', in E. Sandoz (ed.) *Eric Voegelin's Thought: A Critical Appraisal,* Durham, N.C.: Duke University Press.

Seglow, I. (1977) 'Work at a research programme', in P. R. Gleichman *et al.* (eds), *Human Figurations: Essays for Norbert Elias,* Amsterdam: Amsterdams Sociologisch Tijdschrift.

Skinner, Q. (1978) *The Foundations of Modern Political Thought,* 2 vols, Cambridge: Cambridge University Press.

Skocpol, T. (1979) *States and Social Revolutions,* Cambridge: Cambridge University Press.

Somers, M. R. and Gibson, G. D. (1994) 'Reclaiming the Epistemological "Other": Narrative and the Social Constitution of Identity' in C. Calhoun (ed.) *Social Theory and the Politics of Identity,* Oxford: Blackwell.

Springhall, J. (1977) *Youth, Empire and Society: British Youth Movements, 1883–1940,* London: Croom Helm.

Stachura, P. D. (1975) *Nazi Youth in the Weimar Republic,* Oxford: Clio Books.

Strauss, L. (1953) *Natural Right and History,* Chicago: University of Chicago Press.

Szakolczai, A. (1994) 'Thinking Beyond the East West Divide: Foucault, Patocka, and the Care of the Self', *Social Research* 61, 2: 297–323.

—— (1997) Norbert Elias and Franz Borkenau: Intertwined Life-Works, Florence: EUI Working Papers SPS no. 97/8. (forthcoming in *Theory, Culture and Society*).

—— (1998a) *Max Weber and Michel Foucault: Parallel Life-Works,* London: Routledge.

—— (1998b) 'Reappraising Foucault: A Review Essay', *American Journal of Sociology* 103, 5: 1402–10.

—— (forthcoming) 'The Spiritual Character of Modernity: Preemption, Crisis and Return', in S. Barnes and E. Hankiss (eds) *Europe after 1989: A Culture in Crisis?,* Washington, D.C.: Georgetown University Press.

Tabboni, S. (1993) *Norbert Elias: Un ritratto intellettuale,* Bologna: Il Mulino.

Talmon, J. L. (1986 [1952]) *The Origins of Totalitarian Democracy,* Harmondsworth: Penguin.

Tarde, G. (1969) *On Communication and Social Influence,* ed. T. N. Clark, Chicago: University of Chicago Press.

Tashjean, J. E. (1962) 'Franz Borkenau: A Study of his Social and Political Ideas', Unpublished doctoral dissertation, Georgetown University.

—— (1983) 'The Sino-Soviet Split: Borkenau's Predictive Analysis of 1952', *China Quarterly* 24, 342–5.

—— (1984) 'Borkenau: The Rediscovery of a Thinker', *Partisan Review* 51, 2: 289–300.

Tenbruck, F. H. (1980) 'The Problem of Thematic Unity in the Works of Max Weber', *British Journal of Sociology* 31, 3: 316–51.

Treiber, H. (1993) 'Nietzsche's Monastery for Freer Spirits and Weber's Sect', in H. Lehmann and G. Roth (eds), *Weber's Protestant Ethic: Origins, Evidence, Contexts*, Cambridge: Cambridge University Press.

Tribe, K. (1989) 'The *Geschichtliche Grundbegriffe* Project: From History of Ideas to Conceptual History', *Comparative Study of Society and History* 13, 1: 180–4.

Troeltsch, E. (1915) *The Social Teaching of the Christian Churches*, London: George Allen.

Tully, J. (ed.) (1988) *Meaning and Context: Quentin Skinner and his Critics*, Cambridge: Polity.

Turner, E. (1985) 'Prologue: From the Ndembu to Broadway', in V. Turner, *On the Edge of the Bush*, Tucson: University of Arizona Press,

—— (1992) 'Prologue: Exploring the Trail', in *Blazing the Trail: Way Marks in the Exploration of Symbols*, Tucson: University of Arizona Press.

Turner, F. J. (1996 [1920]) *The Frontier in American History*, New York: Dover.

Turner, S. P. (1982) 'Bunyan's Cage and Weber's "Casing"', *Sociological Inquiry* 52, 1: 84–7.

Turner, V. (1967) 'Betwixt and Between: The Liminal Period in *Rites de Passage*', in *The Forest of Symbols*, New York: Cornell University Press.

—— (1969) *The Ritual Process*, Chicago: Aldine.

—— (1975) *Revelation and Divination in Ndembu Ritual*, Ithaca: Cornell University Press.

—— (1982) *From Ritual to Theatre: The Human Seriousness of Play*, New York: PAJ Publications.

—— (1985) 'Experience and Performance: Towards a New Processual Anthropology', in *On the Edge of the Bush*, Tucson: University of Arizona Press.

—— (1992) 'Morality and Liminality', in *Blazing the Trail: Way Marks in the Exploration of Symbols*, Tucson: University of Arizona Press.

Turner, V. and Turner, E. (1978) *Image and Pilgrimage in Christian Culture*, New York: Columbia University Press.

van Gennep, A. (1960 [1909]) *The Rites of Passage*, Chicago: University of Chicago Press.

van Krieken, R. (1990) 'The Organization of the Soul: Elias and Foucault on Discipline and the Self', *Archives Européennes de Sociologie* 31, 2: 353–71.

—— (1998) *Norbert Elias*, London: Routledge.

Voegelin, E. (1924) 'Über Max Weber', *Deutsche Vierteljahrsschrift* 3, 2: 177–93.

—— (1930) 'Max Weber', *Kölner Vierteljahrshefte* 9, 1–2: 1–16.

—— (1944a) 'Nietzsche, the Crisis and the War', *Journal of Politics* 6, 2: 177–212.

—— (1944b) 'Political Theory and the Pattern of General History', *American Political Science Review* 38, 4: 746–54.

—— (1949) 'A Simplification of History', *Review of Politics* 11, 262–3.

—— (1952) 'Gnostische Politik', *Merkur* 6, 4: 301–17.

—— (1962) 'World-Empire and the Unity of Mankind', *International Affairs* 38, 2: 170–88.

—— (1970) 'Equivalences of Experience and Symbolization in History', in L. Pareyson (ed.), *Eternitá e storia*, Florence: Valecchi.

—— (1971) 'On Hegel: A Study in Sorcery', *Studium Generale*, 24: 335–68.

—— (1980) *Conversations with Eric Voegelin*, R. E. O'Connor ed., Montreal: Thomas More Institute Papers.

—— (1981) 'In Memoriam Alfred Schutz', in P. J. Opitz and G. Sebba (eds) *The Philosophy of Order*, Stuttgart: Klett-Cotta.

—— (1984) 'Autobiographical Statement at Age Eighty-Two', in F. Lawrence (ed.) *The Beginning and the Beyond*, Chico, Calif.: Scholars Press.

—— (1990a) *Published Essays 1966–1985*, ed. E. Sandoz, Baton Rouge: Louisiana State University Press.

—— (1990b) *What Is History? and Other Late Unpublished Writings*, ed. T. A. Hollweck and P. Caringella, Baton Rouge: Louisiana State University Press.

—— (1994) *Das Volk Gottes*, ed. P. J. Opitz, Munich: Wilhelm Fink.

—— (1995) *Die Grösse Max Webers*, ed. P. J. Opitz, Munich: Wilhelm Fink.

—— (1995 [1928]) *On the Form of the American Mind*, Baton Rouge: Louisiana State University Press.

—— (1996) 'Nietzsche and Pascal', *Nietzsche-Studien* 25, 128–71.

—— (1999) 'Political Science and the Intellectuals', *Voegelin Research News* 5, 1 (vax2.concordia.ca/~vorenews).

Voegelin, E. *et al.* (1993) *Briefwechsel über 'Die Neue Wissenschaft der Politik'*, Freiburg: Karl Alber.

Waddell, H. (1987 [1934]) *The Desert Fathers*, London: Constable.

Wagner, H. R. (1983) *Alfred Schutz: An Intellectual Biography*, Chicago: University of Chicago Press.

Webb, E. (1981) *Eric Voegelin: Philosopher of History*, Seattle: University of Washington Press.

—— (1997) Review of Michael Franz, *Eric Voegelin and the Politics of Spiritual Revolt*, *Voegelin Research News* 3, 1 (vax2.concordia.ca/~vorenews).

Weber, M. (1977 [1906]) *Critique of Stammler*, New York: Free Press.

—— (1978 [1910]) 'Anticritical Last Word on The Spirit of Capitalism', *American Journal of Sociology* 83, 5: 1105–1131.

—— (1981 [1923]) *General Economic History*, New York, Transaction Books.

—— (1985 [1906]) '"Churches" and "Sects" in North America', *Sociological Theory* 3, 1: 7–13.

Weiss, G. (1997) 'Political Reality and Life-World: The Correspondance between Eric Voegelin and Alfred Schutz, 1938–1959', paper presented at the Second International Conference on the work of Eric Voegelin, 3–6 July 1997, Manchester.

White, L. Jr. (1978) *Medieval Religion and Technology*, Berkeley: University of California Press.

Whitfield, J. H. (1974) 'Introduction', in B. Castiglione, *The Book of the Courtier*, London: Dent.

Wiggershaus, R. (1994) *The Frankfurt School*, Cambridge: Polity.

Wright, E. O. (1997) *Class Counts*, New York: Cambridge University Press.

Wydra, H. (forthcoming) *Continuities in Poland's Permanent Transition*, London: Macmillan.

Yeats, W. B. (1990) *Selected Poems*, London: Macmillan.

Zeitlin, I. M. (1994) *Nietzsche: A Re-examination*, Cambridge: Polity.

Index

Index of subjects